Resource Management for Individuals and Families

Second Edition

ELIZABETH B. GOLDSMITH
Florida State University

 **Wadsworth**
Thomson Learning

Australia • Canada • Denmark • Japan • Mexico • New Zealand • Philippines
Puerto Rico • Singapore • South Africa • Spain • United Kingdom • United States

Publisher:	Peter Marshall
Development Editor:	Laura Graham
Editorial Assistant:	Keynia Johnson
Marketing Manager:	Becky Tollerson
Project Editor:	Sandra Craig
Print Buyer:	Barbara Britton
Permissions Editor:	Robert Kauser
Production:	Martha Emry Production Services
Text and Cover Designer:	Delgado Design, Inc.
Illustrator:	Jim Atherton, Atherton Customs
Compositor:	Parkwood Composition Service
Cover Image:	PhotoDisc, Inc.
Printer/Binder:	R. R. Donnelley/Crawfordsville

Printed in the United States of America

2 3 4 5 6 7 03 02 01 00

For permission to use material from this text, contact us
Web: http://www.thomsonrights.com
Fax: 1-800-730-2215
Phone: 1-800-730-2214

For more information, contact:

Wadsworth/Thomson Learning
10 Davis Drive
Belmont, CA 94002-3098
USA
http://www.wadsworth.com

International Headquarters
Thomson Learning
290 Harbor Drive, 2nd Floor
Stamford, CT 06902-7477
USA

UK/Europe/Middle East
Thomson Learning
Berkshire House
168-173 High Holborn
London WC1V 7AA
United Kingdom

Asia
Thomson Learning
60 Albert Street #15-01
Albert Complex
Singapore 189969

Canada
Nelson/Thomson Learning
1120 Birchmount Road
Scarborough, Ontario M1K 5G4
Canada

Library of Congress Cataloging-in-Publication Data

Goldsmith, Elizabeth B.
  Resource management for individuals and families / Elizabeth Goldsmith.—2nd ed.
    p. cm.
  Originally published: Minneapolis/St. Paul : West Pub. Co., c1996.
  Includes index.
  ISBN 0-534-56493-3
  1. Life skills.   2. Lifestyles.   3. Resource allocation.
  4. Stress management.   5. Time management.   6. Work and family.
  I. Title.
HQ2037.G65 2000
646.7—dc21   99-050282

CONTENTS

preface   vii

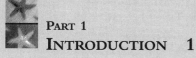

PART 1
INTRODUCTION   1

chapter 1
Management Today   2

What Is Management?   4
  The Management Process   5
  Successful Plans: Putting Management
  into Action   8
  Why Manage?   9
  Who Manages?   10
  Influences on Management Styles   10
  Interdisciplinary Foundation   12
Life Management for Individuals and Families   14
  Managing the Second Half of Life   14
  Singles, Households, and Families   15
  Changes in Family Composition   17
What Lies Ahead?   19
Electronic Resources   19
Summary   20

chapter 2
Management History and Theories   22

The Early Years of Management   23
  Four Eras of Management   28
Theory Overview   30
  Functions of Theory   31
  Theories Ahead   32
Systems Theory   32
  Open and Closed Families   33

Subsystems and System Elements   33
  The Personal System   37
  The Family System   37
  Applications of Systems Theory to Households   38
  Human Ecology and Ecosystems   39
Economic Theory   41
  Optimization and Satisficing   41
  Risk Aversion   43
Electronic Resources   44
Summary   45

PART 2
MANAGEMENT CONCEPTS
AND PRINCIPLES   49

chapter 3
Values, Attitudes, and Goals   50

  Values and Attitudes   52
  Types of Values   54
  Values, Lifestyles, and Consumption   55
  Societal and Cultural Values   59
  Families, Values, Standards, and Households   60
  Attitudes   63
Goals   64
  Goals versus Habits   65
  Goal Attributes   65
  Types of Goals   66
  Setting Goals   67
  College Students' Values and Goals   70
  Motivation   72
Electronic Resources   74
Summary   75

chapter 4

Resources   78

Resources Defined   80

Types of Resources   81

Resources and Economics   82

Resource Attributes and Models   86

Cultural Perceptions of Resources   91

Resources, Families, and Households   92

Consumption and Resources   93

Resource Strategy   94

Electronic Resources   94

Summary   95

chapter 5

Decision Making and Problem Solving   98

Decision Making as Part of Management   100

Steps in Decision Making   102

Models, Rules, and Utility   103

Reference Groups   106

Personal Decision Making   107

Family Decision Making   109

Consumer Decision Making in Families   112

Problem Solving   114

Definition, Analysis, and Plan of Action   114

Uncertainty and Risk   116

Electronic Resources   118

Summary   118

chapter 6

Planning, Implementing, and Evaluating   122

What Is Planning?   125

The Planning Process and Task   125

Need Fulfillment   126

Time, Stress, and Planning   127

Standard Setting   130

Scheduling and Sequencing   131

Attributes of Plans   132

Types of Plans   133

What Is Implementing?   135

Actuating   135

Checking and Controlling   136

What Is Evaluating?   136

Electronic Resources   140

Summary   141

chapter 7

Communication   144

Communication as Part of the Management Process   146

Sending and Receiving   148

Listening   148

Messages   150

Channels   152

Noise   153

Feedback/Response   153

Setting   154

Communication Conflicts   154

In Families   154

Across Cultures   158

Communication in Small Groups   160

Group Discussions and Cohesion   160

Information and Communication Technology   161

Information Overload and Habitual Decision Making   162

Computers and the Human Capacity to Process Information   163

The Role of the Home and the Individual   163

Electronic Resources   164

Summary   165

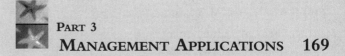

PART 3

MANAGEMENT APPLICATIONS   169

chapter 8

Managing Human Resources   170

Population Shifts: Measuring Human Resources   173

Population Terms and Trends   174

Population Age and Composition   177

Households and Families   178

The Nature of Change   178

Mobility   179

Managing Change   179

Meeting Individual, Family, and Societal Needs   180

Dual-Earner and Dual-Career Couples   181

Children and Child Care   182

Elderly, Elder Care, and Aging   184

The Homeless   186

Individuals with Disabilities   188

Single-Parent and Blended Families   190

Poverty and Low-Income Families   191

Electronic Resources   192

Summary   193

chapter **9**

Managing Time   198

Time as a Resource   201

Discretionary versus Nondiscretionary Time   202

Personal Computers and Time   203

The ABC Method of Time Control   203

Time Perceptions   204

Perceptions of Time across Cultures   208

Biological Time Patterns   210

Quantitative and Qualitative Time Measures   211

Demands, Sequencing, and Standards   213

Electronic Resources   217

Summary   218

chapter **10**

Managing Work and Family   222

Overview of Work and Family   224

The Problem of Work and Family Conflicts   225

Resolving Work and Family Conflicts   226

Family-Supportive Workplace Policies   229

The Meaning of Work and Leisure   230

The Work Ethic   231

Workaholism   232

The Three P's: Procrastination, Parkinson's Law, and Pareto's Principle   232

Workforce Trends Including Home-Based Businesses   233

Volunteer Work   236

Leisure   236

Electronic Resources   239

Summary   241

chapter **11**

Managing Stress and Fatigue   244

Stress: Definition, Theory, and Research   246

Crisis and Adaptation to Stress   247

Decision Making and Stress   252

The Body's Response to Stress   253

Diet, Exercise, and Stress   254

Stress Management   255

Techniques for Reducing Stress   258

Burnout   260

Stress and Non-Events   261

Parents, Children, and Stress   261

College Students and Stress   263

Fatigue: Definition and Sources   264

The Body and Fatigue   265

Systems Theory: Sleep, Energy, and Fatigue   265

Electronic Resources   269

Summary   269

chapter **12**

Managing Environmental Resources   274

The Ecosystem and Environmentalism   277

Problem Recognition   279

Individual and Family Decision Making   281

Environmental Problems and Solutions   282

Water   282

Energy   284

Noise   288

Waste and Recycling   289

Air Quality   290

Electronic Resources   292

Summary   292

chapter **13**

Managing Finances   296

What Is Financial Management?   298

Individuals and Families as Producers and Consumers   299

Income, Net Worth, Budgets, Savings, and Credit   299

Banking, Investments, and Insurance   305

Expenses Related to Children   306

Retirement Planning   308

Financial and Economic Concerns   309

Recession, Depression, Inflation, and Unemployment   310

College Students and Money Management   311

The Gender Gap and the Glass Ceiling   312

Poverty and Wealth   312

Where Does Money Go?   313

Electronic Resources   314

Summary   315

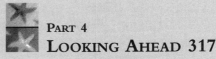

PART 4
LOOKING AHEAD 317

chapter **14**

Future Challenges   318

Technology   321

Computers, Home Automation, and Other Home Innovations   322

Information and Innovation Overload   326

Family and Global Change   327

Quality of Life and Well-Being   328

Multiculturalism   330

Environment   331

Technology, Society, and the Environment   331

Electronic Resources   333

Summary   334

GLOSSARY 337

INDEX 345

PREFACE

The second edition of this book is written to help students plan successful futures and learn how individuals and families manage. Making choices—those made yesterday and those to be made today and tomorrow—and how those choices affect people's lives is a central theme in the book. Sound decision making has never been easy, and it is increasingly difficult as the number of options and amount of information grows. In recognition of this, more coverage is devoted in this edition to how individuals and families respond to and cope with information overload.

This second edition benefits from the feedback given by the students and professors around the world who used the first edition. Special thanks are extended to my students at Florida State University who, through on-campus and distance learning courses, provided helpful comments; to Janice Heckroth of Indiana University and Virginia Vincenti of the University of Wyoming who sent student questions; and to Jing Xiao of the University of Rhode Island who had his students answer three questions about the first edition: What topics should be expanded? What topics should be shortened? What topics should be added? Students and professors in Canada and Europe suggested that more global coverage and examples were needed. This edition endeavored to follow their suggestions as well as those gathered from reviewers and those professors who, at conferences, took the time to tell me what their students liked about the book and what they would like to see in the next edition.

Adapting to change is another central theme in the book, and this second edition makes every effort to include the necessary updates. These were added, however, while keeping in mind that the reviewers, professors, and students emphasized that they did not want the basic structure of the book (i.e., the chapter flow from theory to application to future challenges) changed, but that they did want expanded coverage on certain specific topics.

Across cultures, over and over again, the most popular chapters with students are those on time, stress, and fatigue management. In addition, students found the applied chapters on work and family, human resources management, the environment, and finances to be especially important. Life does not appear to be getting any easier for college students, and in this edition special attention was paid to providing the latest research findings on student life.

The first edition of this book set itself apart from others in its inclusion of the management problems faced by singles and single parents as well as those faced by two-parent families. This approach is even more relevant today, as the number of singles and single parents is increasing and the number of people per household is decreasing. However, the importance of families is not neglected. For example, a new section on family systems has been added to Chapter 2. Throughout the text, the latest population figures are given and discussion is expanded on such related topics as quality of life and well-being.

Part 1 begins with an explanation of management as a process of using resources to achieve goals. The first chapter addresses three questions:

- ◆ What is management?

- ◆ Why manage?

- ◆ Who manages?

The chapter concludes with a discussion of singles, households, families, and changes in family composition. Chapter 2 covers the interdisciplinary, historical, and theoretical foundations of the field.

Part 2 deals with the basic concepts of management: values, attitudes, goals, resources, decision making, and problem solving. This part also discusses how plans are put into action through implementation. A discussion of communication is also included.

Each chapter in Part 3 begins with the verb, *managing*. The specific applications are to human resources, time, work and family, stress and fatigue, environmental resources, and finances. This is a "how-to" section with many helpful suggestions; one section, for example, discusses how to make homes more environmentally friendly. The text goes beyond merely stating the problems and suggests possible solutions.

Thinking about the future is the subject of Part 4. This section brings the book full circle—from the introductory discussions of the history of the study of management and the problems of contemporary families to the management issues on the horizon.

Distinguishing Features

- ◆ **Management as a Process Approach**   Throughout the book, a five-step model is used to illustrate the thinking and action parts of the management process. Beginning with identifying problems, needs, wants, or goals, the model progresses to clarifying values and identifying resources. Then it moves on to deciding, planning, and implementing, and finally ends with accomplishing goals and evaluating. The model takes place within an environmental context and is held together by feedback.

- ◆ **An Emphasis on Systems and Economic Theories**   Rather than relying on only one theory, this text applies many theories to the decision-making behavior of individuals and families. No particular area of the field is overemphasized at the expense of others. This text is meant to be introductory and comprehensive.

- ◆ **Pedagogy**   The most current research and managerial implications are presented in a readable and interesting style. Examples, newspaper articles, advertisements, and photos are included to stimulate student interest.

- ◆ Each chapter begins with a quotation and two *Did You Know* statements. Chapters conclude with an electronic resources section, which contains relevant Web sites, and the following study aids:

  - ◆ *Summary.* A brief review of the major topics discussed.

  - ◆ *Key Terms.* A list of important concepts discussed in each chapter. To help the reader locate them, the key terms appear in boldface type within the chapter text.

  - ◆ *Review Questions.* A list of questions meant to provide the basis for a review of textual material and to encourage thought and discussion on the chapter's content.

◆ *References.* Full citations of references noted in the chapter. An additional list of relevant historic and classic books appears at the end of Chapter 2.

The book concludes with a glossary of the key terms defined in the chapters and an index.

Acknowledgments

A number of people contributed to the inspiration of this book. I am grateful to my major professors at Michigan State University, most notably, Jane Oyer, Margaret Bubolz, and the late Bea Paolucci, and to Sue McGregor of Mt. St. Vincent University for her comments on the Management Process Model.

Much of the historical content of the book was influenced by my sabbaticals in Washington, DC and subsequent visits. I am indebted to Betty Monkman, Curator of the White House, for her guidance regarding technology and the White House discussed in Chapter 1, and Curators Bernard Finn, Anne Golovin, Steve Lubar, Edith Mayo, and Terry Sharrer of the National Museum of American History at the Smithsonian Institution for their critique of the three systems of Household Production/Consumption given in Chapter 2. Special thanks are extended to the Smithsonian Institution Office of Fellowships and Grants and the Herbert Hoover Presidential Library for their support.

The members of Wadsworth's staff should be recognized for their work, and especially for their enthusiasm. Special thanks to Pete Marshall and Laura Graham, who saw the project from beginning to completion, and to Martha Emry, who helped in the final stages.

The reviewers of the first edition of the text did an outstanding job. My thanks are extended to the following:

Maria Canabal
Illinois State University

Elizabeth Carroll
East Carolina University

Lillian Chenowith
Texas Woman's University

Janice Hogan
University of Minnesota

Ruth H. Lytton
*Virginia Polytechnic Institute
and State University*

Teresa Mauldin
University of Georgia

Mary Ann Paynter
Delaware State University at Dover

Alice Pecoraro
Nicholls State University

Pat Stein McCallister
Eastern Illinois University

For reviewing the second edition, special thanks are extended to:

Celia Ray Hayhoe
University of Kentucky

Janice L. Heckroth
Indiana State University of PA

Jeanne M. Hilton
University of Nevada, Reno

Ellen Lacey
Ball State University

Terri Walters
Syracuse University

Most importantly, my deep appreciation and love go to my husband, Ronald, and my sons, David and Andrew, for their support and understanding.

Elizabeth B. Goldsmith

ABOUT THE AUTHOR

Elizabeth B. Goldsmith is an advisor to the White House, the National Park Service, *The Wall Street Journal,* the University of the West Indies, and the United Nations. Her research focuses on women and money, the history and functioning of homes, and environmental issues. Currently, she is Professor of Resource Management and Consumer Economics at Florida State University, where she has won teaching awards. She was recently named Outstanding Alumna at Michigan State University. Dr. Goldsmith has published numerous encyclopedia chapters and journal articles. She served as associate editor of the *Journal of Family and Consumer Sciences* and has presented papers in Australia, Finland, Germany, Great Britain, Malta, Mexico, Northern Ireland, and Sweden.

part 1

Introduction

CHAPTER 1
MANAGEMENT TODAY

CHAPTER 2
MANAGEMENT HISTORY AND THEORIES

chapter **1**

Management Today

MAIN TOPICS

WHAT IS MANAGEMENT?
THE MANAGEMENT PROCESS
SUCCESSFUL PLANS: PUTTING MANAGEMENT INTO ACTION
WHY MANAGE?
WHO MANAGES?
INFLUENCES ON MANAGEMENT STYLES
INTERDISCIPLINARY FOUNDATION

LIFE MANAGEMENT FOR INDIVIDUALS AND FAMILIES
MANAGING THE SECOND HALF OF LIFE
SINGLES, HOUSEHOLDS, AND FAMILIES
CHANGES IN FAMILY COMPOSITION

WHAT LIES AHEAD?

Did you know that...?

... The median age of first marriage in the United States is 25 years for women and 27 years for men.

... In 1900, there were 5 people per household compared to 2.5 in 2000.

> No dream is too high for those with their eyes in the sky.
> —*Buzz Aldrin*

WHAT ARE MY strengths?

Where does my time go?

How can I contribute?

Where do I fit in?

More and more we are faced with these questions as we try to live our lives to the fullest. This book is about choices—the ones made in the past and the ones to be made in the future. When you choose, you are accountable for the resources used and the paths selected. Through our choices our lives are defined and other people's lives are influenced, as is the world in which we live.

According to Stephen Covey, author of *The Seven Habits of Highly Effective People,* "our basic nature is to act, and not be acted upon. As well as enabling us to choose our response to particular circumstances, this empowers us to create circumstances" (1989, p. 75). The study of management explores how human beings react to change and how they cause change to happen. It has been said that the only thing humans can rely on is that things will change. Given the changes expected in technology, biology, medicine, social values, demography, the environment, and international relations, what kind of world are we creating? "No one can say for sure, but one thing is certain: Continuing challenges will tax our collective abilities to deal with them" (Senge, 1999, p. 3).

This book explores past changes and future trends in a rapidly changing world, a world that is becoming increasingly urban and mobile. Today, about half of the people on Earth (3 billion out of 6 billion) live in or around cities. By 2050, an estimated 75 percent of the world's population will be urban dwellers. This switch will have implications for the environment, employment, transportation, and other factors affecting the quality of daily life.

The purpose of this first chapter is to introduce the fundamentals of management as they relate to individuals and families. It begins by asking the question, "What is management?" Some answers will emerge as we examine the management process and see how management can be put into action. Other important questions to be explored include "Why manage?" and "Who manages?" Management does not exist in a vacuum. As you will see, management styles are influenced by several factors, and the study of management draws upon a number of other disciplines. Of necessity, life management must be both versatile and dynamic, for it applies to single adults as well as to families and must adapt to the changing composition of families. This chapter will examine some of these changes and show how the study of life management has adapted to them. The chapter concludes with a description of future chapters, relevant Web sites, and a summary.

WHAT IS MANAGEMENT?

Management is the process of using resources to achieve goals. Another way to express this idea is to say that management is the process of using what one has to get what one wants. The process includes the functioning, actions, thinking, and events that occur over time. Management includes both thought and action; although situations change, the basic principles integral to management remain the same. The importance of knowledge management, the "thinking" part, cannot be underestimated. It is a struggle to learn from past experiences, especially mistakes, and even more of a struggle to apply the knowledge gained to new situations. Thus, there are several challenges inherent in initiating knowledge management, including:

◆ Arrogance (the feeling there is nothing new to learn)
◆ Previous failed attempts (why try again?)
◆ Lack of commitment, drive, and awareness
◆ Lack of support

These and other challenges, concepts, and themes recur throughout the book. They are reflected in the first seven chapter titles: values, attitudes, goals, resources, decision making, problem solving, planning, implementing,

Management takes place at home, in the community, and at work. Everyday life is defined by where we are, what we are doing, who we are with, and how we react and plan.

evaluating, and communication. Then, Chapters 8–14 apply these concepts to the specifics of managing human resources, time, work and family, stress, fatigue, environmental resources, and finances. Central to the discussion in each chapter is how choices are made and acted upon given different personalities and situations.

Thus, the study of management is about how individuals and families decide, plan, and act in order to fulfill needs and accomplish goals in an increasingly complex society. According to Peter Drucker, management's "task is to make people capable of joint performance, to make their strengths effective and their weaknesses irrelevant" (1989, p. 229). In a family, management fulfills this task by enabling the family to engage in collective decision making and by providing a framework that supports and maximizes the benefits to family members.

The Management Process

The **management process** involves thinking, action, and results. Since it is results oriented, management is considered an applied social science. The knowledge obtained through the study of management is evaluated in light of its ability to make an individual's or family's management practice more effective. People have a need for results. It is inherently satisfying to commit to and work toward sought outcomes.

Although management is practical, it is not necessarily simplistic. It becomes complex because individuals' and families' choices are constrained by limited resources. How people handle these constraints is what makes the study of management so interesting. If everyone had equal resources and abilities, the same dreams and wishes, and the same drive and ambition, then there would not be much to discuss. Everyone would lead identical lives.

In actuality, each individual has his or her own resource mix, attitudes, talents, and skills that are brought to bear on situations. Additionally, individuals respond to both external and internal forces in different ways. Internal

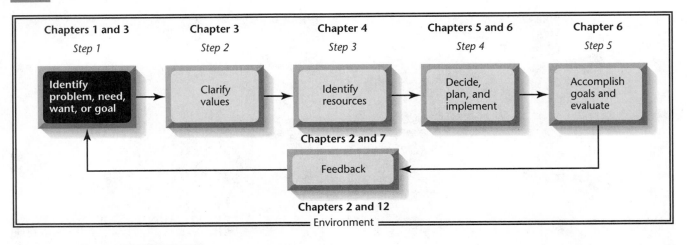

Chapters 1 and 3	Chapter 3	Chapter 4	Chapters 5 and 6	Chapter 6
Step 1	*Step 2*	*Step 3*	*Step 4*	*Step 5*

Identify problem, need, want, or goal → Clarify values → Identify resources → Decide, plan, and implement → Accomplish goals and evaluate

Chapters 2 and 7

Feedback

Chapters 2 and 12

Environment

FIGURE 1.1
The Management Process

forces are the internal drives behind our actions. External forces include the ups and downs of the economy, the condition of the environment, and the rules and laws of society. Consequently, management has to be viewed within the context of the greater life environment, which is constantly changing along with the person who is also reacting and changing.

The purpose of this chapter is to provide an overview of the management process; each aspect of the process will be examined in depth later in the book. Figure 1.1 provides a model of the management process and indicates the chapters in which each step is discussed. Each part of the model plays a critical role in the reinforcing circle, or loop, of the management process.

The process begins with a problem, need, want, or goal. The person initiating the management process identifies a problem or something that he or she desires. **Problems** are questions, dilemmas, or situations that require solving. **Needs** are things that are necessary. **Wants** are things that are desired or wished for, such as a million dollars. In general conversation, the words *needs* and *wants* are sometimes used interchangeably, but in management they are viewed as distinct. A need is something required to survive or to sustain life. According to Dennis Bristow and John Mowen (personal communication, April 4, 1994), there are four types of needs:

1. *Physical needs:* A person's need to sustain life, obtain sensory pleasures, and maintain or enhance her or his physical characteristics (e.g., muscle tone and physical beauty)

2. *Social needs:* An individual's need for relations and interactions with other people; the desire to be included in a group

3. *Wealth needs:* An individual's need to obtain money, goods, property, and other assets with monetary value that are transmittable between two or more people

4. *Information needs:* A person's need to gain knowledge and investigate, explore, study, and/or understand phenomena; the need to satisfy intellectual curiosity and engage in cognitive activity

For example, people need food, air, and shelter to survive. Wants are more specific; they are things or activities that make people feel comfortable and satisfied. Thus, a person may be hungry (a need) but may want to satisfy that hunger with a specific food, such as an apple or a slice of pizza. **Goals** are end results that require action. A college diploma is a goal of most college students, and passing courses is the action required to reach that goal. In the greater scheme of life, goals are arranged in a hierarchy from fairly ordinary to extraordinary.

Once the problem, need, want, or goal has been identified, the individual or family moves to the next step, which is the clarification of values. What do they really want and does it fit into their value system? **Values** are principles that guide behavior, such as honesty or loyalty. **Clarification** means to make clear, to make easier to understand, or to elaborate. As they move through the management process, individuals need to clearly identify what they want to achieve and to ensure that their goal-seeking behavior is compatible with their values. For example, an individual may desire more money, but robbing a bank to get it may not fit the person's or society's value system. Management is based on values and goal-seeking behavior; without these the process would be aimless and misdirected.

The next step in Figure 1.1 involves identifying resources or finding out what the person has to work with. **Resources** are whatever is available to be used. Information, time, skills, human and mechanical energy, and money are examples of resources.

The quantitative and/or qualitative criteria that reconcile resources with demands are known as **standards;** standards also provide measures of values and goals (DeMerchant, 1993). Standards are set by individuals and families for themselves, and they are also set by friends, employers, schools, and governments. For example, governments establish speed limits as part of their traffic standards, and schools and businesses establish appearance or dress codes as standards for their students and employees. During the management process, standards may have to be adjusted. Thus, standard setting is dynamic, meaning that it is subject to change. What is acceptable one year may not be acceptable the next. For example, organizations may allow casual dress every day, or only on Fridays. Or, a school may set school uniforms as the standard one year and do away with the practice the next.

Deciding, planning, and implementing comprise the next step in the process. **Decision making** involves choosing between two or more alternatives. **Planning** is a series of decisions leading to action, and **implementing** is putting plans into action. Plans give focus and direction to the pursuit of wants, needs, and goals. Throughout this step, evaluation takes place and adjustments are made as needed. For example, an individual planning a trip may select a new route or time of arrival as circumstances change.

In the last step of the management process, goals are accomplished or fulfilled, and the process as a whole is evaluated. Individuals are pleased when they achieve their hard-sought goals, but they often overlook evaluation, which in many ways is the most important step in the process. Was the problem solved? What was learned? Which decisions or plans worked and which ones failed? What adjustments should have been made? The answers to these questions are part of the **feedback** (information that returns to the system) that enables the individual's overall management knowledge and ability to grow.

The management process is never stagnant. "It deals with action and application; and its test are results," says Peter Drucker (1989, p. 231). One learns and grows from each decision. New situations provide opportunities for advancement and self-learning. By evaluating past experiences, people learn how to approach the world and discover where their skills and talents lie. In many ways, the study of management is a discovery of self and of how others deal with the world.

So far the management process has been described primarily as an internally driven system (people's problems, wants, needs, and goals motivate them to act), but it should be kept in mind that the process takes place in the larger context of the external environment. For example, a person at a busy fitness center may want to use the treadmill, but will have to wait if someone else is using it. The environment, therefore, can present limitations or barriers to an individual's or family's course of action. As previously noted, the rules and laws of society also affect how wants and needs are fulfilled and what goals are feasible. Thus, the management process must be viewed within an environmental context as Figure 1.1 indicates. Environment refers to everything outside the individual.

Two other comments about the management process are necessary at this juncture. First, in certain situations and decisions (especially hurried ones), the steps may not progress in exactly the order shown in Figure 1.1; sometimes several steps may occur simultaneously. Second, although understanding the individual components of the process is important, the management process is far more than a set of concepts. The essence of the process is that the concepts are interrelated. The process may start with a problem or a need and end with a solution, but the critical element is what happens in between. From the first step to the last, management knowledge, skills, and tools are used. **Management tools** are measuring devices, techniques, or instruments that are used to arrive at decisions and plans of action; examples include clocks, lists, forms, calendars, budgets, and timetables. Are you a list maker? Are you very conscious of what time it is? Did you know that the mechanical clock was invented 500 years ago in the fourteenth century? Before that, people did not think of time in fixed units, but more as a progression, a cycle based on nature. And, nature is not precisely linear; it ebbs and flows in an inexact way. For example, depending on where you live, the first day of spring (March 21) may be covered with snow. The calendar says it is spring; nature says it is not. In this case, using weather as a time measure may be more appropriate than using a calendar.

Successful Plans: Putting Management into Action

Planning is the operalization of choices. This is the stage when people say, "okay, we know what we want, now how are we going to get there?" So, a particularly critical management skill is the ability to create and execute an effective plan. Planning offers several benefits; it:

- ◆ Highlights important problems and opportunities
- ◆ Invests resources in the right tasks
- ◆ Encourages the development of goals
- ◆ Makes decision making more efficient and effective
- ◆ Motivates and coordinates efforts
- ◆ Provides a feeling of growth and accomplishment
- ◆ Involves others

How much planning is necessary? The answer depends on the situation and individual's goals, resources, levels of motivation, and abilities. One fundamental management principle is that planning skill increases with knowledge, practice, and effort. The more individuals plan, listen to feedback, and evaluate their decisions, the stronger their management skills become.

To be successful, a plan needs to be realistic, clear, flexible, and well thought out and executed. The experience of job hunting provides a good example of how planning works and how feedback can help individuals make adjustments to their plans. Most college students want to graduate and get a good job that uses their skills, education, and training. Beyond this generalization, an individual student's career goals become more specific.

For example, Kaitlan's goal is to be employed in a state government job in human services when she graduates. Her bachelor of science degree and senior year internship serve as her knowledge, skills, contacts, and tools base. She is computer literate and knows how to analyze data and reports. In terms of values, she wants to serve people in a meaningful and caring way, and she especially likes working with children. As part of her career plan, she wants a job that will start soon after her May graduation. In January she begins filling out applications, sending out résumés, and interviewing. But, many of her letters and applications go unnoticed, and she receives very few responses. By April she begins adjusting her plan to include more than government jobs. She applies for jobs in nearby states, in the human resources departments at various companies, and through the career services center on campus. At Kaitlan's first interview, the interviewer tells her (provides feedback) that she should rewrite her résumé so that it highlights her past work experiences more clearly. So Kaitlan rewrites it and has three more interviews. In June she is hired and begins work in July; her job is not what she had envisioned, but it does use her skills and provides potential for growth. She is pleased to be working with families and children, and in hindsight she is glad she has had two months off between graduation and the start of her new job. Kaitlan feels that managing this first professional job search has taught her skills, such as the need to be flexible and listen to interviewers' feedback, that will help her the next time she looks for a job.

Why Manage?

The answer to the question "Why manage?" is that people have no other choice. Certainly, life involves nonmanaged actions, such as everyday activities that do not require a lot of thought or planning (e.g., getting up in the morning and brushing one's teeth), but the bigger things that most people want, such as a job and a family life require management skills. Essentially, management takes people from where they are to where they want to go. Having a future to work toward is integral to people's sense of well-being. They need to feel in control of their lives. Being in control is only one of the many benefits management offers. Management also provides new ways of critiquing life situations and offers new perspectives on the nature of change. When you are frustrated or confused, management supplies constructive order, reduces chaos, and suggests steps to follow. In the previous example, familiarity with the management process helped Kaitlan plan, make adjustments, and overcome discouragement.

As a field of study, management is exciting and challenging because it is:

◆ Change oriented

◆ Economically, culturally, and socially significant

◆ Dynamic, intriguing, and complex

◆ Personally and professionally rewarding

◆ Integral to developing leadership and teamwork skills and encourages community involvement

Furthermore, the study of management provides a great deal of insight into a major portion of human behavior—the decisions made and the actions taken based on those decisions. A knowledge of management will help students of human behavior to better understand themselves and the actions of those around them.

Few subjects are more positive and more encouraging than management or more appropriate for college students who are about to embark on new life paths. According to Peter Drucker, "practically all people with schooling beyond high school, in all developed countries—in the United States the figure is 90 percent—will spend all their working lives as employees of managed organizations and could not make their living without them" (1986, p. 352). As this quotation suggests, management is applicable to all life stages. The ever changing environment coupled with their own changing needs impels individuals to constantly search for new courses of action, goals, and solutions to problems. It is important to realize that despite difficulties, new ideas do spread and new options open up all the time.

Who Manages?

The answer to the question "Who manages?" should be obvious by now. Everyone does. Management is such a natural and normal part of life that few people stop to think about how they do it. The management process should be employed every time a school, career, or personal decision is made. Individuals consider their needs and wants, their resources, their preferences, the situation, the other people involved, and so on. Then, they create a plan of action and implement it.

The individual making decisions lies at the heart of the management experience. As Figure 1.1 illustrates, however, management is much more than decision making; it is a multifaceted process involving many concepts, actions, and reactions. Besides those already mentioned, management includes organizing, scheduling, synthesizing, analyzing, resolving tension, negotiating, reaching agreement, mediating, problem solving, and communicating. In other words, although management is fundamental to human life, it is often a difficult process. Consider the decision Jason has to face at age 24. Should he stay at home and live with his parents while he works and builds up his savings, or should he rent an apartment and try to make it on his own even though the rent will take nearly all of his earnings? If he decides to live with his parents, should he stay for six months? A year? What factors should Jason consider besides money in making his decision?

Throughout this book most examples will involve individuals, households, and families, but the basic principles are applicable to all walks of life. As mentioned previously, management is particularly applicable to career situations. Being on time, organizing and finishing work, and scheduling appointments are behaviors that take place in the office as well as in the home.

Influences on Management Styles

Whether at home or at work, people are constantly searching for ways to do things more efficiently and effectively. Commuters try to find routes that will cut 10 minutes off their travel time, and retirees try to find ways to stretch their dollars further. Although everyone manages, each person has his or her own **management style,** or characteristic way of making decisions and acting. Five factors influence management styles:

1. History influences the way decisions are made and the options considered. This includes the history of individuals, families, and societies.

2. Biology dictates basic physiological needs such as food, shelter, air, and water.

3. Culture provides a systematic way in which to fulfill needs. As social beings, people care about each other.

4. Personality is the sum total of individual characteristics, enduring traits, and ways of interacting. For example, personality affects how a person interacts with the environment.

5. Technology applies method and materials to the achievement of objectives. Technology includes laws, techniques, tools, material objects, and processes that help people get what they want.

Maslow's Hierarchy of Needs

Of these, the most fundamental influence is biology. According to psychologist Abraham Maslow (1908–1970), physiological needs (similar to those described earlier in the chapter by Bristow and Mowen) must be met before higher-order needs are undertaken. He hypothesized that each individual has a series of needs ranging from low-order needs to higher-order needs (see Figure 1.2). In Maslow's hierarchy of needs, physiological needs (e.g., thirst, hunger) must be at least partially met before higher-order needs such as safety, belongingness and love, esteem, and self-actualization can be fulfilled (Maslow, 1954). The highest level of need, self-actualization, means to fulfill one's highest potential. Self-actualizers fully integrate the components of their personality, or self. Another way to say this is they attain self-realization, the process in which individuals have the opportunity to invest their talents in activities which they find meaningful.

Of the other factors influencing management style, history, culture, and personality help define human needs and aspirations. Technology provides the means by which the human race progresses.

FIGURE 1.2
Maslow's Hierarchy of Needs

Technology

Because technology plays a significant role in management and will play a larger one in the future, a few comments are in order here, and the topic will be covered in more detail later in the book. It is important to study technology because "if we are to have a fuller understanding of the social and economic context of the family, it is necessary to explore its technological environment" (Burton, 1992, p. 383). Technology differs from the other influences on management style (i.e., history, culture, and personality) in that it is usually visible; technological advances are easily observed and measured. For example, one television set per household used to be the standard. Now American households average 2.8 televisions, and 65 percent of all households are wired for cable ("At Home and At Play," 1999). Currently 96 percent of U.S. households have corded telephones, and 26 percent have wireless phones. And, Europe is well ahead of the United States in telephone technology. Finland leads the list with 58 percent of residents having wireless phones, followed by Norway, Sweden, Italy, Britain, and France (Elstrom, 1999).

Collectively, Americans spend 1.2 billion hours per week on the telephone. Thus, the telephone is both a time saver and a time user. Before the invention of the telephone, how did people spend those 1.2 billion hours per week? E-mail and the Internet have added a whole new dimension to communication. Over 40 percent of American homes have personal computers.

Technology by itself is neither good nor bad, nor is it neutral (Wilson, 1994). It is the use of the technology that determines its worth. The most documented house in the United States, the White House, provides some examples of this phenomenon. In 1879, President Rutherford B. Hayes had the first telephone installed in the White House, but it was rarely used because hardly anyone else in Washington had a telephone, so there was no one to call or to call in (Seale, 1986). When the typewriter was introduced to the White House in 1880, it was put to more immediate use. Previously, all presidential correspondence had to be handwritten by a clerk, so the typewriter was clearly a useful innovation. In 1891, during Benjamin Harrison's administration, electric lights were installed in the White House (Seale, 1986). The president was afraid of being shocked, however, so he refused to operate the electric lights and summoned servants to turn them off and on.

More recently, many people were not sure that the first microwave ovens were really safe and useful. Today, microwave ovens are pervasive. According to Nye, technology is more than a system of machines: "each technology is an extension of human lives; someone makes it, someone owns it, some oppose it, many use it, and all interpret it" (1990, p. ix). Further, today's technologies constantly crisscross, so that a discovery in one industry may revolutionize another industry and its technology (Drucker, 1999). It is becoming increasingly important, then, to be knowledgeable in a variety of fields and to keep up with developments in other disciplines.

Interdisciplinary Foundation

As the previous section explained, various factors (e.g., history, biology, culture, personality, and technology) influence individuals' management style. But the field of resource management is even broader than these influences suggest. Due to space considerations, the following discussion will be limited to management's connections to anthropology, psychology, sociology, and economics, but it is important to note that a number of other disciplines have also contributed. These include agriculture, philosophy, organizational behavior, marketing, biology, chemistry, engineering, and physics. For example, philosophy contributes to our understanding of values, marketing to the consumption decisions made by individuals and families, and engineering to the mechanics and functioning of the home.

Anthropology

The word *anthropology* comes from the Greek *anthropo* (man) and *logy* (science). Simply defined, anthropology is the science of human beings. Anthropologists seek to study and interpret the characteristics of a particular population or activity in its place in time. Of anthropology's many subfields, cultural anthropology is the most relevant to management.

Culture affects what people learn and how they behave. Culture applies to management on two distinct levels: as a set of general attributes of people in a society or group and as material culture, or the objects and tools individuals and families use. The main social group discussed in this book is the family, and the focus will be on objects associated with the family and home use.

Culture also refers to patterns. Repetitive patterns of living are of interest to those who study management. The characteristic way or pattern in which an individual conducts her or his life is called a **lifestyle**. Needs, wants, tastes, styles, and preferences all contribute to lifestyles.

Psychology

The word *psychology* is formed by combining *psyche* (the mind) and *logy* (science). Psychology focuses on how the individual thinks and behaves.

Social psychology and cognitive psychology are particularly relevant to the study of management. Social psychology is the study of individual behavior within a group; it examines attitudes, problem solving, social influences, leaders and followers, and communication. These topics will be discussed in depth in future chapters. Cognitive psychology explains the nature of human intelligence and how people think. It is dominated by the information processing approach, which analyzes thinking processes as a sequence of ordered stages. Values, attitudes, and decision making are integral to cognitive psychology as well as to management.

Sociology

Whereas psychology focuses on the individual or the individual operating in groups, sociology emphasizes the collective behavior of groups. *Sociology* comes from the Latin *socius* (companion or associate) and *logy* (science). Sociology applies the scientific method to the study of human society, specifically, the social behavior of institutions, organizations, and groups. It explores why some groups function the way they do. For example, sociological studies investigate the norms and roles of retired workers, schoolchildren, and employed women. Because the family is a societal group, sociology coupled with family relations contributes much to our understanding of family managerial behavior. Families usually share common goals or purposes and interact in the pursuance of these objectives. Each member of the family is perceived by others as a member, and all members are bound together by traditions and networks. Sociologists study customs, structures, and institutions, as well as how individuals function in groups and organizations.

Economics

Economics is the social science concerned with the production, development, and management of material wealth at different levels: households, businesses, or nations. Specifically, it covers human resource planning, labor market changes, and cost/benefit analyses. For the purposes of resource management, the most relevant topics are those related to human resource planning, financial management, households, and specifically microeconomics, which focuses on the behavior of individual consumers.

Conclusion

Management does not exist in isolation. It deals with people, their values, and their growth and development, and in so doing, it concerns itself with the social structure and the community. For example, how to provide shelter for the homeless is an ongoing community management concern.

Concepts integral to management, such as attitudes, decision making, and planning, are also integral to other disciplines. Knowledge from anthropology, psychology, sociology, economics, and other disciplines provide direction and strength to management research and theory. The next section shows how these theoretical aspects of management can be applied to contemporary problems.

LIFE MANAGEMENT FOR INDIVIDUALS AND FAMILIES

Management principles can be applied to individuals, families, groups, organizations, governments, and businesses. The emphasis throughout this book is on individual and family management. This section discusses life management and provides definitions of several key family and household terms.

Life management encompasses all the decisions a person or family will make and the way their values, goals, and resource use affect their decision making. It refers to more than just specific goal achievement. In life management:

> people are seen as possessing a "self" which helps regulate their actions. . . . Another basic premise is that humans assess situations, speculate about the implications of self and others, take the role of others in order to conduct concerted action, and engage in a process of asking and answering "what if . . .?" questions before engaging in social actions. (Kaplan & Hennon, 1992, p. 127)

Thus, life management includes all the events, situations, and decisions that make up a lifestyle. Life management is a holistic approach that looks at management as a process that evolves over a life span. As the quotation from Kaplan and Hennon illustrates, the process takes place in a social context as part of the environment that surrounds individuals and families.

Managing the Second Half of Life

The second half of life presents its own unique challenges. Patterns (personal, family, work, leisure) established in the first half of life may no longer suffice. Children grow up and leave, jobs prove less challenging or an expected promotion does not come through or early retirement is offered. Individuals may find themselves having spent their first 25 years getting educated, the next 25 on the job, and then face the prospect of 40 years of retirement. How they react to this scenario has a great deal to do with their personality and the details of the actual situation, such as finances and health. Even if they remain employed, work may be redefined by the workers themselves or by the demands of the workplace. Many people question the nature of their work at midlife; most do not want to stay in the same job for 30 years. Unless they manage options or find new opportunities, they may deteriorate, become bored, "retire on the job," lose all joy in work and in life, and become a burden to themselves and those around them (Drucker, 1999, pp. 188–189). Possible solutions to workplace ennui include:

◆ Enriching the present job by taking advantage of training opportunities or travel, teaming up with colleagues on projects

◆ Starting a second or different career or moving to another organization or locale

◆ Developing a parallel career; keeping the basic job but adding another track such as a part-time job, possibly an outgrowth of a hobby or interest area

◆ Joining in a nonprofit activity such as community service, politics, school boards, neighborhood associations, and so on

Combined with the obvious changes that may occur during the second half of life regarding families, health, or jobs, more subtle changes may take place, such as redefining success or determining what is important. It is imperative that people at all ages feel that they are making a contribution at home, at the workplace, and/or in the community. In addition, as more workers become knowledge workers, the need to retire has become less evident than when most people were manual laborers and the physical limitations of age prevented continued employment. Now that work is less physically defined and people are living longer, and as more people work in their homes (through the advent of computers), a societal redefinition of retirement is underway. Whatever happens, it will affect how singles, households, and families function, which is the subject of the next section.

Singles, Households, and Families

Management can be an individual or a group activity. Traditionally, the study of management has focused primarily on the family, but with the growing number of single adults, it is equally important to reflect on their lifestyles and needs. The number of single adults is increasing for several reasons. For one thing, the population is aging, resulting in more elderly singles. In addition, the age at first marriage is rising, so there are many more young adult singles. See Figure 1.3.

In 1900, the average life expectancy in the United States was 47, and only 3 percent of the population lived past 65. Now, the average life expectancy is 75, and 12 percent of the population is over 65 (Beck, 1992). A boy born in 2000 will reach 73 on average; his sister will live into her 80s.

According to the Census Bureau, the median age at first marriage for females rose from 20.3 in 1960 to 25 in 2000. The corresponding figures for males are 22.8 and 27. In the year 2000, a U.S. woman on average will have her first child at age 26. This is a later age than that of her mother when she had her first child, but curiously, age 26 is the average age of the woman's

Grow up, buy a house, have a kid—and perhaps a wedding. Why marriage may be optional. BY PAT WINGERT

I DO, I DO—MAYBE

ON A PLEASANT SUNday evening in Santa Cruz, Calif., 10-year-old Lena stretches out on the brown carpet as she pencils vocabulary words in her fifth-grade workbook. Her parents, Amy Pine and Bob Campbell, sip camomile tea in the airy living room of their three-bedroom ranch. Amy is a psychotherapist. Bob runs a nonprofit organization in nearby San Jose. They fit the pattern of the typical American family in every respect but one: although they have lived together for 15 years and are solidly committed to each other and to their daughter, Amy and Bob are not married. "This is a marriage in heart and spirit," Amy says. "It's just that we didn't need to have it sanctioned by the government."

Getting married used to be a prerequisite for the most important decisions of life: having sex, living together and making babies. Today it's common for unmarried couples to move in together, pick out china, buy a dog—even conceive a child—without bothering with the legalities. The rules of courtship and mating are changing steadily as the century nears its close, and by 2025, when the children of the millennium begin to settle down, the venerable institution of marriage may be more flexible and less manda-tory than ever. Although Americans still overwhelmingly prefer marriage to being single, cohabitation is on the rise: more than 4 million heterosexual couples now live together, up from about 2 million in 1978. Divorce, of course, is still very easy to obtain despite a growing movement to make it tougher. As a result, sociologists now estimate that the percentage of Americans who never marry will grow, from 5 percent to about 10 percent of the population, in years ahead.

The social forces behind these shifts run deep and will last well beyond 2000. The most obvious is the advent of broader career opportunities for women. In the 1950s, says Andrew Cherlin of Johns Hopkins University, "every bread-winner needed a home-maker—they had a need for each other, and that kept most marriages together. Today it's easier for either spouse to walk away if they're unhappy. It isn't that marriage isn't taken seriously today, but it's less necessary." Cohabitation is on the increase because the social taboos against it have weakened. But it can also be a steppingstone to marriage and an attempt to reduce the risk of marital failure by building the relationship before exchanging vows.

The experts all agree that marriage will survive—and the best proof may be the fact that Americans do it so often. Meanwhile, the evidence is mounting that marriage is a plus for most people. Married people are generally happier, healthier and live longer, say researchers Steven Stack and J. Ross Eshleman. Cohabiting is a distant second in creating a sense of well-being. According to University of Wisconsin sociologist Larry Bumpass, the average live-in relationship lasts only about 18 months. That means about three quarters of all the children born to cohabiting couples will see their parents split up, says Bumpass, who worries about "the implications for children of increasingly unstable family relations." Such findings could lead to new emphasis on making marriage work in the new millennium—an important step for adults, but especially for the kids.

With NADINE JOSEPH

Most Americans say they want to get married, and yet cohabitation is rising

PHOTO BY GUY AROCH; HAIR BY DENNIS LANNI FOR BUMBLE AND BUMBLE NYC; MAKEUP BY WADA FOR JED ROOT; STYLING BY JENNIFER ROONEY; SUIT BY HUGO BOSS; DRESS BY YOHJI YAMAMOTO

FIGURE 1.3

Source: © 1998 Newsweek, Inc. All rights reserved. Reprinted by permission.

grandmother when she had her first child (Wingert, Springer, Angell, & Meyer, 1998).

A single lifestyle has both pluses and minuses. For example, on the positive side, single adults may enjoy increased freedom of action and privacy while on the negative side they may experience more loneliness and feel burdened by their inability to share responsibilities. Single people have to take care of everything by themselves. Generalizing about singles is difficult, however, because many singles live with friends or family members and enjoy the support of coworkers and neighbors. Just because individuals are not married does not mean that they live alone or feel lonely; cohabitation has increased in this country.

Many popular images of singles are incorrect or confused. Consider the common belief that the elderly live primarily in the Sun Belt states, especially Florida. Census data reveal that large numbers of elderly singles live in the rural Midwest and that working-age singles cluster in cities such as New York, Washington, Austin, Denver, and San Francisco ("The Singles Scene," 1992). If trends hold true, more elders, along with the rest of the population, will migrate West and South in the future.

People's lifestyles can be categorized by housing units rather than by marital status. According to the Census Bureau, a **household** comprises all persons who occupy a "housing unit," that is, a house, an apartment or other group of rooms, or a single room that constitutes "separate living quarters." A household includes the related family members and all the unrelated persons, if any, such as lodgers, foster children, wards, or employees who share the housing unit. A person living alone or a group of unrelated persons sharing the same housing unit is also counted as a household. Household change generally parallels population change. Household growth in the 1990s was fastest in Nevada, according to the Census Bureau. The smallest gains in new households were in slow-growing states, mainly in the Northeast. Also according to the Census Bureau, **family** refers to a group of two or more persons related by birth, marriage, or adoption and residing together in a household. A family includes among its members the householder. The **householder** is the person (or one of the persons) in whose name the home is owned or rented. If a home is owned or rented jointly by a married couple, either the husband or the wife may be listed first. Prior to 1980, the husband was always considered the household head (householder) in married-couple households.

According to the Census Bureau, since 1980, the percentage of households that are families has declined, and the percentage of people living alone has risen. The average number of people per household in the United States has dropped from 5 persons in 1900 to 2.75 persons in 1980 to 2.63 persons in 1990 to 2.5 persons in 2000. The most dramatic growth in single-person householders is occurring among those aged 45 to 64. More than one in every nine adults aged 15 and over lived alone in 1990, representing a substantial increase since 1970; the number of women living alone increased by 91 percent, whereas the number of men living alone rose by 156 percent (Saluter, 1990).

Changes in Family Composition

To summarize the previous section, there is a growing number of single adults in the United States, and households and families have fewer people on average. However, these changes do not indicate that the number of families is declining. These statistics do indicate significant changes in the composition and size of families. According to an article in *USA Today:*

Families headed by married couples make up just over half of USA households. One in 4 households is made up of a person living alone. One in 4 children is born out of wedlock.

These statistics capture the changes that often are labeled as the breakdown of the family. But experts caution that many shifts reflect huge changes in the population make-up, as well as shifting attitudes about acceptable lifestyles.

While higher divorce and lower remarriage rates contribute to more people living alone, so does longer life expectancy.

"This image of the old-fashioned family is sort of put up as a goal (by) people who think the past is always better than the present," says Arizona State University demographer Paul Glick. "But people have options now they didn't have before. . . . Times have changed." (Usdansky, 1992)

In 1950, families averaged three children compared to one or two children per couple in 2000. Ray Marshall, a former U.S. secretary of labor, has identified another change in family life: "In 1950, 70 percent of American families were headed by men whose wages were the sole source of income. Today only about 10 percent fit that description and fewer than one in eight families consists of a married couple with children in which the mother does not work outside the home" (1991, p. 15). Just as the family has changed, so have social and economic conditions. Marshall suggests that the following have been particularly significant: (1) technological innovations, especially in information, communications, and transportation; (2) the internationalization of the economy; and (3) changes in prevailing attitudes. He also points out that neither the family nor economic conditions were ever as stable as they seem to be in Americans' idealized memories of life in the 1950s. Actually, he says, both have always been in a state of flux.

Another trend is that individuals are increasingly putting off marriage and childbirth to later years and are living long enough to experience single living several times during their life. For example, a woman may be single during her twenties, marry for a few years, divorce, remarry, and then be widowed. When high school classes convene for their twentieth reunion, it is not unusual to find several people who have been married three or four times.

Although the statistics given so far describe conditions in the United States, changes in the composition of families are a global trend. Time-worn traditions of the proper age for marriage and the propriety of divorce are being questioned. In one study of 62 societies, it was found that most young people who divorce do so after four years of marriage, and that most of them eventually remarry (Fisher, 1992). In the United States, a Gallup poll (based on figures from the National Center for Health Statistics) revealed that the average age at second marriage is 39.2 for men and 34.8 for women (Beck, 1992).

Regardless of family stage or type, the main difference between individual and family decision making is that decisions are more complex when made by two or more persons. The bigger the family, the more complicated the decision-making process because more people's needs have to be considered and resources have to stretch further. Family decision making is an important area of study because "the family provides the setting in which essential resources are created, transformed, allocated, and exchanged to meet physical, safety, and higher level needs of individuals" (Rettig & Bubolz, 1983, p. 418).

In conclusion, managing a life, whether as an individual or as a member of family, within the context of the mounting pressures and stresses of everyday existence is not an easy task. As we have seen, not only families but the society and economy in which they live are undergoing dramatic changes.

People try to adapt and to influence these changing situations through the choices they make. Management provides the opportunities to shape future outcomes for the benefit of individuals, families, and communities.

WHAT LIES AHEAD?

This book is divided into four parts. Part 1 includes the present chapter and the next one on management history and theories. These two introductory chapters provide a framework for interpreting the management concepts and applications to come. Part 2 covers management concepts and principles; values, attitudes, and goals; resources; decision making; planning, implementing, and evaluating; and communication. Each chapter in Part 2 will elucidate the steps in the management process model presented in Figure 1.1. Part 3 on management applications has chapters on managing human resources, time, work and family, stress and fatigue, environmental resources, and finances. The book concludes in Part 4 with a chapter on future challenges. Each chapter begins with a quotation, a chapter outline, and a "Did You Know?" section and concludes with electronic resources, a sample Web site, a summary, key terms, review questions, and references. At the end of the book is a glossary and an index.

Electronic Resources

There are innumerable Web sites that touch on management. World and U.S. population figures can be obtained from **www.census.gov** along with social and economic information. There are enough charts and statistics to answer nearly any question about demographic changes. An interesting feature of this

www.census.gov/

U.S. Census Bureau
United States Department of Commerce

Subjects A to Z		
A B C D E F G H I	People	Census 2000 · Estimates · Projections · Housing · Income · International · Poverty · Genealogy · More
J K L M N O P Q		
R S T U V W X Y Z	Business	1997 Economic Census · NAICS · Economic Surveys · Foreign Trade · Government · More
Search	Geography	Create maps · TIGER · Gazetteer · More
Catalog		
Access Tools	News	Releases · Minority Links · New on site · Contacts · More
Jobs@Census		
About the Bureau	Topics	Conversations with America · FedStats · American Community Survey
Related Sites		
American FactFinder		
Publications (PDF)		

Census Tract Street Index
Click Here

Population Clocks
U.S. 273,419,348
World 6,009,839,460
16:34 EDT Sep 03, 1999

State & County QuickFacts
Select a State   ◆
Go!

Latest Economic Indicators

Manufacturers' New Orders

U S C E N S U S B U R E A U
Helping You Make Informed Decisions

Accessibility | Privacy | Quality | Confidentiality | About our new look site is a U.S. and world population update which occurs every five minutes so that you can watch the population grow.

Gallup Organization polls on everything from public opinion polls to surveys on assorted topics are available at **www.gallup.com**. Similarly, results of Roper Organization polls are available at **www.roper.com**.

Updates on employment and the economy can be obtained from Dow Jones Business Information services at **dowjones.com** and business news at **www.cnbc.com**. National and international news services abound, providing articles on trends in singles, households, and families. Two examples are **www.c-span.org** and **www.cnn.com**.

Summary

The study of management is motivated by curiosity and the desire to understand human behavior. This chapter addressed the following questions:

- ◆ What is management?
- ◆ Why manage?
- ◆ Who manages?

Management is the process of using resources to achieve goals. Besides resources and goals, management involves many interacting elements, including problems, needs, wants, values, decision making, planning, implementing, communication, and feedback, all operating within an environmental context.

The unique contribution of management is the insight it provides into decision making and decision implementing. Management is necessary because it provides a sense of direction and purpose. Everyone manages, some with more skill than others. Many of the principles of management are timeless, but the application of management to everyday life is constantly changing. As examples of change, the chapter noted the dramatic increase in the number of single adults and the trend toward marrying at a later age.

The evolving nature of society and technology has made management an increasingly needed and far more complex subject. Given the environmental, economic, and social problems in the world today, the need for skilled managers at all levels has never been greater. Many challenges lie ahead for the thinker and the planner in all of us.

Key Terms

clarification	life management	planning
decision making	lifestyle	problems
family	management	resources
feedback	management process	standards
goals	management style	values
household(er)	management tools	wants
implementing	needs	

Review Questions

1. Why is evaluation, the last step in the management process, so important?

2. Why does the management process involve more than decision making? What other factors or elements are involved?

3. What fields of study have impacted on the study of management? Select one and explain its significance to the field of resource management.

4. How does technology influence management style? Give an example of a technological change in the twentieth century?

5. How have families changed since 1900? For example, has the number of people per household increased or decreased? Also, how did the average age at first marriage change in the twentieth century?

References

At home and at play. (1999, Summer). *Business Week*, 70.

Beck, M. (1992, December 7). The new middle age. *Newsweek*, 51.

Burton, J. (1992). Household technology: Implications for research and policy. *Journal of Family and Economic Issues*, *13*(4), 383–394.

Covey, S. R. (1989). *The seven habits of highly effective people*. New York: Simon & Schuster.

DeMerchant, E. (1993, February). Standards: An analysis of definitions, frameworks and implications. *Proceedings of the Eastern Regional Home Management—Family Economics Conference*, Blacksburg, VA.

Drucker, P. F. (1986). *The frontiers of management*. New York: E. P. Dutton.

_____. (1989). *The new realities*. New York: Harper & Row.

_____. (1999). *Management challenges for the 21st century*. New York: Harper Collins.

Elstrom, P. (1999, May 13). Special report: Telecommunications. *Newsweek*, 175.

Fisher, H. S. (1992). *Anatomy of love: The natural history of monogamy, adultery, and divorce*. New York: W. W. Norton.

Kaplan, L. & Hennon, C. (1992). Remarriage education: The personal reflections program. *Family Relations, 41*, 127–134.

Marshall, R. (1991). *The state of families, 3: Losing direction, families, human resource development, and economic perfor-mance*. Milwaukee, WI: Family Service America.

Maslow, A. (1954). *Motivation and personality*. New York: Harper & Row.

Nye, D. (1990). *Electrifying America: Social meanings of a new technology, 1880–1942*. Cambridge, MA: MIT Press.

Rettig, K. & Bubolz, M. (1983). Perceptual indicators of family well-being. *Social Indicators Research, 12*, 417–438.

Saluter, A. F. (1990). Marital status and living arrangements: March 1990. *Current population reports*, Series P-20, No. 450. Washington, DC: Department of Commerce, Bureau of the Census, 1–13.

Seale, W. (1986). *The president's house*. Washington, DC: White House Historical Association, 494–495, 596–597.

Senge, P., Kleimer, A., Roberts, C., Ross, R., Roth, G., & Smith, B. (1999). *The dance of change*. New York: Doubleday.

The singles scene. (1992, July). *American Demographics*, 18–19.

U.S. Bureau of the Census. (1989). *Current population reports*, Consumer Income Series P-60, No. 169-RD. Washington, DC: U.S. Government Printing Office.

Usdansky, M. (1992, May 30). Diverse fits nation better than normal. *USA Today*.

Wilson, B. (1994). Final thoughts. *Educom Review, 29*(1), 15.

Wingert, P., Springer, K., Angell, E., & Meyer, M. (1998, November 2). Tomorrow's child. *Newsweek*, 54–64.

chapter 2

Management History and Theories

MAIN TOPICS

THE EARLY YEARS OF MANAGEMENT
FOUR ERAS OF MANAGEMENT

THEORY OVERVIEW
FUNCTIONS OF THEORY
THEORIES AHEAD

SYSTEMS THEORY
OPEN AND CLOSED FAMILIES
SUBSYSTEMS AND SYSTEM ELEMENTS
THE PERSONAL SYSTEM
THE FAMILY SYSTEM
APPLICATIONS OF SYSTEMS THEORY TO HOUSEHOLDS
HUMAN ECOLOGY AND ECOSYSTEMS

ECONOMIC THEORY
OPTIMIZATION AND SATISFICING
RISK AVERSION

Did you know that...?

. . . As people age, they report that their homes say more about them than their clothes or jewelry.

. . . A hundred years ago, there was about one servant for every 15 households in the United States.

The journey is the reward.

—*Greg Norman*

VARIOUS THEORIES HAVE been formulated to explain managerial behavior and to help us understand how and why people plan, decide, and act the way they do. This chapter explores the nature of theory and its application to management. It also covers the history of the study of resource management as it relates to individuals, households, and families, along with changes in the U.S. home during the twentieth century. A knowledge of the evolution of management theory provides a useful background for understanding the management process diagrammed in Figure 1.1, which is repeated here as Figure 2.1. This chapter specifically addresses the feedback and environment components of the model.

THE EARLY YEARS OF MANAGEMENT

Although managers and management have existed since the beginning of organized civilization, the earliest records of management are found on the walls of cave dwellings in western Europe. These cave drawings indicated which members of the societal unit hunted, gathered food, and reared children. Much later, in ancient Greece and Rome, home management was the subject of philosophical discussions. The Bible also refers in several verses to the importance of keeping an orderly home. Since the Middle Ages, numerous books about

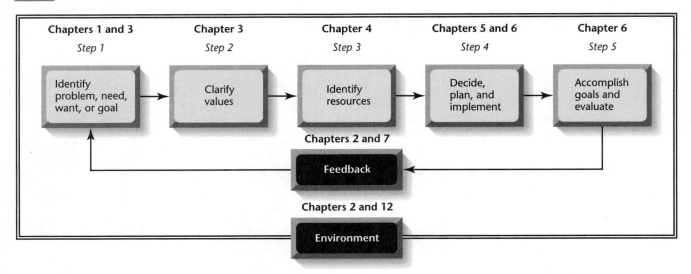

| Chapters 1 and 3 | Chapter 3 | Chapter 4 | Chapters 5 and 6 | Chapter 6 |
| Step 1 | Step 2 | Step 3 | Step 4 | Step 5 |

Identify problem, need, want, or goal → Clarify values → Identify resources → Decide, plan, and implement → Accomplish goals and evaluate

Chapters 2 and 7

Feedback

Chapters 2 and 12

Environment

FIGURE 2.1
The Management Process Model

Philadelphia-born Frederick Winslow Taylor, the well-educated son of a lawyer, became a machinist whose factory-floor observations prompted him to decry workers who "soldiered"—the slackers of his day. His Principles of Scientific Management, *published in 1911, offered solutions for improving industrial efficiency, from piecework incentives to time cards and worksheets.*

household management have been published. A contemporary book summarizes the household accounts of an estate in medieval England (Woolgar, 1993).

Management emerged as a formal subject of study in the United States in the nineteenth century. Across the nation, high school and college courses were taught on a wide range of topics. The courses and the home care books written for the general public offered advice for healthful living; among other things, they extolled the virtues of early rising, cleanliness, sunshine, and fresh air. The first textbook to mention household management in the title was Maria Parloa's *First Principles of Household Management and Cookery,* published in 1879. Parloa advised that "a bed that has been made up a week or more is not fit to sleep in; as moisture gathers, which often proves fatal to persons sleeping in one" (Parloa, 1879, p. 7).

By the early twentieth century, management had become a popular subject of discourse and part of the discipline of home economics, which was founded at the Lake Placid Conferences, held in New York from 1899 to 1908. Authors Lillian Gilbreth and Christine Frederick toured the United States and Europe on the lecture circuit spreading the word about the new scientific methods of efficient home management and household production (Gilbreth, 1927; Frederick, 1918). Government- and industry-sponsored experimental kitchens and college residential laboratories (more commonly known as home management houses) were set up to record the time required and the human and mechanical energy used to perform household tasks. Two of the earliest colleges with residence courses were Stout Institute in Wisconsin (now the University of Wisconsin, Stout) and the University of Illinois. Florida State University was unique in that it was the first college to build a house specifically for home management. Although course content has changed greatly, some colleges and universities still offer residence courses or research laboratory experiences, although this is increasingly rare.

During the early decades of the twentieth century, management practitioners borrowed some of the new techniques that were being used in the workplace and applied them to the home. Frederick Taylor (1856–1915), known as the father of management and famous for his time and motion studies, proposed scientific management principles designed to maximize production efficiency. By carefully studying the most efficient ways assembly line jobs could be performed and implementing changes to increase efficiency, he was able to achieve significant productivity improvements (Taylor, 1911). His influence went beyond business to the application of his scientific management principles to nonprofit organizations and government agencies and facilities, including the Watertown Arsenal of the U.S. Army. Others observing his work applied the same principles to the home by redesigning floor plans, standardizing and updating equipment, and suggesting better work methods (e.g., saving steps and using less time and human energy in such tasks as keeping household accounts, making beds, washing dishes, and cooking). These improved work methods in the home, known as **work simplification**, became an integral part of the study of management.

application of Taylor's research

At the same time, the American home was changing rapidly. Of course, regional and individual variations existed, but in general the century between 1900 and the present can be divided into three eras—premodern, modern, and postmodern. Tables 2.1, 2.2, and 2.3 summarize the main characteristics of household production and consumption patterns in representative decades. Notice that in 1900 most houses did not have indoor plumbing. Although Thomas Edison had invented the incandescent lightbulb in 1879, only 8 percent

TABLE 2.1
**Household Production/
Consumption System I:
Premodern (early 1900s)**

Typical families in the early 1900s made most of their own clothes, food, and household cleaning products. They were likely to buy such basics as soap, flour, and baking powder.

◆ *Household work:* Hands-on, arduous, specific, repetitive.

◆ *Kitchen/laundry equipment:* Inside sink (probably only cold water), stove, washtub or wringer washer, possibly an icebox.

◆ *Bathroom equipment:* Outdoor privy, indoor slop buckets, bathtubs or buckets for washing filled with water heated on the stove; the rich and/or city dwellers might have indoor plumbing.

◆ *Servants:* One servant for every 15 households.*

◆ *Shopping:* Home delivery is common—doctors, peddlers, and tailors come to the home; groceries, ice, baked goods, and dairy products are all delivered. At stores, shop owners take products off the shelf and hand them to the customer. Catalog shopping becomes popular; catalogs offer everything from medicines to whole houses. Beginning of exposure to media advertising and brands.

◆ *Electricity:* Newly introduced, rare in homes except those of the rich, particularly those who live in cities. Mostly used for lighting.

◆ *Lighting:* Kerosene (mostly lower and working class, rural), gas (upper, middle class, urban), candles, and some electricity.

*R. S. Cowan, *More Work for Mother* (New York: Basic Books, 1983), pp. 99 and 240.

TABLE 2.2
**Household Production/
Consumption System II:
Modern (1950s)**

Typical families in the mid-twentieth century bought most of their clothing, food, and household cleaning products from stores.

◆ *Household work:* Hands-on and machine-aided, somewhat arduous, specific, repetitive.

◆ *Kitchen/laundry equipment:* Sink (with hot and cold water), stove, refrigerator, washing machine, perhaps a dryer and a dishwasher.

◆ *Bathroom equipment:* Sink, toilet, bathtub/shower (one or two bathrooms in the average new home).

◆ *Servants:* One to every 42 households.*

◆ *Shopping:* Home delivery less common than in the early 1900s. Customers serve themselves at stores. Moderate exposure to media advertising and brands. Shopping centers begin.

◆ *Electricity:* In over 80 percent of homes.†

◆ *Lighting:* Electric most common, kerosene still used in some rural areas.

*R. S. Cowan, *More Work for Mother* (New York: Basic Books, 1983), pp. 99 and 240.
†*Historical Statistics of the United States* (Washington, D.C.: U.S. Government Printing Office, 1975).

of U.S. homes had electricity by 1907 (Cowan, 1983). Kitchen and laundry equipment were primitive, and housework was backbreaking labor. Furthermore, it increasingly had to be done by the sole adult woman in the household because by the late nineteenth century, servants were disappearing as they found more lucrative employment in the growing number of factories and shops. Also, American families were experiencing a radical change in the way things were bought and made. According to historian Susan Strasser, the period from 1885 to 1915 was a time of "massive transformation. . . . During this period there was a transformation in the factory and in the distribution process. All the really major innovations came in during this time" (Goldsmith, 1993, p. 47). The automobile was introduced, creating a veritable revolution in transportation, and the marketplace and consumer demand were also transformed. There were about 8,000 cars (horseless carriages) in 1900 and less than 10 miles of concrete road in the United States. One of the main changes affecting the home was the switch from making most goods at home to purchasing mass-produced items at the store. Things that used to take all day to make (e.g., soap and bread) could now be bought in minutes. A time revolution, as well as an economic, social, and technological one, was taking place.

In 1900, the economy was strong and prices were low. It was a good time to be a consumer. "In Chicago, you could buy a mahogany parlor table for $3.95 and a sofa for $9.98. In Denver, a good suit cost $10.65, while a turtleneck sweater went for eight cents" ("Only Yesterday," 1999). From 1910 to

Typical families in the early twenty-first century rely heavily on stores for food, clothing, and household cleaning products and on restaurants for meals. Purchase of prepared and frozen food is common.

◆ *Household work:* Hands-on and machine-aided, somewhat arduous, specific, repetitive.

◆ *Kitchen/laundry equipment:* Sink, stove, dishwasher, microwave oven, refrigerator, washing machine, dryer.

◆ *Bathroom equipment:* Sink, toilet, bathtub/shower (multiple bathrooms and sinks common in average new home; also whirlpool baths widely available).

◆ *Servants:* Rare, partially replaced by child care centers and cleaning services.

◆ *Shopping:* Home delivery expands with toll-free catalog shopping by phone and the use of Internet shopping using computers. Stores with customer self-service usual. Malls, multipurpose superstores common. Pervasive exposure to media advertising and brands.

◆ *Electricity:* In nearly all homes.

◆ *Lighting:* Electricity most common.

1940, the United States and other industrialized nations underwent a great expansion of high school education. Students were encouraged to graduate from high school. They worked less on farms and after graduation more went to work in towns and in factories. In the 1930s and 1940s, daily chores in middle-class homes included shoveling coal into furnaces, washing and drying dishes, carrying laundry out to be hung on clotheslines, canning fruits and vegetables, and mending clothes.

By the 1950s, most houses had indoor plumbing, electricity, modern kitchen and laundry equipment. As shopping centers began to spring up, home delivery became less common, and families drove to the store to shop. In the 1990s, household equipment became more sophisticated, and shopping easier, but even today families must devote many hours each week to household tasks and food preparation.

These household and consumption changes have been accompanied by changes in management, which has expanded beyond its initial emphasis on efficiency and economy in the home to include much more. No longer is management primarily concerned with household tasks and the streamlining of work methods in the home, although the home continues to be central to most peoples lives. For example, when asked which one or two of a dozen items says the most about you, Americans rank home number one, ahead of their jobs, hobbies, and so forth. And, as people age they place more value on their home ("There's No Place Like Home," 1997).

Since the 1950s, the emphasis has been on resource use and decision making encompassing a myriad of individual, family, and societal concerns from teenage pregnancy to elder care. In other words, there is more of an emphasis on "life management." Accordingly, the discipline is no longer referred to as home management, but as resource management or, simply, as management. Many important theoretical and research efforts have contributed to management's evolution. Unfortunately, they cannot all be discussed here, but a list of landmark books and other references appears at the end of this chapter as an aid to further study.

Four Eras of Management

To help describe management's development in the twentieth century, several theorists have organized the field's history into chronological categories. For example, Gross, Crandall, and Knoll (1980) conceptualized home management as having six stages of development, and Berger (1984) used these stages as a framework for reviewing management research between 1909 and 1984. Carole Vickers (1986) introduced a simpler version that divided family/home management history into four principal eras:

1. *Era one (c. 1900–1930s)*: Health, sanitation, hygiene, and the importance of household production as a legitimate form of economic production
2. *Era two (c. 1940s–early 1950s)*: Household equipment, efficiency, step saving, task simplification, and standardized work units
3. *Era three (c. 1950s–1960s)*: Family values, goals, standards, resources, decision making, organization and process, optimization of families, gradual swing away from work performance in the home
4. *Era four (c. 1970s–1980s)*: Development of a systems framework emphasizing the interconnections among family, home, and the greater society

Leading theorists Ruth Deacon and Francille Firebaugh (1988) showed how systems theory could be applied to individual and family management problems. Today, the systems framework continues to be the main theory used in the study of management. In addition, theorists have become increasingly aware of the role economics plays in the management behavior and choices of individuals and families. Later sections of this chapter will examine the contributions of systems and economic theory to management in more detail.

Legislation Policy and Research

The evolution of management in the twentieth century has been affected by legislation, policy, and research as well as by technological, economic, and societal changes. In 1914, the Smith-Lever Act was passed to improve life in rural America by providing funds for extension programs through the Department of Agriculture. The Smith-Hughes Act, passed in 1917, provided funding for the training of teachers in primary and secondary schools in what was then called home economics. In 1925, the Purnell Act was passed, which extended the Smith-Lever Act and provided funds for economic and sociological investigations to develop and improve rural home life. The grants were administered by the U.S. Bureau of Home Economics, then part of the U.S. Department of Agriculture (USDA). Currently, the USDA as well as many other government agencies in the United States and in other countries, associations, and private foundations fund management research for both urban and rural populations. Employment opportunities in resource management exist in government at the county, state, and federal level through the Cooperative Extension Service administered through the USDA.

Although early vacuum cleaners were heavy and cumbersome by today's standards, they helped change the domestic duties of women by mechanizing the previously tedious chore of carpet cleaning. No longer was it necessary for homemakers to drag their heavy rugs outside to be pummeled with a carpet beater. (Courtesy of the Hoover Company, North Canton, Ohio.)

During the 1920s, there was a great deal of discussion about the nature of management from a variety of sources, including business, government, and education. For example, it was concluded at the first worldwide Management Congress held in Prague in 1922 that management principles were universal and could be applied to a variety of business and nonbusiness situations (Drucker, 1999). Since then, there have been numerous other conferences, acts, and policies that have had an impact on individuals and families, and many of these will be discussed throughout the book. Certainly, consumer protection legislation improved greatly during the twentieth century. From the 1970s to the 1990s there was a resurgence of interest in improving human rights worldwide. During the twentieth century, the emphasis from the management perspective was on improving living standards, quality of life, and well-being through a variety of means, including improvements in health and nutrition, welfare, child labor laws, education, and work leave policies. Within a topic such as welfare reform, there is imbedded a wide range of factors critical to its success, such as prevention of child abuse and neglect, financial support for children, child care, availability of transportation, education and employment, using social indicators for evaluation and policy analysis, and community-based planning. Each of these require research to determine human needs and the best ways of addressing them.

Research is the collection, processing, and analysis of information. Because management falls within the realm of applied social science, the results of research studies should be useful and made available to citizens and policy makers.

What topics are covered in management research? According to Israelsen, most management research falls into one of two categories: (1) financial/economic resources and (2) human/household resources. He states:

> Specific financial resources research topics have included income and expenditure, impact of women's employment upon family income, financial management, budgeting, debt, saving, financial security and retirement, financial satisfaction, financial support from kin, adolescents and money, determination of living standards, marriage and money issues (resource exchange, conflict over money, marital adjustment and money), economic impact of divorce upon women, and financial decision-making.
>
> The study of human and household resources has historically dealt with topics such as the effect of women's employment upon family life, division of household work between family members, time use/management, household production, household tasks, household satisfaction, household management styles, adolescents and work, and decision-making. (Israelsen, 1990, p. 4)

One of the most studied topics has been time use. Researchers have explored time spent in housework, home-based paid work, and child care; who does what and when; and how factors such as employment, income, and size of family affect time use, demands, and household production and consumption (e.g., Bryant, 1992; Davey, 1971; Goebel & Hennon, 1982; Goldsmith, 1977; Hafstrom & Paynter, 1991; Hafstrom & Schram, 1983; McCullough & Zick, 1992; Owen, 1991; Sanik, 1981; Schnittgrund, 1980; Stafford, 1983; Walker & Woods, 1976; Warren, 1940; Wilson, 1929; Winter, Puspitawati, Heck, & Stafford, 1993). Recently, attention has turned to the interchange between work and family, including the effects of home-based business on the family. Examples of recent studies conducted at Cornell University's College of Human Ecology (**www.human.cornell.edu/faculty/research**, 1999) include the following:

◆ The experiences and expectations of working families

◆ Cultural images of working families

◆ Interlocking careers

◆ Couples' retirement transitions

◆ Midlife transitions and psychological coping

THEORY OVERVIEW

The study of management is a combination of theory, concepts, technique, research, and practice. There is not one management theory or framework, but several. As discussed in Chapter 1, management is an interdisciplinary field that borrows concepts and theories from related disciplines.

Theory is an organized system of ideas or beliefs that can be measured; it is a system of assumptions or principles. A theory summarizes what is known about a phenomenon and permits the formation of **hypotheses**, or predictions about future occurrences. For example, a mother may hypothesize that buying back-to-school clothes for her 13-year-old daughter is a waste of time unless they shop together, because she has observed that whatever she buys on her own will not fit her daughter or suit her taste. The mother's prediction of her daughter's response is based on past purchasing mistakes. Likewise, other theories and hypotheses about human behavior are based on observations, past experience, and research. Theories are useful because they reduce wasted time and effort and provide ways of structuring one's thoughts and knowledge about behaviors. Manual Castells, author of *The Information Age* and a professor at the University of California at Berkeley, adds that all major trends of change are related and that we can make sense of their interrelationship. Further, he says:

> I believe, in spite of a long tradition of sometimes tragic intellectual errors, that observing, analyzing and theorizing is a way of helping to build a different, better world. Not by providing the answers that will be specific to each society . . . but by raising some relevant questions. (Vol. 1, 1996)

Functions of Theory

The primary function of theory is to organize the facts and situations that people observe every day. Theories help individuals make sense of the events that occur around them. For example, observations can be made about the way people behave in situations requiring the allocation of resources, planning, and the implementation and evaluation of decisions. A theory of management not only attempts to explain the behavior of people in general, it also seeks to provide an understanding of a single individual's or family's behavior.

Comprehension of behavior provides the basis for two other functions of theory: (1) to predict future behavior (as in the mother/daughter clothes-buying example) and (2) to control or alter behavior (Arndt, 1984). People are constantly making predictions about their own and others' behavior. For example, they assume they will like or dislike oysters based on a past experience of eating them. Some of these predictions are so automatic that people do not even think about them. When they look at a restaurant menu, they unconsciously skip over the salad section if they never eat salads. However, when an unconscious prediction turns out differently than expected (e.g., a friend who is always late shows up ahead of time), the predictor realizes that he or she has made a prediction and that the prediction was wrong. In the case of the early arriving friend, the predictor is pleasantly surprised.

Behavior has many aspects. Predicting behavior is one aspect, controlling behavior is another. Although the word *control* sometimes has a negative connotation as in brainwashing or mind control, in management it has a more prosaic meaning. **Controlling** refers to the things people do to check their course of action. For example, you may be concerned over whether you have enough money in your bank account to cover your credit cards or whether you can get a better grade on the next test. These concerns involve both predictions and possible alterations of behavior.

As a final comment on the function of theory, consider Kurt Lewin's statement that "There is nothing so practical as a good theory." Theories provide a useful way to organize information. Without theories the prediction of future events would be nearly impossible.

Theories Ahead

Before a new theory can be promoted, the theorist must first develop definitions of key terms, formulate statements or assumptions, and then test the theory. One of the problems in developing and explaining theories is that they are abstract, but once a theory is put into action and the subsequent behavior can be observed, the thought processes behind the behavior become more understandable.

Because so many studies and books have used systems theory, most of this chapter will now focus on its components and applications. The remainder of the chapter will examine the application of economic theory—specifically, optimization, satisficing, and risk aversion—to the study of management. Other theories specific to resource exchange, time, stress, and fatigue will be covered in future chapters.

SYSTEMS THEORY

The dynamic and ongoing nature of systems theory makes it particularly applicable to managerial thought and behavior. One of the reasons systems theory has endured is its versatility—it fits nearly every situation. The principle underlying systems theory is that the whole is greater than the sum of its parts. This emphasis on the whole and the interconnectedness of its different parts is appropriate for the eclectic, interdisciplinary field of management. Also, since individuals and families are part of larger behavioral and environmental systems, it makes sense to view them as part of a whole rather than as isolated units.

Systems theory emphasizes not only interconnectedness but also the interactions between different systems. It focuses on the behavior of feedback and its complexity. The circle in the drawing represents the circular nature of systems with its feedback loop, the fundamental building block of all systems. A **system** is an integrated set of parts that function together for some end purpose or result. Systems may be comprised of living or nonliving things. Since management focuses on human behavior, the emphasis in this book is on living systems in the context of environments, in particular the home and community environments.

A system, as a whole, has characteristics that set it apart from other systems. For example, a family is a system. Families share things in common with other families, such as streets, neighborhoods, or schools, but at the same time they have distinct traditions, ways of living, and consumption patterns. The place or point where independent systems or diverse groups interact is called the **interface**. A doctor's office may serve as the interface between a patient's home and medical services.

Boundaries are the limits or borders between systems. They separate one domain from another. Everyone has personal and family boundaries. Boundaries may be visible, as in fences and doors, or invisible, as in rules of behaving or unmarked borderlines between properties. For example, young children learn early in life where their yard stops and their neighbor's begins. They carry this lesson about boundaries into adulthood. Thus, boundaries maintain functions and influence human behavior.

Homes and workplaces are filled with visible and invisible boundaries. One of the survival skills necessary for any new employee is to learn where the boundaries are—who talks to whom, how flexible lunch breaks are, and which doors are kept open and which remain closed. In a home situation, consider how quickly visiting relatives learn house rules and behavior, such as when breakfast is ready, who gets the bathroom first, and how loud and how long the television can be played. The boundaries of a system determine what is allowed and what is not.

Open and Closed Families

Some families are more open to the outside environment than other families; in other words, they more freely exchange information and materials with outside influences. To use systems terminology, families can be categorized as mostly morphogenic or morphostatic. **Morphogenic systems** are adaptive to change and are relatively open. In an open system, matter and energy are freely exchanged between the system and its environment. Its boundaries are permeable. In contrast, **morphostatic systems** are resistant to change. They are stable and relatively closed.

A relatively open family may have neighborhood children in and out of the house much of the day, chat with neighbors often, spend a lot of time on the telephone, entertain often, and leave the blinds open. A relatively closed family may not know neighbors' names, keep the blinds shut, and keep to themselves. Even without meeting the new family on the block, neighbors may be able to surmise something about their relative openness by the changes they make to the yard or the exterior appearance of the house. At the same time, a quick prediction based only on appearances may turn out to be wrong. A seven-foot-high fence may be a sign that a family is closed or simply indicate that they have a large dog.

Although a family's overall style will be open or closed, variations exist within families, and boundaries can exist between family members. For example, one member of a family may not speak to another. Some family members may be very open and gregarious, whereas others are more private and take a more contemplative approach to life. Within families, each member sets her or his own boundaries of space and privacy. Conflict can occur when boundaries are not respected. Think how often the plots of television soap operas revolve around a violation of privacy, such as parents reading a teenager's diary or mail or one family member's overhearing another's supposedly private conversation.

In addition, situations can alter the way a family interacts with others and their environment. For example, a family crisis can turn a relatively open family into a closed family, at least temporarily. Closure may be a protective mechanism until an adjustment period has passed. Systems theory has the attribute of emphasizing the adaptive nature of families.

Subsystems and System Elements

A **subsystem** is a part of a larger system. Individuals and families are subsystems of communities. Communities are subsystems of counties, which are subsystems of states, and so on. Each system at each level has a reason for existing. This interconnectedness of systems is the reason management is no longer limited to the infrastructure of the home; theorists realize that decisions made in the home ultimately affect the community, the country, and the world and vice versa. Families and economic institutions have always been closely related. Families supply work and society supplies wages that families use to buy goods and services and pay taxes. Thus, each subsystem affects other systems. This emphasis on how the interaction of parts affects the whole is the essence of systems theory.

Inputs, Throughputs, and Outputs   *Systems Elements*

Management has borrowed several systems terms from computer terminology and applied them to the individual and the family. Three of these terms—inputs, throughputs, and outputs—form the basic elements in systems theory as it is applied to management.

Inputs are whatever is brought into the system (i.e., things, ideas, information). The processing of inputs is called **throughput,** or transformation. Any system is subject to a succession of different states, and the transitions from one state to another are called **transformations** (Sieburg, 1985). **Outputs** refer to the end results or products, leftovers, and waste.

Figure 2.2 presents a managerial action model showing the interaction of inputs, throughputs, and outputs. In the model, inputs such as resources and demands are transformed through planning and deciding into the outputs of met demands, altered resources, and satisfaction/dissatisfaction. **Demands** are events or goals that require action. For example, if a landlord demands that rent be paid on time, tenants need to respond to this demand. *Facilitating* means to make something easier. It helps move the managerial process along. **Sequencing** occurs when one thing follows another as in a series of events. For example, scenes in a play follow in sequence. In resource management, events occur in sequence to ensure a successful outcome. Before writing a check to the landlord, the tenant determines that he has enough money in his checking account to cover the rent. This process is facilitated if the tenant has kept his account balanced and his records up-to-date. Calculating whether he has enough money in the account after the check is written would be placing events out of sequence.

Sharpe and Winter (1991) applied inputs, throughputs (transformations), and outputs to the concept of managerial effectiveness. They hypothesized that effective management leads to satisfactory outcomes. They thought that there are many potential ways to be a more effective manager. For example, they hypothesized that managerial effectiveness increases when the manager has goals (inputs) that are clear, actionable, and verifiable and when the manager gener-

FIGURE 2.2
Managerial Action Using the Systems Approach

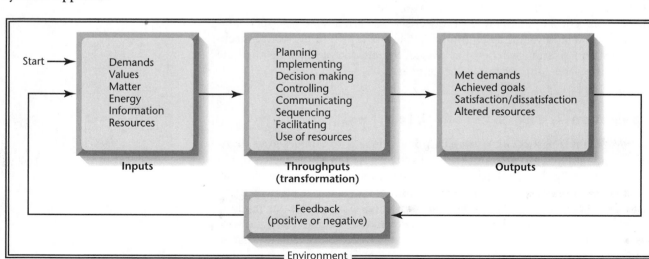

ates workable alternatives (transformations). Increased efficiency in the use of time and evaluation are two output hypotheses. These hypotheses illustrate how input, throughput, and output can be applied to management.

Feedback

Feedback occurs when part of the output is returned to the input in the form of information. The term *feedback* was introduced in Chapter 1 as part of the management process diagrammed in Figure 1.1. It also appeared earlier in this chapter in Figure 2.1. Figure 2.3 shows a model focusing specifically on the feedback loop. This model begins with a current assessment of the performance or situation and then proceeds to the establishment of objectives and goals. As in most management models, an evaluation component leads to further feedback. The feedback loop is important because it reinforces the concept that feedback affects future decisions and the allocation of resources. The model in Figure 2.3 also demonstrates that feedback is not an end in itself, but a process or operation.

There are two kinds of feedback: positive and negative. In general conversation, the words *positive* and *negative* connote good and bad, but in systems terminology the words are used differently. **Positive feedback** is information put into the system that anticipates and promotes change; thus, it indicates that a new course of action is needed. **Negative feedback** is information put into the system that indicates that the system is deviating from its normal course and that corrective measures may be necessary if the desired steady state is to be maintained. Individuals and families use feedback to make future decisions. For example, negative feedback may reinforce that a previous decision was right and that no further change is needed.

To illustrate positive feedback, consider the situation of John, a college student who receives a B+ on a midterm exam in a course where the grade is based on the midterm and the final exam. Since John wants to get an A in the course, his midterm grade indicates that he will have to study harder for the final to earn an A in the course. Therefore, the B+ grade (although it is a disappointment) gives John positive feedback. Since he enjoys the class and thinks he is capable of getting an A, he plans to study harder to improve his grade. Kevin, sitting next to John, also gets a B+ on the midterm, but he decides to put his energies elsewhere and is prepared to settle for a B in the course. Thus, the test grade gave Kevin negative feedback; he chooses to maintain the system by studying at his current pace and not trying to change it.

Feedback serves an important function. People use feedback to learn if they are doing and saying the right things. Their future decisions hinge on the type

The return of info about the result of managerial action

FIGURE 2.3
Model of the Feedback Loop in Management

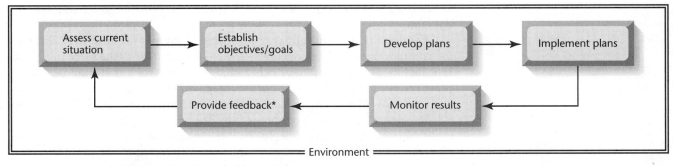

*Feedback is the return of information about the result of managerial action.

of feedback they receive and how they act on that feedback. The concept of feedback will be covered more extensively in the chapter on communication.

Entropy

According to systems theory, each system has a tendency to run down and possibly misfunction as its energy flow ebbs and becomes less structured. This tendency toward disorder or randomness is called **entropy**. It is more likely to occur in a closed system than in an open system because a closed system receives few inputs from outside and thus has no source for renewed energy (Sieburg, 1985). For example, an executive who works 60-hour weeks and eventually wears down and needs a vacation is experiencing entropy. The vacation revitalizes the executive, and she returns with renewed energy and vigor. In a system, entropy can refer to a lack of energy as well as a lack of information. Entropy unchecked leads to disorganization and disruption, order is destroyed.

Homeostasis

Generally, systems try to remain balanced. This tendency to maintain balance is called **homeostasis.** It works as a control device. When something gets out of control, tension is created, and the system becomes unbalanced, triggering the homeostasis mechanism. For example, people who have a Monday through Friday workweek use the weekend to renew their sense of balance and get their home and family life back in order. They run errands, answer mail, wash clothes, mow their lawns, and spend time with their families and friends. By Sunday night, they hope there will be a feeling of homeostasis—a sense that things are back under control and in order for the week ahead.

Equifinality and Multifinality

The concepts of equifinality and multifinality are also important in systems theory. **Equifinality** refers to the phenomenon in which different circumstances and opportunities may lead to similar outcomes. **Multifinality** refers to the phenomenon in which the same initial circumstances or conditions may lead to different conclusions or outcomes.

For example, consider the situation of two friends, Brett and Nick, who are high school seniors deciding which college to attend. Although they have been accepted by the same colleges and have the same backgrounds and career goals, Brett chooses to stay at home and attend a community college, and Nick chooses to go away to a four-year college. This different outcome given the same initial conditions is an example of multifinality. Now, consider the situation of Megan and Tia, two students who have never met. Even though they have totally different backgrounds and ambitions, they end up choosing the same college—an example of equifinality, a similar outcome given different initial conditions.

Equifinality and multifinality are useful concepts because they illustrate the complex nature of management. Different outcomes to the same initial surface factors may indicate that other factors are at work that may not be apparent to the outside observer. For example, individual tastes, preferences, and attitudes play a large part in decisions and outcomes. Nick might be ready for a four-year college away from home, but Brett may not. Expense might be another consideration in their decisions. Megan and Tia may have more in common than is readily apparent, or both may be attracted to the same feature of a particular college.

The Personal System

The goal of personal systems management is to recognize and to make productive the specific strengths and abilities of each individual. Respect for the uniqueness of the qualities of each individual is a critical part of management. Each person is a system composed of many subsystems, including the (1) biological/physiological, (2) behavioral, (3) psychological, and (4) social subsystems. Each subsystem in turn has many components. For example, values and ethics are part of the psychological subsystem; they provide integrity and direction to decisions, guiding individuals through the many moral dilemmas they encounter each day. For example, after a day of shopping, Kayla examines her receipts and discovers that the salesperson at the music store neglected to charge her for one of the compact discs she purchased. Will Kayla go back and pay for the extra disc? Her decision will be guided by the values and ethics of her psychological subsystem.

Each individual's personal system exists within a greater system of relationships, friendships, and family. Inputs to the personal system include other people, the environment, heredity, and past experiences, all of which help shape the individual's personal management style. Due to the dynamic nature of systems, the individual is always changing and always interpreting feedback.

Industry and government are interested in how people's attitudes change. The Gallup organization regularly monitors people's attitudes on a variety of subjects, including conditions in the United States and in their personal lives. In one survey, respondents reported that they were more satisfied with their personal lives than with the way things were going overall in the United States. Since the beginning of the 1980s, Gallup polls have consistently indicated that about 80 percent of Americans are satisfied with the way things are going in their lives (Newport & Hueber, 1990). Newport and Hueber conclude from this that Americans have a remarkable ability to think positively about their own personal life situations, even while seeing things about them in a more negative light. In another survey, the Roper organization found that as people age their home becomes more important to them, and clothes and jewelry become less important as a means of defining self.

The Family System

The goal of family system management is to recognize and to make productive the specific strengths and abilities of each family. In family systems, boundaries change over time as families change.

Interactions within families are qualitatively and quantitatively different from interactions among other groups. According to McCubbin and his colleagues (1997), families are especially resilient because: (1) they establish patterns of functioning after being challenged and confronted by risk factors, referred to as elasticity, and (2) have the ability to recover quickly from a misfortune, trauma, or transitional event, an ability referred to as buoyancy.

The discovery of factors that enhance a family's resiliency is a subject of interest to researchers. McCubbin and his colleagues predict that the twenty-first century will be characterized as the era of family transformation and stress. They have identified ten general resiliency factors that will help families survive and prosper.

1. Family problem-solving communication
2. Equality

3. Spirituality

4. Flexibility

5. Truthfulness

6. Hope

7. Family hardiness

8. Family time and routines

9. Social support

10. Health

Family systems theory also emphasizes the importance of family history, a psychological perspective introduced by Murray Bowen in the 1970s and set forth more recently by Monica McGoldrick in *You Can Go Home Again*. McGoldrick emphasizes that people and their problems do not exist in a vacuum but are part of a broad family system. Thus, family patterns of working, relating, and dealing with stress can reverberate through generations (Shellenbarger, 1998). She says that:

> The "family" comprises the entire emotional system of at least three and increasingly four generations, who move through life together, even though they often live in different places. As a family we share a common past and an anticipated future. The patterns of family life cycle are changing dramatically, so that there is less continuity than ever before between the demands on current families and the patterns of past generations. Thus it is easy to lose all sense of connection with what has come before in your family, and this can be a serious loss. (McGoldrick, 1995, p. 30.)

Further, McGoldrick says:

> While each family is unique in its particular history, all families are alike in their underlying patterns. Famous families may, because they are in the spotlight, have certain responses to their notoriety, but all families have basic ways they deal with love, pain, and conflict; make sense of life and death; cross time, class, and cultural barriers. All families must find ways of dealing with loss and of integrating new members.

Applications of Systems Theory to Households

The previous two sections have focused on the management of personal and family lives. Systems theory and terminology can also apply to homes. For example, the concepts of inputs, throughputs, outputs, and feedback can be applied to both simple and complex household operations.

An example of a simple household operation is doing the laundry. Water, detergent, and clothes are inputs into the washing machine. The throughput is the cleansing, rinsing, and spinning action, and the outputs are dirty wastewater and clean clothes. If the clothes are not clean, this signals (provides feedback) that something is wrong with the system and a change is needed.

More complex household operations include preparing meals, establishing schedules, and caring for children. For example, meal preparation involves deciding what to eat, shopping (the average grocery store offers more than 30,000 different products), food preparation, serving, eating, and cleaning up. Setting schedules requires communication and the coordination of activities, people, and time. Child care involves innumerable decisions, tasks, and responsibilities plus emotional factors.

The model in Figure 2.4 illustrates the many facets of household production and consumption. In the model, the inputs to the household are rented, leased, provided by the community, or owned. Raw materials, market goods and services, and durables are inputs to the household system. These various inputs lead to the production of goods and services that may be consumed or given as gifts, sold, or bartered. This activity contributes to household well-being and the desired end result (output, goal) of improved human resources. As this model demonstrates, household production/consumption does more than satisfy immediate needs—it provides for an increased human capability, a provision for the future.

Human Ecology and Ecosystems

Conditions in the greater environment have an important influence on how households and families function. The study of how living things relate to their natural environment is called **ecology**. Adding the word *human* produces the term **human ecology**, which simply stated means humans interacting with their environment. A more comprehensive definition of human ecology is that it is the study of how humans—as social, physical, and biological beings—interact with each other and with their physical, sociocultural, aesthetic, and biological environments as well as with the material and human resources of these environments (Bubolz & Sontag, 1988).

Human ecology views humans and their near environments as integrated wholes, mutually influencing each other (Bubolz & Sontag, 1988). The **environment** is the sum of the external conditions influencing the life of an organism or population (Naar, 1990). In this book, the emphasis is on the quality of life conditions for individuals and families.

The *environment* is essentially everything that surrounds humans, but this concept is so broad that theorists have divided the environment into the

FIGURE 2.4
Model of the Household Production/Consumption System

Source: F. M. Magrabi, Y. S. Chung, S. S. Cha, and S. Young, *The Economics of the Household* (New York: Praeger, 1991), p. 7. Greenwood Publishing Group, Inc., Westport, CT. © 1991.

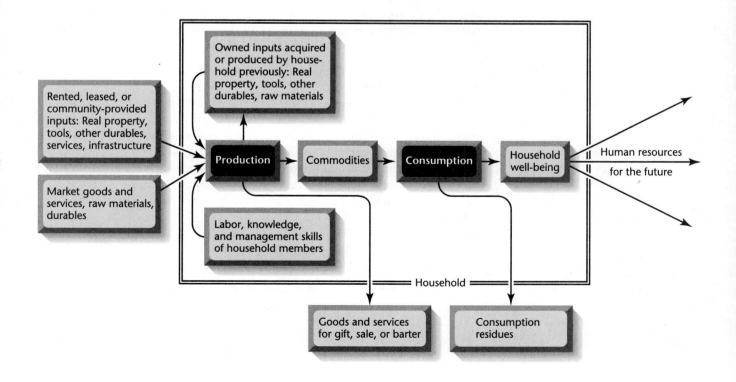

microenvironment and the macroenvironment. The **microenvironment** (also called the microhabitat or near environment) is the environment that closely surrounds individuals and families. Apartments, sorority and fraternity houses, classrooms, libraries, and dormitory rooms are part of a college student's microenvironment. The **macroenvironment** (also called the macrohabitat or far environment) surrounds and encompasses the microenvironment. Sky, trees, and oceans are part of the macroenvironment.

Family Ecosystem

The **family ecosystem** is the subsystem of human ecology that emphasizes the interactions between families and environments. According to Paolucci, Hall, and Axinn (1977), the family ecosystem has three basic elements:

1. *Organisms:* These are the family members.
2. *Environments:* Both the natural and human-built environments are included.
3. *Family organization:* This functions to transform energy in the form of information into family decisions and actions.

The ecosystem approach is useful because it emphasizes the interaction between families and the conditions that surround them. A change in a single component of the family ecosystem has an impact on the other parts. For example, if one family member has an alcohol or drug abuse problem, it will affect everyone else in the family.

Figure 2.5 illustrates the many ways family organisms (O) and environments (E) relate to one another. The example of alcohol or drug abuse internal to the family is depicted as O ↔ O, family organism affecting family organism. Examples of E → O are fires or hurricanes destroying homes and communities. A family's decision to cut down a tree in the yard is an example of O → E. A tropical storm hitting a deserted island is an example of E ↔ E. The study of management emphasizes human interactions with environments, which are diagrammed as O ↔ E. Most management situations involve individuals or families interacting with each other and with factors in their environment.

Global Ecosystems

Global ecosystems encompass all the family ecosystems and are regulated by interactive physical, social, political, economic, chemical, and biological processes. To begin to understand the global ecosystem, one must understand the dynamics of family ecosystems. For instance, each family contributes to the greater society and is a microcosm of the larger social system in which it exists. Jesse Jackson's quilt metaphor is an excellent illustration of those concepts. He said that "America is not like a blanket—one piece of unbroken cloth, the same color, the same texture, the same size. America is more like a

FIGURE 2.5

Interdependence of the Components of a Family Ecosystem

Source: B. Paolucci, O. Hall, and N. Axinn, *Family Decision Making: An Ecosystem Approach* (New York: Macmillan College Publishing Company, 1977), p. 16.

E ——————→ O	Environment affecting family organisms (members)
O ——————→ E	Family organisms affecting environment
O ←——————→ O	Family organisms affecting family organisms
E ←——————→ E	Environment affecting environment
O ←——————→ E	Reciprocal effect of family organisms and environments

quilt—many pieces, many colors, many sizes, all woven and held together by a common thread" (Jackson, 1988). Each patch in the quilt adds a special nuance of color, pattern, strength, utility, and texture to the finished product. Collectively, the sum of all the parts is infinitely more interesting than the individual pieces. Each extended family and each nation benefits from the combined strength of their various people and cultures.

Millions of family ecosystems combine to form national ecosystems that in turn make up the global ecosystem. Human ecology emphasizes the global interdependence of individuals, families, and communities, with the resources of natural, constructed, and behavioral environments, for the purpose of wise decision making and use of resources essential to human development and the quality of life and the environment (Bubolz & Sontag, 1988).

In homes, family ecosystems interact with the systems that supply food, heat, health care, information, water, gas, electricity, clothing, and transportation. These same systems operate in the global ecosystem on a much larger scale. The welfare of nations depends on these life support systems. For example, maintaining an adequate food supply is a concern at the household level, the natural level, and the global level.

International environmental issues will dominate the global policy agenda of the twenty-first century. Long-range solutions to environmental problems will require planning and cooperation among nations. Since planning is a fundamental part of management, this field will play an increasingly vital role in encouraging the conservation of resources and the promotion of informed and sound health and environmental attitudes and practices at the individual, family, and household levels.

ECONOMIC THEORY

Although systems theory has been the dominant influence on management in the last few decades, the application of economic theory to management has attracted renewed attention. According to Sherman Hanna (1989), "The most obvious application of economic theory to family resource management is in terms of the maximization of satisfaction or utility subject to resource constraints. The potential application of the economic framework is very wise, extending to all consumer purchases of products and services, and also including labor force, fertility, and even marriage decisions."

Economic theory assumes that individuals seek to maximize satisfaction from the decisions they make. It also assumes that individuals are rational (use reason in making decisions) and will act in their own self-interest. Economic theory focuses on the interaction between buyers and sellers. Economists are basically concerned with the nature of exchange, for example, what things cost and what is gained in return.

Optimization and Satisficing

Economic theory includes many subtheories. One of these is **optimization**, which means obtaining the best result, such as maximizing profit for a business or maximizing satisfaction for a household (Hanna, 1989). In other words, optimization refers to the effective use of resources to gain the most satisfaction. Although in theory individuals and families will seek to optimize their resources, in reality they often do not behave in optimizing ways. For example, they may not buy the low-cost generic product in a grocery store even though it has the same quality as a more expensive brand name product. Or they may not buy the lowest-cost airplane ticket because they do not want to fly at an inconvenient time or do not plan far enough ahead to get the lowest price. Comparison shopping can save money, but some people may feel it is not worth the aggravation, time, energy, and patience required.

Intensive information seeking is an important aspect of optimization theory. Since economic theory emphasizes the measurable and the rational, information seeking is heralded as a logical course of action. Theorists reason that the more people know, the more informed (better) their decisions will be. This makes intuitive sense, but not everyone does what is reasonable and logical all the time. Besides even the best informed decisions can go wrong. For example, Randall and Elaine spent months researching which car to buy. They read articles about new cars, checked the recommendations of *Consumer Reports* magazine, and then went out and bought the worst car of their married life. Apparently, the marketplace is less than perfect (i.e., an individual car can be poorly manufactured even though the model is highly recommended). Furthermore, people must consider the possible outcomes in deciding how much planning and implementing effort is optimal. Expending considerable effort to obtain information about a choice that will have little long-term effect on the family may not be a wise use of time and other resources.

Attempts have been made to integrate economic and social systems theories. For example, mate selection is an intriguing example of a decision that is not entirely based on reason. Nevertheless, Gary S. Becker, professor of economics at the University of Chicago and winner of the Nobel Prize in economics, posits that the economic forces that influence people to get married and have children are as powerful as the forces that govern decisions to buy a new car or change jobs ("Family Values," 1992–1993). Others disagree. They argue that selecting a mate, having children, and other highly personal choices are more emotional than rational. Less controversial is the use of optimization theory by household and business managers. Decisions that are largely objective, such as which refrigerator or laser printer to purchase, may be well suited to a short information search and a rational decision. Thus, optimization may be most useful in simple, straightforward situations involving a short information search and little emotion. Whether it is applicable in decision situations such as mate selection, as suggested by Becker, is open to debate. But since the basic point of optimization is the maximization of satisfaction through obtaining the best result, the theory should be applicable to a variety of situations.

Satisficing refers to picking the first good alternative that presents itself (Simon, 1959). The individual stops searching once it appears that an initial choice will suffice. This strategy makes sense when time and choices are limited. Someone with a flat tire who is late to work may not want to take the time to comparison shop for tires. She will probably buy a tire as quickly as possible so she can proceed on her way.

Applying economic theory to personal consumption is complicated because "values other than efficiency are important for many people, including satisfaction derived from the process rather than the end-product, and creation of unique products not available from the market" (Hanna, 1989). Thus, shopping in and of itself is an enjoyable activity for many individuals, and this should be considered in discussions of rational economic behavior. The fastest choice may not be the best choice if shopping itself creates satisfaction. Furthermore, according to Hanna (1989), "in the business world, firms that do not adopt more efficient ways of doing things will not survive in the long run, but households can just muddle along using inefficient techniques." This quote makes one wonder: How efficient do households have to be to exist and function? How much of economic theory, with its emphasis on rationality and logic, can be applied to households and families? These types of questions fuel management research.

Risk Aversion

The possibility of experiencing harm, suffering, danger, or loss is known as **risk.** Although we tend to associate risk with physical danger, it can also involve such things as losing money, energy, time, or reputation. In the last section, car-buyers Randall and Elaine experienced consumer risk, but risk can also take other forms, including health and safety risk, educational risk, relationship risk, occupational risk, and financial risk. Foxall, Goldsmith, and Brown (1998) have identified several types of perceived risk that affect decision making:

- ◆ *Functional or performance risk:* The possibility that a choice may not turn out as desired or have the expected benefits
- ◆ *Financial risk:* The possibility that substantial amounts of money may be lost
- ◆ *Physical risk:* The possibility that harm may come from a choice
- ◆ *Psychological risk:* The possibility that a choice may damage a person's image of self or self-esteem
- ◆ *Social risk:* The possibility that a choice will not be approved by others, or may cause social embarrassment or rejection
- ◆ *Time risk:* The possibility that the ability to satisfy wants will decline over time

This is not to imply that risk is all bad. Changing jobs is a risk, and traveling involves risk. Indeed, many people like a certain degree of risk, otherwise games, gambling, and competition would not exist. For these people, risk provides a little excitement and release from tedium. One person may dream of winning the lottery and quitting his boring job. Another may take up skydiving to spice up her life. As these examples suggest, risk is not an absolute. The perception of risk varies from person to person. One individual may think riding down the Grand Canyon on the back of a mule is an exciting adventure, whereas another may view it as foolhardy.

Trying to avoid the dire outcomes associated with risk is a rational course of behavior. In economic theory, the avoidance of risk is called **risk aversion.** Risk-averse individuals and families seek to minimize problems and maximize satisfaction by avoiding risk. For example, a risk-averse individual who dislikes heights and enclosed spaces would avoid riding elevators to the top of tall buildings. Just as different people perceive risk differently, the amount of risk aversion varies from person to person, family to family, and situation to situation. Although some people feel comfortable betting on horse races or playing slot machines, others would never dream of spending money on gambling. The amount of risk a person is likely to take also varies by life cycle stage. A person who is 18 years old is likely to take more risks than someone who is 84. People's resources also affect the amount of risk they are likely to assume.

What constitutes a risk depends on the individual.

The greater the resources, the more confident an individual will feel about taking a risk. If the decision fails, the individual will not feel the loss as keenly as someone with fewer remaining resources.

Yet even people with substantial resources may be wary of risk or feel uncertain in new situations. Ultimately, an individual's management skills may affect both his or her perception of the uncertain situation and the decision that he or she makes (Jensen, 1987). The decision maker estimates how much risk the situation involves and tries to turn an uncertain outcome to his or her advantage. Hopefully, "the process of problem definition, setting goals, developing alternative courses of action, deciding among alternatives, carrying out the activity and evaluating the results will bring about increased satisfaction even under conditions of uncertainty" (Jensen, 1987). Understanding the principles of perceived risk and being sensitive to the presence of risk can help the decision maker use risk-reduction strategies (e.g., gathering more information or following safe procedures) more effectively (Foxall, Goldsmith, & Brown, 1998). Chapter 5 discusses the relation of risk and uncertainty to decision making in more detail.

To conclude, risk aversion as an economic theory provides insight into the study of management. The fundamental principle of the maximization of satisfaction through the avoidance of risk provides plausible explanations for many types of decisions.

Electronic Resources

For information on historic homes, go to **www.nr.nps.gov**, the Web site of the National Register of Historic Places, or **www.nps.gov** for the National Park Service with links to the past. If you are interested in researching your **genealogy** (an account of the descent of a person or family from an ancestor or ancestors), before going on the Web, begin by writing down what you know about your parents, grandparents, or other relatives, including their full names, birthdates, birthplaces, wedding dates, and dates of death. Search your house for information in old books, photograph albums, clothes, trunks, attics, and so forth. Talk to older relatives about their older relatives and explore outside resources. To involve relatives who live at a distance, send them photocopies of photographs or other evidence you want them to identify or verify.

One resource in the United States is **census.gov** (similar government sources exist in other countries). Also, all states have a Vital Statistics Division of the State Department of Health, which may provide useful information, usually for a fee. Other resources include immigration, marriage, church, and military service records. Or, contact the Web sites or go in person to visit libraries and archives, religious organizations that keep records, and genealogical societies. In addition, the World Wide Web has a wealth of genealogical information including:

- ◆ **www.genhomepage.com**, The Genealogy Home Page™ sponsored by Family Tree Maker online.
- ◆ **www.ancestors.com**, which is the home page for Ancestors, a PBS series on genealogy. Information is given about genealogical organizations by state and how to research a family tree.
- ◆ **www.cyndislist.com** has more than 41,000 links that are categorized and cross-referenced into different categories.
- ◆ **www.ngsgenealogy.org** is the National Genealogical Society's Web site that contains library records.

www.genhomepage.com

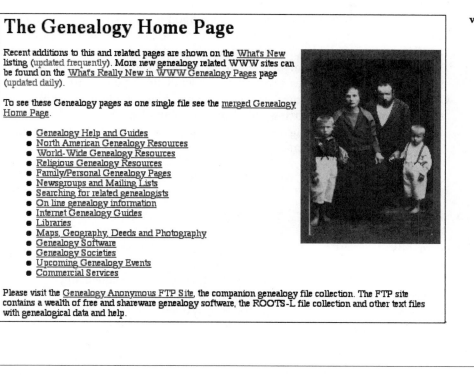

The Genealogy Home Page

Recent additions to this and related pages are shown on the What's New listing (updated frequently). More new genealogy related WWW sites can be found on the What's Really New in WWW Genealogy Pages page (updated daily).

To see these Genealogy pages as one single file see the merged Genealogy Home Page.

- Genealogy Help and Guides
- North American Genealogy Resources
- World-Wide Genealogy Resources
- Religious Genealogy Resources
- Family/Personal Genealogy Pages
- Newsgroups and Mailing Lists
- Searching for related genealogists
- On line genealogy information
- Internet Genealogy Guides
- Libraries
- Maps, Geography, Deeds and Photography
- Genealogy Software
- Genealogy Societies
- Upcoming Genealogy Events
- Commercial Services

Please visit the Genealogy Anonymous FTP Site, the companion genealogy file collection. The FTP site contains a wealth of free and shareware genealogy software, the ROOTS-L file collection and other text files with genealogical data and help.

Summary

This chapter discussed the historical background of management and the basics of theory along with the specifics of systems theory and economic theory. The study of management as taught and practiced today has its roots in the nineteenth century. As it has adjusted to technological, social, and economic changes in the twentieth century, the field has necessarily become far more complex than it was originally. One particularly significant change in the twentieth century was the transformation of the home from being primarily a producer to being primarily a consumer of goods and services. Not only has the amount of household production declined, but the types of products it does produce and consume have changed significantly.

The study of management relies heavily on systems theory. In systems theory, each part contributes to the behavior of the whole and the whole is greater than the sum of its parts. Two types of feedback—positive and negative—are integral to this theory. The chapter presented a model of a feedback loop as well as a model showing the interaction of the components of a household production/consumption system.

Gallup polls have attempted to measure individuals' satisfaction with their personal lives and have found that Americans tend to be more satisfied with their personal affairs than with overall conditions in the United States. The chapter emphasized the importance of the interdependence of families and environments within the global ecosystem. Environments, near and far, provide the setting for human interactions, although individuals and families vary in the degree to which they are open or closed to the environment.

The chapter also examined the economic theories of optimization, satisficing, and risk aversion. In optimization, the individual increases her or his chance for satisfaction and minimizes problems in a rational way by searching for information. In satisficing, the first good choice that presents itself is selected. In risk aversion, the goal is to maximize satisfaction by avoiding risks.

Underlying both systems theory and economic theory is the belief that behavior is not random and it occurs for some reason or reasons. One of the few absolutely undisputable principles in resource management is that most behavior is rational and that individual preferences and situations play a great part in behavior. Theories provide useful ways to organize information, allowing for predicting future behavior. They do not explain everything, but they provide valuable starting points and frameworks. The next chapter goes beyond the realm of the theoretical to explore how values affect decision making and how goals drive managerial behavior.

Key Terms

boundaries	hypotheses	positive feedback
controlling	inputs	risk
demands	interface	risk aversion
ecology	macroenvironment	satisficing
entropy	microenvironment	sequencing
environment	morphogenic systems	subsystem
equifinality	morphostatic systems	system
family ecosystem	multifinality	theory
genealogy	negative feedback	throughputs
homeostasis	optimization	transformation
human ecology	outputs	work simplification

Review Questions

1. Compare and contrast typical homes and household tasks in 1900, 1950, and 2000.

2. "There is nothing so practical as a good theory," says Kurt Lewin. Explain why theory is useful.

3. What is the difference between positive and negative feedback?

4. How is a family a system? According to McCubbin and his coauthors, why are families especially resilient?

5. What are the assumptions underlying economic theory?

References

Arndt, W. (1974). *Theories of personality*. New York: Macmillan.

Berger, P. S. (1984). Home management research: State of the art 1909–1984. *Home Economics Research Journal, 12*(3), 252–264.

Bryant, K. (1992). Human capital, time use, and other family behavior. *Journal of Family and Economic Issues, 13*(4), 395–406.

Bubolz, M. M. & Sontag, S. (1988). Integration in home economics and human ecology. *Journal of Consumer Studies and Home Economics, 12*, 1–14.

Castells, M. (1996). *The information age*, Vol. 1. Cambridge, MA: Blackwell.

Cowan, R. (1983). *More work for mother*. New York: Basic Books.

Davey, A. (1971). Relationship of family interaction to family environment. Unpublished Ph.D. thesis, Michigan State University, East Lansing.

Deacon, R. E. & Firebaugh, F. M. (1988). *Family resource management: Principles and applications* (2nd ed.). Boston: Allyn & Bacon.

Drucker, P. (1999). *Management challenges for the 21st century*. New York: Harper Business.

Family values. (December 26, 1992–January 8, 1993). *The Economist, 325*(7791), 37–40.

Foxall, G., Goldsmith, R., & Brown, S. (1998). *Consumer*

psychology for marketing. London: Routledge.

Frederick, C. (1918). *The new housekeeping.* New York: Doubleday.

Gilbreth, L. (1927). *The homemaker and her job.* New York: D. Appleton.

Goebel, K. P. & Hennon, D. B. (1982). An empirical investigation of the relationship among wife's employment status, stage in the family life cycle, meal preparation time, and expenditures for meals away from home. *Journal of Consumer Studies and Home Economics, 6,* 63–78.

Goldsmith, E. (1977). Time use of beginning families with employed and unemployed wives. Unpublished Ph.D. thesis, Michigan State University, East Lansing.

Goldsmith, E. (1993). Home economics: The discovered discipline. *Journal of Home Economics, 85(4),* 45–48.

Gross, I. H., Crandall, E. W., & Knoll, M. M. (1980). *Management for modern families* (4th ed.). Englewood Cliffs, NJ: Prentice-Hall.

Hafstrom, J. & Paynter, M. (1991). Time use satisfaction: Home, farm, and labor force workload. *Lifestyles: Family and Economic Issues, 12(2),* 131–143.

Hafstrom, J. L. & Schram, V. R. (1983). Housework time of wives: Pressures, facilitators, constraints. *Home Economics Research Journal, 11,* 245–254.

Hanna, S. (1989). Optimization for family resource management. *Proceedings, Southeastern Regional Family Economics/Home Management Association.*

Israelsen, C. (1990). Family resource management research 1930–1990. *Financial Counseling and Planning, 1,* 3–39.

Jackson, J. (1988, July 23). Address to 1984 democratic national convention. *Congress Quarterly Weekly Report, 46(30),* 2057.

Jensen, H. (1987). Household risk management and human resources. In R. E. Deacon & W. E. Huffman (Eds.), *Human Resources Research, 1887–1987: Proceedings.* College of Home Economics, Iowa State University, 161–171.

McCubbin, H., McCubbin, M., Thompson, A., Hans, S., & Allen, C. (1997, Fall). Families Under Stress: What makes them resilient? *Journal of Family and Consumer Sciences,* 2–11.

McCullough, J. & Zick, C. (1992). The roles of role strain, economic resources and time demands in explaining mother's life satisfaction. *Journal of Family and Economic Issues, 13(1),* 23–44.

Marshall, R. (1991). *The state of families, 3.* Milwaukee, WI: Family Service America.

McGoldrick, M. (1995). *You can go home again.* New York: W. W. Norton.

Naar, J. (1990). *Design for a livable planet.* New York: Harper & Row.

Newport, F. & Hueber, G. (1990). Satisfaction levels and approval of President Bush. *Gallup Poll Monthly.*

Owen, A. (1991). Time and time again: Implications of time

perception theory. *Lifestyles: Family and Economic Issues, 12(4),* 345–349.

Paolucci, B., Hall, O., & Axinn, N. (1977). *Family decision making: An ecosystem approach.* New York: John Wiley & Sons.

Parloa, M. (1879). *First principles of household management and cookery.* Boston: Houghton, Osgood.

Rettig, K. & Bubolz, M. (1983). Perceptual indicators of family well-being. *Social Indicators Research, 12,* 417–438.

Sanik, M. M. (1981). A division of household work: A decade comparison, 1967–1977. *Home Economics Research Journal, 10,* 175–180.

Schnittgrund, K. (1980). Productive time of household heads. *Journal of Consumer Studies and Home Economics, 4,* 239–248.

Sharpe, D. L. & Winter, M. (1991). Toward working hypotheses of effective management: Conditions, thought processes and behaviors. *Lifestyles: Family and Economics Issues, 12(4),* 303–323.

Shellanbarger, S. (1998, April 28). *Work and family. The Wall Street Journal,* B1.

Sieburg, E. (1985). *Family communication.* New York: Gardner Press.

Simon, H. (1959). Theories of decision-making in economics and behavioral sciences. *American Economic Review, 49,* 253–283.

Stafford, K. (1983). The effects of wife's employment time on household work time. *Home Economics Research Journal, 11,* 257–266.

Taylor, F. W. (1911). *Principles of scientific management.* New York: Harper & Brothers.

There's no place like home. (1997, January). *American Demographics,* 26.

Vickers, C. (1984). Themes in home management. *In Themes in Home Economics and Their Impact on Families, 1909–1984.* Washington, DC: American Home Economics Association.

Walker, K. E. & Woods, M. E. (1976). *Time use: A measure of household production of family goods and services.* Washington, DC: American Home Economics Association.

Warren, J. (1940). Use of time in its relation to home management. Cornell University Agricultural Experiment Station Bulletin 734.

Wilson, M. (1929). Use of time by Oregon farm homemakers. Oregon Agricultural Experiment Station 256.

Winter, M., Puspitawati, H., Heck, R., & Stafford, K. (1993). Time-management strategies used by households with home-based work. *Journal of Family and Economic Issues, 14(1),* 69–92.

Woolgar, C. (1993). *Household accounts from medieval England.* Oxford: Oxford University Press.

For Further Reading*

Andrews, B. R. (1935). *Economics of the household*. New York: Macmillan.

Becker, G. S. (1981). *A treatise on the family*. Cambridge, MA: Harvard University Press.

Beecher, C. (1841). *Treatise on domestic economy*. Boston: Marsh, Capen, Lyon, & Webb.

Bonde, R. L. (1944). *Management in daily living*. New York: Macmillan.

Bratton, E. C. (1971). *Home management is*. Boston: Ginn.

Cushman, E. M. (1945). *Management in homes*. New York: Macmillan.

Fitzsimmons, C. & Williams, F. (1973). *The family economy, nature and management of resources*. Ann Arbor, MI: Edwards Brothers.

Gilbreth, L., Thomas, O. M., & Clymer, E. (1955). *Management in the home*. New York: Dodd, Mead.

Goodyear, M. R. & Klohr, M. C. (1965). *Managing for effective living* (2nd ed.). New York: Wiley.

Kyrk, H. (1933). *Economic problems of the family*. New York: Harper & Row.

Kyrk, H. (1953). *The family in the American economy*. Chicago: University of Chicago Press.

Liston, M. (1993). *History of family economics research: 1862–1962*. Ames, IA: University Publications, Iowa State University.

Magrabi, F. M., Chung, Y. S., Cha, S. S., & Yang, S. (1991). *The economics of household consumption*. New York: Praeger.

May, E. E., Waggoner, N. R., & Boethke, E. M. (1974). *Independent living for the handicapped and the elderly*. Boston: Houghton Mifflin.

Oppenheim, I. (1976). *Management of the modern home* (2nd ed.). New York: Macmillan.

Paolucci, B., Hall, O. A. & Axinn, N. (1977). *Family decision making: An ecological approach*. New York: John Wiley.

Reid, M. G. (1934). *Economics of household production*. New York: John Wiley.

Rice, A. S. & Tucker, S. M. (1986). *Family life management* (6th ed.). New York: Macmillan.

Richards, E. H. (1900). *The cost of living as modified by sanitary science*. New York: John Wiley.

Stage, S. & Vincent, V. (1997). *Rethinking home economics*. Ithaca, NY: Cornell University.

Starr, M. C. (1968). *Management for better living*. Lexington, MA: D. C. Heath.

Steidl, R. E. & Bratton, E. C. (1968). *Work in the home*. New York: John Wiley & Sons.

Swanson, B. B. (1981). *Introduction to home management*. New York: Macmillan.

Talbot, M. & Breckinridge, S. (1919). *The modern household*. Boston: Whitcomb & Barrows.

*When a book has appeared in several editions, the newest is cited. This list of seminal works (textbooks, popular books, and reference books) is intended to supplement those already cited in the reference list; it is not meant to be comprehensive. In addition, management articles can be found in the *Journal of Family and Consumer Sciences* (formerly the *Journal of Home Economics*), *Family and Consumer Sciences Research Journal* (formerly the *Home Economics Research Journal*), *Journal of Marriage and the Family, Journal of Consumer Affairs, Journal of Family and Economic Issues, Journal of Consumer Studies, Kappa Omicron Nu Forum, Canadian Home Economics Journal,* and in the journals of allied fields. Other sources for management theory, research, and applications are theses and dissertations, Agricultural Experiment Station Bulletins, the *Family Economics Review* and other government publications, and conference proceedings.

part 2

Management Concepts and Principles

CHAPTER 3
VALUES, ATTITUDES, AND GOALS

CHAPTER 4
RESOURCES

CHAPTER 5
DECISION MAKING AND PROBLEM SOLVING

CHAPTER 6
PLANNING, IMPLEMENTING, AND EVALUATING

CHAPTER 7
COMMUNICATION

Values, Attitudes, and Goals

MAIN TOPICS

VALUES AND ATTITUDES
TYPES OF VALUES
VALUES, LIFESTYLES, AND CONSUMPTION
SOCIETAL AND CULTURAL VALUES
FAMILIES, VALUES, STANDARDS, AND HOUSEHOLDS
ATTITUDES

GOALS
GOALS VERSUS HABITS
GOAL ATTRIBUTES
TYPES OF GOALS
SETTING GOALS
COLLEGE STUDENTS' VALUES AND GOALS
MOTIVATION

Did you know that...?

. . . About 23 percent of New Year's resolutions are broken the first week, 45 percent by the end of January.

. . . On average, nearly one-third of college freshmen do not return for their sophomore year.

> A good beginning makes a good ending.
>
> —*English Proverb*

VALUES, ATTITUDES, AND goals underlie interpersonal relationships and lifestyle choices, such as whom people choose to live with, what they consume, and what work they do. People who report being happy when they are 20 years old report being equally happy when they are 70. Conversely, 20-year-olds who report being unhappy at 20 are still unhappy at age 70 (McIntosh, Martin, & Jones, 1997). It has also been found that the process of pursuing goals leads to happiness (Csikszentmihalyi, 1997). This chapter explores these and related concepts.

As noted in Chapter 1, management is the process of using resources to achieve goals. The goals people seek and the way they perceive and use resources are affected by their values and attitudes. This chapter focuses on steps 1 and 2 in the management process model (see Figure 3.1).

The chapter begins with a discussion of values and attitudes and then proceeds to goals. The values and goals of college students in particular are examined. Since the successful achievement of goals is closely linked to motivation, it plays an important part in this chapter. Consider the motivation and achievement of Charles Lindbergh, the first aviator to fly nonstop across the Atlantic Ocean from the United States to Europe. Discussing his flight in an article in the *New York Times* on May 13, 1927, he said:

> We (that's my ship and I) took off rather suddenly. We had a report somewhere around 4 o'clock in the afternoon before the weather would be fine, so we thought we would try it.

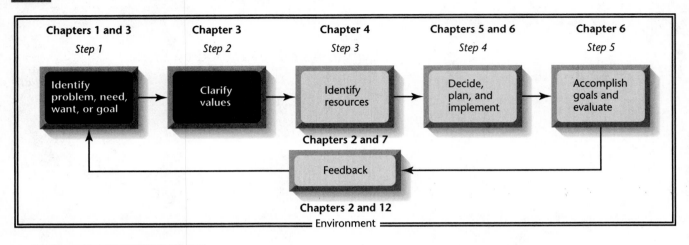

FIGURE 3.1
The Management Process Model

In the same article, F. Scott Fitzgerald, the renowned novelist, described the flight of the *Spirit of Saint Louis* more eloquently:

> In the spring of '27 something bright and alien flashed across the sky. A young Minnesotan [Lindbergh] who seemed to have had nothing to do with his generation did a heroic thing, and for a moment people set down their glasses in country clubs and speakeasies and thought of their old best dreams.

In the 1980s, articles in *Business Week, Science,* and *Time* questioned whether the spirit of invention, technological advance, and adventure epitomized by Lindbergh's solo flight was declining (Mansfield et al., 1988). But in the 1990s, widespread innovations in computers and telecommunications spurred new hope that technology and the spirit of adventure were still very much alive. There's no denying that the twentieth century brought an incredible amount of innovation and progress to our world.

The pace of innovation stands only to increase as we enter the twenty-first century. Business will change more in the next 10 years than it has in the past 50, driven by the Internet, personal computers, innovative software, and new generations of digital devices. The industrial revolution of the nineteenth century was about enhancing muscle power. The current revolution—the digital revolution—is about enhancing the power of the mind (*Business Week,* 1999, Summer, p. 1).

Encouraging the reader to think about the issues surrounding goals and personal and societal values, to set priorities, to seize opportunities, and to move forward are the behavioral goals of this chapter.

VALUES AND ATTITUDES

Values are principles that guide behavior. For example, a person who values honesty will try to act in honest ways. Values are deep-seated psychological constructs that direct individual preferences and strategies for goal achievement. They form the foundation for behavior, including goal-seeking behavior. Each person has an internally integrated value system called a **value orientation,** which is expressed in part in the way he or she makes judgments. A person's judgments are based on the value meanings derived from his or her feelings (the **affective domain**) and thinking (the **cognitive domain**) about events, situations, groups of people, and things. Both the affective and the cognitive domains are based on previous experience. Thus, valuing is an ongoing, never-ending process that forms an integral part of an individual's personality and behavioral systems. Different generations may hold slightly different values, as shown in Table 3.1.

Behavior is what people actually do. The word *behavior* implies action. Often a gap exists between values (the ideal) and behavior (the actual). For example, someone may say that he is on a strict weight-reducing diet, yet stuff his grocery cart with candy bars. Another person may say that she thinks a speed limit of 55 MPH is a good idea, yet habitually drives much faster. Knowing of the gap between values and behavior, researchers are careful to ask survey questions not only about values and attitudes, but also about actual behavior.

Attitudes are concepts that may express values, serve as a means of evaluation, or demonstrate feeling in regard to some idea, person, object, event, situation, or relationship. They are states of mind or feelings, likes, and dislikes about some matter. Everyone has her or his own unique set of attitudes, but the number of attitudes varies from person to person. One person may have attitudes on everything and everybody, whereas someone else may have few attitudes. Think how dull television talk shows would be if the guests and the audience had no attitudes or opinions to express. Attitudes can range from the significant to the petty.

Charles Lindbergh with his plane, the Spirit of Saint Louis, *ready to start on his attempt to cross the Atlantic.*

TABLE 3.1
Values of Three Generations

Percent of U.S. adults who say selected things are very much a part of the American Dream, by generation.

	Matures[*]	Boomers[†]	Xers[‡]
Having a happy marriage	77%	74%	70%
Living in a decent, secure community	75	81	71
Owning your own home	74	79	81
Having children	64	59	51
Unlimited opportunity to pursue dreams	63	71	70
College education for self	50	56	63
Being a winner	45	40	50
Living where everyone shares my values	41	38	28
Becoming wealthy	33	37	46

[*]Matures (everyone born before 1945)
[†]Boomers (born between 1946 and 1964)
[‡]Xers (twenty-somethings)
Source: Yankelovich Partners. Copyright 1998 © Primedia Intertec. Used with permission.

Sometimes values and attitudes are confused. They do share the characteristic that both are abstract. In addition, both can be either explicit, meaning that they are held at the conscious level and are readily verbalized, or implicit, meaning that they are held subconsciously and can only be identified by behavior. But values and attitudes also differ in several respects. Whereas values are fairly constant (as deep-seated psychological constructs), attitudes are more transitory and subject to change. Values represent broad tendencies and highly prized beliefs (e.g., helpfulness, courage, and ambition), whereas attitudes are narrower predispositions (e.g., having a particular attitude about a clothing style, rap music, or modern art). Advertising plays on both values and attitudes by appealing to people's feelings about cleanliness, youthfulness, power, and prestige.

Goals are end results, the purpose toward which much behavior is directed. Goals are linked to deadlines, accomplishments, completion, or achievement. They are most likely to be attained if they are specific and stated in measurable terms. For example, rather than merely hoping to finish a race, an experienced runner is likely to set a goal of cutting X number of seconds off his or her best recorded time. Goals give shape, meaning, and direction to people's lives. A life without goals would be aimless.

Every day people engage in a complex series of decisions that reflect their attitudes, values, and goals. If students value good grades, they decide to spend time studying. Attitudes often occupy a middle ground between values and goals. Students who hate studying (an attitude) are going to have difficulty working out the relationship between their value of intellect and their goal of attaining good grades.

Types of Values

Because the world is filled with an almost infinite array of different stimuli, one of the most basic human functions is to classify concepts, objects, and events into clusters or groups. In so doing, people simplify their world and lay the groundwork for interpretation and action. For example, values can be classified in four different ways:

1. Absolute and relative
2. Intrinsic and extrinsic
3. Traditional, personal, and professional
4. Instrumental and terminal

Each of these will be discussed in the following sections.

Absolute and Relative Values

Absolute values are extreme and definitive; such values can be described in terms of black and white, as in the phrase "honesty is the best policy." People who hold honesty as an absolute value would say that honesty is right in all situations. **Relative values** are interpreted based on the context. They can be visualized as shades of gray that depend on the situation for definition. A person who holds honesty as a relative value will usually be honest, but in certain situations will put friendship, politeness, or consideration first. For example, if a friend gets a terrible haircut and asks how it looks, Person X, who has absolute values, will respond that the haircut is awful. Person Y, who has relative values, will simply say that her friend's hair might be a little short. In this situation, Person Y is placing the values of friendship and sensitivity over the value of total honesty.

People with more relative values tend to seek additional information about an event or situation. They want more details or knowledge before expressing an opinion or taking action.

Intrinsic and Extrinsic Values

Values can also be classified as **intrinsic values,** which are ends in themselves, or **extrinsic values,** which derive their worth or meaning from someone or something else. A couple finding their own way around a foreign city might find that experience intrinsically rewarding. They are demonstrating the values of independence and self-reliance. On the other hand, winning an Academy Award has extrinsic value because in this case a group of people have rewarded an individual for professional excellence.

Traditional, Personal, and Professional Values

Traditional values are those commonly held by the predominant society in which one lives. A traditional value or societal standard widely held in the United States and Canada is that children should begin going to school around the age of five or six. Another value of these two nations is that education is important and a key to future success. Personal values are values individuals hold for themselves, such as courage (standing up for one's beliefs) and forgiveness (the ability to pardon others). Many people pride themselves on their personal values. Professional values are related to jobs and careers, for example, being ambitious, capable, or logical. The same value can fall into all three categories. For example, a society, an individual, and a profession may all hold politeness as a value. Conversely, societal, personal, and professional values may be in conflict. For example, employees who place a high value on honesty and integrity might expose the wrongdoing of the company or government agency for which they work. Their values are in conflict with the values and procedures of their employer.

One of the goals of a job interview is to determine if there is an appropriate fit between the prospective employee's values and those of the organization. To help determine this, some organizations give psychological tests to applicants.

Instrumental and Terminal Values

Milton Rokeach, one of the most prolific and respected authorities on values, divided values into two types: terminal values and instrumental values (see Table 3.2). Terminal values are preferences for end states of existence, such as equality, freedom, or a comfortable life. Instrumental values are preferences for general modes of conduct, such as being helpful, loving, or intellectual. An individual taking the Rokeach Value Survey is asked to rank the values in each list from 1 (most important) to 18 (least important).

Rokeach defined values as global beliefs that guide actions and judgments across a variety of situations. He concluded that values are individual attributes that affect attitudes, motivation, needs, and perceptions (Rokeach, 1973).

Values, Lifestyles, and Consumption

Values are formed from experiences over time and are influenced by many sources, including parents, siblings, friends, teachers, religions, organizations, the media, and others. Shopping behaviors provide an example of values in action.

A person who comparison shops has different values (and perhaps resources) than a person who buys the first thing she or he sees. Choosing what to buy and where to shop are examples of consumption decisions based on values and lifestyle. Consider the differences between the consumption styles of college students Chelsea and Anthea. Chelsea usually shops at The Gap, but if she does not have much money to spend, she goes to Old Navy or another less expensive store. She goes clothes shopping every week. Anthea prefers department stores and tries

TABLE 3.2
Terminal and Instrumental Values

Terminal Values (end states of existence)	Instrumental Values (modes of conduct)
A comfortable life (a prosperous life)	Ambitious (hard-working, aspiring)
An exciting life (a stimulating, active life)	Broadminded (open-minded)
A sense of accomplishment (lasting contribution)	Capable (competent, effective)
A world at peace (free of war and conflict)	Cheerful (lighthearted, joyful)
A world of beauty (nature and the arts)	Clean (neat, tidy)
Equality (brotherhood, equal opportunity)	Courageous (standing up for your beliefs)
Family security (taking care of loved ones)	Forgiving (willing to pardon others)
Freedom (independence, free choice)	Helpful (working for others' welfare)
Happiness (contentedness)	Honest (sincere, truthful)
Inner harmony (freedom from inner conflict)	Imaginative (daring, creative)
Mature love (sexual and spiritual intimacy)	Independent (self-reliant, self-sufficient)
National security (protection from attack)	Intellectual (intelligent, reflective)
Pleasure (an enjoyable, leisurely life)	Logical (consistent, rational)
Salvation (saved, eternal life)	Loving (affectionate, tender)
Self-respect (self-esteem)	Obedient (dutiful, respectful)
Social recognition (respect, admiration)	Polite (courteous, well-mannered)
True friendship (close companionship)	Responsible (dependable, reliable)
Wisdom (a mature understanding of life)	Self-controlled (restrained, self-disciplined)

Source: From The University of Chicago Press, from "The Role of Values in Public Opinion Research," by Milton Rokeach, *Public Opinion Quarterly*, 32:554, Winter 1968–1969.

to find what she needs as quickly as possible so she can leave. She sees shopping as a chore, so she only goes a few times a year and has turned to shopping over the Internet.

VALS Research

One of the most famous values and lifestyles research projects was the VALS project (VALS stands for Values and Lifestyles) developed in the 1970s and 1980s by SRI International and Arnold Mitchell (Mitchell, 1983). The purpose of VALS research was to track shifts in consumer values and lifestyles. Based on the findings from the VALS research, U.S. consumers were divided into four major groups:

1. Need-driven consumers who purchase primarily to satisfy basic, subsistence needs. They constitute about 11 percent of the population.

2. Outer-directed consumers who are influenced by a desire to impress other people. They make up about 67 percent of the population.

3. Inner-directed consumers who are motivated by a desire for self-awareness. About 20 percent of the population fall into this group.

4. Combined outer- and inner-directed consumers who integrate social and self orientations. They account for about 2 percent of the population.

In the VALS system, values refer to a wide array of an individual's beliefs, hopes, desires, aspirations, and prejudices. Marketers, retailers, and advertisers used the VALS research to help them design advertisements, displays, and products that attract the type of consumer they wanted to reach.

In 1989, SRI introduced a newer version, also called VALS™ (Values and Lifestyles), which has a stronger psychological base than the original VALS (see Figure 3.2). Through this base, researchers attempt to determine more enduring attitudes and values. It categorizes U.S. adults into groups based on their psychology and several key demographics, such as yearly income and age. The results of VALS have been found to be consistent in several other countries in addition to the United States. The base is measured by asking respondents the degree to which they agree or disagree with 42 statements, such as the following:

◆ I often crave excitement.
◆ I like outrageous people and things.
◆ I like a lot of variety in my life.
◆ I like being in charge of a group.
◆ I am interested in theories.
◆ I follow the latest trends and fashions.

The entire survey, which you can take if you wish, is on SRI International's Web site (see the Electronic Resources at the end of the chapter).

The answers to the survey questions are designed to classify respondents into three primary self-orientations:

1. *Principle oriented:* These individuals are guided in their choices by their beliefs and principles rather than by feelings, events, or desire for approval. They are information-driven, thoughtful, and have a belief system that they use to run their lives, make decisions, and so forth.

2. *Status oriented:* These individuals are heavily influenced by the actions, approval, and opinions of others. They may own status cars.

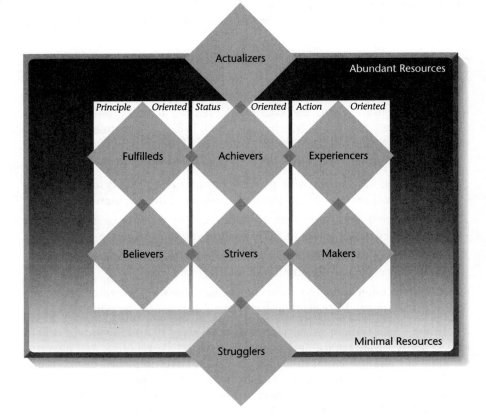

3. *Action oriented:* These individuals desire social or physical activity, variety, and risk taking. They seek stimulation and adventure. They try to make a statement and gain attention through such things as body piercing, bungee jumping, trekking to Nepal, and the like.

These three orientations determine the types of behaviors and goals that individuals pursue. As shown in Figure 3.2, *Actualizers* have the most abundant resources and *Strugglers* have the least resources. Actualizers are in many ways similar to the self-actualization stage in the Maslow hierarchy discussed in Chapter 1. In the VALS Network, they are shown at the very top of the figure because they are above the system. Actualizers have the resources to express different orientations; they do and are interested in a variety of things. They are highly aware of the choices available to them and have the means to do what they want. On the other hand, the Strugglers are at the bottom of the figure. They are barely holding on because they have so few resources; they are just getting by, surviving. Obviously, someone may start out as a struggler and move to other areas in the figure as their resources and attitudes change.

The information derived from VALS has been linked with numerous major databases used by population analysts and consumer product companies. Although it is one of the best values measures, it has a drawback in that it emphasizes individual attitudes and values although most consumption decisions are made by the household or are heavily influenced by several people. For example, two people would probably make the decision to purchase a king-size bed.

This discussion of VALS (both the original and the newer version) has been introduced here to illustrate that values and typologies are not strictly the domain of resource management, but are also an integral part of the fields of marketing and advertising. The study of values has practical implications for the business world as well as the personal world.

Societal and Cultural Values

Although values are enduring and measurable, they are not static. An individual's and society's values can change through an evolutionary process. They may be influenced by all of the following:

◆ Family or societal upset

◆ Technological, economic and cultural changes

◆ Dramatic events, such as war, famine, or disease

◆ Environmental threats

Examples of all of these have occurred in the twentieth century. The Great Depression, which began in October 1929 and lasted through the 1930s, influenced a whole generation to be cautious spenders. Thrift and security remained very important values to these people well after the depression was over. More recently, fear of AIDS and the desire to practice safe sex have prompted many people to use condoms. Personal health and safety are the values that prompt the use (a behavior) of condoms. In regard to environmental safety (a value), people are more aware than ever before of the dangers of environmental threats, such as unclaimed floating barges laden with garbage, oil spills, and polluted air. Corresponding behaviors range from personal accountability (e.g., recycling or joining clean-up crews) to national accountability (e.g., the promotion of environmental legislation and more government enforcement of environmental regulations).

Values are the cornerstones of a society's culture. **Cultural values** are generally held conceptualizations of what is right or wrong in a culture or what is preferred. Customs, manners, and gestures are indicators of cultural values. For example, bowing in deference to one's superiors or elders is customary in South Korea but would be unusual in the United States. Bowing is the outward behavior that reflects the underlying value of deference or respect. People in Western cultures such as Canada, the United States, Australia, and most countries in Western Europe customarily eat three meals a day, whereas eating five meals a day is customary in East and Southeast Asian cultures. Even the meaning of gestures (a behavior) varies by culture. For example, the hand sign for "okay" in the United States is considered an obscene gesture in some Latin American countries.

Understanding cultural differences can be helpful in a variety of contexts, including the planning of workplaces, transportation systems, and homes. For instance, supervisors who keep a close watch on their workers may be viewed as caring in some cultures, but overbearing and belittling in others. Cultures also vary in the types of mass transit they prefer and the amount of crowding people will accept in subways and trains. Typical cultural values and standards of comfort, function, and beauty influence floor plans of homes and interior designs.

For example, consider the differences between values in the United States and Japan. The Japanese tend to be more concerned with consensus and are group oriented. Consequently, Japanese businesses offer their employees more security and long-term employment than most American businesses. A study comparing the work values of American and Japanese men found significant differences (Engel, 1988). Japanese men placed a higher value on group involvement and loyalty to their employer and country. American men placed more emphasis on individualism, independence, and self-sufficiency and tended to believe that education and hard work led to success. These cultural differences in values start in the home. A study comparing Japanese-American parenting styles with the practices of Americans of European ancestry found that ethnicity does affect how parents interact with and rear their children; child-rearing techniques varied considerably between the two groups (O'Reilly, Tokuno, & Ebata, 1986).

Why cultural differences exist between Japan and the United States given their common bond of a strong industrial base is not clear, but the answers appear to lie in historical, religious, and political differences. As contacts between the countries increase through mass media, travel, and business exchange, the values gap appears to be narrowing (O'Reilly, Tokuno, & Ebata, 1986).

One does not have to cross national borders to find cultural differences in values, attitudes, and behavior, however. They exist everywhere within countries. Regional food preferences are a good example. The food in northern Italy is quite different from the food in southern Italy. In the United States, grits are a favorite food in the South, but are rarely eaten elsewhere. Different regions also perceive and use time differently. A study conducted by Hilton Hotels Corporation found that 48 percent of the people living on the West Coast of the United States make time for their ideal weekend compared with 38 percent of those on the East Coast (Rigdon, 1991). When asked about their goals, 72 percent of westerners said personal goals, such as vacations and hobbies, were among their top priorities for the 1990s compared with 55 percent of easterners. The study concluded that easterners appear to be always working whereas westerners work hard but also play hard.

Families, Values, Standards, and Households

All families have values and value orientations, and the way they maintain their homes is an expression of those values. As Chapter 1 explained, standards are the quantitative and/or qualitative criteria used to measure values and goals and reconcile resources with demands. Different family members may have different time and household work standards. What is "on time" to one family member may not be "on time" to another. And a teenager's standard of a clean bedroom may not be the same as his parents'. Standards also vary greatly between households. Dennis, a 13-year-old, told his parents about the variations he had observed in the household cleaning standards of his three friends:

> We don't like going to Daryl's house because it is sterile. It is so clean it is spooky, like nobody lives there and we are afraid to touch anything. They even clean the driveway. The only things in Daryl's room are a bed, a dresser, and a desk. Steve's house is a mess because they have that awful dog tearing up everything. Brent's house is about like ours, somewhere in the middle. So we usually end up at our house, sometimes at Brent's.

The physical and emotional quality of home and family life has been a subject of debate across time and across cultures. Two national surveys about family values and patterns of behavior indicated that people in the United States think the family is falling apart everywhere but in their own home. This paradox is called the "I'm OK, but you're not" syndrome. According to one survey, "four out of five Americans claim they wouldn't give up Thanksgiving dinner with their family for $1,000." Nevertheless, two out of three Americans say that family values have grown weaker. The researchers summed up this paradox as follows: "Some of this is real change. . . . But some is the same pattern you find when you ask people about schools or crime or members of Congress. Everyone else's is terrible, but theirs is OK."

Value Formation and Socialization

Values are shared by most members of a society and are passed on to younger members by senior members. Families, especially parents, play a fundamental role in forming children's values. The ability to cope with and adjust to life problems and demands is based on the psychological foundations of early family experience. One study of college students found that the more positive the family experience, the more likely the students were to have a positive attitude and believe they were in control of their lives (Parish & Nunn, 1988). Parents perceive that within their society certain competencies and values are important for their child's growth and development. For example, parents influence their children's dress and grooming standards, manners and speech, and educational motivation. Thus, the culture's child-rearing patterns reflect the parents' and the greater society's values and the environmental context in which the parents live. As the society changes, so do the values parents impart to their children. A study examined changes in values in children in the United States from 1964 to 1984 and found that parents in more recent years desired their children to have more autonomy or self-direction (having good sense and sound judgment, and being honest, responsible, and considerate) and were less concerned with conformity or obedience (obeying parents, having good manners, being neat and clean, and acting according to sex-role norms) (Alwin, 1989).

The process by which children learn the rules of a society is called **socialization**. Although the family is the primary socializer of children, parents are not the only influence. Values are affected by a host of variables, conditions, and sources, such as the media, friends, and extended family. Furthermore, to imply that socialization is only a childhood experience would be misleading. Although socialization starts in infancy, it is a lifelong process influenced by many sources.

A subsystem of socialization is called consumer socialization; through this process, people acquire the skills, attitudes, and information necessary to function in the marketplace. Children initially learn much of their consumption behavior, such as store and brand preferences, from accompanying their parents on shopping trips. By adolescence, children are likely to shop with friends. In fact, going shopping with friends has become such a popular teen activity that some malls in the United States have limited teen shopping hours. This practice raises an interesting societal values question, "Should stores be able to restrict who shops in them?"

The New Traditionalism

Besides the dominant social and cultural trends, there are often counterbalancing subdominant trends. For example, the value of traditionalism (going back to basics) appears to run in cycles. It is estimated that 29 percent of Americans can be called "heartlanders" or *traditionalists*. They hold traditional views, specifically believing in the value of small town and country life (Ray, 1997). Traditionalists are a smaller group within the U.S. population than *modernists* (47 percent), who place a high value on personal success, consumerism, materialism, and technological rationality. The other main group is the *cultural creatures* (24 percent) who put a strong emphasis on having new and unique experiences, and are attuned to global issues, and social causes.

Figure 3.3 shows an advertisement for *Good Housekeeping* magazine that suggests that many families adopt a lifestyle called the "New Traditionalism." According to the advertisement, the new traditionalist family is made up of conscientious consumers who read labels, are brand conscious, and take environmental concerns seriously. Further, according to the advertisement, the new traditionalists put their trust in *Good Housekeeping* because they share the magazine's value orientation. As this illustrates, a medium such as a magazine can have a value orientation just as individuals and families have. Newspapers,

FIGURE 3.3
The New Traditionalists
Source: Reprinted by permission. Copyright 1989 The Hearst Corporation. All rights reserved.

THE NEW TRADITIONALISTS.

THEY'RE THE CUSTODIANS OF THE GREAT AMERICAN BRANDS.

Diane and Ian Ingersoll are today's pioneers. They design and build Shaker furniture. They live a simple, solid family life. And suddenly their furniture, and their lifestyle, has a whole new following.

The Ingersolls embody the most powerful social force in America today – the New Traditionalist movement. For

marketers – it signals the end of "conspicuous consumption" and the trend to "conscientious consumption."

New Traditionalists shop more strategically, more conscientiously than most people – they read labels, they take environmental concerns seriously, they stay more loyal to the products they know and trust. And at a time of

diminishing brand loyalty, they are the true custodians of America's brands.

They put their trust in Good Housekeeping, because we have always stood for the values they are seeking. No one speaks to the New Traditionalist with the authority of Good Housekeeping – the Magazine, the Institute, and the Seal.

AMERICA BELIEVES IN GOOD HOUSEKEEPING

books, television and radio shows also have value stances. For example, many magazines and newspapers will not publish cigarette advertisements.

The renewed interest in traditionalism is not the exclusive domain of one magazine. Clothing and home furnishings retailers have noticed a renewed interest in traditional patterns, styles, and fabrics. The new traditionalists put the well-being of families and children ahead of ostentatious consumption. A car advertisement directed to the new traditionalists would emphasize the car's safety (e.g., airbags, low accident rate) over its speed. According to Levin (1989), middle-class traditionalists also tend to make prudent provisions for the future in the form of savings and investments and believe that individuals and governments alike should pay their bills.

Another survey identified six types of families, including one called "traditionalists." According to this survey, the largest group, representing 24 percent of all families, are the "family enthusiasts," who embody nearly all of the traditional values and some other characteristics as well. Family enthusiasts like to stay within the proper bounds of society and do not want to be seen as too far out. As a group, they are young and optimistic. Overall, the survey's respondents said that values are best taught by parents in the home.

Attitudes

As noted earlier in this chapter, *attitudes* are favorable or unfavorable feelings or ideas about some matter. They are expressions of likes and dislikes. People have attitudes about other people, objects, and issues. Examples of attitudes are prejudice about racial or cultural issues, notions about the characteristics of rich people versus poor people, and ideas about war, space exploration, or politics. Letters to the editor in newspapers and magazines and Internet chat rooms are filled with attitudes and opinions.

Attitudes are learned. Just as with values, children learn their attitudes primarily from their families, but in time those attitudes are also shaped by other environmental influences. As they develop into adults, "men and women accumulate information that shapes their perceptions of their roles as men and women, their roles as parents, their behaviors, their attitudes and their belief systems" (Palkovitz & Copes, 1988, pp. 191–192). For example, household management practices (ways of planning and doing work in the home, standards of cleanliness, and assigning tasks) are learned first in childhood. Adults choose to accept, reject, or modify the household management practices they learned in their youth.

Once learned, attitudes influence behavior. Two experts on the effects of attitudes on behavior, Icek Ajzen and Martin Fishbein (1980), developed a theory of reasoned action that assumes that human beings are usually quite rational and make systematic use of the information available to them. Ajzen and Fishbein posit that individuals consider the implications of their actions before they decide to engage in a given behavior or not. In their theory, a person's intention to perform (or not to perform) a behavior is the immediate determinant of the action. The individual's positive or negative evaluation of performing a behavior is her or his attitude toward the behavior. The second factor in the intention to act is called the subjective norm. This refers to the person's perception of the social pressures put on him or her to perform or not perform the behavior in question. Ease or difficulty of behavior is also a factor. Thus, intention to behave a certain way will be affected by whether the

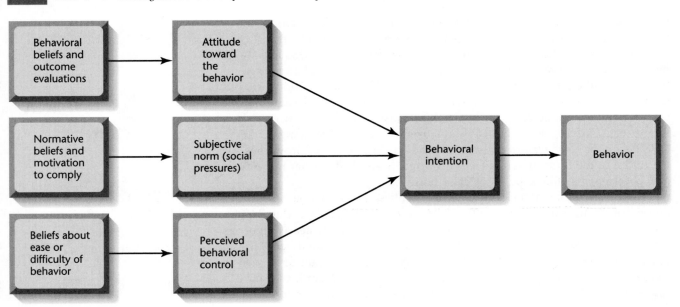

FIGURE 3.4

**The Theory of Planned
Behavior**

Sources: Based upon Ajzen, I. (1985). "From
Intentions to Actions: A Theory of Planned
Behavior." In J. Kuhl and J. Beckman (Eds.), *Action-
Control: From Cognition to Behavior* (pp. 11–39). New
York: Springer, Ajzen, I., and Fishbein, M. (1980).
Understanding Attitudes and Predicting Social Behavior.
Englewood Cliffs, NJ: Prentice-Hall.

person evaluates the behavior as positive, by what other people think, and if
the action is perceived as easy or difficult. As Figure 3.4 illustrates, beliefs
shape attitudes and subjective norms, which in turn lead to intention and then
actual behavior.

Since attitudes are not directly observable, they must be determined by research or by observation of behavior although care should be taken in infer-
ring attitudes and values based solely on behavior. For example, the distance
between two people who are talking with each other may be indicative of their
attitudes (likes and dislikes) toward each other, but it may also reflect cultural
standards of behavior. Chapter 7 has more on this topic. As another example,
work behavior is often easy to observe. Is the person a loner? Or a team
player? Is a person always late? Or early? Reliable? Or unreliable? Is the person's work neat? Or sloppy? Attitudes about time, independence, control, obedience to authority, and conformity to rules all affect work behavior.

GOALS

Some attitudes and values are held more strongly than others. Likewise, some
goals are pursued more strongly than others. This section explores the nature
of goals and motivation. If goals (defined earlier as end results) are to be
achieved, they must be specific and realistic.

Figure 3.5 shows the relationship between values and goals. Once a goal
has been identified, values provide the impetus—the start—toward goal attainment. A person fulfills a desire or a need by engaging in goal-seeking behavior leading, one hopes, to goal achievement. The seeking of goals requires
energy, commitment, and motivation. As the figure shows, not all goals are
reached; some have to be reformulated or dropped. Accordingly, flexibility is
one of the most important characteristics of goal setting. Knowing when to let
go of unrealistic or unattainable goals is an important step in the management
process. Goals should be constantly reevaluated and updated. If goals are not
fully committed to, they have little chance of succeeding.

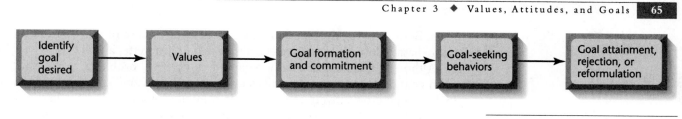

FIGURE 3.5
Interactive Values—Goals Model

Goals versus Habits

Goals are things people are trying to accomplish. Not all behavior is goal directed or goal activated; some of it is simply basic survival behavior or habit, such as watching television. **Habits** are repetitive, often unconscious patterns of behavior. Confucious said that "the nature of men is always the same, it is their habits that separate them." In other words, habits are unique to the individual. They can be either good or bad. Whining and overeating are bad habits. Treating others with respect and courtesy are good habits.

Goals encompass more than just the fulfillment of immediate wants and needs. For example, graduating from law school is a goal, but eating a hamburger is not—it is the fulfillment of a need, hunger. Mihaly Csikzentmihalyi, author of *Flow: The Psychology of Optimal Experience,* says that:

> The earliest explanations of human behavior, starting with Aristotle, assumed that actions were motivated by goals. Modern psychology, however, has shown that much of what people do can be explained more parsimoniously by simpler, often unconscious causes. . . . I do not claim that most people most of the time act the way they do because they are trying to achieve goals; but only that when they do so, they experience a sense of control which is absent when behavior is not motivated by consciously chosen goals. (1990, p. 242)

Goal Attributes

Not all goals are created equal, each has certain characteristics or attributes. For example, goals vary in:

- *Intensity:* Commitment, how much the goal is desired
- *Complexity:* The number of the goal's interrelationships
- *Priority:* How important the goal is
- *Timing:* How long it will take to attain the goal

These goal attributes are demonstrated by the behaviors of Roger and Stephanie. Roger, a 20-year-old, worked for eight years on a paper route and after school jobs and saved every penny to buy a Corvette. Stephanie, a 22-year-old, made finding the best job her top priority her senior year in college and put that goal before everything else.

Goals influence action in four ways (Locke, 1968):

1. By directing attention
2. By fostering strategy development
3. By mobilizing effort
4. By increasing persistence

In the preceding examples, Roger and Stephanie directed their attention, developed strategies, mobilized effort, and persisted until they reached their

Striving for goals has often been compared to climbing a mountain.

goals. Both were highly goal driven. Goals provide a sense of purpose and direct behavior toward a positive end result (e.g., a Corvette, a job).

Although goals are generally regarded as positive, problems can surface when goal conflict occurs in families or other groups. Conflict develops when goals compete or subvert each other. If a family's goal is to eat a leisurely Sunday dinner together, conflict may arise if their teenage children would rather skip dinner and spend the afternoon with their friends.

Types of Goals

For purposes of discussion, it is useful to assign goals to categories. Among the ways goals can be categorized are the following:

- ◆ *By time:* short term, intermediate, or long term
- ◆ *By role:* personal, professional, societal, or familial
- ◆ *By type:* primary or secondary

Each category will be discussed in the following sections.

Goals and Time

Goals can be separated into short-term, intermediate, and long-term goals.

- ◆ Short-term goals usually take less than three months to accomplish.
- ◆ Intermediate goals can usually be achieved in three months to one year.
- ◆ Long-range goals usually take more than one year to achieve.

A Fall-semester college junior may have a short-term goal of finishing current coursework, an intermediate goal of finishing the year, and a long-term goal of graduating. College students are assumed to be long-term planners. For example, job recruiters typically ask college interviewees, "What do you plan to be doing five years from now?" With this question, the recruiter finds out whether the student has thought ahead, is a realistic planner, and is ambitious.

Sometimes people think of goals as a luxury reserved for the wealthy and better educated. Certainly, setting long-term goals implies a secure future or at least one partially under control. Low-income families do not always have the resource base to think beyond short-term goals. In the VALS typology discussed earlier, they may be strugglers; their attention is focused on immediate survival. In terms of Maslow's hierarchy of needs, they are concerned with the physiological and safety levels of the hierarchy. For them, planning a year in the future would be a luxury. At the other extreme are celebrities who may have managers or agents who plan their schedules five years or more in advance.

Goals and Roles

Another way to categorize goals is by role. In this typology, goals can be personal, professional, societal, or familial. Personal goals include such things as learning how to swing dance, ski, skydive, or ride a horse. Professional goals are related to one's job or career; they might include improving computer skills, writing a contract, or conducting an interview. Societal goals are commonly held by the greater society; they include such goals as having a full-time job by a certain age, marrying, having children, and retiring. Familial goals are related to being a son, daughter, parent, or other family member. At any one time, a person might be achieving personal and professional goals while considering or reacting to societal or familial goals.

An individual can have one or two goals or dozens. People who are professionally oriented may have lots of career goals and ignore personal goals. Other people may have no professional or career goals (their job is simply something to do to earn money, and they go home at five o'clock and forget about it) and are only interested in personal or family goals. Management comes into play because goals must be prioritized and strategies developed. What is most important? And how does someone go about getting what she or he wants?

Goals by Type: Primary and Secondary Goals

Goals can also be categorized as primary and secondary (Dillard et al., 1989):

- Primary goals are formed to influence process and progress.
- Secondary goals motivate the individual and ultimately lead to and complement the primary goal.

For example, if a person's primary goal is to attain a college degree, then his or her secondary goals would include being accepted into a college, passing courses, and completing graduation requirements. Secondary goals are smaller ones that motivate and collectively add up to the primary goals.

Setting Goals

The beneficial effect of goal setting on task performance is one of the most validated concepts in psychology. Ninety percent of the reported studies have found that goal setting has positive or partially positive effects on task performance (Locke, Shaw, Saar, & Latham, 1981). Simply stated, people accomplish more when they set goals. A study of survivors of concentration camps found that those who had a purpose for living and well-defined goals were able to withstand greater deprivation, including starvation and torture, than those without goals (Powell & Enright, 1990). Many of the survivors said that their main goal was to see their families again.

To be helpful, goals should have certain characteristics. First, goals must be reasonable, affordable, and within the resources of the goal setter. For example, a person who wants to buy a house must have the resources to make a down payment and meet the monthly payments. Saying that goals should be realistic and attainable does not mean that they should be too easy to accomplish. Indeed, goals should present some challenge for the goal setter.

Goals should also be clearly formed and simply stated. When asked about his formula for success, J. Paul Getty, one of the richest men in the world, said: "Rise Early. Work Late. Strike Oil." The importance of having clear, specific goals cannot be overemphasized. The goal of buying a new car is too vague because it cannot be visualized. The goal of buying a certain type of car in one year is effective, however, because it allows the mind to form a specific picture of the car and focuses attention on actions and a time frame for achieving the goal. When the person sees advertisements for that particular car or passes one in a parking lot, her decision to try to buy that car will be reinforced. Of course, during the year, she may decide on another model, but at least initially visualizing a specific car can be helpful.

Goals provide an avenue for freedom, a sense of control, and, as noted before, a sense of direction and purpose. A lack of initiative and direction can lead to unstable goals, however (Robbins, Payne, & Chartrand, 1990). In that case, the person will vacillate and change goals frequently without reason, thereby losing the sense of purpose goals can provide.

Optimism, Goals, and Well-Being

In *Learned Optimism,* Martin Seligman writes that optimism is essential for a good and successful life. Optimism is necessary for achieving goals because it allows an individual to use the wisdom won by a lifetime of trial and error to better effect (Seligman, 1991). According to Seligman, flexible optimism—optimism with its eyes open—provides limitless benefits. He adds that habits of thinking and living need not go on forever; in other words people do not have to be stuck with their pasts, but can learn from them. Seligman points out that "the most significant finding in psychology in the last twenty years is that individuals choose the way they think" (1991, p. 8).

In the pursuit of understanding the linkages between health and illness, other researchers have explored the relationship between optimism and general well-being. For example, a study of attorneys revealed a significant relationship between optimism and general well-being. Optimism was defined in this study as the degree to which one has a favorable approach to the world (Sweetman, Munz, & Wheeler, 1993). An optimist is more likely to think that goals are reachable.

Selection of Goals: Importance of Challenge

How does a person choose which goals to pursue? The study of management assumes that if someone devotes the required resources, plans well, and makes the sacrifices necessary, almost anything can be achieved. Consequently, people should aim high and set goals that force them to do their best. Setting specific and challenging goals leads to higher performance than setting easy goals (Locke, Shaw, Saari, & Latham, 1981). By creating a challenge, goals affect performance by directing attention, mobilizing effort, increasing persistence, and motivating strategy development.

Anthony, who is single and age 25, listed his goals for the next five years as follows:

- ◆ *Career/work:* Own a fitness center
- ◆ *Home:* Have a nice apartment
- ◆ *Personal:* Date someone seriously, have lots of friends
- ◆ *Leisure:* Work out everyday

Do Anthony's goals seem realistic for someone who works full-time in a gym and has a college degree in nutrition and fitness? How much does it cost to open a fitness center? To rent an apartment? What secondary goals does he need to accomplish in order to reach his primary goal of owning a center?

Anthony's goal of owning a fitness center has created a very real challenge for him and forced him to develop strategies to achieve it. Anthony's strategies include learning all he can from the gym where he now works before opening his own fitness center and fulfilling his secondary goals of paying off his college loans and credit cards and saving money. According to Csikszentmihalyi, "of all the virtues we can learn no trait is more useful, more essential for survival, and more likely to improve the quality of life than the ability to transform adversity into an enjoyable challenge" (1990, p. 200).

Plans for Attaining Goals

Once goals are set, a plan for achieving them must be developed. Planning includes all managerial activities that determine results and the appropriate means to achieve those results. It involves the following four steps:

1. Set specific goals and prioritize them.

2. State the goals clearly and positively. For example, "I will be a nonsmoker by January 1"—not "I will stop smoking." "I will lose five pounds"—not "I will lose weight."

Set standards

3. Forecast possible future events and the resources that will be needed to deal with them. This entails determining both the level of material resources that will be needed and the amount of effort that will be required.

4. Implement the plan by following through with goal-directed activity. (Chapter 6 discusses goal implementation, as well as evaluation, in more detail.)

Note that the planning process begins with prioritizing goals. Prioritizing involves ranking goals by the degree of commitment to them. Commitment is the sense of obligation one feels toward the goal. If a goal is not enticing or inspiring, something is wrong, and the goal will not serve its function of motivating the person to greater effort. Prioritizing forces people to decide what they really want and how they are going to get it.

A New Years tradition in many countries is to make resolutions, which are types of goals. About 23 percent of New Year's resolutions are broken in the first week, 45 percent by the end of January (Norcross & Prochaska, 1998). The reasons for failure are as stated in points one through four; willpower is not enough, resolutions need to be chosen wisely, and a plan to work on them every day devised. Even the smallest step makes a difference in the long run.

Obstacles to Goal Achievement

Crises happen. All the goal setting in the world cannot stop unplanned events from altering the course of resource use. Obstacles to achieving goals include, but are not limited to, the following: time, parents, family, rules, peers, social customs, demands, imagination, money, health, and natural disasters (e.g., hurricanes, tornadoes, floods).

Obstacles alone do not determine the fate of human goal-seeking behavior. Instead, the way people perceive and react to obstacles will determine whether they will reach their goals. One way to overcome obstacles is to divide larger

Crisis events affect people's lives. Previously set goals can be altered by a crisis event such as a hurricane.

goals into smaller ones, which allow a person to make progress a little at a time. It also helps to find a trusted, nonjudgmental friend who is willing to talk about one's goals and periodically check on how projects are going. Monitoring one's progress by marking deadlines on a calendar is useful as well. Everyone should also become aware of when blocks are likely to occur. Is it at the start of projects? In the middle? At the end? Note that this may vary from person to person. Finally, goals need to be reevaluated. Resistance to goals may mean it is time to change them or to take a break. Pursuing goals requires energy.

Needs for Achievement: the n Ach Factor

In a classic study, David McClelland, a Harvard psychologist, stressed that individuals vary in their need for achievement, which he called "n Ach" (McClelland, 1961). He found that each individual has a different level of motivation for overcoming obstacles, desiring success, and expending effort to seek out difficult tasks and do them well as quickly as possible. He emphasized that the achievement motive can be expressed as a desire to perform in terms of a standard of excellence or to be successful in competitive situations.

A person possessing high n Ach takes moderate risks, not high risks as one might assume. This phenomenon can be demonstrated by the ring-toss game. Low achievers will stand very near the peg and drop the rings over it or stand far away and wildly throw the ring. High achievers will carefully calculate the exact distance from the peg that will challenge their abilities, yet still give them a chance for success. Thus, low achievers take a low or high risk and high achievers take a moderate risk. Research indicates that this pattern holds true in most walks of life and for children as well as for adults.

Lifestyles, Goals, and Feedback

Each person has a basic notion of what he or she wants in the way of food, shelter, and companionship; these basic needs evolve into a more complicated set of needs that combine to form a lifestyle. Likewise, goals often start simple and evolve into more complicated notions. A recent college graduate might want a job, any job, to get started and then as time goes by develop a more specific definition of what a good job is.

Forming short-term goals is a way to conserve the time and energy needed to reach long-term goals. Short-term goals have the advantage that they can be completed fairly rapidly, giving the person a sense of accomplishment. An author, for example, might write newspaper and magazine articles during the same time period he is writing a novel so that he always has something in process, in the mail, or in print.

Individuals and families need feedback to determine if their goals are viable or need to be changed. Goals are generally thought of as positives in life, but they can be self-defeating if they are too difficult. Goals can also have a negative effect if they cause people to be so single-minded that they do not see other possible goals or courses of action that might be better. Both depression over failure to be an overnight success and a single-minded focus on today without a thought of the future can be self-defeating. Listening to feedback helps keep goals realistic and on track.

College Students' Values and Goals

College students' values and goals have been the subject of many studies. In recent years, researchers have found that overall college men and women have similar goal and value orientations. For example, Hammersla and McMahan (1990) studied 303 college students and found that women were about as goal oriented as men.

They found that college students placed a high value on relationships with members of the opposite sex and said they were willing to sacrifice most other goals for the relationships should that be necessary. Two other researchers found that college women rated personal development and social skills higher than college men did (Kaufman & Creamer, 1991). In their study, women students were more likely than men students to invest significant effort on relations with peers.

In a study of work attitudes, over two-thirds of college men and women endorsed "equal emphasis on family and career" and 90 percent expected husband and wife to participate equally in the care and discipline of children (Phillips & Johnston, 1985). Sometimes it is difficult to coordinate family life with other drives and goals, however. For example, Raina and Vats (1990) observed that achievement and prestige are top priorities for men. More research is needed on the choices, sacrifices, and tensions between goal achievement and interpersonal relationships among both men and women (Hammersla & McMahan, 1990).

For many students, the college years serve as a transition stage between living at home with parents and living on their own—a physical and emotional bridge between childhood and adulthood. In reflecting back on their relationship with their parents, women undergraduates in one study reported spending more time with their mothers than with their fathers (Miller & Lane, 1991). Both male and female students said they received more positive treatment from their mothers and experienced more positive emotions and closeness with their mothers than with their fathers. Further, the Miller and Lane study found that individuation and well-being were facilitated when students had close, personal relationships with parents rather than distancing relationships. Thus, a close family relationship led to a more successful adjustment to college life for students.

The Miller and Lane findings seem to indicate that fathers have contributed less than mothers to their children's sense of well-being, but to cite the results of only one study on such an important topic would be misleading. Study after study documents the importance of both the mother and the father to a child's development. One series of studies on college students' career expectations found that fathers had an important influence on their sons' and daughters' career expectations, specifically, their salary and work hour expectations (Goldsmith, Hoffman, & Hoffacker, 1993; Hoffman, Goldsmith, & Hoffacker, 1992; Hoffman, Hoffacker, & Goldsmith, 1992).

Another study by Flanagan (1990) revealed the association between parents' current career status and children's goals. She found that mothers and fathers who received promotions (those moving up in their careers) were the most likely to expect their children to go to college. Parents who were temporarily laid off were least likely to encourage their sons and daughters to go to college. Adolescents whose parents received promotions had clear, consistent goals, whereas adolescents whose parents were laid off had a limited view of future options.

Because college is a transitory stage, goal instability is not unusual during the college years. For example, students may change their majors and career choices many times. One study found that the degree of goal instability was associated with the prediction of adjustment during entry to college. For example, goal instability was related to personal control and esteem, but was also related to depression and anxiety (Robbins, Payne, & Chartrand, 1990). In other words, goal instability is not unusual for college students and can even be helpful, but it can also be uncomfortable for the individual experiencing it.

In another study it was found that nearly one-third of college freshman do not return for their sophomore year. The main reasons they do not return are job opportunities, financial circumstances, and personal situations. (Cravatta, 1997). The no-return rate was much higher for community colleges than for four-year universities.

Although college students have the same array of values as the general population, the media and social scientists over the years have attempted to categorize the general typology of college students by decade or generation. For example, students of the 1950s have been described as conservative and conforming, as holders of traditional values with only slight concern for societal problems. After graduation, supposedly, these students went on to become the "organization man" who obeyed the law, fulfilled obligations, and strove to get ahead (Whyte, 1957). Some commentators disagree with this characterization. David Halberstam, author of *The Fifties* (1993), writes that the 1950s were a decade of enormous change, some good, some bad, but certainly not boring or rule driven. As examples of change, he notes that the 1950s were the era of the Korean War, the development of the hydrogen bomb, and significant advances in civil rights.

The late 1960s and early 1970s are considered years of unrest and change, characterized by the advent of the peace movement, the women's liberation movement, and other societal causes. College students challenged traditional ways of doing things, questioned material gain, and extolled the virtues of individual rights and freedom. Values changed on campuses, exemplified by the widespread introduction of coed dormitories and the end of dress codes and curfews.

In the 1980s, the college culture moved back to material goals; students flooded business schools and became more egocentric and less committed to broader sociopolitical change. The students of the 80s grew up during the downsizing of certain businesses; they saw or experienced social and personal insecurities. As a result, they became more savvy and more skeptical (Stoneman, 1998).

Students of the 1990s enjoyed the benefits of a strong economy and a good labor market. They had more money than their predecessors. Colleges realized that standard dormitory-style living was becoming less attractive to students. Some built or renovated dormitories; others allowed privatized on-campus apartments.

How will current students compare with those of previous generations? One trend is the growing concern over crime in society and substance abuse on campuses and the subsequent increase in more secure and substance-free dormitories on campuses (Seligmann, 1991). Another trend is increasing acceptance of fragmentation and extreme individuality. The unifying value of today's college students is "I want to decide something for myself and on my own, and not try to be part of the crowd" (Stoneman, 1998).

Motivation

Thomas Edison tried 3,000 ways to create a light bulb before he found one that worked. A motivated person has to take risks and overcome obstacles in order to achieve goals. The word *motivation* comes from the Latin word *movere,* which means "to move." In management, **motivation** refers to movement toward goals or other desired outcomes and also to vigor, drive, persistence, creativity, direction, and sustained energy.

Motivated individuals work hard. However, motivation is not just a personal construct; it is the driving force behind companies and organizations. Car salespeople try to sell a certain number of cars per month to reach a quota. Real estate salespeople try to sell so many houses in a year so they can be on the "million dollar seller list." Girl Scouts try to sell enough boxes of cookies so they can go to camp. Goal setting's potential for improving productivity is so well established that it is rarely questioned as a management technique.

Motivation is a process rather than an end state. The process begins with an unsatisfied need that creates tension. This tension drives a person to undertake a search (for resources or information), which leads to the need being satisfied and the tension reduced (Robbins, 1991). Hence, the person does not feel satisfied until her or his need is fulfilled or the goal attained.

Internal and external factors contribute to the motivation to achieve goals. **Intrinsic motivation** involves the underlying causes and the internal need for competence and self-determination. It refers to the pleasure or value a person derives from the content of work or activity. If a student works hard in school, the satisfaction he or she derives from learning and mastering a subject provides the intrinsic motivation to keep learning. **Extrinsic motivation** involves forces external to the individual—environmental factors such as titles, raises, preferred offices, promotions, and other forms of rewards. For a student, extrinsic motivators include "A" grades, the honor roll, the dean's list, the honor society, scholarships, and other forms of recognition for academic performance.

Both intrinsic and extrinsic motivation are important for goal achievement. Children need to experience both types. They should feel good about learning (intrinsic), and they should also feel that their efforts are recognized by others (extrinsic). In the home, the family members who do housework should feel good about living in a clean house and that their cleaning effort is noticed and appreciated by other family members.

One of the unsolved mysteries of life is why some people have more intrinsic motivation than others. These people work hard regardless of the number and quality of external rewards. Are the answers in genetics? In early childhood or work experiences? In temperament? Psychologists and others are searching for the answers to these questions. Martin Seligman, a psychologist and the author of *Learned Optimism* mentioned earlier in the chapter, says that:

> A composer can have all the talent of a Mozart and a passionate desire to succeed, but if he believes he cannot compose music, he will come to nothing. He will not try hard enough. He will give up too soon when the elusive right melody takes too long to materialize. Success requires persistence, the ability to not give up in the face of failure. (1991, p. 101)

Far more is known about the workings of extrinsic motivation than about intrinsic motivation. For example, extrinsic rewards are most effective if:

◆ They are specific.
◆ They are given immediately after a good work performance.
◆ They are valued by the receiver.
◆ They are equitable.

What one person perceives as a reward may not be perceived as desirable by another. For example, a trip at the company's expense to a convention might be valued by one employee, but considered a burden by another. As another example, a child who does not like candy will not view a candy bar as a reward. Rewards should be appropriate to the individual and at the same time be perceived as equitable by the family or organization.

Electronic Resources

There are many Web sites, some interactive, that discuss values and attitudes. The main polling organizations, such as Gallup (**www.gallup.com**), Roper (**www.roper.com**) and Yankelovich, Skelly, and White (**www.ysw.com**), report regularly on the state of values and attitudes in the United States and in other countries. As more companies (the primary financial supporters of the polling organizations) sell globally, the polling organizations have found that they need to collect more values and attitude data internationally. Government agencies and politicians also use data from polling organizations.

To join an online discussion of the changing nature of the American character, go to The Wall Street Journal Interactive Edition at **http://wsj.com**. Other newspapers and magazines run similar discussion groups.

For information on population trends and changes in values by age groups, location, gender, and so forth, go to the American Demographic Web site at **www.demographics.com**. This site does not give predictions about values, but rather reports the present state of values held by various groups.

Individuals interested in learning more about and/or taking the SRI International VALS survey described in this chapter can find it at **future.sri.com** by clicking on "To the Survey." Survey takers receive a brief analysis in return.

**http://future.sri.com/vals/
valsindex.html**

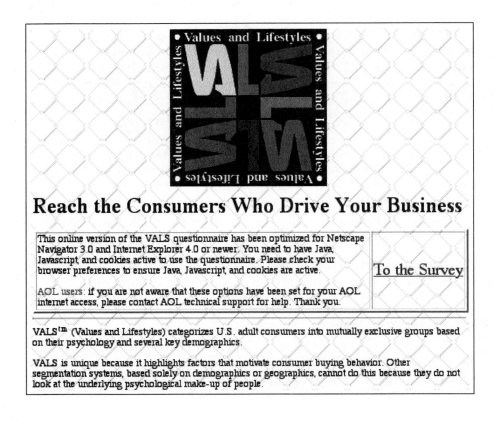

Reach the Consumers Who Drive Your Business

This online version of the VALS questionnaire has been optimized for Netscape Navigator 3.0 and Internet Explorer 4.0 or newer. You need to have Java, Javascript, and cookies active to use the questionnaire. Please check your browser preferences to ensure Java, Javascript, and cookies are active.

AOL users: if you are not aware that these options have been set for your AOL internet access, please contact AOL technical support for help. Thank you.

To the Survey

VALS^{tm} (Values and Lifestyles) categorizes U.S. adult consumers into mutually exclusive groups based on their psychology and several key demographics.

VALS is unique because it highlights factors that motivate consumer buying behavior. Other segmentation systems, based solely on demographics or geographics, cannot do this because they do not look at the underlying psychological make-up of people.

Summary

This chapter explored three of the most important concepts in the management process—values, attitudes, and goals. Values are principles that guide behavior. Families play a fundamental role in the formation and transmission of values. Parents, as the primary socializer of children, greatly influence their children's values. Goals are end results, the things people are working toward. Motivation and optimism are important elements in achieving goals. Attitudes are states of mind or feelings, likes and dislikes, about some matter. They often occupy a middle ground between values and goals.

When two people date or become close friends, one of the things they try to find out about each other is the values, attitudes, and goals they have in common. Do they enjoy the same activities? Do they have similar or compatible views about leisure, work, religion, and politics? Do they have similar reactions to situations and people?

Selecting one's life goals is a complex task that is easier for people who have been raised in a supportive environment. Whether an individual family is supportive depends to a great extent on how much energy and enthusiasm family members invest in each other, especially in each other's goals. The family that encourages their children's development by attending school plays and sporting events, music recitals, award ceremonies, and science and history fairs is a family that recognizes and rewards hard work, performance, and achievement.

To be achievable, goals should be clear, realistic, and challenging, but not overwhelming. Most importantly, goals should be flexible. McMinn (1988) warns, "Don't have such a tenacious grip on the boat that if it begins to sink, you go down with it."

Goals are influenced by outside forces (extrinsic motivation) and forces within the individual (intrinsic motivation). The motivation process starts with an unsatisfied need or unmet demand that creates tension and is resolved with a satisfied need and reduced tension. Goals give direction to life and values serve as a guide. However, goals cannot be set without consideration of resource availability. Resources are the subject of the next chapter.

Key Terms

absolute values	cultural values	intrinsic values
affective domain	extrinsic motivation	motivation
attitudes	extrinsic values	relative values
behavior	habits	socialization
cognitive domain	intrinsic motivation	value orientation

Review Questions

1. How do attitudes differ from values?

2. What purpose does the VALS research serve?

3. Why does Martin Seligman in his book *Learned Optimism* say that optimism is essential for achieving goals?

4. What is the difference between intrinsic and extrinsic motivation? Which one do researchers know more about? Why?

5. Bob Greene, author of *Make the Connection,* says "Each morning when you wake up, take a few moments to state what is important to you, what you wish to accomplish, and the steps you will take that day to work toward your goals. These can be goals that relate to your body and health, or anything else you want to accomplish. The beauty of this daily renewal is that no matter how yesterday went, you have the opportunity to improve on it and better yourself today." What are your goals for today? What steps are you taking? What do you think about Greene's statement regarding the daily renewal aspect of goal setting?

References

Ajzen, I. & Fishbein, M. (1980). *Understanding attitudes and predicting social behavior.* Englewood Cliffs, NJ: Prentice-Hall.

Alwin, D. F. (1989). Changes in qualities in children in the United States, 1964–1984. *Social Science Research, 8,* 195–236.

Business Week (1999, Summer).

Cravatta, M. (1997, November). Hanging on to students. *American Demographics,* 41.

Csikszentmihalyi, M. (1990). *Flow: The psychology of optimal experience.* New York: Harper & Row.

———. (1997). *Finding flow.* NY: Basic Books.

DeMerchant, E. (1993, February). *Standards: An analysis of definitions, frameworks, and implications.* Proceedings of the Eastern Regional Home Management—Family Economics Conference. Blacksburg.

Dillard, J. P., Segrin, C., & Hardin, J. (1989). Primary and secondary goals in the production of interpersonal influence messages. *Communication Monographs, 56,* 19–36.

Engel, J. (1988). Work values of American and Japanese men. *Journal of Social Behavior and Personality, 3*(3), 191–200.

Flanagan, C. A. (1990). Families and schools in hard times. *New Directions for Child Development, 46,* 7–26.

Goldsmith, E., Hoffman, J., & Hoffacker, C. (1993). Insights into the long-term effects of parents' careers on reported parent-offspring closeness. *Journal of Employment Counseling, 30*(2), 50–54.

Halberstam, D. (1993). *The fifties.* New York: Villard.

Hammersla, J. F. & McMahan, L. (1990). University students' priorities and life goals vs. relationships. *Sex Roles, 23*(112), 1–14.

Hoffman, J., Goldsmith, E., & Hoffacker, C. (1992). The influence of parents on female business students' salary and work hour expectations. *Journal of Employment Counseling, 29,* 79–83.

Hoffman, J., Hoffacker, C., & Goldsmith, E. (1992). How closeness affects parental influence on business college students' career choices. *Journal of Career Development, 19*(1), 65–73.

Kaufman, M. & Creamer, D. (1991). Influences of student goals for college on freshman-year quality of effort and growth. *Journal of College Student Development, 32*(2), 197–206.

Levin, D. P. (1989, February 27). Luxury cars lose some status. *New York Times,* B1.

Locke, E. A. (1968). Toward a theory of task motivation and incentives. *Organizational Behavior and Human Performance, 3,* 157–189.

Locke, E., Shaw, K., Saari, L., & Latham, G. (1981). Goal setting and task performance: 1969–1980. *Psychological Bulletin, 90,* 125–152.

McIntosh, W., Martin, L., & Jones, J. (1997). Goal beliefs, life events, and the malleability of people's judgments of their happiness. *Journal of Social Behavior and Personality 12*(2), 567–575.

McMinn, D. J. (1988). *Strategic living.* New York: Baker House.

Mansfield, E., Romeo, A., Schwartz, M., Teece, D., Wagner, S., & Brach, P. (1988). *Technology transfer, productivity and economic policy.* New York: W. W. Norton.

McClelland, D. (1961). *The achieving society.* New York: Van Nostrand Reinhold.

Miller, J. B. & Lane, M. (1991). Relations between young adults and their parents. *Journal of Adolescence, 14,* 179–194.

Mitchell, A. (1983). *The nine American lifestyles: Who we are and where we're going.* New York: Macmillan.

Norcross, J. & Prochaska, J. (1998). *Changing for good.* New York: Avon.

O'Reilly, J. P., Tokuno, K., & Ebata, A. (1986). Cultural differences between Americans of Japanese and European ancestry in parental valuing of social competence. *Journal of Comparative Family Studies, 17*(1), 87–95.

Palkovitz, R. & Copes, M. (1988). Changes in attitudes, beliefs, and expectations associated with the transition to parenthood. *Marriage and Family Review, 12*(3/4), 183–197.

Parish, T. A. & Nunn, G. D. (1988). The importance of the family in forming life values and personal values. *Journal of Psychology, 122*(5), 519–521.

Phillips, S. D. & Johnston, S. L. (1985). Attitudes toward work roles for women. *Journal of College Student Personnel, 26,* 334–338.

Powell, T. J. & Enright, S. J. (1990). *Anxiety and stress management.* London: Routledge, 115–119.

Raina, M. K. & Vats, A. (1990). Life goals of Indian and American college students. *International Journal of Intercultural Relations, 14,* 57–71.

Ray, P. (1997). The emerging culture. *American Demographics, 29–34, 56.*

Rigdon, J. (1991, August 14). Managers who switch coasts must adapt to different approaches to use of time. *Wall Street Journal,* B1.

Robbins, S. B. (1991). *Organizational behavior* (4th ed.). Englewood Cliffs, NJ: Prentice-Hall.

Robbins, S. B., Payne, E. C., & Chartrand, J. M. (1990). Goal instability and later life adjustment. *Psychology and Aging, 5*(3), 447–450.

Rokeach, M. J. (1973). *The nature of human values.* New York: Free Press.

Seligman, M. (1991). *Learned optimism.* New York: Knopf.

Seligmann, J. (1991, December 16). College without chemicals, *Newsweek,* 59.

Stoneman, B. (1998, December 4). Beyond rocking the ages: An interview with J. Walter Smith. *American Demographics,* 1–7.

Sweetman, M., Munz, D., & Wheeler, R. (1993). Optimism, hardiness, and exploratory style as predictors of general well-being among attorneys. *Social Indicators Research, 29,* 153–161.

Whyte, W. H. (1957). *The organization man.* Garden City, New York: Doubleday.

chapter **4**

Resources

MAIN TOPICS

RESOURCES DEFINED
TYPES OF RESOURCES
RESOURCES AND ECONOMICS
RESOURCE ATTRIBUTES AND MODELS
CULTURAL PERCEPTIONS OF RESOURCES

RESOURCES, FAMILIES, AND HOUSEHOLDS
CONSUMPTION AND RESOURCES
RESOURCE STRATEGY

Did you know that...?

...Men are spending more time with their children.

...The most likely meal eaten out is dinner.

> You already possess all you need to be happy; all you
> need is the awareness of what you have.
> —*Sarah Ban Breathnach*

SOCIETY IS DEPENDENT on an ever increasing array of resources. To wash clothes, people no longer go down to the stream and rinse them out. They use washers and dryers, detergent and softeners, electricity, and piped-in water to get clothes clean. Or, they may drop their clothes at the laundry and exchange money for human time and energy. Many management activities have been transformed from simple but labor-intensive actions to complex processes requiring investments of time, human and mechanical energy, and money.

As another example, the resource use of college students over the past few decades has changed considerably. Middle-aged parents remember themselves as cash-strapped, existing for weeks on peanut-butter sandwiches, living in run-down dormitories and apartments, but today's college students have more cash and credit. For example:

- More than half of students at four-year colleges have cars and computers.
- Two-thirds have credit cards and telephone calling cards.
- Seventy percent have cable TV.

- ◆ Seventy-five percent ate at a fast food restaurant in the past week.
- ◆ Fifty percent bought dishwashing detergent in the past month (compelling anthropological evidence that students also buy and cook food).
- ◆ Forty-seven percent shopped at a mall in the past week (Speer, 1998).

The college market is growing. More than 14 million students were enrolled in U.S. higher-education institutions in 1998, according to the National Center for Education Statistics, and that number is expected to grow 13 percent by 2007, to 16 million. When they graduate, college graduates have higher than average lifetime earnings (compared to the general population), and they spend more money on virtually everything. Money is just one of the resources used by college students.

This chapter will explore the subject of resources from a variety of theoretical and applied viewpoints. Resource theory analyzes, predicts, and explains the nature of resources as well as their perception, exchange, and use. During economic hard times such as the recession of the early 1990s, stretching resources to meet individual and family needs was a practical concern. Economic good times, such as those in the late 90s, also required thoughtful resource use. Identifying resources (and then deciding how to allocate them) is an integral part of the management process, as Figure 4.1 shows.

RESOURCES DEFINED

Resources are what is available to be used. They are assets—anything with a real or perceived value used to attain or satisfy something. Not all resource use is directed toward long-term goals; some resources are used to provide for more immediate wants and needs. For example, a librarian spending five dollars on lunch is satisfying hunger, an immediate need. The cost of buying lunch is weighed against the time and expense involved in making and bringing a lunch to the library.

FIGURE 4.1
The Management Process Model

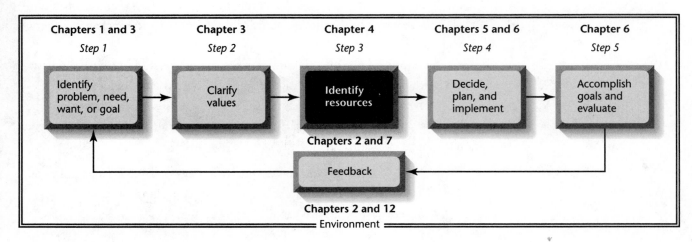

In management, time, energy, and money usually receive the most attention, and these resources will be referred to throughout this chapter and the book as a whole. But resources can take other forms. A sense of humor or a pleasant personality is a resource. Knowledge is a resource. A high school diploma is a resource. Everyone has a unique set of resources and uses those resources differently.

Resourcefulness is the ability to recognize and use resources effectively. A resourceful person skillfully uses resources to cope with daily challenges. When resourceful people encounter a problem, they solve it or find a way around it, rather than being defeated by it. Resourcefulness is learned in families, schools, work situations, and social organizations. For example, if the electrical power goes out at home, children observe how their parents cope and substitute alternative sources of energy and light. In an office, if the copy machine breaks down, the employees substitute temporary alternative resources (e.g., using the machine in another office or going to a copy center). Along with families, schools and community youth organizations, such as Boy Scouts, Girl Scouts, 4-H, and the YMCA and YWCA, encourage the development of resourcefulness in children.

One of the most basic concepts in management is that material resources are limited, so decisions have to be made about their allocation. By helping individuals learn to be more resourceful, resource management can contribute significantly to their quality of life. It is not enough to win millions of dollars, as lottery winners who have lost all their money will attest; more important to one's lifestyle in the long run is what one does with the money to retain it and make it grow.

Types of Resources

Resources can be classified in several ways. One way is to categorize them as intangible or tangible. **Intangible resources** are incapable of being touched; examples include integrity, confidence, and literacy. **Tangible resources** are real, touchable, or capable of being appraised; some examples are jewelry, land, and houses. Obviously, tangible resources are easier to observe and measure than intangibles.

Resources can also be classified as human or material. **Human resources** are the skills, talents, and abilities that people possess. Such resources increase through use. For example, the more a person rides a bicycle, the better bicycle rider he or she becomes. Examples of human resources are knowledge, health, feelings, and caring.

The sum total of human resources, all the capabilities and traits that people use to achieve goals and other resources, is called **human capital.** Investing in human capital is a lifelong personal goal for many people and a professional goal for those employed in the helping professions (e.g., counseling, education, and social work). Government also invests in human capital through such programs as free school lunches and Head Start. As another example, employers and employees create value, based not only on some unit of labor in the current moment, but on their entire store of knowledge and experience—their human capital.

> It's said that a tourist once spotted Pablo Picasso sketching in a Paris cafe and asked if he would sketch her, offering to pay him fair value. In a matter of minutes, Picasso was finished. When she asked what she owed him, Picasso told her 5,000 francs.
>
> "But it only took you a few minutes," the tourist said.
>
> "No," said Picasso, "it took me all my life." (Kay, 1999)

Our knowledge-based economy is full of Picassos. What goes into a personal or professional decision is not just the time immediately absorbed. It is the years of experience and education accrued by the person that is applied to the situation at hand.

One of the goals of education is to increase human capital. By going to college, students invest in their human capital development. When parents pay tuition fees and alumni provide scholarships, they are also investing in students' human capital.

Although everyone has human capital and the potential for growth and development, only 4 to 10 percent of human potential is used according to one estimate (Peters & Waterman, 1982). How accurate is this estimate? What happens to the remainder? How can the remaining 90+ percent be tapped? Scientists have a long way to go before they will completely understand the boundaries and potentials of human capital.

Material resources include natural phenomena, such as fertile soil, petroleum, and rivers, and human-made items, such as buildings, money, and computers. Material resources decrease through use; that is, buildings deteriorate, money is spent, and computers break down or become outdated.

Lifestyles are based on a combination of human and material resources. **Resource stock** is the sum of readily available resources an individual possesses. Each individual has a resource stock that she or he draws on to make and implement decisions.

Resources and Economics

Regardless of type, resources have the power to satisfy wants and enhance lives. Individuals use resources differently at different times in their life span. For example, parents have a difficult time understanding why their children "waste money" on candy and poor-quality toys, because the parents would make different choices. In childhood, much resource use is directed to the satisfaction of immediate personal wants and needs; hence, candy is a good purchase in the mind of a 5-year-old.

This book is primarily about management, not economics. Nevertheless, most decisions are affected by economic realities. For example, many people would like to go on a trip abroad, but how many can afford to go on the spur of the moment? Everyone is a consumer, if not of trips, of food and shelter. Patterns in food consumption are an interesting case in point. Over the last decade, the levels of eating out and bringing prepared foods into the home have risen sharply. According to the National Restaurant Association, in the United States, almost half of all adults (46 percent) are restaurant patrons during a typical day. In an average month, 78 percent of U.S. households used some form of carryout or delivery. The likelihood of patronizing restaurants is highest among younger consumers: about 6 out of 10 18-to-24-year-olds are restaurant patrons on a typical day, compared to 3 out of 10 adults over 65. The most likely meal to be eaten out is dinner (see Figure 4.2). The number of African-American-owned and women-owned eating and drinking establishments increased at double-digit rates over the past decade, with sales also rising dramatically. Saturday is the most popular day to eat out. Monday is the least popular. August is the most popular month to eat out. One out of five takeout food consumers is a daily user.

As Chapter 1 explained, economics refers to the production, development, and management of material wealth. It is also concerned with distribution and consumption. Any economic system must address three questions:

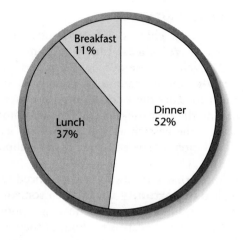

FIGURE 4.2
Distribution of Restaurant Customer Traffic, 1997*

*Commercial establishments only

Source: National Restaurant Association 1998 Pocket Factbook. Web site: www.restaurant.org

1. What goods and services are going to be produced?
2. How are the goods and services produced?
3. Who will get these goods and services?

Scarcity, which means a shortage or an insufficient amount or supply, lies at the heart of these questions. For example, in the 1980s, toy stores experienced a run on Cabbage Patch dolls for Christmas. Evening news programs showed parents fighting over dolls and told of the disappointment of children who did not receive one. In this instance, the demand far outweighed the supply, creating a shortage. A year later, stores had an oversupply of the same dolls, which were no longer in great demand. In the 1990s, a similar run on another set of toys, Beanie Babies, happened with the same problems of overdemand and undersupply.

Scarce goods are economic goods. Food, clothing, and shelter are examples of economic goods. So are parks, trees, and clean air. Leisure is also an economic good because most people feel they do not have enough leisure time. Juliet Schor, author of *The Overworked American,* writes:

> When surveyed, Americans report that they have only sixteen and a half hours of leisure a week, after the obligations of job and household are taken care of. Working hours are already longer than they were forty years ago. If present trends continue, by the end of the century Americans will be spending as much time at their jobs as they did back in the nineteen twenties . . . . U.S. manufacturing employees currently work 320 more hours—the equivalent of over two months—than their counterparts in West Germany or France. (1991, pp. 1–2)

Economic thinking recognizes that obtaining any scarce good involves a cost, which leads individuals and families to economizing behavior and goal setting. People use their skills, energy, and ingenuity to produce economic goods. They struggle constantly to lessen scarcity and better provide for their needs.

No society has enough economic goods or resources to satisfy everyone's wants and desires; nor does any individual have enough income or wealth to satisfy her or his every want or desire. Scarcity exists as long as people cannot purchase everything at zero price. Theoretically, the richest person and the poorest person in the world experience scarcity. Each person defines for himself or herself what constitutes scarcity. A related concept is availability. Resources are described as being available or not depending on how scarce or abundant they are.

Choice and Opportunity Costs

Scarcity forces people to make choices and decisions about the allocation of resources. Should a person save for a car, tuition, or something else? If so, how much should be saved? Each of these decisions involves a cost; for example, saving for a car means that money cannot be spent on a ski trip. Economics assumes that people will consider these costs as they attempt to better their living conditions by making the best use of their time and money. Management offers a guide for making the best choices about how to use and allocate resources such as time and money. The end goal of these choices is maximizing satisfaction.

The highest-valued alternative that must be sacrificed to satisfy a want or attain something is called **opportunity cost.** When someone quits a paid job to stay home with children, he or she is experiencing opportunity costs. One way to conceptualize opportunity costs is to think of them as tradeoffs. Life is full of tradeoffs. Choosing one activity over another involves a tradeoff. For example, choosing to buy one product over another may involve a tradeoff between quality and cost. To get a desired good or outcome, it is necessary to trade off some other desired good or outcome, for example, time with friends versus time with family. Tradeoffs, then, require sacrifice—something must be given up to gain something else. In short, there is no free lunch.

The basic activities of any household include many examples of resource tradeoffs. In each household, the manager (or managers) must decide how the family resources of time, labor, and money will be allocated. Among other things, the manager must decide which aspects of household production should be carried out by the unpaid work of household members or obtained through market goods and services. A restaurant meal could replace a home-cooked dinner, for example, or a gardener could be hired to care for the lawn and a housekeeper to care for the house. Often a household's tradeoffs are between time and money. Obtaining goods or services from outside is more costly than producing them within the household. Buying frozen pre-prepared meals at the store costs more than cooking at home, and sending clothes to the laundry costs more than washing them at home. But as time becomes an increasingly scarce commodity more families are choosing time-saving options and relying on time-saving equipment such as microwave ovens and dishwashers.

Laws of Supply and Demand

Scarcity affects the price or worth of a resource. According to the law of demand, as the price of a good or service rises, the quantity demanded of that good or service falls. Conversely, as the price falls, the quantity demanded will rise.

The law of supply is the law of demand in reverse. According to the law of supply, as the supply of a good or service goes up, the price goes down. Conversely, as the supply goes down, the price goes up.

Aren't more people likely to apply for a job that pays $50 an hour than for one that pays $1 an hour? Isn't a one-of-a-kind Louis XV desk more valuable than a mass-produced desk from a discount store? Thus, the price paid for goods and services is influenced by supply and demand. In economic theory, the right price is reached when supply and demand are equal.

When prices change radically, they are probably reacting to real or perceived changes in supply or demand. For example, if the weather is too wet and the peanut crop is destroyed, the price of peanut butter will skyrocket. Grocery shoppers will watch for sales on peanut butter and stock up or substitute another sandwich ingredient for the high-priced peanut butter.

Economic Well-Being

Economic well-being is the degree to which individuals and families have economic adequacy and security. It refers to the desire or extent of protection against economic risks, such as loss of employment, illness, bankruptcy, bank failures, poverty, and destitution in old age (McGregor & Goldsmith, 1998). It is a function of many variables in combination, including money income, financial assets, human capital, durable goods and services, time, ability to manage, control over financial affairs and resources, values, job security, retirement plans, ability to adjust to changes, and lifestyle decisions. Economic well-being is often used as a measure of quality of life. Each person and each family defines what constitutes economic well-being for them. Based on the results of a study of the financial well-being of adults in an eight-state region, researchers came to the following conclusion:

> When working with families and individuals in matters of financial concern, it is critical to recognize that although income is important in predicting perceived economic well-being, other factors contribute to this perception. These perceptions, attitudes, and skills affect the use of resources and how environmental factors are perceived. Each family has a distinctive composition and is predisposed to characteristic modes of thought reflecting the circumstances unique to it. (Kratzer & Keefe, 1993, p. 43)

Allocation and Recognition of Resources

Management is the process of using resources to attain goals through planning and of taking the steps necessary to meet goals. A crucial part of the management process is the allocation of resources to appropriate goals. As explained in the previous chapter, goals can be prioritized and divided into short-term, intermediate, and long-term goals. In theory, resources should be allocated to meet the most important goals first, but in practice, resources are often diverted to more immediate needs or demands.

Everyone has different types and amounts of resources and different life demands. As explained in the previous chapter, many people who live from day-to-day do not have the luxury of allocating resources toward long-term goals. Their resources have to go to basic survival needs.

Resource recognition is the realization of the skills, talents, and materials one possesses. Lack of resource recognition is often a problem for teenagers. As they develop their adult identity, they become more aware and more confident about their resources and how to allocate them. One of the goals of education is to help students become aware of their strengths and how to capitalize on them.

Regulation of Resources

Who should control resources? Many conflicts, from family feuds to full-scale wars, have been fought over this question. How should resources be divided? Which resources should be publicly held? Which should be privately held? **Private resources** are owned and/or controlled by an individual, family, or group. **Public resources** are owned and used by all the people in a locality or country; a national park and a county-owned swimming pool are examples.

In 1776, Adam Smith advanced a theory justifying capitalism in his book *An Inquiry into the Nature and Causes of the Wealth of Nations.* He argued that with economic freedom individuals will follow their own self-interest to fulfill themselves and their families, thereby benefiting society as a whole.

Smith used the term *laissez-faire* to suggest that government should leave business alone. According to him, the "invisible hand" of competition would guide the marketplace. To a certain extent, society still adheres to much of Smith's laissez-faire theory, but societal and economic developments in the twentieth century have led many people to believe that government needs to serve to a certain degree as a regulator of the economy. How much governmental regulation is desirable in such areas as health care and welfare reform is an ongoing public debate that continues in the twenty-first century.

Economic Resources and Employee Benefits

Economic resources refer to wealth in any form, including credit, money, benefits, and stocks and bonds. Household equipment, cars, savings, property, and investments are forms of wealth, whereas commissions, wages, interest, dividends, bonuses, pensions, and royalties are forms of money income. Wealth is a measure of what has been accumulated, whereas income is earned or given to the recipient (e.g., child support, alimony, and government transfer payments such as welfare payments).

Employee benefits are goods and services that are part of an individual's or family's resource base. When determining personal and family assets, the value of benefits should be estimated along with income and wealth. About 95 percent of employees in medium and larger U.S. firms and businesses receive benefits (Garman & Forgue, 1993). Typical employee benefits are health insurance, life insurance, paid vacations and sick leave, and retirement programs. Many employers offer cafeteria plans, which allow employees to choose the benefits they want. For example, employees may add a dental plan or a child-care assistance plan to their basic benefit package.

Resource Attributes and Models

In a household, someone has to decide what will be done; by whom it will be done; when, where, and how it will be done; and which resources will be required. The person (or persons) who does this is the manager. He or she makes decisions about how money is spent, initiates goals, sets objectives, makes plans, keeps records and timetables, makes doctor and dentist appointments, and performs a host of other tasks. The manager may be one person, or management responsibilities may be split among several people. As children grow older and more independent, they take on more responsibility for scheduling their own time, money, and work. According to Bryant (1990), performance of household management activities leads to direct satisfaction (leisure, comfort) or indirect satisfaction (work completed).

The characteristic way an individual or family manages their resources is shaped by five forces:

1. Psychological/personality forces (including value orientations) that shape individual choices and preferences
2. Economic forces that regulate the exchange of money, energy, materials, services, and information
3. Technological forces that generate problem-solving inventions, tools, and methods
4. Sociocultural forces that regulate mores, norms, and customs
5. Political-legal forces that allocate power and provide constraining and protecting laws and regulations

These forces constantly interact with each other; any decision about resource allocation will be affected by several or all of these forces.

Attributes

Household resources can be classified as human (time, skills, energy of members) or physical. Resources also have certain other characteristics or attributes (adapted and expanded from Paolucci, Hall, & Axinn, 1977):

◆ Resources are interdependent.

◆ Sometimes resources are exchangeable.

◆ Material resources are limited.

◆ Resource use relies on the person's ability to process information and make decisions.

◆ Sometimes resources can be stored. Examples include fuel, books, furniture, and clothes.

Resources can also be characterized by their affective, cognitive, and psychomotor attributes. Affective attributes refer to feelings about or expressions of resource use. Expressions of love, gratitude, and caring are examples of affective attributes. Which resources are shared and with whom are affected by feelings. Someone is more likely to share private information with a friend, for example, than with a stranger.

Cognitive attributes refer to the knowledge aspects of resource use. Existing knowledge based on past learning and experiences is applied to new situations. The ability to synthesize (bring together information and knowledge), analyze, and evaluate new situations is a crucial part of the cognitive attribute. A resourceful person has a high degree of cognitive ability.

Psychomotor attributes refer to physical reactions to mental stimuli, such as the capacity to respond to threats or to perform work. Being able to respond quickly and appropriately to physical and mental demands is also a part of being resourceful.

Activities such as learning and teaching require all three attributes. For example, teaching others to use computers requires good hand-eye coordination (psychomotor ability), knowledge (cognitive ability), and the ability to communicate in an interesting way (affective ability). Most jobs require all three attributes (e.g., surgeon, nurse, and child care worker).

Foa & Foa Resource Model

Anything that can be used is a resource, but this concept is too expansive to be very helpful. By arranging the main types of resources in an interactive model, they can be examined in a meaningful and systematic way. One such model is the Foa & Foa Resource Model, which illustrates the interdependence of resources (Figure 4.3). Resource theory was first promulgated by Uriel Foa in 1971 and explained further in 1974 in a book entitled *Social Structures of the Mind,* which he published with Edna Foa. The theory provides a framework for understanding social interactions and the relationships that form between individuals in everyday life (Converse, 1993). These relationships provide the means by which individuals can obtain needed resources—love, services, goods, money, information, and status—from others. In the model, the resources at the top of the circle (love, status, and services) are more particularistic than the ones at the bottom (information, money, and goods). In other words, people are more selective when exchanging love (only with family and friends) than

FIGURE 4.3
Foa & Foa Model
of Resource Exchange

Source: Foa, U., Converse, J., Tornblom, K., and Foa, E. (Eds.) (1993). *Resource Theory: Explorations and Applications.* San Diego: Academic Press. Reprinted with permission.

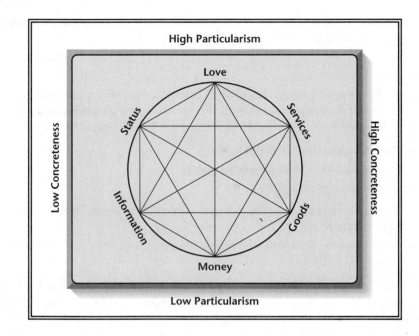

when exchanging money (with nearly anyone, including store clerks and bank tellers). In the model, resources close to each other on the circle are more likely to be exchanged than those opposite each other. For example, a mother who loves her baby provides care by feeding or diapering the baby (a service). Note that love and money are directly opposite each other.

Several researchers have attempted to apply the Foa & Foa model to different populations and situations to see how well it works in reality. For example, Kathryn Rettig, Sharon Danes, and Jean Bauer used the model in a study of the problems of economically stressed farm families. They found that "family life quality is negatively affected by economic hardship, particularly for women" (1993, p. 149). Further, the study revealed that "the exchanges of services in the family setting were perceived by women to be less satisfying, compared to men, at the time of most severe stress" (p. 149). The researchers concluded that resource theory is useful in exploring questions of quality of life and economic hardship. In an earlier article on the Foa & Foa model, they stated:

> Each person has a unique motivational state for engaging in resource exchanges which results from a combination of past and present experiences. The larger the amount of a resource possessed by a person, the more power one has with this resource and the more likely it is to be given to others. (1991, p. 274)

Using the Foa & Foa Resource Model in a study of older women, Rosemary Blieszner (1993) found a distinction between how the women interacted with close versus casual friends. Specifically, the means for giving and receiving love and status were higher for close friends than for casual friends; thus, Blieszner's results lend support to the proposition that people reserve exchanges of particularistic resources for special relationships. The next section describes an extension of the Foa & Foa Resource Model.

The Resource Model of Motivation (RMM)

Based on the work of the Foas, Dennis Bristow and John Mowen developed another resource model which also illustrates the interaction of resources. This model, called the Resource Model of Motivation (RMM), appears in Figure 4.4. Note that it differs from the Foa & Foa model mainly in the types and configuration of the resources. According to Bristow (personal communication, April 4, 1994):

> The RMM is founded upon the premise that in order to function properly, humans engage in exchange activities to protect and enhance certain fundamental assets (resources). Broadly defined, resources can be operationalized as available, accumulative assets that one can use to achieve one's goals. Such assets must be transmittable or exchangeable between individuals. . . . Further, as is posited in the RMM, resources are said to exist in an interdependent system. As such, it is argued that as resource levels or amounts change, imbalances in the system occur. For example, if an individual is strongly motivated to accumulate wealth resources (e.g., stocks and bonds, large sums of money, fine art collections, etc.) and engages in activities to that end, activities directed at developing or maintaining social resources (e.g., friendships, intimate relationships, etc.) may necessarily decrease. In essence, the four resources in the RMM exist in a dynamic and interrelated system.

In the RMM, the four fundamental resource needs are physical resources, social resources, informational resources, and wealth, which were defined in Chapter 1 in the discussion of needs. In the RMM, self-concept is in the center, and the resource exchange is encompassed within an individual's environment and time. In the RMM, time is envisioned as a finite temporal space in which activities are performed. Research studies examining how well the RMM works are underway.

Other Resource Allocation Factors: Utility and Accessibility

A basic concept in management is that resources are not useful unless they are perceived as useful. **Utility** is the value, worth, applicability, productiveness, or, simply, usefulness of a resource. Utility is in the eye of the beholder. For example, a papier-mâché castle made by a 10-year-old boy may not have any market value, but to him it has great value and is useful in play.

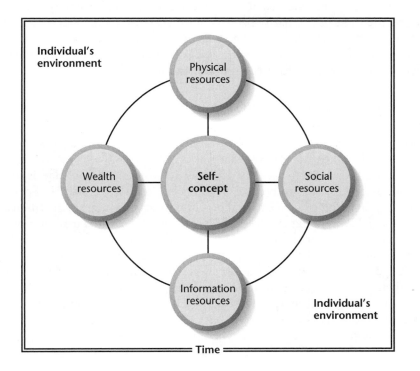

FIGURE 4.4
The Resource Management Model of Motivation

Source: Adapted from Dennis Bristow and John Mowen, *The Resource Management Model of Motivation,* Proceedings of the Society of Consumer Psychology Annual Meeting, St. Petersburg, Florida, February 17, 1994.

Economists and anthropologists recognize different kinds of utility, such as time, place, form, and diminishing utility, and also observe that various cultures view resources and utility differently. The concept of utility is learned and subjective. Time utility refers to the availability of a resource when it is needed. Arriving at a closed store with a fistful of dollars is a frustrating and useless activity. Place utility refers to location. Form utility means that the resource is in an accessible and usable form. Diminishing utility refers to the concept that the first use is more desirable than a later use. Drinking beer is a classic example. The first sip is more tasty and satisfying than subsequent sips, and if too much is drunk, there is an undesirable negative effect.

To be useful, a resource has to be accessible. Telephone answering machines and car phones make messages and other information more accessible. As another example, money locked up in a bank vault overnight is not useful; with the invention of the automatic teller machine, however, money is accessible day or night. The 24-hour grocery store, 24-hour catalog shopping services, and Internet shopping have also expanded accessibility. The general trend is toward greater accessibility of resources.

Decision Making and Resources

In making any decision, an individual considers accessibility and other resource attributes. By finding out all the information possible about a person, place, or situation before making a decision, some potential problems can be avoided. In deciding which college to attend, for example, a student considers location, tuition costs, housing options, and availability of courses. Decision making uses up a vital resource, however—time. A basic economic principle is that the total cost of an item is equal to its monetary cost plus its time cost.

To save time, consumers rely on established shopping behaviors (e.g., going to the same stores, buying the same brands). They are open to change when they have the time, when they perceive a need for a change, and when they realize there is a disparity between what they want and what they are getting. When the motivation for change is present, new alternatives are considered. From an economic standpoint, the best alternative is the one providing the most benefit for the least cost in time and money.

Knowledge and Education: Vital Resources

The question of what is our greatest resource has been debated by scholars and writers from a variety of fields. Is it money, possessions, land, or something else? Peter Drucker (1999) says that our primary resource is knowledge and the leading social groups will be knowledge workers. Knowledge is gained through experience or study. E. F. Schumacher, author of *Small Is Beautiful,* says that education is the most vital of all resources. He states that "all history as well as all current experience—points to the fact that it is man, not nature, who provides the primary resource: that the key factor of all economic development comes out of the mind of man" (1973, p. 79). Schumacher suggests that the development of nations should not start with goods, but with people and their education, organization, and discipline. An educated population leads to economic development through expanded work opportunities and better planning skills. Schumacher says, therefore, that investing in human capital should come before other types of investment.

Cultural Perceptions of Resources

Culture is the sum of all socially transmitted behavior patterns, beliefs, arts, expectations, institutions, and all other products of human work and thought characteristic of a group, community, or population. Language, ideas, customs, taboos, codes, tools, techniques, music, rituals, and ceremonies are all part of culture. In families, culture is transmitted from one generation to another. Members of cultural groups share common interests and goals. As explained in the previous chapter, cultural values are generally held concepts of right or wrong that are shared by members of cultural groups.

In general, cultures have the following six attributes:

1. They develop over time.
2. They supply boundaries or limits of acceptable behavior that affect how individuals think and act.
3. They provide a sense of belonging, identity, and security. Saying "I am an African American," or "I am Catholic," or "I am a member of the Smith family" implies an identification with a cultural group.
4. They are so pervasive that they are often taken for granted. Familiar traditions, such as turkey at Thanksgiving or a decorated tree at Christmas, are expressions of culture and provide a sense of continuity and identity to individual and family life.
5. They can be constrictive. In a teenage clique, members may feel forced to act, dress, and think alike. Conformity to the group may take precedence over the identity of the individual.
6. They can be enriching or expressive. Culture can provide a style or a format for intellectual, social, or artistic expression.

Attributes 5 and 6 may seem contradictory, but they demonstrate that culture can be many things. Culture can mold people and at the same time provide a means for individual expression.

The boundaries cultures set are called **norms.** Norms, which are based on cultural values, are rules that specify, delineate, encourage, and prohibit certain behaviors in certain situations. One norm of the classroom is for students to sit in chairs at desks. Standing on the desks would go against the norm. Norms are useful because they guide behavior, letting people know how to act in given situations. Manners and etiquette are other types of norms.

Culture evolves slowly over time. Technological and other innovations change the way things are normally done. The electrification of the home, the introduction of computers, and the automobile have all changed the way lives are conducted.

Cultures and Subcultures

Usually, a single dominant culture provides the major influence on behavior. Citizens of a certain nation share a common language, customs, and history. Subcultures, or subsystems of the dominant culture, may have a strong influence also. These subcultures may have a religious, ethnic, political, racial, social, or economic base. Individuals can belong to a dominant culture and several subcultures at the same time.

Culture is transmitted through a variety of channels, including parents, schools, community organizations, churches, employers, and government. An individual may live and travel in many different cultures. Individuals may change their language, form of dress, or way of acting as they move between different cultural systems. They may dress and act a certain way at work and dress and act quite differently at home.

RESOURCES, FAMILIES, AND HOUSEHOLDS

During the past 20 years, families and households have undergone vast changes. The principal developments include increased labor force participation of women, smaller family size, more divorces, more single-parent families, the aging of populations, internationalization of the economy, changes in prevailing values and attitudes, and technological innovations, especially in communications, information, and transportation. Nearly every social and economic institution has been altered. In the United States, according to Ray Marshall, a former secretary of labor:

> We have moved from an economy in which economic success depended heavily on natural resources and economies of scale to one that is more competitive and knowledge intensive. In the economy of the 1990s and beyond, success depends mainly on the quality of human resources, and the quality of human resources depends heavily on what happens to families. (1991, pp. 103–104)

Marshall identified several economic and labor market changes associated with the dramatic changes in families and households:

◆ There has been a decline in the proportion of family households, especially those classified as "traditional," (i.e., married families with children). These families have also become smaller. Simultaneously, nonfamily and single-person households have proliferated.

◆ Fertility rates have declined because women are having fewer children and at older ages.

◆ Despite their decline, a substantial majority of Americans live in family households.

In the late 1990s, men were spending more time with their children. The Changing Workforce survey of 2,877 workers showed that fathers were spending a half-hour more each workday, and one more hour each day off, caring for and doing things with their children than in 1977 (Shellenbarger, 1998).

As families become more mobile and both parents increasingly work outside the home, raising children is becoming more difficult, and the family must rely more on outside resources. As social historian Barbara Whitehead says, ". . . raising children isn't an individual act. It is a social and communal enterprise, involving kin, neighbors, other parents, friends, and many other unrelated adults. Typically, hermits don't raise kids; villagers do" (1990, p. 5). First Lady Hillary Rodham Clinton's book *It Takes a Village* expressed a similar point of view.

Some solutions to family problems lie in changes in family and work policies in the private and public sectors. The Family and Medical Leave Act, enacted in 1993, is one example of a public policy designed to strengthen families. Through this act, men and women workers in companies with more than 50 employees can take up to three months unpaid leave for the birth or adoption of a child or the care of a critically ill family member. Essentially, workers will not have to choose between their job security and their family's well-being during times of family crises, emergencies, or upheaval. Besides public policies, employers, schools, friends, extended family, and community and religious organizations can also help support families. Chapter 8 discusses specific human resource problems of families, and Chapter 10 has more details about The Family and Medical Leave Act.

Consumption and Resources

The United States has been called a throwaway society or a consumer society. To **consume** means to destroy, use, or expend. The enormous productive capacities and market forces of the United States have been committed to satisfying human needs and desires often with little overall regard to the future of life on the planet. Figure 4.5 illustrates how much more land, water, fossil fuels, and forest products a person in the United States consumes compared to a person in China.

If this course of consumerism continues, waste will become an increasingly difficult problem. Although some waste cannot be helped, much packaging and many products themselves are unnecessary. For a while, a U.S. appliance manufacturer sold $25 lamps that were designed to be discarded when the bulbs burned out. Lighters, razors, and disposable cameras are made for a single use and then thrown away. Convenience has come to be valued over cost per use and sensitivity to the environment.

From the perspective of resource conservation, is the use of disposables a good thing? Obviously, no. The customs and values of U.S. culture traditionally supported thrift and conservation. Planned obsolescence and unnecessary waste are at odds with these values. Many people are beginning to question or reject the notion of the throwaway society as evidenced by a widespread acceptance of recycling and the increased purchasing of products made from recycled materials.

FIGURE 4.5
Resource Use in the United States and China Compared

Source: As adapted by Francis Sizer and Eleanor Whitney, *Nutrition: Concepts and Controversies,* Eighth Edition (Belmont, CA: Wadsworth, 2000).

	Land for crops, pasture, forests	Water	Fossil fuel (oil equivalents)	Forest products

In the United States, one person depends on these amounts of resources each year:

 3.2 hectares

2.5 million liters

 8,000 liters

14 tons

In China, one person depends on:

0.5 hectares

460,000 liters

 413 liters

 0.03 tons

Resource Strategy

Underlying much of management is the concept of strategy. A **strategy** is a plan of action, a way of conducting and following through on operations. Strategy implies the careful thinking out of details and the consideration of outcomes. Usually, the word *strategy* is associated with military or business management operations, yet it has many applications for individual, household, and family management as well. Strategy revolves around the following questions:

◆ What do I want to accomplish? Or, what do I want to create?

◆ What is important?

◆ How will a plan contribute to goal achievement?

A successful resource strategy incorporates planning what is owned versus what is desired. If a couple wants to buy a new house, they have to form a strategy to save for the down payment. A person who wants to lose weight should reevaluate her or his eating and exercise habits to form a weight-loss strategy. The person would set a timetable and a goal for weight reduction. Similar plans of action or strategy could be set up to reduce household waste or unnecessary spending. Finding a job also involves strategy.

Electronic Resources

www.eatright.org

Resource use affects all aspects of life; hence, the number of potential Web sites is almost limitless. A few select Web sites are featured here. To learn more about how organizations look at human capital development and operational excellence, go to the Web site of the Society for Organizational Learning at **www.fieldbook.com/resources.html**. For more information about human capital, see the report entitled "A Solid Investment: Making Full Use of the Nation's Human Capital," from the U.S. Department of Labor Glass Ceiling Commission at **www.ilr.cornell.edu/library/e_archive/glassceiling**.

A growing area of interest in resource management is the field of health care management. For example, information on women's health can be obtained from **www.acog.org** (American Academy of Obstetricians and Gynecologists), **www.nof.org** (National Osteoporosis Foundation), and **www.aaos.org**

(American Academy of Orthopaedic Surgeons). Information on maintaining healthy weight for men and women is available at **www.navigator.tufts.edu** (Tufts University Nutrition Navigator), **www.eatright.org** (American Dietetic Association), **www.nhlbi.nih.gov** (National Heart, Lung, and Blood Institute), and **www.acefitness.org** (American Council on Exercise). The Department of Health and Human Services' health resource guide can be found at **www.healthfinder.gov**. For information about Healthy People 2010, an alliance of over 600 health organizations promoting health and disease prevention in the twenty-first century, visit their Web site at **www.health.gov/healthypeople**.

Summary

Resources are central to the management process. Without human and material resources, there would be nothing to manage. For individuals, resources are the essential means to attain goals and meet demands. For families and households, resource use provides a lifespace and a lifestyle around which an individual's and family's needs are met. Knowledge and education are vital resources.

This chapter has covered many types, models, and levels of resources. Resources can be looked at from an economic or a cultural viewpoint. Because of scarcity, an individual tries to make choices which maximize benefits and minimize costs. The way a person goes about doing this is culturally defined.

Resource management is concerned with all these topics. The next chapter takes the information presented so far and puts it together in the decision-making process. Later in the book, the resource concepts covered in the present chapter will be applied to specific environmental and human problems. Management provides a way of looking at problems in an organized, rational, and still compassionate manner. Material goods and wealth are not the sole determinants of happiness. Wealth and goods can help assure an easier life, but not necessarily a happy one. The elusive nature of happiness and the search to find the right life balance underlie the study of management. Individuals make decisions purposefully, always seeking to better their circumstances. This constant striving drives people to seek better solutions and explains the "why" behind much of human behavior.

Key Terms

consume	material resources	resource stock
culture	norms	scarcity
economic well-being	opportunity cost	strategy
human capital	private resources	tangible resources
human resources	public resources	utility
intangible resources	resourcefulness	

Review Questions

1. What is the relationship between supply and demand?
2. What does the story about Picasso and the tourist illustrate about the nature of human capital? Name one skill, talent, or ability that you have built up over the years.

3. What do the Foa & Foa Resource Model and the RMM illustrate?

4. Why is the United States called a throwaway society? How does U.S. consumption compare to that of China?

5. What role does strategy play in resource management? A college senior in sociology, Alison, figures that she will need a minimum starting salary of $26,000 to live in Charleston, based on a budget she developed. She wants to live in Charleston because she has friends there, but she is having trouble finding a job because she goes to school 500 miles away. Alison's main expense is that she will need at least $600 a month for rent. If you were Alison what would you do next? In other words, what would your strategy be?

References

Blieszner, R. (1993). Resource exchange in the social networks of elderly women. U. Foa, J. Converse, K. Tornblom, & E. Foa (Eds.), *Resource theory: Explorations and applications.* San Diego: Academic Press.

Bryant, W. K. (1990). *The economic organization of the household.* Cambridge and New York: Cambridge University Press.

Converse, J. (1993). Preface. In U. Foa, J. Converse, K. Tornblom, & E. Foa (Eds.), *Resource theory: Explorations and applications.* San Diego: Academic Press.

Drucker, P. (1999). *Management challenges for the 21st century.* NY: Harper Books.

Foa, U. (1971). Interpersonal and economic resources. *Science 171*, 347.

Foa, U., Converse, J., Tornblom, K., & Foa, E. (Eds.) (1993). *Resource theory: Explorations and applications.* San Diego: Academic Press.

Foa, U. & Foa, E. (1974). *Societal structures of the mind.* Springfield, IL: Charles C. Thomas.

Garman, T. & Forgue, R. (1993). *Personal Finance.* New York: Houghton Mifflin.

Heilbroner, R. (1990, February). *American Demographics, 12*(2), 9.

Kay, I. (1999, January 18). *The Wall Street Journal.*

Kratzer, C. Y. & Keefe, D. (1993). Towards development of an ecological model for predicting perceived economic well-being. In C. Y. Kratzer (Ed.), *Change and exchange: The Proceedings of the Southeastern Regional Association of Family Economics—Home management,* Roanoke, Virginia, 35–45.

Marshall, R. (1991). *The state of families, 3: Losing direction, families, human resource development, and economic performance.* Milwaukee, WI: Family Service America.

McGregor, S. and Goldsmith, E. (1998, Summer). Expanding our understanding of quality of life, standard of living, and well-being. *Journal of Family and Consumer Science, 22,* 2–6.

Paolucci, B., Hall, O., & Axinn, N. (1977). *Family decision making: An ecosystem approach.* New York: John Wiley & Sons.

Peters, T. & Waterman, R. (1982). *In search of excellence.* New York: Harper & Row.

Rettig, K., Danes, S., & Bauer, J. (1991). Family life quality: Theory and assessment in economically stressed farm families. *Social Indicators Research, 24,* 269–299.

_____. (1993). Gender differences in perceived family life quality among economically stressed farm families. In U. Foa, J. Converse, K. Tornblom, & E. Foa (Eds.), *Resource Theory: Explorations and applications.* San Diego: Academic Press, 123–155.

Schor, J. B. (1991). *The overworked American: The unexpected decline of leisure.* New York: Basic Books.

Schumacher, E. F. (1973). *Small is beautiful.* New York: Harper & Row.

Shellenbarger, S. (1998, April 15). Work and family. *The Wall Street Journal,* B1.

Smith, A. (1776). *An inquiry into the nature and causes of the wealth of nations.* New York: Modern Library (1973 edition).

Speer, T. (1998, March). College come-ons. *American Demographics.*

Whitehead, B. D. (1990, Spring/Summer). The family in a friendly culture. *Family Affairs, 2*(1–2), 5.

chapter 5

Decision Making and Problem Solving

MAIN TOPICS

DECISION MAKING AS PART OF MANAGEMENT
STEPS IN DECISION MAKING
MODELS, RULES, AND UTILITY
REFERENCE GROUPS
PERSONAL DECISION MAKING
FAMILY DECISION MAKING
CONSUMER DECISION MAKING IN FAMILIES

PROBLEM SOLVING
DEFINITION, ANALYSIS, AND PLAN OF ACTION
UNCERTAINTY AND RISK

Did you know that...?

. . . Thirty-four new food products are launched each day in the United States.

. . . Mothers typically perform tasks from 17 occupations.

> If we really want to live, we'd better start at once to try.
> —*W. H. Auden*

WHAT IS A good decision? How can bad decisions be avoided? Good decisions meet several criteria—quality, acceptance, flexibility, and clarity. Quality means that the decision meets some standard, objective, or goal. Acceptance signifies that the key players in the decision acknowledge that it is reasonable and workable. If the decision does not meet some standard, objective, or goal or if someone involved in the decision does not accept it, then the decision is likely to be ineffective. Therefore, a family's decisions are more likely to succeed if they have the support of family members and are linked to an agreed-upon standard, objective, or goal. In other words, in families as in other groups, decisions that are cocreated have a better chance of success than ones that are individually created. Flexibility means that the decision not only should be appropriate to the situation but should be able to adjust if the situation changes. For example, becoming engaged to be married may seem like a good decision under certain circumstances, but when attitudes or circumstances change (e.g., compatibility wanes, expectations change, another love interest comes into the picture), the couple may choose to break the engagement or wait a while. Clarity refers to how clear the decision is. Vague decisions do not work because they lack definition and commitment.

Decisions are conclusions or judgments about some issue or matter. Management recognizes the influence of values on decisions and the role of goals in providing direction to decisions. The decision process begins when a change or a thing is desired.

Decision making, the process of making a choice between two or more alternatives, is an integral part of the overall management process (see Figure 5.1). In systems terminology, decision making is part of the transformation process incorporating various inputs and culminating in outputs. Sometimes the process involves negotiation or bargaining with others. The previous chapters on values, attitudes, goals, and resources have laid the groundwork for a full discussion of the decision-making process. This chapter begins by explaining the relationship between decision making and management and then describes the steps in decision making. Decision models and rules are examined, along with their application to individuals and families. The chapter explains the difference between decision making and problem solving and explores the concepts of risk and uncertainty.

DECISION MAKING AS PART OF MANAGEMENT

Should I share an apartment or live alone? Should I take the risk of going with a small start-up firm or take a job with a more established company? Decisions arise from such situations. They require effort. People have to want something they do not have and they have to make decisions and plans to bridge the gap between what is and what could be.

Decision making is essential to maintaining and improving life conditions. Values guide decisions. A decision maker values an issue or a life condition enough to spend time thinking about it. Values also influence decision makers because they realize that the choices they make will have positive or negative consequences.

FIGURE 5.1
The Management Process Model

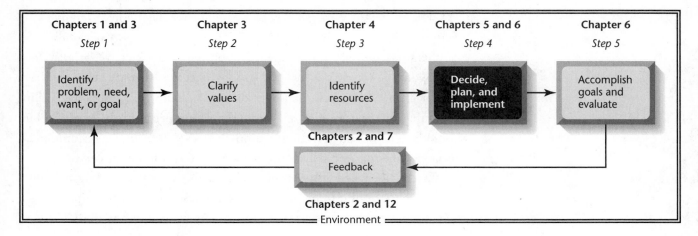

Decisions vary in intensity and importance. The purpose and content of decisions are related to other aspects of the management process, such as planning, implementing, and cost/benefit analysis. For example, each decision entails a cost in time and energy and sometimes money. Decision makers try to minimize the costs and maximize the benefits of a decision.

This desire to maximize positive outcomes and to minimize mistakes motivates individuals to make the best decisions that they can. Curiously, the plots of many movies, books, and television shows feature individuals who do just the opposite. These characters make decisions that minimize positive outcomes and maximize mistakes. Watching the characters disentangle themselves from their mistakes and put their lives back in order can be interesting and enlightening. Observing how others make decisions and solve problems in television, movies, books, and real life can help sharpen an individual's own decision-making and problem-solving skills.

Decision situations present both problems and opportunities. In analyzing decision situations, individuals appraise alternatives and identify useful information and resources. An important resource is time. An individual or family can save time by eliminating alternatives that do not fit their values. Why waste time considering an alternative that is morally or ethically unacceptable? Ralph Keeney (1988), a values expert, suggests that if "we begin with values, we might not even think of situations as decision problems, but rather as decision opportunities. Periodically, we might examine achievement on the basis of our values and ask, 'can we do better?'" (p. 466).

Since it is value based, decision making is highly personalized. Each individual's personality and usual modes of thinking and acting influence the way he or she makes decisions. Each person's decision making also tends to follow a pattern, with successful decisions being repeated again and again. The characteristic way that a person makes decisions is called her or his **decision-making style**. Thus, decision-making styles are affected by individuals' values, knowledge, ability, and motivation. The types of decisions made, the speed at which decisions are made, and the amount of information gathered before

Maximizing positive outcomes?

making a decision are all part of a person's style. For example, some individuals are quick deciders, others are more deliberate. Differences in style are also evident in the evaluation phase at the end of the decision-making process. Some individuals look back and agonize over every thought and action, whereas others think about past decisions only for a few minutes and then go on.

Some decision styles are irritating. Suppose you go to a meeting and the boss asks your opinion. You invest time and effort and present an opinion, then find out the decision had already been made. How would you feel? Similarly, in a family, how do children feel if their opinions are asked only to find out that their parents had already made the decision?

Steps in Decision Making

Decision making involves a series of steps that result in the choice of an alternative. The process can be long or short. Obviously, more time will be spent deciding where to build a new home than in choosing which movie to see. When the process is long and complicated and includes a sequence of intentions, it constitutes a **decision plan**. Decision plans can be specific or general. For example, Zak's plan to buy his favorite cereal and milk at the grocery store this afternoon is a specific decision plan. Jennifer's plan to buy a car next year is a general decision plan because she does not know what kind of car she wants or exactly when she will buy it. Since decision making is a transformation process, the inputs, such as how much money and time Zak and Jennifer have, will affect the decisions.

Decision makers use different strategies for different situations. The strategy selected will depend on (1) the decision involved, (2) the characteristics of the decision task, and (3) the decision-making style of the decider. In general, though, most people follow six steps in making decisions. The acronym DECIDE provides an easy way to remember these steps (adapted from Malhotra, 1991):

- ◆ Define the decision (distill and define the issue).
- ◆ Estimate resources.
- ◆ Consider alternatives.
- ◆ Imagine (visualize) the consequences of alternative courses of action.
- ◆ Develop an action plan and implement it.
- ◆ Evaluate the decision.

These steps are discussed in detail in the next paragraphs.

Step 1: Define the Decision

In defining the decision, the individual should take into account the purpose of the needed behavior, the relevant background information, what information is needed, and how it will be used in decision making. In so doing, the layers of a potential decision are peeled back to reveal the core of the situation. Once the decision has been defined, the decision maker can move on to the next step.

Step 2: Estimate the Resources Needed

The decision maker has to decide what resources will be needed. As discussed in the previous chapter, resources include time, energy, money, information, and anything else that is useful to the decision and subsequent planning and action. The number of possible alternatives is limited by the resources possessed or anticipated in the future. A ski vacation in Utah is out of the question if a person has only a hundred dollars to spend.

Step 3: Consider Alternatives *important; may be hard for bad decision makers*

Given the limitations on their resources, individuals seldom consider all alternatives. For example, test-driving every car on the market before choosing one would be impractical. Instead, a prospective buyer would eliminate many models because of their cost, accessibility, features, and style or because they did not suit his tastes and preferences; then, he would test-drive just a few cars. Narrowing down the possibilities to one or two acceptable alternatives is an important part of the decision process.

Step 4: Imagine the Consequences of Alternative Courses of Action

Imagining or thinking through the most likely alternatives is the next step. Envisioning what will happen if a certain decision is made is so enjoyable or distasteful that some people get stuck on this step. For example, in consumer decision making, this step is called **prepurchase expectations**, which are beliefs about the anticipated performance of a product or service. Before buying, an individual tries to imagine how much pleasure or pain he or she will get from the purchase.

Step 5: Develop an Action Plan and Implement It

Once an alternative is selected, a course of action, a strategy, must be developed. Putting the decision into action is called *implementation*. During this step, the decision maker monitors the progress being made and evaluates how well implementation is proceeding. Are things going as planned? On schedule? Are adjustments to the plan necessary?

Step 6: Evaluate the Decision

After the process has been completed, the decision maker looks back to judge how successful the decision was. "Did I make the right decision?" "Should I have done something else?" she or he wonders. In consumer decision making, this step is called **postpurchase dissonance**. After a major purchase, such as a car, the buyer is likely to seek some reinforcement for the decision by talking to other owners of the same model or reading advertisements or news stories about the car. Being assured that the right decision was made reduces doubt or anxiety.

Models, Rules, and Utility

Although change is a necessary part of life, many individuals are reluctant to change and continue to follow existing plans. Adhering to established goals and objectives and the plans, strategies, and tactics devised for attaining those goals is referred to as "maintaining the status quo." According to Silver and Mitchell (1990), when faced with uncertain alternatives, most people tend to stay with the status quo. But if a person, family, or organization wants to change or to understand the mechanisms of decision making, they may find decision-making models useful. These models assume that rational decision makers will evaluate alternatives and then make the best possible choice.

Because decision making is an abstract concept, decision-making models are useful because they provide a way to visualize how the elements of a decision interact. Figure 5.2 shows the Central-Satellite and Chain models, and Figure 5.3 provides examples of these models.

In the Central-Satellite Model, a central decision is surrounded by decisions that are offshoots of the central decision. In the Chain Model, each decision builds on the previous one, forming a sequence of decisions, such as the steps involved in preparing a meal (see Figure 5.3). Generally, the Chain Model is appropriate for smaller, systematic decisions, whereas the Central-Satellite Model is suitable for larger, more complicated situations. Businesses such as catering services or conference and wedding planning services use both models to organize receptions, banquets, meetings, and events.

As illustrated in Figure 5.4, values lie at the base of decisions. Two other concepts in management, resources and goals, also play important roles. Decision trees are commonly used in business strategy sessions, but they can also be used by individuals in personal and professional decision making. The model shows that people select alternatives based on their goals and perception of available resources and that values underlie decisions. A more usual method used by many individuals in choosing between alternatives (e.g., whether to move to one locale over another, which job offer to select) is to make pro and con lists.

Decision Rules

Models operate on certain principles or rules of logic. **Decision rules** are principles that guide decision making. One decision rule is that decision makers will seek the best outcomes. Another decision rule is that individuals will

FIGURE 5.2
Central–Satellite and Chain Models

Source: B. Paolucci, O. A. Hall, and N. Axinn, *Family Decision Making: An Ecosystem Approach* (New York: Macmillan College Publishing Company, 1977), p. 106. Reprinted with the permission of Simon & Schuster, Inc. All rights reserved.

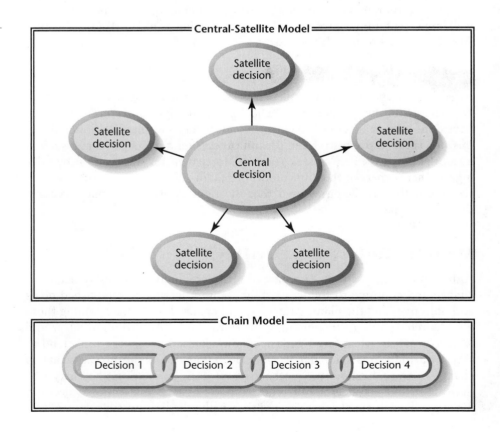

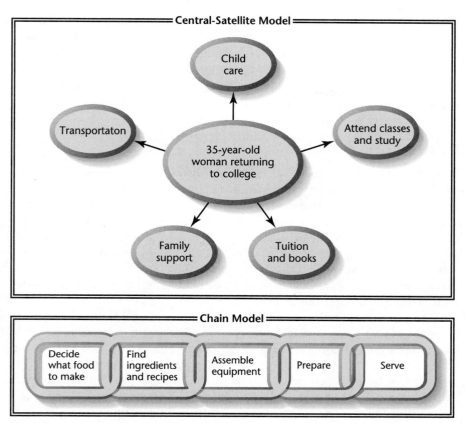

FIGURE 5.3
Examples of Decision Situations Using the Central-Satellite and Chain Models

try to use their time to best advantage, wasting as little as possible. However, this varies by situation and by culture. In a study of Chinese students it was found that they were not very time conscious, but they were quite price and quality conscious (Fan & Xiao, 1998).

Utility

One of the most important decision rules is the necessity to optimize utility or the usefulness of decisions. The concept of utility underlies much of the study of economics and is strongly associated with the study of management.

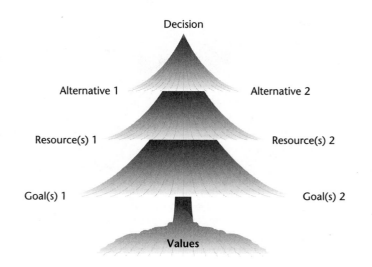

FIGURE 5.4
A Decision Tree: Values Lie at the Root of All Decisions

Rational decision makers are assumed to seek the maximum utility (satisfaction) from the decisions they make. Also, the utility concept focuses on how choices are made and on how that process can be improved. A related decision rule is that consumers have limited information; they may not be aware of all the alternatives that exist. The next section on reference groups provides one explanation of why individuals may have only partial knowledge.

Reference Groups

Each decision has a history. For example, Alison orders pepperoni pizza because she knows from past experience that she likes it. Besides past experiences, past and present relationships affect an individual's decision making. If Alison begins dating Trae, who is a vegetarian, and he prefers pizza with cheese, green peppers, olives, and onions, they have several options: they can order two pizzas, or they can order a pizza that is half pepperoni and half vegetarian, or Allison can learn to skip the pepperoni. This simple joint decision-making situation illustrates how many choices exist and how individual tastes and relationships affect those choices.

The people who influence an individual or provide guidance or advice are members of that person's **reference groups.** Trae and Alison are members of each other's reference groups. The diagram in Figure 5.5 illustrates a typical college student's reference groups. An individual does not have to be present in person or be geographically close to be a member of a reference group. A person is considered part of a reference group if the memory of her or his values and attitudes affects someone's decision making. For example, Rob, a

FIGURE 5.5
**A College Student's
Reference Groups**

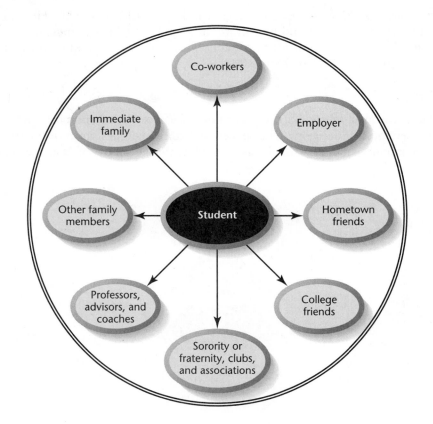

newspaper editor, has not seen his high school journalism teacher for many years, but she is still a member of Rob's reference group because he thinks of her often and remembers what she taught him when he makes decisions about his paper.

Reference groups can be divided into two types, primary and secondary, depending on the amount of contact the individual has with a person or group. An individual has regular contact with the people in primary reference groups. Family, coworkers, and close friends fall into this category. Secondary reference groups include those individuals and groups with whom contact is infrequent, such as distant relatives, organizations, and professional associations.

The influence of reference groups on decision making and behavior cannot be overestimated. For example, one study showed that family members' smoking behavior influenced college students' smoking behavior. The study compared Oregon college students in 1963–1964 with students in 1986–1987 (Gray & Donatelle, 1990). In 1963–1964, the student respondents said their smoking behavior was most influenced by whether their father, mother, or older sister smoked. In 1986–1987, students who smoked were most likely to say they had been influenced by an older brother or brothers who smoked. The authors concluded that factors that influence smokers appear to change over time. When students in 1986–1987 were asked why they smoked, the main reasons they gave were peer smoking and stress.

Personal Decision Making

Although all decisions—from which car to buy to whether to smoke—are influenced by others, ultimately the individual is responsible for his or her own decisions. Individuals begin learning how to make decisions at an early age. During the socialization process, children are given the opportunity to make choices and to learn from decision situations. By the time they become adults, most people assume they are competent decision makers. In reality, however, this assumption may fall short if there is a difference between the actual and perceived quality of decisions. The actual quality of decisions refers to what is truly happening. The perceived quality of decisions refers to what an individual thinks is happening in the decision process. Potentially, then, a person could deceive themselves into thinking that a poor decision is a good one or at least an acceptable one. Experience and improved decision-making skills can narrow the gap between the perceived and the actual.

Decision-making style is affected not only by an individual's socialization, knowledge, ability, and motivation, but also by his or her personality traits, such as compulsiveness, open-mindedness, innovativeness, self-confidence, and courage. Another factor that can affect decision-making style is self-esteem. Low self-esteem often results in indecisiveness. In other words, someone who is unsure of her or his ability to make sound decisions is likely to be indecisive. Indecisiveness can be a major problem for individuals, families, and organizations. Possible causes of indecisiveness are:

- Fear of the unknown
- Procrastination
- Fear of making a wrong decision or mistake
- Fear of acting on one's own
- Lack of "good judgment"

◆ Feeling overwhelmed

◆ Fear of taking responsibility or standing alone on an issue

◆ Overdependency on other people's opinions

Indecisiveness and the Peter Principle

Although some individuals always seem to be indecisive, others are indecisive only in certain situations. Lawrence J. Peter and Raymond Hall (1969) proposed an explanation for indecisive behavior. They suggested that people can reach a point in their work in which they can no longer successfully function. Specifically, they said that people tend to be promoted until they reach a level beyond their competence—a point at which they can no longer make and implement effective decisions. They called this phenomenon the **"Peter Principle."** Even though the Peter Principle is pervasive, it can be avoided by fitting the right person to the right job and by making performance expectations clear from the outset. Examples of this principle can be found in a variety of organizations and settings, including the home and the community.

Avoiding Decisions

Being indecisive is linked to another decision-making phenomenon—avoidance. Passing the decision-making buck is one way individuals avoid decisions. According to Delaney (1982), avoidance typically results in statements such as the following:

◆ "I thought you were going to settle this."

◆ "That's not my job."

◆ "You're the boss. Don't ask me what I think, just tell me what to do."

◆ "Why is it up to me?"

Failure to assign clear responsibility for tasks in the home or the office may lead to some of these remarks. When chores are not assigned and the dishes are not done or the garbage is not taken out, family members may all say "That's not my job." Parents and children need to have a clear understanding of who will do what in the home. At the same time, tasks, chores, and duties are not static. Nonperformance may result because goals and priorities have changed; they are no longer commonly held beliefs of how to act. There is a fundamental difference between compliance and commitment. Complying means going along with some idea or action. Commitment means that people believe in the idea or action. High commitment workplaces and households are more productive and more comfortable places to be.

Decidophobia

Not making decisions is also a decision. **Decidophobia** is the fear of making decisions, specifically the fear of failure. A person with decidophobia is frozen and cannot choose an alternative or form a plan of action. Such people see decisions as problems, not as opportunities. One way to overcome decidophobia is to utilize the decision-making models and the DECIDE acronym, which divide decisions into parts. Often it is easier to break a big decision into smaller parts and make those decisions first. Another way to overcome decidophobia is to moderate expectations.

Decidophobia is a learned behavior, a type of helplessness or dependency on others or a form of perfectionism. To avoid establishing this pattern, young children should be given the opportunity to experience decision making (e.g., choosing the red shirt or the blue shirt, the apple or the orange) at an early age so that they can develop decision-making skills. Setting up a variety of activity areas or learning centers in preschools or kindergartens is an excellent way to provide children with early decision-making experiences. During free time, the children can choose the activity they want to engage in, whom they want to be with, and what they want to accomplish—all useful life preparation skills.

Intuition

Intuition plays a part in decision making. One way to increase decision making acumen is to trust feelings and instincts (Kaye, 1996). As mentioned earlier in the chapter, a multistep approach is not always necessary to select a course of action. Sometimes decisions are influenced by **intuition,** or the sense of knowing what to do without going through rational processes. For example, Brad accompanies Kirsten, his wife, to two out-of-state interviews. Brad likes one state but cannot stand the other, although he cannot give specific reasons for his feelings. Fortunately, Kirsten gets offers from both employers, and she and Brad choose the state they both feel good about. Since it is difficult to measure, intuition is one of the least scientific aspects of decision making, but it is still recognized as an important factor.

Family Decision Making

The main difference between personal and family decision making is that the latter is more complex. The more people involved in making a decision or potentially affected by a decision, the more complex the decision process is likely to be. Consider, for example, how difficult it can be for five coworkers to decide where to go to lunch or for a group of friends to decide which movie to see. Similar difficulties can arise in a family setting, depending on how many family members are involved in each decision. In a simple situation, only one family member is involved in making a decision, and everyone else simply accepts whatever that person decides. For example, one person may suggest going to the school basketball game, and the entire family agrees and accepts the decision. In a more complex situation, each family member may suggest a different course of action. Instead of agreeing to go to the basketball game together, the family members go off in different directions: the teenage son goes to the basketball game, the mother to a PTA meeting, the daughter to a friend's house, and the father to a club meeting. If the family has only one car, this is going to be a difficult situation to manage. These examples illustrate two of the questions raised by family decision making: Will the manager alone make most of the decisions or does each family member have a say? Are most decisions made smoothly or is conflict more usual?

Homes and families can provide a base for cooperation, coordination, and negotiation. Family members bring to this base their own needs and wants, but sometimes one family member's needs and wants are in conflict with another's. When conflict rather than harmony is characteristic of the home or family, the decision-making process becomes more complicated.

A practical example of a family decision making situation is who does what in the home. As Table 5.1 shows, women are more likely to do the laundry, prepare meals, shop for groceries, clean the house, care for children, buy gifts, make decisions about furniture and decoration, pay bills, and wash

TABLE 5.1
Who Does What in the Home

As I read a list of common household chores, please tell me how much of each job you usually do yourself? If I read a chore that does not apply to your household, just tell me. First, how about . . . do you usually do all of this yourself, most of it, about half, less than half, or none?

Percentage Saying They Do All or Most of Each Chore

	Men	Women
Doing laundry	27%	79%
Preparing meals	26	78
Paying bills	47	65
Making decisions about savings or investments	41	38
Washing dishes	31	68
Doing yard work	63	21
Making minor home repairs	74	16
Grocery shopping	26	72
Cleaning the house	22	69
Keeping the car in good condition	81	22
Caring for children on daily basis*	12	72
Taking care of children when they're sick*	10	78
Disciplining children*	28	42
Buying gifts for birthdays and holidays	24	78
Making decisions about vacations and entertainment	25	34
Making decisions about furniture and decoration	18	60

*Based only on those respondents with children living at home.

Source: L. DeStefano and D. Colsanto. "Unlike 1975, today most Americans think men have it better," *The Gallup Poll Monthly*, February 1990, p. 31. Reprinted with permission.

dishes. Men are more likely to do yard work, make minor home repairs, and keep the car in good condition. An in-depth study of 20 moderate- to middle-income dual-career couples with children found a similar division of household tasks (Coltrane, 1989). Coltrane concluded: "Generally, mothers were more likely than fathers to act as managers for cooking, cleaning, and child care, but over half of the couples showed responsibility in all areas" (p. 480).

Another study found that mothers typically performed tasks from 17 occupations, including chef, social worker, psychologist, and property manager. It claimed that combined median annual salary for a mother's multitasking should be more than $500,000 (*Wall Street Journal,* 1999).

A developing trend is more shared responsibility in the home. For example, the chart in Table 5.1 shows that women are more likely to do more or most of the grocery shopping than men. Newer studies support this general division of labor, but note that in more and more cases, activities such as child care and grocery shopping are shared. For example, one study revealed that 14 percent of men and women share grocery shopping. In response to this and the research finding that men are more likely to buy whatever they see, Audrey Guskey, a marketing professor at Duquesne University, says that stores court men with end-of-aisle displays of chips, beer, and soft drinks—items men commonly buy on impulse (Meyer, 1997).

Families, Environment, and the Elbing Model

According to Marshall (1991), "the future of American families is not predetermined, but depends heavily on the choices made by families, employers and especially public institutions" (p. 5). Consequently, family decision making is strongly influenced by families' awareness of what is feasible and acceptable in the environment in which they live. Alvar Elbing developed a model (see Figure 5.6) to illustrate how two individuals in a family make decisions given their reference groups, perceived and acceptable alternatives, and environmental constraints. The Elbing Model demonstrates that decisions are influenced by many factors and considerations. The XYZ section in the center of the model represents the solution, because alternatives are perceived by both individuals and are acceptable in the environment.

Accommodation, Consensual, and De Facto

There are three types or styles of family decision making: accommodation, consensual, and de facto. In **accommodation,** the family reaches an agreement by accepting the point of view of the dominant person. Power is a critical factor in accommodation. In **consensual decision making,** the family reaches a mutual agreement equally acceptable to all individuals involved. **De facto decision making** is characterized by a lack of dissent rather than by active assent. It usually occurs when no one really cares about the outcome of the decision. For instance, no one in a family may have strong feelings about which television show to watch.

Families in which the husband and wife share equally in making most of the decisions are **syncratic.** Families can also be **autonomic,** which means that an equal number of decisions are made by each spouse. Thus, in syncratic

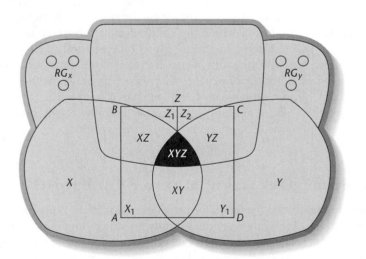

FIGURE 5.6
The Elbing Model for Viewing Alternatives in a Family Decision Situation

Source: Adapted from Alvar O. Elbing, Jr., "A Model for Viewing Decision Making in Interaction Situations form an Historical Perspective." In Alvar Elbing, *Behavioral Decisions in Organizations.* Copyright © 1970 by Scott, Foresman and Company.

ABCD: Family decision situation
X: Family member
Y: Family member
Z: Environment
RG_x: Reference group for member X
RG_y: Reference group for member Y
XZ: Alternatives perceived by X and acceptable in existing environment.
YZ: Alternatives perceived by Y and acceptable in existing environment.
XY: Alternatives perceived by both X and Y but *not* acceptable in the environment.
X_1 and Y_1: Alternatives perceived by one member but not acceptable in the environment.
Z_1 and Z_2: Acceptable alternatives not perceived by family members.
Solution
XYZ: Alternatives perceived by both family members and acceptable in the environment.

families the decisions are shared, whereas in autonomic families the spouses make an equal number of separate decisions.

According to a classic study by Blood and Wolfe (1960), the partner who commands the greater amount of material resources will achieve greater power in spousal decision making. Newer studies suggest that decision-making power in couples is also related to their emotional interdependence and ability to control each other and influence the ultimate degree of consensus. For example, Godwin and Scanzoni (1989) theorized that the more modern the gender role preference of the wife, the less control her husband had. Their study of 188 married couples revealed that socioemotional factors affected both coerciveness and control. Specifically, emotional bonding contributes to spouses' influence over each other and also to whether they reach a consensus. "Spouses who reached higher levels of consensus included husbands who had patterns of previous cooperativeness during conflict situations, more equitable economic resources of the spouses, wives whose communication styles were less coercive, and spouses who demonstrated greater control" (p. 943). Further, husbands who were committed to the marital relationship were more likely to respond positively to their wives' suggestions, ideas, and directives.

In conclusion, it appears that explaining decision-making power (who decides what and to what extent) in couples is more complicated than simply looking at who contributes the greater amount of resources. Other important factors include how close the husband and the wife are, the degree of cooperativeness and communication between them, and their levels of education. For example, a study in India revealed that literate women participated to a greater extent in decisions related to health and size of the family, their children's education, and the family's investments and savings than did illiterate women (Mohanty, 1996).

The types of decision making discussed so far have involved couple-centered families in which most decisions are made by the spouses. An alternative to this is child-centered families in which the children make or affect most of the decisions of the whole family, including the choice of foods, television shows, and activities. Actually, the difference between couple-centered and child-centered families is not absolute, for children affect decisions in every family. Nevertheless, children do have more influence in some families than in others. The next section will discuss family and couple consumer decision making and show how children influence parents' buying behaviors.

Consumer Decision Making in Families

Decision making in the marketplace provides an excellent illustration of family decision making. How an individual family spends money may not seem that important, but, collectively, family spending amounts to billions of dollars when multiplied across all families. For this reason, manufacturers and advertisers spend enormous amounts of money on consumer research to determine who decides what in a family and why. In short, consumer decision making is big business and the driving force behind the well-being of national economies.

Families must decide (1) what to buy, (2) where to shop, (3) how much to pay, (4) when to buy, and (5) who should buy. The first decision is the most important—families have to decide if they want to buy something. This decision leads to the other four. Deciding what to buy is more difficult when there are countless brands to consider. For example, 34 new food products are launched each day in the United States (Mogelonsky, 1998).

The family decision-making process involves eight distinct roles (see Table 5.2). These roles provide a way of conceptualizing how family members make decisions—some family members are buyers, others users, others influencers, and so on. For example, a mother or father buys disposable diapers, the baby uses them, and the parent who changes the diaper disposes of it.

Family decision-making purchases can involve conflict. For example, a couple may differ about the amount of money to spend, the brand or type of good to buy, the stores to shop in, or who should make the purchase. Conflict will decrease if the couple agrees on which goals are desirable. Purchasing decisions may be influenced by a number of variables, including reference groups, work life, leisure pursuits, culture, subculture, social class, stage in the life cycle, mobility, geographical location, and children. For instance, young families with preschool children have different buying decisions to make than retired couples. Joint decision making is most common among the middle class, whereas autonomous decision making is most likely in the upper and lower classes (Loudon & Della Bitta, 1988).

Children have a significant influence on their parents' buying habits. A study by Infocus Environmental of Princeton, New Jersey, found that one-third of parents changed their shopping habits because of environmental information their children gave them (Schlossberg, 1992). When questioned

---

TABLE 5.2
Eight Roles in Family Decision Making

There are eight distinct roles in the family decision-making process. A look at these provides further insight into how family members interact in their various consumption-related roles:

1. *Influencers:* Family member(s) who provide information to other members about a product or service

2. *Gatekeepers:* Family member(s) who control the flow of information about a product or service into the family

3. *Deciders:* Family member(s) with the power to determine unilaterally or jointly whether or not to purchase a specific product or service

4. *Buyers:* Family member(s) who make the actual purchase of a particular product or service

5. *Preparers:* Family member(s) who transform the product into a form suitable for consumption by other family members

6. *Users:* Family member(s) who use or consume a particular product or service

7. *Maintainers:* Family member(s) who service or repair the product so that it will provide continued satisfaction

8. *Disposers:* Family member(s) who initiate or carry out the disposal or discontinuation of a particular product or service

The number and identity of the family members who fill these roles vary from family to family and product to product.

Source: Leon G. Schiffman and Leslie Lazar Kanuk, *Consumer Behavior,* 4th ed. (Englewood Cliffs, N.J.: Prentice-Hall, 1991), p. 341. Adapted with permission of Prentice-Hall, Englewood Cliffs, New Jersey.

about their information source, the children said they learned about the environment in school. In a study reported in *Marketing News* (Schlossberg, 1992) children affect their parents' buying and shopping habits by encouraging them to purchase items in recyclable packaging (24 percent) and to avoid products in containers that are not recyclable or biodegradable (17 percent). The study concluded that children are influencing far more than the particular foods their parents purchase and that they are having a significant impact on their parents' environmental consciousness.

PROBLEM SOLVING

Problems are questions or situations that present uncertainty, risk, perplexity, or difficulty. **Problem solving** involves making many decisions that lead to a resolution of the problem. In some disciplines the terms *decision making* and *problem solving* are used interchangeably, but in resource management they are used differently. Decision making encompasses all sorts of situations (many of them routine), needs, and wants, whereas problem solving implies that a certain degree of difficulty or risk is involved.

As noted earlier, the more people involved in a decision, the more complex the decision process. Thus, family problem solving is usually more complex than individual problem solving. Because problems arise from difficulty, they put even more strain on families than routine decision making. If any family member has hidden agendas or demands, problem definition or analysis can be extremely difficult. Skilled family managers can often spot potential problem areas and try to resolve them before they become full-blown problems involving intense family conflict.

Definition, Analysis, and Plan of Action

Usually people do not spontaneously become aware of a problem and then suddenly decide to search for and analyze relevant information (Fay & Wallace, 1987). Instead, the person or family is motivated by dissatisfaction with the current state of things. As motivated processes, problem awareness and analysis are subject to five levels of motivation influences:

1. Needs, motives, and goals of the problem solver
2. Perceptions and beliefs of the problem solver
3. Values of the problem solver
4. Resources of the problem solver
5. Learning, background, and previous experience of the problem solver

These influences affect the way a person defines a problem and makes decisions to solve the problem.

Problem Definition

Problem recognition or definition is the first step in problem solving. The person has to recognize the problem as such before engaging in purposeful behavior to resolve the situation. Problem definition is a creative process requiring the individual to see common threads and sense important cause and effect relationships. For example, the person needs to uncover the underlying symptoms that have caused the problem. How does one go about this? According to David Nylen, "problems are best defined in the form of questions. Doing so provides clear direction for the rest of the process. The task of the decision maker becomes one of providing a solution or decision that will answer the question. . . . The final decision must fulfill and reflect the underlying cause of the situation" (1990, pp. 51–52).

Complicated problems demand more energy and attention because their cause (or causes) may be hidden or multifaceted. Once the problem is defined, then the individual can move on to the next step in problem solving—problem analysis. As a practical example, the next sections will show how Michelle engages in problem solving after her boss tells her that she has been denied a promotion because she lacks administrative experience.

Problem Analysis

Depending on the type of problem and the individuals involved, problems can be viewed as messes or as experiences that simply require a logical and reasonable response. For example, after being denied a promotion, Michelle could respond or act in many ways. She knows she has a problem (the problem is clearly defined); now she has to decide what she is going to do about it.

No two problems are the same because each involves its own unique timing, individuals, and circumstances, and stems from a specific situation. To solve complicated problems, the individual needs to systematically follow the decision steps discussed earlier in this chapter. Taking shortcuts in the decision process will only result in incomplete information that will complicate the problem situation further. Since many complex problems involve the interaction of subproblems, one approach is to divide the problem into subproblems and analyze each separately.

Plan of Action

Once the defining and analyzing phases are over, the individual designs a plan of action. Planning involves putting together the activities or steps to follow. The objective of planning is to produce systems or solutions that can provide satisfaction to the problem solver and other participants in the problem.

Michelle decides to get administrative experience so that the next time an opening occurs she will be qualified. Her subproblems include whether her current workplace can provide the necessary experience or whether she will have to get experience elsewhere. Perhaps her boss could be more explicit about the work experience she needs. Michelle also turns to her colleagues, friends, and family for advice. After she considers their advice and her own perception of the problem, she forms a plan of action. Forming a plan makes her feel more in control of things. Resource management as a discipline encourages individuals to gather as much information as possible, objectively examine their problems and options, and form a plan of action that will help get them what they want.

Motivation is a key part of problem solving. The motivation to solve the problem will depend on the amount of discrepancy between the desired and the actual state and the importance of the problem. Most people will not waste inordinate amounts of time on minor daily decisions such as what to wear or what to eat. Routine decisions such as these are rarely problems. They can become problems, however, if the person defines them as a problem or if the decision has a far-reaching impact. For example, what to wear to a job interview or what to serve at a banquet for 500 people may become major problems involving substantial amounts of money and a variety of alternative choices and consequences.

Another essential part of problem solving is the search for information. The search leads to the formation of alternative courses of action and evaluation. Looking within oneself for information for decisions is called an **internal search**. Michelle did this first. After her boss told her she had been denied the promotion, she went back to her office, shut the door, and thought over the problem. An internal search is easier and more common than an **external search**, which involves gathering information from family, friends, other people, and the media. When Michelle asked others for advice, she engaged in an external search. As part of her external search, she watched a television news report and read magazine articles about how many people around the country were being laid off from their jobs due to corporate downsizing or were turning to home-based work because they were tired of working for someone else or commuting. This information helped Michelle put her failure to receive a promotion in perspective. She reasoned that at least she had a job that she liked, and she felt sure that given time and effort she would be promoted. As in Michelle's case, complex problem solving usually requires both internal and external searches.

As the search proceeds, the problem becomes more narrowly defined and refined. At all times, decisions should be linked to the primary goal sought. If the goal is landing the best job possible, the job seeker continually looks for information, work experience, and contacts leading to that goal. The desired end state is a solution. According to Lollie McLean, "Spend only 5 percent of your energy on talking about the problem, and 95 percent of your energy on solving the problem" (**www.lollie.com**). Michelle would be well advised to spend time getting the training she needs to get ahead, if not at her present job, at another organization.

Uncertainty and Risk

The problems associated with career advancement and job hunting are good examples of uncertainty and risk. In both cases, the individual searches for information to reduce the levels of uncertainty and risk. The more an employee or job seeker knows about a company, such as its policies and track record, the more confident he or she will be on the job or at job interviews. Increased knowledge and ability reduce an individual's perceptions of uncertainty and risk.

Risk and uncertainty were introduced in Chapter 2 in the discussion of risk aversion theory. This theory says that rational people will try to reduce or avoid risk and that risk is subjective in that individuals define the level of risk and uncertainty they can handle. For example, a blind date is a risk. To reduce the amount of risk and uncertainty, the couple will try to find out as much as possible about each other before going out on the date.

Uncertainty is the state or feeling of being in doubt. *Risk* is the possibility of pain, harm, or loss from a decision. Risk is subjective; that is, each person defines what risk is. A person weighing uncertainty and risk is judging the **probability,** or likelihood, of a good or bad outcome. Shopping, particularly catalog or internet shopping, involves risk and the consideration of probable outcomes.

An individual's perception of uncertainty leads to the perception of risk. For example, John, a recent college graduate, may be uncertain whether to wear shorts and a T-shirt or a sports shirt and slacks to his first company picnic. He may also be uncertain about the weather the day of the picnic. If he thinks it may rain, he might try to reduce his risk of getting wet by taking a hat and a jacket. Although deciding what to wear to a picnic is not a high-risk venture, John wants to dress appropriately so that he will fit in. In contrast, Sam, one of John's coworkers, has not even given a thought to what he will wear to the picnic. His perception of risk in this problem situation is minimal; in fact, he does not even think of dressing for the picnic as a problem situation. At the picnic, Sam is the only person wearing shorts, and for the next two months, he must endure gentle ribbing about his "bony knees" and plaid shorts. Risk can be perceived as occurring before, during, or after a decision.

Types of Risks

As discussed in Chapter 2, there are five main types of risks that affect decision making: functional or performance risk, financial risk, physical risk, psychological risk, social risk, and time risk. In the last example, John was seeking to reduce physical, psychological, financial, and social risks. If he worries about the best time to arrive at the picnic, then he would add time risk to his list of concerns. To reduce risk, people search for information or behave in ways that will lessen their uncertainty, such as asking others for advice or repeating behaviors that have worked for them in the past.

At-Risk Children

Certainly, many individual, family, and societal problems are far more difficult than what to wear to an event. A disturbing societal problem that is much in the news is at-risk children. An estimated seven million children, one in four of those aged 10 to 17 in the United States, engage in high-risk behaviors and are in "jeopardy of not growing into responsible adults who can effectively parent, work, or vote" (Dryfoos, 1991). According to Dryfoos, high-risk children are likely to be low achievers, drug abusers, premature parents, or in trouble with the law. Many of these children live in high-stress family situations and have little parental support and supervision.

Questions have been raised about what schools can do to help at-risk children (Katz, Dalton, & Giacquinta, 1994). A consensus is forming that school programs as they currently exist cannot solve the rapidly rising incidence of depression and stress emerging from dysfunctional families. New types of school-based support programs and curricula are suggested as a means for dealing with educational, health, and life issues of at-risk populations. In New York State, the Home and Career Skills (HCS) curriculum concentrates on developing the critical thinking skills of students so that they can make rational decisions and prepare to meet their responsibilities as members of families, consumers, home managers, and wage earners (Katz, Dalton, & Giacquinta, 1994). Similar curricula are being used in other states under various names, including Life Management Skills.

In addition, families, both nuclear and extended, and community groups and health organizations need to do all they can to reduce the number of at-risk children and give children the best possible start in life. Helping children learn to make responsible decisions at an early age is a good starting point, followed by continued attention and support through the later years. For those in the helping professions, the emphasis when working with families is to assist them in making their own decisions and solving their own problems, not imposing the professionals' own decision solutions.

Electronic Resources

Decision making is an all-encompassing topic and there are a wide variety of Web sites to explore. Many decisions are based on inputs such as information, and the Internet is increasingly the easiest source for information on many topis. For example:

- ◆ Finding an apartment: **www.apartmentlinks.net** (enter the zip code and Apartment Center will list apartments in that area)
- ◆ Moving: **www:moving.mall.com** (a database of over 120,000 moving-related U.S. companies)
- ◆ Exploring the world: **www:nationalgeographic.com**
- ◆ Waking up in the morning: **www.mrwakeup.com**
- ◆ Getting the news: **www.go.com**
- ◆ Checking the stock prices: **www.stockpoint.com**
- ◆ Comparing CD or book (including college textbook) prices: **www.amazon.com** or **www.varsitybooks.com**
- ◆ Checking auction prices, selling or making bids: **www.ebay.com**
- ◆ Comparing car prices and models: **www.carpoint.com**
- ◆ Checking different home remodeling options, including flooring, wallpaper, and cabinets: **www:totalhomenetwork.com**
- ◆ Listening to music and playing along using a computer keyboard: **www.spottedantelope.com**

www.ask.com
"Ask Jeeves" is a popular Web site that offers answers to general questions.

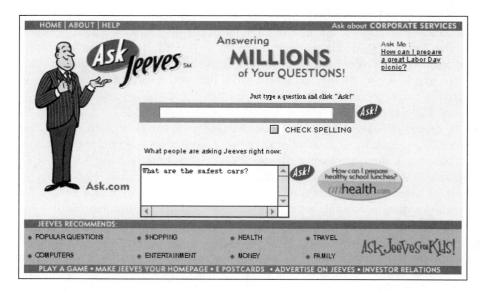

Summary

Everyone makes decisions and solves problems. People try to choose the best alternatives from the choices available; in so doing, they seek to reduce uncertainty and risk and increase the probability of good outcomes.

Decision making is central to the management process. The acronym DECIDE is an easy way to remember the six steps of decision making. The Elbing Model of family decision making demonstrates that each decision has a history and is influenced by members of reference groups. The Central-Satellite and Chain models of decision making show the interrelationships among decisions. The decision tree illustrates that values underlie decisions and that resources and goals affect the alternatives considered. Decision making involves rules and rational patterns of thought as well as intuition.

Individuals and families seek to maximize their satisfaction through sound decision making. Families may engage in individual (husband- or wife-dominated), couple-centered, or child-centered decision making. Decision making is an art or skill that can be improved through reasoning and practice rather than avoidance. Decidophobia is the fear of making decisions, specifically the fear of failure.

Much of a person's success depends upon his or her ability to identify the causes of problems and develop workable solutions for resolving them. Problem solving differs from decision making in that problem solving involves difficulty, perplexity, risk, and uncertainty, whereas decision making refers to all sorts of situations, needs, and wants (some problematic, others not).

In order to be effective, decisions need to be implemented, evaluated, and communicated. Planning, implementing, and evaluating are the subjects of the next chapter, and communication will be discussed in Chapter 7.

Key Terms

accommodation
autonomic
consensual decision
    making
decidophobia
decisions
decision-making
    style
decision plan

decision rules
de facto decision
    making
external search
internal search
intuition
Peter Principle
postpurchase
    dissonance

prepurchase
    expectations
probability
problem solving
reference groups
syncratic
uncertainty

Review Questions

1. What is a "good" decision? What are the possible consequences when the criteria discussed in the first paragraph of the chapter are not met?

2. What does each letter in the acronym DECIDE represent?

3. What is the Peter Principle? How is it related to decision making?

4. What does the Elbing Model illustrate?

5. What is the difference between decision making and problem solving? What is a decision you are trying to make right now? What is a problem you are trying to solve?

References

Blood, R. O. & Wolfe, D. M. (1960). *Husbands and wives.* New York: Free Press.

Coltrane, S. (1989). Household labor and the routine production of gender. *Social Problems, 36*(5), 473–490.

Delaney, W. A. (1982, December). Why are people indecisive? *Supervisory Management,* 450.

Dryfoos, J. G. (1991). School-based social and health services for at-risk students. *Urban Education, 26*(1), 118–137.

Fan, J. & Xiao, J. (1998). Consumer decision-making styles of young adult consumers. *Journal of Consumer Affairs, 32*(2), 273–292.

Fay, C. H. & Wallace, M. J. (1987). *Research based decisions.* New York: Random House, 32.

Godwin, D. D. & Scanzoni, J. (1989). Couple consensus during marital joint decision making: A context, process, outcome model. *Journal of Marriage and the Family, 5,* 943–956.

Gray, N. L. & Donatelle, R. L. (1990). A comparative analysis of factors influencing smoking behaviors of college students: 1963–1987. *Journal of Drug Education, 20*(3), 247–255.

Katz, E., Dalton, S., & Giacquinta, J. (1994). Status risk taking and receptivity of home economics teachers to a statewide curriculum innovation. *Home Economics Research Journal, 22*(4), 401–421.

Kaye, H. (1996). *Decision power.* Englewood Cliffs, NJ: Prentice-Hall.

Keeney, R. L. (1988). Value-focused thinking and the study of values. In D. E. Beal, H. Raiffe, & A. Tuersky (Eds.), *Decision Making* (p. 466). Cambridge: Cambridge University Press.

Loudon, D. & Della Bitta, A. J. (1988). *Consumer behavior: Concepts and applications.* New York: McGraw-Hill, 304–305.

Malhotra, N. K. (1991). Mnemonics in marketing: A pedagogical tool. *Journal of the Academy of Marketing Science, 19*(2), 141–149 and adaptation of DECIDE acronym from Malhotra, N. K. (1992). *Marketing research: An applied orientation.* Englewood Cliffs, NJ: Prentice-Hall.

Marshall, R. (1991). *The state of families, 3: Losing direction.* Milwaukee, WI: Family Service America.

Meyer, M. (1997, August). The grocery gender gap. *Good Housekeeping,* 147.

Mogelonsky, M. (1998, August). Product overload? *American Demographics.*

Mohanty, M. (1996, Spring). Women in India: The relationship of literacy and participation in household decision making. *Journal of Family and Consumer Sciences,* 42–43.

Nylen, D. W. (1990). *Marketing decision making handbook.* Englewood Cliffs, NJ: Prentice-Hall.

Peter, L. J. & Hall, R. (1969). *The peter principle.* New York: William Morrow.

Schiffman, L. G. & Kanuk, L. L. (1991). *Consumer behavior* (4th ed.). Englewood Cliffs, NJ: Prentice-Hall.

Schlossberg, A. (1992, March 2). Kids teach parents how to change their buying habits. *Marketing News,* 8.

Silver, W. S. & Mitchell, T. R. (1990). The status quo tendency in decision making. *Organizational Dynamics, 18,* 34–46.

Wall Street Journal. (1999, May 6), A1.

chapter 6

Planning, Implementing, and Evaluating

MAIN TOPICS

WHAT IS PLANNING?
THE PLANNING PROCESS AND TASK
NEED FULFILLMENT
TIME, STRESS, AND PLANNING
STANDARD SETTING
SCHEDULING AND SEQUENCING
ATTRIBUTES OF PLANS
TYPES OF PLANS

WHAT IS IMPLEMENTING?
ACTUATING
CHECKING AND CONTROLLING

WHAT IS EVALUATING?

Did you know that...?

. . . Fifty-nine percent of all supermarket purchases are unplanned.

. . . Families today live months ahead of themselves.

The journey of one thousand miles begins with a single step.

—*Lao-Tse*

COLLEGE PLANS, FINANCIAL plans, real estate development plans, lunch plans, weekend plans, wedding plans, national health care plans, and affirmative action plans are just a few examples of the wide variety of plans that exist. As the list indicates, plans can range from the mundane to the significant, but all plans are important to the individuals involved. Without plans there would be no birthday cakes or gifts under Christmas trees; nor would there be any roads or businesses. In short, life as we know it could not exist without planning.

In fact, planning is so crucial to human existence that it has been the subject of sayings and fables since ancient times. Think how often you have heard someone say, "If you fail to plan, you are planning to fail." Countless generations of children have heard the story of the industrious ant who planned ahead and stored food for the winter while the foolish grasshopper frolicked in the sun. Of course, when winter came, the grasshopper's failure to think ahead proved fatal.

As the ant and the grasshopper story indicates, planning is prevention—a good plan is a management tool that can save countless hours in revising, restructuring, and other ineffective actions. The amount of planning needed varies, however, from situation to situation and from individual to individual. Planning needs also change over the life cycle. For example, the oldest members of the baby boom generation turned 50 in 1996, so a large segment of the population is seriously planning for retirement.

Like individuals, families make plans, and their plans involve the same type of considerations (i.e., time, energy, personnel, cost, schedules) as other plans. For example, family tasks and responsibilities are planned and assigned. A family's plan may include who will drive the children to school, who will pick up groceries for dinner, who will take the garbage out, and so on. Yet, despite the amount of planning that families do, how often do they sit down and really think about all they do and evaluate the effectiveness of their planning?

This chapter addresses several questions: How are plans made? How can they be more effective? What are the forces that drive planning behavior? As social and economic conditions worldwide are transformed, these questions are becoming more and more critical. The world's growing population is straining its resources, increasing the necessity for better planning. In the consumer area, life is moving so fast that individuals are having trouble devising enough plans to handle all the choices and changes that confront them. Several years ago, the *Wall Street Journal* highlighted this problem:

> Mr. Cialdini, the psychologist, believes that consumers are resorting increasingly to what he calls "click whir" behavior. Life has become so complex that consumers can't possibly analyze the merits of all of their decisions, he says. So they are more susceptible to certain cues and symbols like "discount" or "last day of sale" and take less time to analyze fundamental questions like need or cost. When we react to symbols instead of information, then what we do doesn't make sense anymore, he says. (August 4, 1987)

As this chapter will show, situations, events, and other factors affect planning, implementing, and evaluating. Besides exploring the complex nature of planning and implementing, the chapter also examines the motivating forces behind these processes. Why do people plan? What are they trying to accomplish? How successful are their plans? Key topics include the influence of personality and style on planning, as well as social contexts and environments. Examples of planning, implementing, and evaluating will be given, providing a blend of theory and practice. With real-world examples, this chapter provides an important learning resource for students of individual and family management.

This chapter also contributes to the understanding of the management process model first presented in Chapter 1 and repeated here in Figure 6.1. Planning is a process (a subsystem) within the larger process (system) of management. Step 4 in the model is "decide, plan, and implement," and step 5 is concerned with accomplishing goals and evaluation. Thus, this chapter explains the culmination of the management process.

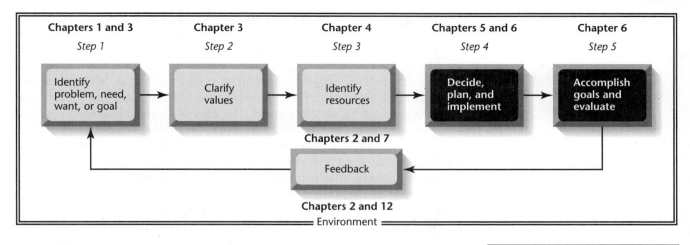

FIGURE 6.1
The Management Process Model

WHAT IS PLANNING?

Planning is a process involving a series of decisions leading to need or goal fulfillment. A **plan** is a detailed schema, program, strategy, or method worked out beforehand for the accomplishment of a desired end result. For example, a student planning to graduate in June follows a plan of action that entails completing required courses and filling out the paperwork necessary to ensure graduation. As the graduation date nears, he must rent or buy a cap and gown. Plans such as graduation plans require a systematic approach to problem solving and goal attainment.

The Planning Process and Task

This chapter follows the chapter on decision making because planning is a more complex process than decision making. A **process** is a system of operations that work together to produce an end result. The word *process* implies movement or change. Something is happening—steps are being taken.

Planning is a thinking and information-gathering process involving a series of decisions. It is a process because formulating plans requires several steps, such as information gathering, sorting, and prioritizing; then, based on this information, the planner must decide which plan is most likely to succeed. The decision and steps are not random, but proceed in an orderly, logical sequence. For example, after living in a dormitory for a semester, a college student may decide to move into an apartment the next semester, but she will not move out of the dormitory without doing some planning. She must decide how much rent she can afford, whether she will look for roommates or live alone, and in what parts of town she would like to live. Before finally selecting an apartment, she will probably look at several apartments.

To help understand the rule of planning in management behavior, researchers have constructed models that depict the various stages of the planning process. The principal aim of such models is to predict future behavior: How does a person normally plan? Will the plan be repeated?

Figure 6.2 shows one such model of the planning process. In the model, the first step is awareness—an individual becomes aware that a plan is needed. In the next step, the person gathers and analyzes information. In the third step, the information is put into the context of the situation, including consideration of others, and a plan is formed. The plan is a series of decisions, including decisions about resource allocations. Finally, in the fourth and fifth steps, the plan is implemented and evaluated. As the model shows, plans are made within an environmental context—the person considers what is possible within his or her environment. A beach party is not a practical plan in Minneapolis in the winter, for example, nor is a sit-down dinner with five courses a good choice for a 4-year-old's birthday party.

When individuals and families plan, their main task is to figure out what needs to be done and how to go about doing it. In a competitive world where there are many demands on people's time, energy, money, and ability, survival and growth require accurate knowledge, decisions, and implementation. How should people act? Where should they go? How can they prioritize among conflicting activities and responsibilities? How do they choose between work and family duties?

A plan should have a purpose. It should be going somewhere. What does the planner hope to achieve? Management theory stresses the necessity of planning if an individual or a family hopes to achieve the goals they have set. One of the reasons individuals and families engage in planning activity is to help them visualize what may or may not happen. Among the questions they may consider are the following:

◆ Will others cooperate?
◆ Is there enough money?
◆ Is there enough time?
◆ Is there enough information?

By reviewing these questions, the planner is trying to anticipate problems before they arise. Answers to these questions may lead directly to implementation of the plan or to more planning and different courses of action.

Need Fulfillment

Generally, people arrive at their needs through a complex subjective assessment based on their inherent motivations and their perceptions of the external world (Foxall, Goldsmith, & Brown, 1998). For example, if a new product is

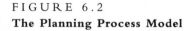

FIGURE 6.2
The Planning Process Model

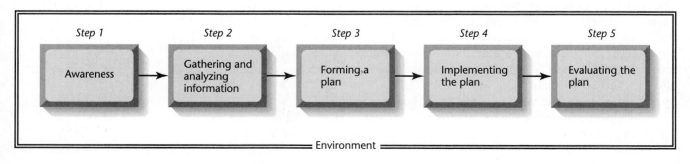

to succeed, consumers must perceive that it will satisfy some need or combination of needs. Likewise in management theory, if a plan is to succeed, individuals must perceive that the plan and its implementation will be useful and will satisfy some need or combination of needs.

Time, Stress, and Planning

Planning takes time, but sometimes time is in short supply. Individuals, families, and organizations may become so caught up in everyday activities and crises that they have no time to plan. In that case, they are victims of **Gresham's Law of Planning**, which comes from the better-known Gresham's law (Simon, 1993). Thomas Gresham, a financial adviser of Queen Elizabeth I, observed that "bad money drives out good," so that "if two coins have the same nominal value but are made from metals of unequal value, the cheaper will tend to drive the other out of circulation" (*Encyclopedia Britannica,* Vol. 5, 1989, p. 489). Applying Gresham's Law of Planning to management, Herbert Simon observed that "short-term concerns create priorities and deadlines that absorb managerial attention and energy at the expense of long-range concerns" (1993, p. 139).

There are a number of indicators that families have less and less time that they can devote to planning. One of the ways they are coping with time stress is to plan further ahead than ever before. Families today live months ahead of themselves.

> They rent next year's summer home before Thanksgiving; buy Christmas concert tickets in the summer; apply to favorite schools for next year; even before this year's class has had a chance to warm the seats. . . . In Chicago, Robin Cohn has her children's after school activities planned for the next eight months; all that is in question is whether her son, a third grader, will play soccer or basketball this spring. "And we'll decide that in a week or two," she says. (Kronholz, 1997, p. A1)

Part of the reason that families plan so far ahead is that many of them are competing for the same activities. Too many have found that planning is necessary if they are to get what they want. They have learned that many organization's schedule around the egalitarian principle of first-come, first-served, so the first come earlier and earlier. The price to be paid for all this planning ahead is a lack of spontaneity.

The paradox of planning is that it can create stress and also relieve stress. Stress is relieved when people are more relaxed once a decision is made, for example, once the cruise tickets are bought and a trip can go on as scheduled. But, what happens when the cruise, for which tickets were bought six months ahead, is canceled when a hurricane hits right where the ship is going? Stress can arise from feeling too boxed in, too committed, or too rigid so that changes or new opportunities cannot be readily taken advantage of.

> Certainly, people who live entirely for the moment haven't got it right, says Chicago's Mr. Csikszentmihalyi. But those who spend their lives planning their lives don't either. "You end up finding that you have squandered opportunities for really living in order to prepare yourself for living in the future," he says. (Kronholz, 1997, A1)

Thus, planning is affected by time constraints and stress. But there are other factors that affect planning, such as situational aspects and personality characteristics, including motivation. These will be discussed next.

Situational Factors

Situational factors, including environmental context, shape wants, needs, and goals. These factors can include a specific precipitating circumstance, such as a broken computer. Until the computer breaks down, the owner has no need to consider how to fix or replace it, but now he must either have the computer repaired or buy a new one. Individuals and families continually respond to such changes in situations or circumstances. Something (a problem, need, want, or goal) motivates them to plan and act. For example, they may drive up to a restaurant and find it is closed. They then must formulate a new plan of where to go and what to eat. Among the situational influences to be considered in making plans are the following:

- ◆ *Physical surroundings:* Location, decor, lighting, cleanliness, sound, heat, or cold.
- ◆ *Social surroundings:* Other people, crowding, and relationships.
- ◆ *Time:* Time of day, month, year, and season.
- ◆ *Task:* The reason the person is there. What needs to be done?

The importance of situational influences cannot be overestimated:

> At a more immediate level, is our behavior determined more by our internal attributes (personality traits, attitudes, beliefs, values, self-concept) or situational forces? While many people assume their behavior is largely determined by their internal attributes, social psychological research, with its interpersonal orientation, demonstrates that situational factors often have a very powerful effect on what we do. Situational forces are particularly visible in studies of helping in emergencies, conformity, and pressure to comply with orders to behave in hurtful ways.
>
> Three general conclusions can be drawn from these studies. First, our behavior is dramatically influenced by what other people do in the same situation; they serve as models and provide information about how to interpret the situation and what the consequences of various behaviors are. Second, most people are genuinely unaware of how strongly their behavior has been influenced by the behavior of others. And third, it is very difficult for the average person to resist pressures to comply to the wishes of others. (Bingham, 1991, p. 36)

Personal Traits and Characteristics

Although situational factors are important, the person making the decision lies at the heart of the planning process. The planning and implementing that will take place will be based on how that individual assesses the situation. Thus, personality plays a crucial role in planning.

According to Foxall, Goldsmith, and Brown (1998), **personality** refers either to an extensive range of separate behavior traits (honesty, perseverance, and hostility, for instance) or to overall types of character and response (extrovert versus introvert). **Introverts** tend to think about themselves first; their thoughts are directed inward. **Extroverts** are less interested in self and more interested in others and in the environment. People are rarely either completely introverted or extroverted, but they do tend to exhibit more traits of one than the other.

How does being introverted or extroverted affect planning? One difference is in the way information is gathered and processed. For example, after purchasing a camera, an introverted person might be more likely to read the instruction booklet or figure out through trial and error how to operate it, whereas an extroverted person might be more inclined to ask for help from the camera store owner or friends.

Many other personality factors also affect planning. For example, is the individual primarily a dreamer or a realist? Consistent or inconsistent? Precise or imprecise? Impatient or patient?

Besides personality differentials, some individuals are simply more expert than others in planning. They have more foresight, organizational and analytical skills, and imagination. They are motivated to change things and do not accept the status quo. Perhaps their families provided more models of planning behavior than the families of less expert planners. Planning ability varies between professions as well as between individuals. Consider the range of planning skills necessary in day care centers, hospitals, urban and regional planning, and air traffic control.

The ability to perform tasks successfully and dependably is called **expertise.** It increases as the person acquires more detailed knowledge, has more contact with experts, and develops more memory and experience. Naturally, it follows that young children have less expertise in most subjects and situations than adults.

Experts recall more information about messages and situations and are more likely to draw conclusions and make comparisons rapidly. Thus, experts not only have more access to information, but they tend to recall, reorganize, and return messages to a greater extent than others. Expertise affects beliefs and planning style, which in turn affect intentions to behave and actual behavior.

In a family, one family member may have more mechanical ability than the others and is therefore expected to fix things, whereas another may have more planning ability and is therefore in charge of organizing family events. Other family members will check with the organizer before scheduling events of their own.

Motivational Factors

Motivated planning behavior is thinking activity that is directed toward a particular goal or objective. Achievement-motivated people set goals for themselves and work hard toward attaining those goals (McClelland & Winter, 1969). They are able to keep goals in mind as they plan and complete tasks.

Motivation has three main aspects:

1. The goal or objective must be attractive and desired.
2. The goal or objective seeker must be persistent.
3. The seeker becomes discontented if she or he does not reach the goal or objective.

Persistence refers to a person's staying power; it is the personality trait of not giving up when faced with adversity. Psychological factors, such as depression, may affect motivation and persistence—in a job search, for example (Smith & Price, 1992).

According to Maslow's theory of the hierarchy of needs, which was introduced in Chapter 1, a person attempts to satisfy a more basic need (such as shelter) before directing behavior to higher needs (Maslow, 1943; Maslow, 1954). Maslow proposed that the typical adult satisfies about 85 percent of physiological needs; 70 percent of safety and security needs; 50 percent of belongingness, social, and love needs; 40 percent of esteem needs; and 10 percent of self-actualization needs. In the years since Maslow introduced his theory, many people have criticized his percentages, in particular, the percentage for self-actualization, which they think is too high. Nevertheless, Maslow's basic theory—that needs motivate human behavior and that unsatisfied needs lead to frustration and stress—is still widely accepted.

Applying Maslow's theory to planning, one might say that a person is motivated to plan and act by some state, condition, or situation, perhaps a social drive (the need to be liked or more popular), or a physiological drive (hunger or thirst). Figure 6.3 provides a model and an example of motivated planning behavior. The example of a hungry person eating to satisfy his or her hunger is a simple one. Achievement motivation can be far more profound. Think of all the individuals and the steps involved in planning a new museum or a space shuttle mission. Many organizations use flow charts to graphically illustrate how an operation, such as the development of a new car or a community, is progressing.

Some people seem especially oriented toward the achievement of goals. Achievement-motivated people, such as Donald Trump, Bill Gates, and Hillary Rodham Clinton, continually set new goals and develop new aspirations. They refuse to rest on their laurels. This characteristic explains why individuals who have made millions in a business venture will, upon selling it, immediately look for another venture to invest their energy in—money was not their primary objective. Rather, the obtaining of it (the process) was the motivator. For such people, the excitement is in the chase; they value each success more for its message "I've succeeded" than as a vehicle for obtaining life's luxuries. Thus, motivation is an internal drive that is fueled by the process of striving for and attaining goals. Planners have to be motivated; they must want their plans to succeed.

Standard Setting

Standards are another important part of the planning process. Standards were defined in Chapter 1 as quantitative and/or qualitative criteria that reconcile resources with demands and serve as measures of values and goals (DeMerchant, 1993). The procedures, conduct, and rules of individuals, families, and organizations all incorporate standards. For example, an industry may set a certain standard or level of excellence.

In planning, standards provide the criteria for action. The standards that are set affect the assessment and allocation of resources, leading to the clarification of demands, decisions, plans, and action. It is important that the plan fit the standards of the individual or situation. In business, a poorly thought-out management plan will not meet the standards set by the company. Likewise, a poorly devised personal or family plan of action may not meet the standards of most families. For example, a 14-year-old son bringing home an "F" grade in science may not meet the standards for educational achievement set by the family. Standards emanate from the values and the goals of family members. What do they want and how do they want to go about getting what they want? What makes sense to them?

Standards evolve or develop over time. A newly married couple gradually develops compatible standards and defines what constitutes a comfortable life

FIGURE 6.3
Motivated Planning Behavior:
Model and Example

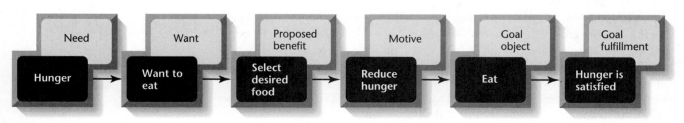

Need	Want	Proposed benefit	Motive	Goal object	Goal fulfillment
Hunger	Want to eat	Select desired food	Reduce hunger	Eat	Hunger is satisfied

together. They explore what they value and define what they want as individuals and what they want as a couple. Over the course of their married life, they may go from a tiny apartment to a large house, from a small income to a large income, and at the end of their married life back to a small apartment again and a reduced income. Throughout these changes, the couple's standards will adjust to their needs, life stage, and resources.

Scheduling and Sequencing

Almost all plans include schedules or sequences of events and activities. "**Scheduling** refers to the specification of sets of time bounded projected activities which are sufficient for the achievement of a desired goal set" (Avery & Stafford, 1991, p. 327). Written plans with deadlines or end points, diaries, lists, and timetables are all examples of schedules. Consider list making. A list may be a series of activities or appointments, such as 8:00–11:00, go to classes; 11:00 see advisor; 11:30–12:30 lunch; 12:30–5:00 work. Another common type of list is a grocery list. The generally accepted belief that writing a grocery list will eliminate or lessen impulse buying has been challenged by two researchers, Jeffrey Inman of the University of Wisconsin-Madison and Russell Winer of the University of California at Berkeley. They found that list makers are just as likely to make spontaneous purchases as those who shop without them (Inman & Winer, 1999). According to a report on their study in *American Demographics*, 59 percent of all supermarket purchases are unplanned.

Scheduling involves the mental process of sequencing. Sequencing is the ordering of activities and resources necessary to achieve goals. One action succeeds another until the need or the goal is fulfilled. Activities or tasks can be independent, dovetailed, interdependent, or overlapped. These four types will be discussed next.

Independent activities take place one at a time. They stand alone. For example, a person who watches television, then does an hour of homework, and then gets ready for bed is engaged in three independent activities. Each activity is independent of the others because the person could choose to go straight to bed and not watch television or do homework. In other words, none of the activities depends on the others.

Dovetailing occurs when two or more activities take place at the same time; some examples are eating popcorn and watching a movie, doing homework and listening to the radio, and talking on the telephone while making dinner. People often think dovetailing is a desirable way of organizing activity and getting a lot done in a short time, but it can be ineffective if it leads to unacceptable consequences. Sometimes people try to do too many activities at once. Trying to talk on the telephone, answer the doorbell, cook dinner, and watch a small child all at the same time can result in a burned dinner and a crying child. As this example suggests, dovetailing can be a useful time management tool, but it is not a panacea. Doing more at the same time does not necessarily produce better outcomes. Each individual must decide how many activities she or he can reasonably handle at once.

Overlapping activities involve a combination of activities that require intermittent and/or concurrent attention. For example, college students with children combine child care with schoolwork, going back and forth between the activities.

Activities are **interdependent** when one activity must be completed before another can take place. In other words, one activity builds on another and

Dovetailing means doing two or more activities at the same time. This mother is trying to do too much.

is not effective in isolation. For example, hiring someone before a position exists and money is allocated for a salary would be senseless. Similarly, a newspaper article is not complete until the main people involved in the story are interviewed or at least contacted for comment.

It is not always easy to differentiate among overlapping, dovetailing, and interdependent activities. People may switch back and forth among the three types of activities in a short period of time. Regardless of type, the behavioral goal of scheduling and sequencing is to provide the desired flow between activities.

Sequencing and scheduling preferences are closely associated with the personality or temperament of the planner as well as with the task itself. How many college students have exactly the same class schedule? Even when they have the same class schedule, it is highly unlikely that they will also eat, socialize, and sleep at exactly the same time. In a family, plans should accommodate the different scheduling needs and preferences of the individuals in the household.

Attributes of Plans

Workable plans have the following attributes: they are clear, flexible, adaptive, realistic, appropriate, and goal directed. Clear plans are understood by everyone. For example, when an advertisement for a concert says that the concert will start at 8:00 P.M., the audience assumes that it will start promptly and that they should plan to get there ahead of time. In this situation, the concertgoer's plans will have to be flexible because traffic and parking conditions are not totally predictable. Is arriving 10 to 15 minutes ahead of time suitable? If several people are going to the concert together, how will they adjust their schedules to be ready on time? Adaptive refers to the ability of the plan to respond to unanticipated events that may occur. Realistic implies that the plan is feasible and likely to work. Being appropriate means that the plan is suited to the situation and the people involved.

As has been suggested throughout this chapter, successful plans are goal directed. Specific, challenging goals lead to higher task performance than do specific, unchallenging goals, vague goals, or no goals (Locke, et al., 1994).

Types of Plans

Many different types of plans exist. Plans can be categorized by time, such as short-term and long-term plans. Plans can also be distinguished by the parties involved: individuals, households, organizations, communities, or nations. This chapter will concentrate on three types of plans (directional, contingency, and strategic) that are commonly associated with individual and family resource management. Given different situations, a manager can pick the best type of plan.

Directional plans progress along a linear path to long-term goal fulfillment. Plans to graduate from high school and then graduate from college and then go to law school to become an attorney are examples of directional plans. Because a certain degree of work experience is a prerequisite for a higher-level position, career planning is usually directional, although less so than formerly because people today change jobs more frequently than in the past.

Contingency plans are backup or secondary plans to be used in case the first plan does not work. The military is known for contingency plans, if one strategy does not work, they have several others ready to initiate. Similarly, chess players think of several different potential ways to respond to an opponent's move.

Organizations often use a contingency approach. The basic idea behind this approach is that there is no single best way to manage; a method that is successful in one situation may not be successful in another. Therefore, a business manager will devise several plans after assessing the characteristics of the individuals and groups involved, the organizational structure, and his or her own leadership style (Ivancevich & Matteson, 1990). If one plan is not successful, the manager will try another. Likewise, in a family, the manager (or managers) sizes up the situation, the family members and others involved, and prepares several plans leading to a solution. Here again, the manager will be prepared to substitute another plan if the first does not work.

As an example of how an individual uses the contingency approach, consider Shannon, a 22-year-old who applied to eight different graduate schools. Her plan was to apply to three schools known to be hard to get into, two schools that were moderately difficult to get into, and three easy-to-get-into schools. Shannon wanted to be sure that by September she would be accepted by at least one school, and she did everything she could to ensure that result.

As explained in Chapter 4, a strategy is a plan of action, a way of conducting and following through on operations. **Strategic plans** use a directional approach and include both a proactive search for new opportunities and a reactive solution to existing problems (Wheeler & Hunger, 1987). *Proactive* and *reactive* are discussed in detail in the next section, but here they mean simply that the strategic planner utilizes a forward-looking approach while realizing that past business must also be concluded.

Strategic planning focuses attention on the initial stages of the decision-making processes—the opportunities and occasions for choice and the design of new action strategies (Simon, 1993). To conclude, strategic plans are often associated with the military, business, or politics, but they also occur in individual and family life. For example, job hunting involves many strategies, such as résumé writing (a record of one's past achievements and experience), reading, prioritizing, and responding to job announcements.

Proactive versus Reactive

Proactive means taking responsibility for one's own life. According to Covey (1989), "our behavior is a function of our decisions, not our conditions. We can subordinate feelings to values. We have the initiative and the responsibility to make things happen" (p. 71). Proactive people accept responsibility for their own actions; they do not blame others or circumstances for their behavior. "Proactive management involves change-oriented planning where the desired change is conceived by a person or family and the implementation of the change alters the environment" (Dollahite, 1991, p. 374). Thus, in proactive management, the individual or family is actively seeking solutions to problems by forming plans including strategic plans.

Reactive people are often overly affected by outside forces, such as changes in the weather or the bad attitudes of their coworkers. According to Covey (1989), "when people treat them well, they feel well; when people don't, they become defensive or protective. Reactive people build their emotional lives around the behavior of others, empowering the weaknesses of other people to control them" (p. 72). Proactive people also notice the weather or the social conditions around them, but they respond differently than reactive people. Values such as honesty and self-respect drive the behaviors of proactive people more than outside forces. Other people's opinions matter less to proactive people than they do to reactive people. As Eleanor Roosevelt said, "No one can hurt you without your consent."

Typical phrases used by proactive and reactive people are listed in Table 6.1. Notice that the reactive person says "I can't," whereas the proactive person says "I choose." Proactive people believe their lives are the sum total of the choices they have made. Planners with proactive styles approach life challenges more assertively than reactive people do. Management theory supports the notion that effective managers tend to be proactive and goal oriented (Sharpe & Winter, 1991). Proactive management can help a person or family avoid crises or stress through active anticipation of events to come. In proactive management, an "individual or a family actively clarifies values, makes plans, sets goals, organizes activities, and makes changes before experiencing stressors" (Dollahite, 1991, p. 374).

Planning Summary

The three types of plans discussed in this section—directional, contingency, and strategic—are not limited to individuals and families. They are potentially applicable to all organizations and situations. For example, Coca-Cola, in a strategic move to market its product worldwide, seized the opportunity to go

TABLE 6.1
Reactive versus Proactive Language

Reactive Language	Proactive Language
There's nothing I can do.	Let's look at our alternatives.
That's just the way I am.	I can choose a different approach.
They make me so mad.	I control my own feelings.
They won't allow that.	I can create an effective presentation.
I have to do that.	I will choose an appropriate response.
I can't.	I choose.
I must.	I prefer.
If only.	I will.

global rather than being confined to the United States. Airlines are constantly searching for more profitable routes. Fast-food restaurants look for new locations and new products in order to expand their share of the market. Likewise, individuals and families try to maximize their chances at improving their lives. For example, a proactive, goal-setting foreign service officer will try to get an appointment overseas in a desired location rather than wait to be assigned anywhere the government decides to send him or her.

The specific planning mode used (directional, contingency, or strategic) reflects the individual's or the family's perceptions of what type of plan will be most suitable. Key decisions flow from the dominant planning mode and the choice of a proactive or reactive approach.

What Is Implementing?

Implementing means putting plans and procedures into action and controlling the action. Controlling takes place because once plans are activated, they need to be checked to make sure that they are leading to the desired end state. As everyone knows, it is easier to make plans than to initiate and monitor them. Environmental, economic, social, and a variety of other forces and conditions can positively or negatively affect the outcome of the most carefully prepared plan. For example, planning a dream house and building an affordable house are two different things.

The factors that affect implementing are the same ones that affect planning: situations, personal traits and characteristics, and motivational factors. Possible blocks to successful implementation include:

- ◆ Other people. They may not believe in the same plans you do, or they may drag their feet.
- ◆ Costs and other restrictions.
- ◆ Competition. Perhaps there are competing plans that are better. For example, 14 architects may be invited to submit plans for a new university building—only one will be selected.
- ◆ Crises. Long-term plans may be put on hold if resources are required for more immediate needs.
- ◆ Procrastination or lack of motivation.
- ◆ Close mindedness.

Several strategies can be employed to avoid these blocks. The main strategy is to intelligently size up the situations that arise and respond accordingly. In the end, implementing requires a scanning sensibility—a monitoring of your actions and the actions of those around you. **Scanning** is an activity in which individuals or families "read the world," looking for signals and clues (i.e., information, messages, feedback) that could have strategic implications. Three of the elements that play into this—actuating, checking, and controlling—are discussed next.

Actuating

Actuating refers to putting plans into effect, action, or motion. For example, Mike, a teenager, has been reading car advertisements and talking for months with friends about buying a used car. Finally, he decides he is ready to look at some cars.

Plans can be actuated in stages. A teacher may interview for a job in January that does not start until August. Within the family system, parents might start saving for their child's college education soon after the child's birth and add money to the college fund at each birthday.

Positive and negative feedback (discussed in Chapter 2) play a large part in actuating. Feedback from others may prevent a person from actuating a plan—she or he may want to wait until the time seems to be right. Also, if things are going well, an individual may decide not to "rock the boat" and let things simply evolve for a while. Other times, a more active and controlling approach is necessary.

Checking and Controlling

Once the plan is activated, different situations or personal factors may indicate the need for corrective action. To be successful, plans need to be checked and rechecked. This checking or **adjusting** activity is a type of controlling. For example, a person may make a reservation months in advance of an important event, but reconfirm the reservation a day or two before the event.

Checking is defined in management as determining if actions are in compliance with standards and sequencing. An individual determines whether plans are unfolding as they should, in the right sequence, and in a timely fashion. If a check reveals that they are not, a correction is necessary.

Changes in planning and implementing can occur, for example, when an individual goes grocery shopping with a list. The list is a plan of action, but, while shopping (actuating the plan) the shopper may make several changes, such as substituting one product for another or adding several more items to the grocery cart. In this way, the list serves as a guide. Most plans can be envisioned as a guide—a mental plan of action.

If overdone, checking can produce undesirable effects. Too much checking by the planner or by the recipient of the plan can lead to frustration, resentment, or pressure. Consider the frustration potential of a person on a diet who checks his or her weight several times a day. Or consider how employees feel when the boss stands over them when they are trying to complete a task. Or how an interviewer feels when a potential employee keeps calling about the results of an interview. In the latter case, too much checking can ruin the person's chances for employment. The goal is to have a sufficient amount of checking to ensure a positive outcome (e.g., a weight loss, a completed task, or a job), but neither too much nor too little.

Controlling also takes time. Therefore, the implementer has to weigh the costs against the benefits of spending time and energy on checking. Controlling is most effective at significant milestones or critical points in a plan. Teachers and professors do this by giving tests or assignments at appropriate intervals of learning. This is their way of checking learning progress.

As with so many other aspects of management, the key to successful planning and implementing is a balance between wants, goals, and actions. Particularly in the checking phase, achieving a balance is essential to obtaining a successful outcome.

WHAT IS EVALUATING?

The word *evaluation* comes from an Old French verb, évaluer, meaning to be worthy or to have value. To evaluate means to determine the worth of an effort. Thus, **evaluation** is a process of judging or examining the cost, value, or worth of a plan or decision based on such criteria as standards, met demands, or goals. It occurs throughout the management process: in setting goals in the first place and at each step along the way. As discussed earlier, people may encounter obstacles to goal achievement, such as crises and unplanned-for events.

Since judgments are subjective, evaluations can turn out to be flawed or biased. To ensure better end results, people engage in assessments. **Assessment** involves the gathering of information about results, the comparison of those results with the results of the past, and the open discussion of the meaning of those results, the ways that they have been gathered, and their implications for the next moves of the family or the individual (Senge, 1999).

Progressive steps leading to the final evaluation phase of planning can be explained through storytelling (a detailed explanation of the probable sequence of events) or they can be charted. One charting method is called **storyboarding,** a planning technique used by advertisers, movie screenwriters, and television scriptwriters to show the main scenes in a commercial, movie, or television show. A storyboard is a comic-strip type presentation complete with pictures, dialogue, and words to describe the action (Levinson, 1999). Storyboarding can be used as a planning technique in other situations to show the consecutive steps that lead to desired outcomes. It allows a person to visualize the steps to be taken.

Figure 6.4 shows a storyboard from a commercial. Use the blank spaces provided in Figure 6.5 to create your own storyboard. The last frame should be your desired outcome.

At the end of the management process, a final evaluation takes place. If a goal is achieved, the manager can look back with satisfaction on how things turned out. Other possible outcomes are the achievement of a new or a substitute goal (not the ones initially set), the solution to a problem, the satisfaction of a need or want, or perhaps none of these. Whether the outcomes are effective or ineffective, the manager should review what went right and what went wrong with the process so that she or he can learn from it for future decisions. Since evaluation can be painful, people often ignore this step and proceed immediately to the next problem or goal. Nevertheless, looking back and evaluating past decisions are crucial steps in becoming a better manager. Improving management skills is important because competence in problem solving has been identified as an essential part of healthy marriages and family systems (Rettig & Bubolz, 1983).

SFX: CAR AND FOOT TRAFFIC AMBIENCE
VO: Why did the chicken cross the road?
To open a 7/24 Savings Plan at San
    Diego Trust.
Because with $500 in savings . . .

. . . he can avoid getting henpecked by
monthly charges on a checking account.
What's more, he can access his nest egg
    through our huge ATM network . . .
SFX: BANK AMBIENCE
    . . . and round-the-clock phone service.

VO: And of course, the interest he'll earn on
    savings isn't just chicken feed.
So open a 7/24 Savings Plan at San Diego
    Trust.
And give yourself a good reason to . . .
SFX: COCKA DOODLE DOO

FIGURE 6.4

A Sample Storyboard Layout

Source: Reprinted by permission of Wells Fargo
Bank.

Desired outcome or goal: _____

_____

Steps: What do you have to do first, second, third, and so on to reach the desired outcome? Use words or draw pictures to illustrate the main steps or actions needed to reach your goal. *Note:* You may need less than eight steps (frames).

1
2

3
4

5
6

7
8

Desired outcome or goal should be written or drawn in here.

FIGURE 6.5
Storyboarding: A Planning Technique

Electronic Resources

If someone has a planning problem, there are many organizations, radio call-in shows and individuals willing to take on the burden or to give advice. An industry has evolved wherein a lot of people make their living by solving other people's problems. For example, the National Association of Professional Organizers (**www.napo.net**) can step in and assist with organizing homes and businesses by designing systems and finding a place for everything.

For insurance problems, there is the National Association of Public Insurance Adjusters who will recommend people that can organize a homeowner's insurance claim in the case of a major property loss from such causes as fire, explosion, and tornadoes (**www.napia.com**). Claims assistance professionals who serve as advocates for people whose health insurance claims have been denied can be reached at **www.claims.org**, the Alliance of Claims Assistance Professionals.

General advice on how to plan the moving of household goods more efficiently can be found at the Web sites of major moving companies. Moving coordinators can be hired to help, especially elderly people, with packing and unpacking. Details about moving coordinators can be found through the National Association of Professional Organizers. Estate organizers, professionals who help implement an estate plan for someone who is still alive or help settle the estate of someone who has recently died, can also be reached through the National Association of Professional Organizers. Banks, accountants, and financial planners also offer assistance with estate planning. For legal advice, a site to check is the American Bar Association at **www.aba.org**.

www.census.gov/population/ www/projections/nathh.html
Government plans are based on the projections of changes in households and families.

U.S. Census Bureau

National Households and Families Projections

Projections of the numbers of households and families at the national level are produced periodically by the Population Projections Program of the Census Bureau. These projections are based on national population projections and assumptions about future household structure and family composition. The output tables include data on various factors related to household and family structure such as age of householder, the number of persons in households, household type (both family and non-family), race and Hispanic origin, persons living alone, and families with children under age 18.

- Methodology
- Consistency issues

National Households and Families Projections, 1995 to 2010 (Series 1, 2, and 3, except where noted):

1. Projections of Households by Type
2. Percent Distribution of Projected Households by Type
3. Projections of Households by Type of Household and Age of Householder
4. Projections of Households by Type, Race, and Hispanic Origin, Series 3 Only
5. Projections of Families with Children under 18 by Type
6. Projections of the Number of Persons Living Alone by Age and Sex
7. Projections of the Marital Status of the Population by Age and Sex

Summary

Resource management theory focuses on conscious decision making, leading to the formation and implementation of plans to achieve goals. Planning, implementing, and evaluating were the main subjects of this chapter. They represent both mental and physical activity. Planning begins with mentally organizing activities to accomplish a desired end state. It requires vision, energy, and motivation to succeed. Implementing includes both actuating and controlling.

Planning and implementing require an ability to order and sequence steps in a rational manner. Personality, situations, standards, and the environment all affect planning outcomes. Proactive and reactive personality types differ in how they approach planning. Their language reflects these differences. Scanning is an activity in which individuals or families "read the world" by searching for signals or clues that have strategic implications. Assessment involves the gathering of information about results. Storyboarding was introduced as a technique for visualizing the steps in planning leading to a desired outcome.

People vary in their planning expertise. Planning ability can be increased through experience and maturity. As Emerson said, "that which we persist in doing becomes easier—not that the nature of the task has changed, but our ability to do has increased."

Key Terms

actuating	extroverts	personality
adjusting	Gresham's Law of	plan
assessment	Planning	proactive
checking	independent activities	process
contingency plans	interdependent	reactive
directional plans	activities	scanning
dovetailing	introverts	scheduling
evaluation	overlapping activities	storyboarding
expertise	persistence	strategic plans

Review Questions

1. What are some of the difficulties a person might face when trying to set priorities for a plan of action?

2. What influences affect planning? Include a discussion of Gresham's Law of Planning in your answer.

3. What is the difference between proactive and reactive styles?

4. How can implementation be blocked?

5. The musician John Lennon wrote a song lyric that said, "Life is what happens to you while you're busy making other plans." What do you think he meant by this? What is your opinion about how much of life can be planned and how much just happens? Give an example of something you planned to do, but "life" got in the way.

References

Avery, R. & Stafford, K. (1991). Toward a scheduling congruity theory of family resource management. *Lifestyles: Family and Economic Issues, 12*(4), 325–344.

Bingham, J. (1991). *Social psychology* (2nd ed.). New York: Harper Collins.

Covey, S. (1989). *The 7 habits of highly effective people.* New York: Simon & Schuster.

DeMerchant, E. (1993, February). Standards: An analysis of definitions, frameworks and implications. In C. Y. Kratzar (Ed.), *Proceedings of the Southeastern Regional Home Management Association of Family Economics* (pp. 13–22). Roanoke, VA: Virginia Polytechnic Institute.

Dollahite, D. (1991, Winter). Family resource management and family stress theories: Toward conceptualization integration. *Lifestyles: Family and Economic Issues, 12*(4), 361–377.

Foxall, G., Goldsmith, R., & Brown, S. (1998). *Consumer psychology for marketing.* London: Routledge.

Inman, J. & Winer, R. (1999, May 6). Shoppers are impulsive. *Tallahassee Democrat.*

Ivancevich, J. M. & Matteson, M. T. (1990). *Organizational behavior and management.* Homewood, IL: Richard D. Irwin.

Kronholz, J. (1997, November 20). We're all living in future tense—And it's tense indeed, *The Wall Street Journal,* A1.

Levinson, J. (1999). Guerilla advertising. New York: Houghton Mifflin.

Locke, E., Smith, K., Erez, M., Chah, D., & Schaffer, A. (1994). The effects of intra-individual goal conflict on performance. *Journal of Management, 20*(1), 67–91.

McClelland, D. & Winter, D. (1969). *Motivating economic achievement.* New York: Macmillan.

Maslow, A. (1943, July). A theory of human motivation. *Psychological Review,* 370–396.

Maslow, A. (1954). *Motivation and personality.* New York: Harper & Row.

Morris, B. (1987, August 4). As a favored pastime, shopping ranks high with most Americans. *Wall Street Journal.*

Rettig, K. & Bubolz, M. (1983). Perceptual indicators of family well-being. *Social Indicators Research, 12,* 417–438.

Senge, P., Kleiner, A., Roberts, C., Ross, R., Roth, G., & Smith, B. (1999). The dance of change. New York: Doubleday.

Sharpe, D. & Winter, M. (1991). Toward working hypotheses of effective management: Conditions, thought processes, and behaviors. *Lifestyles: Family and Economic Issues, 12*(4), 303–323.

Simon, H. A. (1993). Strategy and organizational evolution. *Strategic Management Journal, 14,* 131–142.

Smith, S. & Price, S. (1992). Women and plant closings: Unemployment, re-employment, and job training enrollment following dislocation. *Journal of Family and Economic Issues, 13*(1), 45–72.

Wheeler, T. & Hunger, J. (1987). *Strategic management* (2nd ed.) Reading, Massachusetts: Addison-Wesley.

chapter **7**

Communication

MAIN TOPICS

COMMUNICATION AS PART OF THE MANAGEMENT PROCESS
SENDING AND RECEIVING
LISTENING
MESSAGES
CHANNELS
NOISE
FEEDBACK/RESPONSE
SETTING

COMMUNICATION CONFLICTS
IN FAMILIES
ACROSS CULTURES

COMMUNICATION IN SMALL GROUPS
GROUP DISCUSSIONS AND COHESION

INFORMATION AND COMMUNICATION TECHNOLOGY
INFORMATION OVERLOAD AND HABITUAL DECISION MAKING
COMPUTERS AND THE HUMAN CAPACITY TO PROCESS
   INFORMATION
THE ROLE OF THE HOME AND THE INDIVIDUAL

Did you know that…?

...The average person spends 70 percent of his or her working hours in some form of communication.

...The 80 muscles in the face create over 7,000 expressions.

He who listens, understands.

—West African proverb

COMMUNICATION IS AN integral part of every step of the management process. Feedback connects the steps together forming a loop, as shown in Figure 7.1.

Although communication and feedback are normally thought of as verbal, both can be nonverbal as well. For example, a look can often convey more than words. This chapter will examine both verbal and nonverbal communication. Other topics to be covered include the process of communication, conflict, information overload, and the value of listening. Communication is recognized as an important area of study in family resource management because the breakdown of communication is the primary cause of family breakups (Williams, 1997).

Encouraging the reader to communicate more effectively is the behavioral goal of this chapter. Presenting the types, forms, and problems of communication in families, in small groups, and in professional settings is the informational goal. By the chapter's conclusion, readers should be more aware of how they and others communicate. The chapter begins with a discussion of communication as part of the management process.

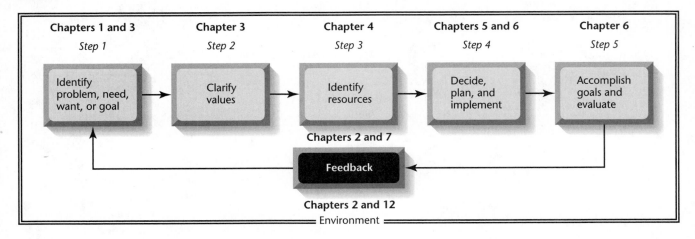

FIGURE 7.1
**The Management Process
Model**

COMMUNICATION AS PART OF THE MANAGEMENT PROCESS

Communication is the process of transmitting a message from a sender to a receiver. **Interference** is anything that distorts or interrupts messages. Effective communication occurs when the receiver interprets the sender's message in the same way the speaker intended it.

Because information transmission is an integral part of management, to be effective, a manager has to be an effective communicator. In systems terminology, communication is part of the transformation process—transforming inputs into outputs. In transforming information resources (inputs), communication uses up time and energy. The average person spends approximately 70 percent of his or her waking hours in some form of communication—writing, reading, speaking, and listening (Robbins, 1989). Given this time investment, it follows that one of the forces most likely to inhibit successful life management is a lack of effective communication.

Much of a manager's time must be devoted to goal setting, which also requires effective communication. Goal setting is a sequence that starts with thinking and proceeds to acting, which includes communicating goals to others and engaging their support and interest. As part of this process, managers need to communicate several key decisions, including the following: (1) What goals will be sought? (2) Which goals have the highest priority? (3) How are the goals related? (4) How long will it take to achieve the goals? (5) Who should be accountable for achieving the goals? The answers to these questions guide the present and future behavior of individuals, families, and other groups.

Effective communicators have a number of characteristics, including the following:

- ◆ Sensitivity to others
- ◆ A tendency to ask, persuade, or explain rather than telling, demanding, or threatening
- ◆ Openness to differing opinions

◆ The ability to pass along information, giving advance notice of impending changes and plans

These characteristics are important in both family and professional life. Talking through problems and listening carefully to what other family members have to say adds to family cohesiveness. In professional life, communication skills can be crucial to getting ahead. Peter Drucker, an expert in business management, says:

> Your success as an employee—and I'm talking of much more than getting promoted—will depend on your ability to communicate with people and to present your own thoughts and ideas to them so they will both understand what you are driving at and be persuaded. (1977, pp. 262–263)

As Drucker's comments indicate, communication is indeed a process rather than a finished end state, and as such, it allows individuals to share information, ideas, and feelings. For example, consider the following conversation between Heather and Sam, two college students who have been friends for over a year, but have never dated each other:

Sam: I haven't seen you around for weeks. Where have you been?

Heather: I've been working on two projects and they've taken all my time. I'm worried about my grades.

Sam: Hm. You do look stressed.

Heather: Yes, I am. But it's almost over—everything is due this week.

Sam: You'll do all right. You always worry about your work and then you make A's. Why don't we get together this weekend?

In this exchange, Sam and Heather have communicated information and feelings. Their remarks show that their relationship has a past, present, and future. Sam puts Heather's concerns into perspective. His comments show that he likes her. As the conversation continues, what are some of the responses Heather might give?

Notice that only the verbal communication between Sam and Heather has been presented. Their nonspoken or nonverbal communication is not included. Does Sam smile or grin at Heather? Does he try to show he cares by his tone of voice or stance? Is Heather yawning?

Communication is more than words. It includes senders, receivers, encoding and decoding messages, channels, noise, feedback, and setting. The **channel** is the method by which communication travels from source or sender to receiver. As Figure 7.2 shows, these elements interact to create the total communication environment. Think how different Sam and Heather's conversation would be if it took place in a crowded cafeteria rather than a deserted hallway. A quiet setting allows senders and receivers to concentrate on each other; a noisy setting is full of distractors.

The importance of the setting cannot be overestimated. There are appropriate places and times for discipline, compliments, whispers, shouts, and disputes. Being sensitive to environmental conditions as well as to words is part of being an effective communicator. One way to build a positive environment for communication is for individuals to let others know that they care about them. Providing a climate of acceptance fosters human functioning and teamwork. For example, children need to know that their parents love them. Likewise, employees need to know that their employers are concerned about their welfare. When there is trust, people feel freer to exchange information, ideas, and feelings.

FIGURE 7.2
A Model of the
Communications Process

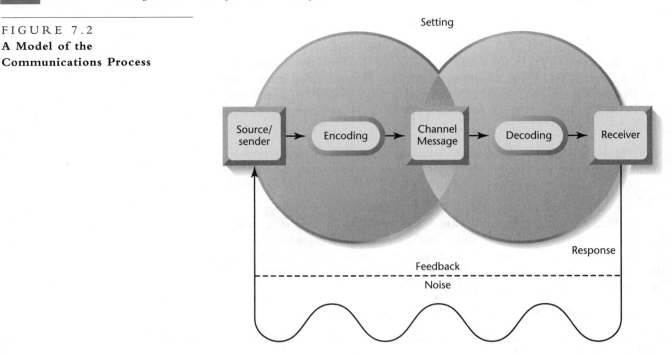

Sending and Receiving

Communication is a two-way process between sender and receiver. **Sending** is saying what one means to say, with agreement between verbal and nonverbal messages. In good sending, the person must know what she or he wants to say and then say it. The sender should make eye contact with the receiver. **Receiving** entails listening to the verbal messages and observing the nonverbal messages. If the message is getting through, the receiver will probably show his or her response through facial expressions. A good sender talks with people, not at them, and considers the listener's feelings, personality, and opinions.

Usually, people are receivers and senders at the same time. Communication is not as simple as one person speaks, another listens and then speaks, and so on. For instance, more than one listener may be involved. Also, the sending and receiving can be simultaneous.

A sender can also be called a **source** or communicator. The receiver is the **destination** or audience. The sender's task is to reach the audience whether it is one person or a million people.

The sender and receiver use four communication functions: encoding, decoding, response, and feedback. **Encoding** is the process of putting thoughts, ideas, or information into symbolic form. **Decoding** is the process by which the receiver assigns meaning to the symbols. **Responses** are the individual reactions that follow the message. Feedback is the total response pattern between sender and receiver. An individual's communication style is closely tied to her or his personality, self-concept, family of origin, and past experiences.

Listening

Whether in the home or office, managers want to be heard by those they manage and also to listen to them. Parents want their children to listen. Conversely, children want their parents to listen to them. In schools, teachers want their students to listen and learn, retain, and use information. Students want to understand what their teachers are saying. To encourage more listening, the sender should make messages and listening attractive. There are several ways to do this. Sometimes humor works, which is why many speeches begin with a joke or humorous anecdote. One way advertisers deliver effective messages is to appeal to potential customers' senses. Think of the senses involved in this appeal from General Foods: "Turn a stormy night into a quiet evening with the after-dinner-mint taste of chocolaty Irish Mocha Mint."

Listeners as well as senders have a job to do. This is one of the reasons listening is considered active rather than passive. To be effective, listeners use certain gestures or mannerisms to communicate interest:

- Leaning forward rather than back
- Nodding occasionally to show comprehension
- Smiling
- Looking directly at the speaker and maintaining eye contact
- Making comments such as "I see," "Go on," "Oh," or "Mm"
- Taking notes or tape recording, if appropriate

A good listener summarizes conversations when they end and lets the sender know his or her message was heard by nodding, smiling, or with some other gesture or response.

Critical Listening

Besides the general, everyday listening everyone does, there are specific types of listening. One of these is **critical listening**, in which the listener evaluates or challenges what is heard. Listening to a political candidate or a spokesperson for a new product requires critical listening. Can their message be believed? Before voting, making a contribution, or buying something new, the listener may:

- Question the communicator's motives. What does he or she want?
- Question the origin and validity of the communicator's ideas.
- Separate fact from fiction.
- Judge the message and the sender. Are they accurate and reliable?

Critical listening takes time. Not all messages require critical listening, however. A sign that it may be necessary is that the message or messenger makes the listener feel uncomfortable or suspicious.

Reflective or Empathetic Listening

Another type of listening is reflective listening. **Reflective listening** or **empathetic listening** involves listening for feelings. **Empathy** is the ability to recognize and identify another's feelings by putting oneself in that person's place. Reflective or empathetic listening is so common that individuals don't examine their skills in this area closely enough. As a reflective listener, the listener's job is to set aside her or his own feelings and enter into the feelings of the person talking. The listener can do this by:

- Identifying the speaker's emotion. Is the person afraid, excited, happy, or frustrated?
- Listening for the details of the story. What is included, and what is left out?

   ◆ Paraphrasing or mirroring the speaker's comments to see if the message is being heard accurately.

   ◆ Letting the other person work through the problem. Talking out feelings is a way to find solutions.

Informational and Pleasurable Listening

Listening does not have to be painful, difficult, or critical; nor does it have to involve the use of counseling skills. Much listening is for information or for fun. Informational listening is done to acquire knowledge or instruction. A news program or a college lecture is primarily informational, but also involves critical listening. Pleasurable listening provides enjoyment, relaxation, satisfaction, diversion, amusement, or delight. Tuning the radio to a favorite station provides pleasurable listening. Watching a television situation comedy show provides escape, amusement, and laughter. Other sources of pleasurable listening are available besides the media. Imagine the happiness of a father hearing his child's first word, a high school student learning she has won a college scholarship, or a person overseas receiving a phone call from home. Often the most pleasurable listening comes from unexpected sources or at an unanticipated time.

Messages

The **message** is the total communication that is sent, listened to, and received. Communication is made up of symbols. **Symbols** are things that suggest something else through association. For example, an engagement ring is a symbol of love and the intention to marry. It communicates a past, present, and future. Symbols, such as an engagement ring, that can be seen are called **visible symbols**.

   An **abstract symbol** stands for ideas rather than objects. Poor communication often springs from misunderstandings of abstract symbols. For example, Matt tells Suzanne he has an "awesome" apartment. By *awesome* he means that it is close to campus and inexpensive, but Suzanne, hearing the word *awesome*, envisions a new, beautifully decorated, spacious apartment. Imagine her surprise when Matt takes her to a crumbling 50-year-old building. Lasting friendships are built on shared abstract symbols—commonalties of interests or appreciation of each other's differences. In the future, Suzanne will suspect Matt's use of the word *awesome*.

Verbal and Nonverbal Symbols

Verbal symbols are words. A **nonverbal symbol** is anything other than words that is used to communicate. Examples of nonverbal symbols include works of art, train whistles, sirens, tone and volume of voice, clothing, personal appearance, gestures, facial expressions, posture, and yawns. For example, yawns may communicate tiredness or boredom, whereas sirens communicate danger or caution. Conventional scientific wisdom said that the role of gestures was to convey meaning. There is an emerging consensus that gestures serve another function—to help people retrieve elusive words from memory. People who gesture a lot may think in spatial terms. "Not everyone talks with their hands. Some people gesture 40 times more than others." (Begley, 1998, p. 69). Communication experts estimate that as many as 93 percent of the messages sent and received are made up of nonverbal symbols

(Mehrabian, 1981)—hence the expression, "It is not what you say, but how you say it."

Table 7.1 describes six aspects of nonverbal communication: artifacts, proxemics, body language, physical characteristics, clothing, and one's touching behavior. **Artifacts** are the type, placement, or rearrangement of objects around a person. A student who sits down at a library table and takes 20 minutes to arrange his belongings before settling down to work communicates something different than a person who takes 20 seconds to set up. **Proxemics** is the distance between speakers. Closeness and whispering imply one type of relationship whereas distance and shouting imply another. Touching behavior includes both touching oneself, such as hairtwisting or rubbing one's face, and touching others, such as shaking hands or hugging. A brief kiss on the cheek, for example, conveys something different than a kiss on the lips.

I-Messages and You-Messages

Verbal messages can be divided into two types: I-messages and You-messages. **I-messages** are statements of fact about how an individual feels or thinks; for example, "I like it when you send me flowers, thanks." **You-messages** are statements that often ascribe blame or judge others, such as "You had better straighten up" or "You had better get it right next time." You-messages can lead to arguments. Family counselors and therapists promote the use of I-messages over the accusatory tone of You-messages as a way to encourage more positive communication in couples and families. Many You-messages can be rephrased into I-messages as in "I hope things will go better next time."

Message Construction

The structure of a message has a lot to do with its potential effectiveness. **Message construction** includes where information should be placed in a message to have maximum impact. The communicator has to decide whether to place the main point of the comment or speech at the beginning or the end and whether to provide solutions or leave the solutions to the audience.

TABLE 7.1
Six Aspects of Nonverbal Communication

1. *Artifacts:* The manipulation of objects in contact with persons. Examples include objects on desks, dishes on tables, purses, backpacks, notebooks, pens, and hammers.

2. *Proxemics:* The distance between two people who are communicating.

3. *Body language:* The way a person moves, smiles, or frowns and uses gestures such as pointing or waving.

4. *Physical characteristics:* The size, posture, and shape of a person's body.

5. *Clothes or other forms of adornment or grooming:* This includes hairstyles, jewelry, cosmetics, and use of aftershave or perfume.

6. *Touching behavior:* How one touches oneself and others while communicating. Examples include shaking hands, hugging, cracking one's knuckles, and tapping one's feet.

Message Content and Complexity

Message content refers to the strategies or information that may be used to communicate an idea or policy to receivers. Determining content is the first step in creating a message. Then the communicator must decide on the best way to get the message across to the audience. Senders must decide how complex the message should be and whether to use humor or sobering statistics. Some messages include an appeal to fear, which seems negative, but can be an effective way to point out potential problems in order to reduce risk or achieve other positive effects. Antidrug public service television spots often use fear as a means of reducing drug use. Toothpaste, life insurance, burglar alarms, and automobile advertisements often include fear messages (see Figure 7.3).

Channels

As mentioned earlier, the channel is the method through which the message travels from sender to receiver. Channels may be direct, as in face-to-face talking, or indirect. In face-to-face channels of communication, the individuals have the advantage of seeing how the other person is reacting to the message,

---

FIGURE 7.3

"STATISTICS FOR PEOPLE INTERESTED IN NOT BECOMING STATISTICS"

A not-so-subtle fear appeal in an automobile ad.

Source: Courtesy of Volvo Cars of America.

"A barrier impact at 35 mph can generate between 80,000 and 120,000 lbs of force."

"In a 30 mph front end collision, a 165 lb man hits the windshield with a force of 3 tons."

"A 10 mph increase in impact speed from 30 to 40 mph means that 79% more energy must be absorbed."

Let a bunch of safety engineers slam enough cars into a wall and statistics like these begin to pile up. The more of them you have to work with, the safer the car you can build.

At Volvo, safety has always been a high priority.

So every year at our Technical Center in Gothenburg, Sweden, we destroy between 70 and 80 Volvos in crash tests. And the statistics we've gathered over the years have helped us make the kinds of innovations that have made Volvo the standard of safety for the automobile industry.

Our now famous steel "safety cage," for instance, surrounds the passenger compartment of a Volvo and is designed to keep it from

© 1984 Volvo of America Corporation.

crumpling during a collision. Every weld in it is strong enough to support the weight of the entire car.

At either end of a Volvo is a built-in safety zone. It's especially designed *to* crumple in order to absorb some of the energy forces of a collision instead of passing them along to the occupants.

To make sure you have protection on all sides in a Volvo, we've placed tubular, steel anti-intrusion bars in all doors.

Even our steering column is designed to collapse upon impact and our laminated windshield is designed to remain intact.

Of course no car can protect you in a crash unless you're wearing the safety innovation that became standard equipment in Volvos back in 1959: the three point safety belt. (Statistics show that fifty percent of the deaths due to road accidents could be avoided if drivers and passengers were wearing them.) So if you're interested in not becoming a highway statistic, take a precaution the next time you take to the highway.

Be sure to fasten your safety belt.

And incidentally, it might be a good idea to be sure it's fastened to a Volvo.

VOLVO
A car you can believe in.

so there is less chance of miscommunication. Radio, television, magazines, newspapers, and signs are **indirect channels** of mass communication. Telephones provide a channel for more personal communications than other types of media because the tone of voice is heard, but telephone communication is still not as clear as face to face.

Channels can also be categorized as social channels or advocate or expert channels. **Social channels** consist of friends, neighbors, and family members. Because of familiarity and proximity, these channels are most likely to involve face-to-face contacts. **Advocate or expert channels** (e.g., experts in a field, salespeople, or people with a cause) are more likely to contact receivers through letters, speeches, or less direct forms of communication.

Noise

Noise is any interference in the communication process that prevents the message from being heard correctly, and it can occur at any point in the process. The sender may send out confusing messages, the channel may be distorted, or the receiver may be distracted.

There are two types of noise: external and internal. **External noise** comes from the environment. An airplane overhead, the hot blinding sun, a howling wind, or lightning are all examples of external noise. Notice that in communication noise includes more than just sounds, as the sun and lightning illustrate. **Internal noise** occurs in the sender's and receiver's minds. They are thinking about something else during the communication—their minds are not on the conversation taking place. Daydreaming during a class lecture or thinking about a family member at work instead of listening to coworkers discuss the copy machine's breakdown are examples of internal noise. Often internal noise occurs when a word or allusion in the current conversation reminds us of something else. Discussing a menu for an awards banquet might trigger thoughts about what to cook for dinner that night at home.

There is more noise today than ever before. Because of all the noise, advertisers are having a difficult time getting customers to notice their messages. On the home front, spouses may wonder if their mates are listening to them when the television is blaring in the background. In today's sped-up world, too many conflicting messages are vying for everyone's attention.

Feedback/Response

In systems terminology, feedback is the return to the input of a part of the output in the form of information. An equally appropriate but simpler definition of feedback is the response process between sender and receiver. Feedback may take a variety of forms. It closes the loop in the communications flow and lets the sender know how the intended message was decoded and received. Feedback begins when one hears or observes what is being said, stores or responds to the information, and listens for the next message. For example, if Joseph gives Alison a compliment and she says "thank you," her response provides feedback. Joseph's message was heard accurately and acknowledged.

Feedback provides a control mechanism for the accuracy of communication. By the recipient's response, the sender can tell if the message was communicated effectively. If Alison bursts into tears, obviously Joseph's compliment was not phrased correctly or received correctly. If he values their relationship, he will restate his comment and try to straighten things out. The advantage of face-to-face conversations is that the feedback is immediate.

Setting

As mentioned in Chapter 2, the greater environment in which individuals and families live has a significant effect on the way they manage. The **setting,** or physical surroundings, is where management messages are communicated. Some settings, such as a church or a boardroom, are more formal than others. Communications should be appropriate for the setting. Public speakers check out the setting before their speech so they can match their speaking voice and microphone volume to the room size and potential audience.

The design of homes, offices, and campuses communicates to the user the type of relationships that will occur in that setting. A campus with winding walkways, fountains, and botanical gardens has a different atmosphere than a campus consisting of high-rise concrete buildings. Indoor lighting and color affect communication. Warm colors, such as red and orange, and bright lights tend to accelerate talking whereas cool colors such as soft blue and green and low lights tend to subdue communication.

The arrangement of furniture and use of plants and art also affect communication. Sofas and chairs with tables, lamps, and plants provide a comfortable homelike atmosphere conducive to personal conversations. For this reason marriage and family therapists' offices have homelike furniture, lamps, and plants to relax clients. If their clients include children, they will have toys and magazines suitable for different age groups. In contrast, row on row of metal tables and chairs, such as those found in a school cafeteria or an unemployment office, create an institutional atmosphere that is not conducive to quiet personal conversations. Even clothing is part of the setting. Research has shown that the style of clothing therapists wear will enhance or detract from their relationship with clients (Heitmeyer & Goldsmith, 1990).

COMMUNICATION CONFLICTS

Many potential communication conflicts and problems can be avoided by applying the general principles already presented on noise, setting, feedback, channels, and messages. But, in addition, certain situations and audiences deserve special attention. This section examines the potential communication conflicts that can occur within families and across cultures.

In Families

In general, the goal of communication is to provide understanding that leads to desired actions. In some cases, however, communication fails and conflict results. **Conflict** is a state of disagreement or disharmony. In poor communication, there is a message struggle or conflict between the sender and the receiver. If survival of the relationship is the ultimate goal, this conflict can pose a definite threat. Negotiations to remedy the conflict are known as **conflict resolution.** The sender, receiver, or another person can initiate conflict resolution.

Conflict is particularly common in families because of the intimate, ongoing nature of the relationships. Family members know each other so well that they notice nonverbal communications (e.g., a raised eyebrow, a strained voice) that strangers would be likely to miss. Hence, conflict is more on the surface and less readily hidden in families. The emotional intensity of family relationships is generally much greater than in small groups, so family communication problems tend to have more serious and painful implications (Sieburg, 1985). Although information should flow easily among family members, sometimes it stagnates and conflict between family members goes on for years.

The number of possible interactions also contributes to communication conflicts in families. Figure 7.4 shows how adding a second child to a family increases the number of interactions. As the number of interactions increases, family members may succumb to interaction fatigue. Because the family system is part of the larger environment, interaction fatigue may also develop at work and affect the family at home or develop at home and spill over into work. Kanter (1977) observed that employees who experience interaction fatigue at work may withdraw from personal contact at home.

Researchers (Liberman et al., 1980, p. 90) have identified several common destructive messages and tactics that characterize ineffective communication within families:

◆ Ordering turns the interaction into a power struggle between partners or between parents and children. "You do this" and "Stop doing that" are examples of ordering.

◆ Threatening is similar to ordering, but it goes further. It can lead to passivity or despair.

◆ Moralizing sends a message of guilt or moral inferiority or suggests that the other person needs guidance or direction. "You should" messages are examples of moralizing.

◆ Providing solutions occurs when words sound like a question as in "Why don't you," but really indicate superiority or a kind of parental guidance.

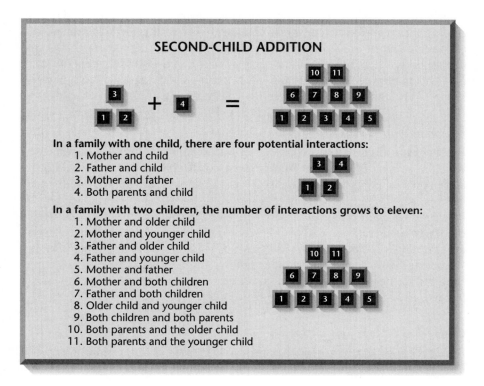

SECOND-CHILD ADDITION

In a family with one child, there are four potential interactions:
1. Mother and child
2. Father and child
3. Mother and father
4. Both parents and child

In a family with two children, the number of interactions grows to eleven:
1. Mother and older child
2. Mother and younger child
3. Father and older child
4. Father and younger child
5. Mother and father
6. Mother and both children
7. Father and both children
8. Older child and younger child
9. Both children and both parents
10. Both parents and the older child
11. Both parents and the younger child

FIGURE 7.4

Potential Interactions in a Family of Four

Source: P. Siegel, "Baby–Hunger Again," *Self,* August 1990, p. 137.

- Lecturing is a more forceful way of providing solutions. You are told what to do or are told you always do things wrong.

- Criticizing can mar relationships and lead to lower self-esteem and dependency in the criticized person.

- Ridiculing generates resistance and resentment. It involves biting and hurtful phrases such as "You're talking like an idiot" or "You're such a mess."

- Analyzing occurs when one person tells another how he or she should think and act. Analyzers are often amateur psychologists who generate anger by invading others' privacy and questioning their motivations, with comments like "You think you know what you are doing, but you don't." Often analyzers are wrong, however.

- Interrogating is used to gain information by relentless questioning. "You're not telling the truth, are you?" is an example of an interrogating question.

- Withdrawing is a way to end conversations. The person may say she or he is tired and going to bed. The "silent treatment" is another tactic.

Do these messages and tactics sound familiar? They should because they are very common. If they are used too frequently, they can impede effective communication and damage relationships. Being able to recognize these tactics helps the recipient understand the sender better. Possibly, the message is not conveying the real problem. The real problem may be with the sender or with the relationship between the sender and the receiver. For example, Luciano L'Abate and Tamar Harel suggest that "relationships that cannot become intimate emotionally may make contact with each other through sporadic and sudden ambushes, uproars, upsets, and conflicts over performance and/or production" (1993, p. 243).

Conversely, the Marital Communication Inventory (Bievenue, 1978) has identified behaviors that indicate satisfying marital communication. They include pleasant mealtime conversations, avoidance of the silent treatment, discussions of work and interests with each other, avoiding saying things that irritate each other, and communicating affection and regard. In general, communication between husbands and wives is most satisfying when both partners feel they are understood and when they agree on essential points.

Interpersonal Conflicts

Interpersonal conflicts are actions by one person that interfere in some way with the actions of another. **Destructive conflicts** are a specific type of interpersonal conflict involving direct verbal attacks on another individual. Yelling, screaming, abuse, attacks on self-esteem, and words leading to breakups are characteristics of destructive conflicts. Conversely, **constructive conflicts** focus on the issue or the problem rather than on the other person's deficits. This type of conflict can open up issues and lead to deeper relationships, clarification, and better understanding of the other person. Thus, not all conflicts are negative. Sometimes conflict is necessary to resolve points of difference, clear the air, or relieve tension.

Gender and Communication

Researchers generally accept that men and women communicate differently, both verbally and nonverbally. As Deborah Tannen, a sociolinguistics professor at Georgetown University and the author of *You Just Don't Understand,* points out, men talk far more than women, especially in public. Men speak more at meetings, in the classroom, and in mixed groups at work.

Women tend to interrogate or question more than men do. Psychiatrist Aaron Beck (1988) points out that wives tend to believe that their marriage is working as long as they and their husbands are talking about it. Conversely, men may think the marriage is not working if they have to talk about it constantly. Generally, women are more comfortable talking about personal matters with family and friends than men are.

According to Tannen, men and women also differ in the way they express their troubles and the way they seek out information. Women resent "men's tendency to offer solutions to problems, men complain about women's refusal to take action to solve the problems they complain about" (1990, pp. 51–52). Men want to solve problems and move on, whereas women hesitate and seek other people's opinions to gain as much information as they can before moving toward a solution. This is one of the reasons women make up the majority of the audience for talk shows. They enjoy considering all the angles to a situation or issue. Men sometimes feel women go to such excess talking over situations that they seem to enjoy wallowing in a problem. Men move to solutions quickly because they derive pleasure from fixing things. Fixing things "reinforces their feeling of being in control, self-sufficient, and able to dominate the world of objects" (1990, p. 70).

Women are more likely than men to ask directions and accept information from others. The classic example is of men driving around lost rather than stopping and asking directions. Men are also more likely to try to get the "best" parking space in a shopping center. At the root of both of these behaviors is concern about status, hierarchy, and connections. According to Tannen, boys as young as age three are using words in their conversations with peers that show they want to be a leader, to be first, and to be best whereas girls of the same age are more interested in getting along with friends and understanding their feelings and opinions. For example, girls are more likely to say "let's" and "we" in their conversations. Boys' conversations are filled with orders, such as "Get up" or "Give it to me," and ridicule, such as "You're a dope" (Beck, 1988, p. 82). Boys are more inclined than girls to threaten, boast, and argue.

Tannen contends that men and women have different but equally valid communication styles. Problems arise when men and women talk to each other and expect a certain kind of response. Because of gender differences in conversation, a woman will not always get the response she desires from men and vice versa. Tannen concludes:

> The biggest mistake people can make is believing there is one right way to listen, to talk, to have a conversation—or a relationship. Nothing hurts more than being told your intentions are bad when you know they are good, or being told you are doing something wrong when you know you're doing it your way. (1990, pp. 297–298)

Tannen's observations have implications for family dynamics and workplace management. As women move into positions of authority, these gender differences in conversation will require greater understanding from both men and women. The solution is not to change styles so everyone speaks alike, but to understand and appreciate the various forms of communication. The realistic approach is to "learn how to interpret each others' messages and explain your own in a way your partner can understand and accept" (1990, p. 297).

Not everyone agrees that men and women have different conversational styles. Certainly, there are individual men and women who do not fit the generalities presented here. Nevertheless, the bulk of communication research supports the contention that conversational styles do differ by gender and that these differences are evidenced as early as the preschool years.

Across Cultures

Just as communication conflicts may occur between men and women, communication conflicts may arise between cultures. These mistakes stem from the failure to understand values, decision patterns, symbols, and spoken and nonverbal languages of other cultures. For example, as companies have expanded internationally, many glaring errors have occurred in product names and packaging. What is appropriate in one country may not be in another. For example:

◆ The car slogan "Body by Fisher" becomes "Corpse by Fisher" in Flemish.

◆ "Come alive with Pepsi" comes out "Pepsi brings your ancestors back from the grave" in Chinese and "Come alive out of the grave" in German.

These examples illustrate problems in translating words. Nonverbal differences between cultures are more subtle. A friendly gesture in one culture may be insulting in another. Manners and etiquette vary around the world. Here are some examples of rude behavior in other cultures:

◆ Pointing at people, in Japan

◆ Eating with your left hand, in some Arab countries

◆ Sitting where people can see the soles of your shoes, in certain cultures

Anthropologist Edward T. Hall has studied how people vary across cultures in communicating trust, warmth, and respect. In his book, *The Silent Language,* he pointed out that "what people do is frequently more important than what they say" (1959, p. 24).

Even the amount of time spent socializing with friends and family varies by culture. The typical American spends 16.3 hours socializing each week compared to 7.5 hours for the typical Japanese (Blinder, 1991).

Also varying is the underlying message. For example, Americans are deal oriented, impatient, and competitive. But, an advertiser wishing to appeal to a Japanese audience would avoid saying:

◆ "Be the first in your neighborhood to own such and such." Japanese do not like to be out of step with their neighbors.

◆ "New, free . . . no strings attached." The average Japanese honors stability rather than "newness" and would be suspicious of something that is given away for free.

The correct social space between people also varies across cultures and by relationships within cultures. Figure 7.5 shows the four distance zones common in the United States. Intimate distance in the United States is less than 18 inches; typically, few people enter this space. Personal space is between 1 1/2 to 4 feet. Americans like to have this amount of personal space around their

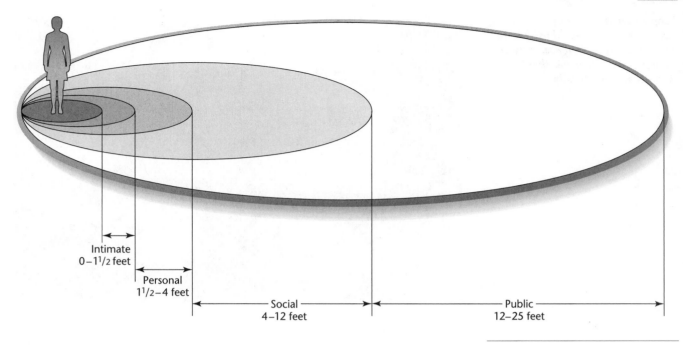

FIGURE 7.5
The Four Distance Zones

bodies; culture dictates that this should not be invaded by strangers. But in some countries, hugs, slaps on the back, and even spitting on the ground near the feet are meant to convey trust and connection (Adams, 1998). In the United States, business tends to be conducted within the social zone of 4 to 7 feet. To visualize this distance, think about the distance between salesclerks and their customers (remember that salesclerks often stand behind counters). In Latin America and the Middle East, people tend to get closer. A businessperson from the United States confronted with this behavior abroad may back away, giving the impression of being cold and unfriendly. According to Hall (1959, p. 209), Latin Americans cannot talk comfortably with one another unless they are very close to the distance that evokes either sexual or hostile feelings in a North American.

Besides language and gestures, symbols are interpreted differently across cultures. Colors, flower arrangements, and numbers all communicate in different ways across cultures. In certain countries, purple is associated with royalty or death, and yellow-green with spring and fertility. However, in Malaysia, green symbolizes the danger and death in the jungle. When a water recreation company in Malaysia used a green corporate symbol, their promotional campaign failed. Flowers can represent death, infidelity, loyalty, or love depending on the type of flower, the occasion, the color, and the country. The number 13 is considered unlucky in the United States—many people will not fly on Friday the thirteenth and most hotels do not have a floor numbered 13. In Europe, thirteenth floors are common.

As the United States and Canada become more involved in exports, international business, and worldwide communications, and as Europe becomes more unified, an awareness of cultural differences and similarities will become more important. Also, the new focus on the dynamics of family diversity and multiculturalism worldwide have renewed interest in cross-cultural communication and cross-group communication. The next section explores communication within small groups.

People's sense of appropriate distance zones are affected by culture. These men from Florence, Italy are standing closer together than American men typically would.

COMMUNICATION IN SMALL GROUPS

One characteristic of all groups is that they share a common goal or purpose. Families are a type of small group joined together by ties of affection and kinship. But there are many other kinds of small groups as well. People get together to solve school, community, work, or environmental problems, for fellowship or support, and for individual and family growth. Once a group has decided on its main goals or purposes, it is ready to proceed.

Groups vary in size, but research indicates that effective group size ranges from 3 to 13 with the ideal size being 5 (Hybels & Weaver, 1989). Larger groups may divide into smaller task force groups or committees to solve problems or to take charge of an issue or fund-raising drive. Groups are too large when some people do not have an opportunity to participate or speak. If this continues to happen, smaller groups are needed. Conversely, groups can become too small or stagnant. When nothing new is contributed time after time, then perhaps a new group should be formed or members added.

Group Discussions and Cohesion

When a group becomes stagnant or cannot find a project that members consider interesting, then it should try brainstorming. In **brainstorming** all group members suggest ideas—no matter how seemingly ridiculous or strange. Afterward, the group examines each idea separately to see if it has merit. Brainstorming is a good way to get the creative juices flowing and introduce some energy into the group.

Once a project has been agreed upon, the group should seek out information. Group members should find out how others have initiated similar ideas or programs. Many times a project or program is phrased as a question; for example, how can a group help homeless families in the community? How can a fourth grade class participate in Earth Day?

After the questions have been discussed, the next stage is to move toward solutions. Groups will discuss and discard many unworkable or unaffordable solutions before they arrive at one or two that group members can agree upon. Next a plan will be initiated. If necessary, an unworkable plan will be thrown out and a new plan developed. Eventually, the group will have to determine which plans are working and whether the group should move on to other projects.

Several factors contribute to group cohesion: the size of the group, the goal achievement orientation, the status and resources of the group, the degree to which members depend on the group for need satisfaction, and the demands or pressures under which the members operate. Too large a group will decrease group cohesion. Successfully achieving a goal will spur the group on to new challenges. For example, a successful fund-raising drive for a new town library may lead to another community fund-raising effort.

In summary, communication is the key to whether groups will function smoothly or not. Families and other types of small groups cannot be successfully managed without some degree of open communication. What needs to be done and who needs to do it should be clearly communicated and negotiated. Closed or poor communication will undermine the family's or the group's cohesiveness and future progress.

INFORMATION AND COMMUNICATION TECHNOLOGY

Much of the previous discussion has focused on group dynamics and communication problems. But, people do not always interact with each other directly; often they interact through machines such as computers, televisions, telephones, and radio. How attentive an individual is to these forms of communication depends on the message, the messenger, and the channel. In addition, different types of media affect different senses. Print media, such as newspapers and magazines, usually affect vision only. The inclusion of perfume samples in magazines affects our sense of smell. Television is multisensory in that it affects both vision and hearing.

One of the greatest technological changes of the nineteenth and twentieth centuries has been the switch from face-to-face conversations to less personal forms of communication. This transformation began in 1876 with the first telephone (patented by a voice teacher, Alexander Graham Bell) and continues today with fax machines, e-mail, and the Internet.

New technologies can help various populations stay more connected and secure. For example:

> Ardith Hammond, 70 years old, living alone in her St. Louis home after having her hip and knee replaced, often worried that she would fall and be unable to get up. "No one would know for days," she says. She didn't want to ask her son or his wife to call every day. So she worked out a routine with a neighbor in which they would turn off their porch lights at the same time nightly as a signal that they were OK, but the neighbor lost interest. Then Ms. Hammond discovered a source of reassurance: technology. She subscribes for $1 a day to a computer telephone service, TelAsure, that dials her twice daily, greets her by name with a recording and asks her to confirm, by pushing buttons on her phone. If she doesn't answer as scheduled, the service alerts family or friends. Does getting called by a computer seem cold? "No," Ms. Hammond says, "where else can you get love and reassurance for $1 a day?" (Schellenbarger, 1999, B1)

Information Overload and Habitual Decision Making

As consumers, individuals are constantly bombarded with information. Some of this information is **passively acquired**, such as through billboards, e-mail, airplane messages, and loudspeakers at K-marts, meaning that the consumer does not seek out the information. Other information is **actively acquired**, meaning that the consumer actively looks for it; for example, scanning fashion advertisements in magazines or actively listening to television commercials.

The degree of effort expended on the information search and the amount of exposure to information vary by person, product, and issue. For example, consumers often react to information (e.g., store displays, advertisements) with **low involvement**, meaning that they tend not to think much about it and may find their attention wandering. In **habitual decision making**, choices are made out of habit without any additional information search. Decisions are made with little conscious effort. This allows the consumer to devote real effort and thought to important decisions requiring more careful scrutiny.

Information overload refers to that uncomfortable state when individuals are exposed to too much information in too short a time—so much that they can not process the information. Rather than ignoring information as one does in low involvement, the person feels overwhelmed by it. Figure 7.6 shows the growth in the number of people using e-mail.

An offshoot of information overload is **information anxiety**, which is the gap between what individuals think they understand and what they actually do understand. Thus, information anxiety refers to the space between data and knowledge. Richard Wurman, author of *Information Anxiety*, observes that people used to have to make a conscious decision to seek information, but now technology permits information to be transmitted without the desire—or often the permission—of the receiver. Adding to the information explosion is the proliferation of communications technology. To deal with information overload, Wurman advises people to accept that they don't

FIGURE 7.6
Growth of E-mail
Source: Bransten (1997, December 8). "Executive," *The Wall Street Journal,* R8.

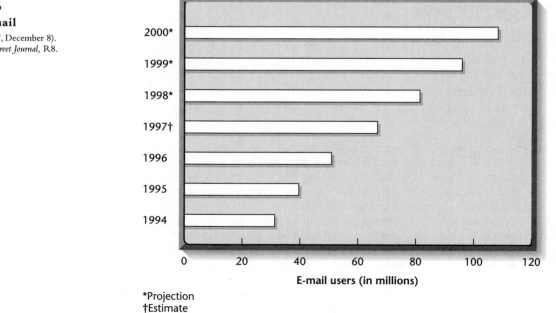

E-mail users (in millions)

*Projection
†Estimate

have to know everything about everything. He recommends that they focus on what matters most.

Computers and the Human Capacity to Process Information

Information that was once stored in people's heads and in books and file cabinets is now being put into digital form on computers. Once this information is stored in a computer's memory, it can be manipulated and accessed over phone lines, transmitted by satellite, and accessed by many different users.

Borrowing computer terminology, the amount of information the human central nervous system can process has been compared to the amount of information a computer can process. It has been estimated that individuals can manage at most seven bits of information (e.g., differentiated sounds, visual stimuli, or recognizable nuances of emotion or thought) at any one time and that the shortest time it takes to discriminate between one set of bits and another is about 1/18 of a second (Csikszentmihalyi, 1990). On the basis of these figures, humans can process at most 126 bits of information per second or 7,560 per minute. In practical terms, this means that an individual cannot process what three people are saying to him or her simultaneously and absorb all the nonverbal cues. These are all estimates since the exact limit of humans' conscious ability to process information is unknown. Nevertheless, it is known that an individual's interest in the message and the message giver influences how much is processed and retained. According to a University of Chicago researcher, Mihaly Csikszentmihalyi, "the mark of a person who is in control of consciousness is the ability to focus attention at will, to be oblivious to distractions, to concentrate for as long as it takes to achieve a goal, and not longer. And the person who can do this usually enjoys the normal course of everyday life" (1990, p. 31).

The Role of the Home and the Individual

As the preceding quotation illustrates, individuals make choices about what to concentrate on and what to ignore. In part, these are conscious decisions by an individual or family about which technologies they will adopt. In the future, more technology-assisted activities will take place in the home, including shopping, investing, banking, and working. Computers have already made it possible for many people to work at home.

Faith Popcorn, a predictor of trends, noted that **cocooning** (the desire to remain at home as a place of coziness, control, peace, insulation, and protection) is already being facilitated by technology such as videocassette recorders and microwave ovens. In many respects, the improved home-based technologies should increase family time spent in the home. Children who miss classes due to illness will be able to tune into their classroom and keep up with their classmates. The increase in home-based technologies are a boon for the elderly, disabled individuals, and others less mobile than the general population, as the previous story about Ardith Hammond illustrated.

Along with these benefits, the innovations in communication technology have some drawbacks. Cost is an obvious problem. New technologies are expensive and may increase the gap between the haves and have-nots in society. Privacy is another issue. As more information is recorded and exchanged, more is known about an individual's buying habits and personal communications. More legislation will be needed to establish ground rules on who will have access to data and under what conditions. Families will have to make decisions about access to data and use of technology as well. Parents will have to decide what technology to adopt and what technology to let children access.

Individuals and families will also have to make decisions about managing information. Theodore Leavitt argues that discrimination is necessary in the use of information and data. Unfortunately, he says, as information becomes more abundant, the less meaning it seems to yield. He draws the analogy that "the greater the variety of good food consumed at a meal, the less you appreciate each dish. The louder the noise, the less clear the message" (1991, p. 6).

Electronic Resources

www.fcc.gov/

As the chapter pointed out, there is more and more unwanted communication. In the United States, the Federal Trade Commission's (FTC) privacy Web site (**www.ftc/privacy**) provides advice on how to stop the spread of personal information and tells you how to remove your name from direct marketing mailing lists. Since it is estimated that the average person receives 34 pounds of junk mail a year, this could be a time-saver for you and a cost-saver for companies who are wasting not only their advertising dollars but also countless trees. In addition, there are numerous Web sites that help consumers reduce the amount of **spam** (unsolicited commercial e-mail, or, in other words,

Internet junk mail) they receive. Each year, the FTC reports on the top dozen spam scams at **www.ftc.gov/opa/1998/9807/dozen.htm**. The Federal Communications Commission can be reached at **www.fcc.gov**. The FCC is actively trying to monitor the Internet.

Since the topic of communication includes all forms of information, there are innumerable business and organizational Web sites that fit this subject. General Web sites such as Yahoo! at **www.yahoo.com** and GeoCities at **www.geocities.com** can yield information on nearly any area of interest.

Summary

Effective managers are effective communicators and it is impossible to manage without communicating. Communication serves as a linkage between the various steps in the management process. Communication can be verbal or nonverbal. Appearance, clothing, facial expressions, gestures, and posture communicate along with words.

Communication skills can be improved through study and application. Listening is an important management skill. Hearing other people's needs and being able to express one's own is the basis of human communication. Communication is satisfying when individuals feel that they are understood and that they understand others.

Five main components exchanged between senders and receivers make up the total communication environment: message, channels, noise, feedback, and setting. Communication conflicts can arise from any of these components or from a combination of them. Family communication differs from other types in its emotional intensity and ongoing nature. Because of these characteristics, communication conflicts in families can be particularly painful and harmful. Destructive messages and tactics such as ridiculing, ordering, or threatening can be harmful to family relationships.

According to Deborah Tannen and other researchers, men and women have different but equally valid conversational styles.

Communication and communication technology are never stagnant. The modes, the messages, and the means are always changing. Information overload is becoming an increasing problem because of these changes. Individuals are constantly being bombarded by messages, some of which are expected (actively acquired information) while others are unanticipated or unwelcome (passively acquired information). There is a limit to how much information humans can consciously process. Future research will provide more insight into the ability to process information and the ways computers can assist further in accessing and storing information. Already computers and other forms of technology and the speed of information have altered the traditional functioning of the home. Since every communication advance has its pluses and minuses, individuals and families must weigh the costs and the benefits.

Key Terms

abstract symbols	artifacts	conflict
actively acquired information	brainstorming	conflict resolution
	channel	constructive conflicts
advocate or expert channels	cocooning	critical listening
	communication	decoding

destination
destructive conflicts
empathetic listening
empathy
encoding
external noise
habitual decision
  making
I-messages
indirect channels
information anxiety
information overload

interference
internal noise
interpersonal conflicts
low involvement
message
message construction
message content
noise
nonverbal symbols
passively acquired
  information
proxemics

receiving
reflective listening
responses
sending
setting
social channels
source
spam
symbols
verbal symbols
visible symbols
You-messages

Review Questions

1. Why is effective listening important?

2. Change the following You-messages into I-messages: "You never clean the apartment." "You never put gasoline in the car." "You always leave everything to the last minute. Why don't you do something on time for a change?"

3. List the destructive communication styles or tactics used in families. Which do you think is the biggest problem? Why?

4. Do you agree with Theodore Leavitt's statement that the more information you are exposed to, the less meaning it seems to have? Explain.

5. Many doors in the brain seem to open onto memories. For example, a whiff of cinnamon may unleash memories of your childhood kitchen. Likewise, gesturing may open a door to a word or a memory especially one with a spatial (high, low, or wide) or movement connotation (here or there). When someone is looking for the right word that connotes motion, for example, hands may help. Do you gesture often? What sorts of gestures do you make? How do members of your family gesture?

References

Adams, D. (1998, December 23). When holding hands help clinch the deal. *Tallahassee Democrat*, 10E.

Beck, A. (1988). *Love is never enough*. New York: Harper & Row.

Begley, S. (1998, November 2). Living hand to mouth. *Newsweek*, 69.

Bievenue, M. (1978). *A counselor's guide to accompany a marital communications inventory*. Saluda, NC: Family Life.

Blinder, A. (1991, July 22). Time is not on America's side. *Business Week*, 12.

Csikzentmihalyi, M. (1990). *Flow: The psychology of optimal experience*. New York: Harper & Row.

Drucker, P. (1977). *People and performance*. New York: Harper College Press, 262–263.

Hall, E. T. (1959). *The silent language*. Greenwich, CT: Fawcett.

Heitmeyer, J. & Goldsmith, E. (1990). Attire as an influence on the perceptions of counselors' characteristics. *Perceptual and Motor Skills, 70*, 923–929.

Hybels, S. & Weaver, R. (1989). *Communicating effectively* (2nd ed.). New York: Random House.

Kanter, R. (1977). *Work and family in the United States: A critical review and agenda for research and policy*. New York: Russell Sage Foundation.

L'Abate, L. & Harel, T. (1993). Deriving, developing, and expanding competence from resource exchange theory. In U. Foa, J. Converse, K. Tornblom, & E. Foa (Eds.), *Resource theory: Explorations and applications*. San Diego: Academic Press, 233–269.

Leavitt, T. (1991). *Thinking about management*. New York: Free Press.

Liberman, R., Wheeler, E., de Visser, L., Kuehnel, J., & Kuehnel, T. (1980). *Handbook of marital therapy*. New York: Plenum Press, 90.

Mehrabian, A. (1981). *Silent messages: Implicit communication of emotions and attitudes* (2nd ed.). Belmont, CA: Wadsworth, 76–77.

Popcorn, F. (1991). *The Popcorn report: Faith Popcorn on the future of your company, your world, your life*. New York: Doubleday.

Robbins, S. P. (1989). *Organizational behavior* (4th ed.). Englewood Cliffs, NJ: Prentice-Hall, 267.

Schellenbarger, S. (1999, April 21). Work and family. *The Wall Street Journal*, B1.

Sieberg, E. (1985). *Family communication*. New York: Gardner Press.

Tannen, D. (1990). *You just don't understand*. New York: Ballentine Books.

Williams, F. (1997, Spring). Divorce decisions: Information and roles for the family and consumer scientist. *Journal of Family and Consumer Sciences*, 59–61, 65.

Wurman, R. (1990). *Information anxiety*. New York: Doubleday.

part 3

Management Applications

CHAPTER 8
MANAGING HUMAN RESOURCES

CHAPTER 9
MANAGING TIME

CHAPTER 10
MANAGING WORK AND FAMILY

CHAPTER 11
MANAGING STRESS AND FATIGUE

CHAPTER 12
MANAGING ENVIRONMENTAL RESOURCES

CHAPTER 13
MANAGING FINANCES

chapter **8**

Managing Human Resources

MAIN TOPICS

POPULATION SHIFTS: MEASURING HUMAN RESOURCES
POPULATION TERMS AND TRENDS
POPULATION AGE AND COMPOSITION
HOUSEHOLDS AND FAMILIES

THE NATURE OF CHANGE
MOBILITY
MANAGING CHANGE

MEETING INDIVIDUAL, FAMILY, AND SOCIETAL NEEDS
DUAL-EARNER AND DUAL-CAREER COUPLES
CHILDREN AND CHILD CARE
ELDERLY, ELDER CARE, AND AGING
THE HOMELESS
INDIVIDUALS WITH DISABILITIES
SINGLE-PARENT AND BLENDED FAMILIES
POVERTY AND LOW-INCOME FAMILIES

Did you know that…?

...Spain has the lowest fertility rate in the world.

...Iowa has the highest percentage of centenarians.

> Do what you can to show you care about other people,
> and you will make our world a better place.
>
> —*Rosalynn Carter*

IN 1900, 1.5 BILLION people inhabited the earth and most of them lived in large cities in Western Europe. Now, the world population is 6 billion and the greatest concentration of people is in Asia. China is the most populous country followed next by India and the United States (see Figure 8.1). Soaring birthrates and sharp population growth have occurred in Ethiopia, Pakistan, and Nigeria. In these countries, the government is having trouble feeding, housing, and educating all the children (Hager, 1998). Although there is a great worldwide gain in population, certain countries are losing population, for example, Russia, Italy, and Germany.

Most of the world's population is concentrated in cities, causing a stress on natural resources and support systems. Many of these cities are called gateway cities because they are located on borders (between countries) or on coastlines. Immigrants often arrive in gateway cities, establish families and businesses, and do not venture further into the interior of countries. Currently, half of the Earth's population lives in cities. As noted in Chapter 1, by 2050, this is predicted to rise to 75 percent.

FIGURE 8.1
**The Ten Most
Populous Countries**

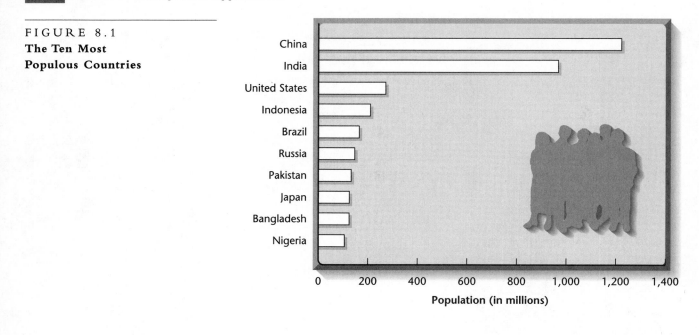

Population (in millions)

Managing human resources in a finite environment is the subject of this chapter. As Chapter 4 explained, resources can be classified as human and material. Human resources include all the capabilities (skills, talents, and abilities) that contribute to achieving goals and responding to demands. Health, vitality, and intelligence are examples of human resources. Human resources can be divided into three main categories:

1. *Cognitive:* knowledge, intelligence, and reasoning
2. *Affective:* emotions and feelings
3. *Psychomotor:* muscular activity associated with mental processes and the ability to do physical work

Many tasks require skills from two or more of these categories. For example, typing requires cognitive and psychomotor skills. Parenting requires all three types of human resources.

Human capital, which was also discussed in Chapter 4, is the sum total of an individual's human resources. Education, training, and practice increase human resources. Developing human capital in oneself and in others is one of the most important management processes covered in this book. Ultimately, the strength of a nation depends on its stock of human resources—the collective ability of its citizens to solve problems creatively and to meet society's demands.

Today, people find themselves immersed in a tangle of worldwide changes in the economy, society, institutions, education, the labor market, and individual lifestyles. Individual concerns must now be viewed in the context of the entire world. The family, as the basic unit of society, has weathered many storms, but many challenges lie ahead.

This chapter goes beyond the theoretical into the realm of population statistics and the practical management problems of certain groups. One important population change is the rapid increase in the percentage of minority groups in the United States. Another significant trend is the maturation of our society. The baby boom generation—children born between 1946 and 1964—has grown up and established family and community roots, cared for teenage children and elderly parents, moved into management positions at work, and bought homes. Another important aspect of the maturation trend is the growth of the over-65 age group, the "graying of America," although it should be pointed out that the whole world is aging, with the trend most pronounced in developed countries. Elderly people today are healthier, more active, and more affluent than those of previous generations.

The twenty-first century promises to be more responsible about the environment and more respectful of individual age and cultural differences than the previous century. To express this concept of respect for cultural diversity, Alvin Toffler, author of *Future Shock*, coined the word *demassification*, which means breaking away from mass society where everyone must be the same. He says we're moving to a "mosaic society" where diversity is recognized and fostered.

This chapter begins Part 3, the management applications section of the book. It starts by examining population trends relevant to the study of individuals and families, including an exploration of how these changes take place. Although management concepts are relevant to all individuals and families, the remainder of this chapter focuses on the particular management needs and concerns of the following populations: dual-earner and dual-career families, children, the elderly, the homeless, individuals with disabilities, single parents, blended families, and poor and low-income families.

POPULATION SHIFTS: MEASURING HUMAN RESOURCES

Certain human resources, such as trust, love, and caring, are difficult to measure, but numbers of people and population shifts can be quantified. The primary source of U.S. population data is the national census, which is taken every 10 years by the Bureau of the Census. The census attempts to count every person living in this country and to collect vital information about family size and community and housing conditions. Based on this information, the government can determine population shifts and formulate policy.

The first census was taken in 1790 when George Washington was president. At that time, 3.9 million people were counted. As Figure 8.1 shows, currently the U.S. population is 271 million. All statistics in this chapter come from the U.S. Bureau of the Census unless otherwise noted.

281 - Mau

Population Terms and Trends

Demography is the study of the characteristics of human populations, that is, their size, growth, distribution, density, movement, and other vital statistics. **Demographics** are data used to describe populations or subgroups. Population figures are affected by three main factors: births, deaths, and immigration.

The birthrate is technically termed fertility. The **fertility rate** is the yearly number of births per 1,000 women of child-bearing age. The technical term for death is **mortality. Immigration** refers to the number of people who enter and settle in a county where they are not native. Without a decided increase in immigration and birthrate, populations can stagnate or decrease. In recent years, the states with the largest population gains have been Texas, Florida, and California.

Birthrates

Worldwide, fertility rates are plummeting. Today, women on average have just half the number of children they did in 1972. In 61 countries, fertility rates are now at or below replacement levels. This does not mean the worldwide population will fall in the immediate future, however, because people are living longer. Globally, the average life span has jumped from 49.5 years in 1972 to 63 years. In addition, as mentioned earlier, the low fertility rate of industrialized nations is offset to some degree by less developed countries, who often have high fertility rates.

Spain has the world's lowest fertility rate. Spanish women have an average 1.15 children in their lifetimes. Unless Spain's immigration rate increases dramatically, it is very likely that Spain's population will shrink over the next 50 years (Longman, 1999). Spain's low fertility rate is explained, in part, by the lack of work and a lackluster economy during the late 1990s. This may turn around.

Over the years, high unemployment and poor economies have been shown to have direct impact on fertility rates in industrialized countries. For example, during the Great Depression of the 1930s, the United States had a low fertility rate. Prior to that, especially from 1880 to 1900, the U.S. population growth rose from the influx of immigrants from Europe.

The U.S. birthrate rose sharply again after World War II. Unlike earlier population increases, which were caused largely by immigration, this growth was primarily due to the births of millions of children. This "baby boom," which ended in 1964, was followed by a period of slow growth that did not pick up again until the late 1980s and early 1990s. In 1988, 3.9 million babies were born—the highest number since 1964. Termed the "baby boomlet," these babies are the children of the "baby boomers."

A distinct trend of the last decade has been the rise in the number of women between the ages of 30 and 35 who have given birth for the first time. One-third of the nation's births are now experienced by women over 30.

A documented trend is a decrease in teen pregnancies. Since 1990, the teen birth rate in the United States has dropped almost 10 percent.

In families, the birth of a baby brings about many changes in time management and consumption patterns. Parents suddenly find themselves the prime targets of advertisers offering a wide array of baby products. Their grocery carts are filled with products they never purchased before: diapers, infant formula, baby food, toys, and baby shampoo. The home environment also changes as baby care equipment is added: strollers, cribs, swings, high chairs, and playpens. Storage of such items and the safety of the child become special concerns.

Beginning in 1892, over 12 million immigrants, mostly from Europe, came through Ellis Island in New York City's harbor.

In response to demographic changes, the marketplace transforms as it tries to keep up with consumer demand. Note the impact on consumption that the baby boom generation has had in the past and will have in the future (Figure 8.2). As noted earlier, the baby boomers have reached middle age—some are already well into it—and are earning income, paying taxes, traveling, and owning material goods. The number of married couples without children is rising due to empty-nest baby-boom households and by delayed childbearing by younger couples.

Mortality

At the other end of the life cycle, about two million people die each year in the United States. Overall, the death rate has been decreasing for several reasons:

- Declining rates of heart disease
- Increases in life expectancy
- Better nutrition and fitness and less smoking
- Improvements in preventive health care
- Improvements in infant mortality rates

Worldwide, the infant mortality rate in developing countries dropped by more than 50 percent from 1900 to 1996 (Vo, 1998).

Between 1970 and 1980, the average American's life expectancy went up three years (Wilkie, 1986). Another rise in average life expectancy happened between 1980 and 2000. In the 1990s, life expectancy was about 71.5 years for men and 78.5 years for women. According to the Census Bureau, the chances of living to 100 are growing. Since 1990, the number of Americans

FIGURE 8.2

The Baby Boom Tidal Wave Moves through Life

Source: Taeuber, C. (1979, June). "A changing America," *American Demographics,* pp. 9–15. Reprinted with permission.

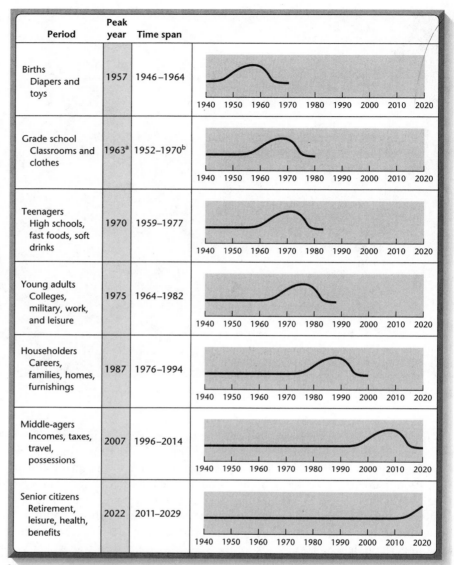

[a] "Peak year" represents the year at which the highest number of persons entered each stage; 1963 reflects the year with the highest number of first graders.
[b] "Time span" represents the years during which all baby boomers entered the stage; the first baby boomer entered grade school in 1952; the last baby boomers entered in 1970.

reaching that age has nearly doubled to 70,000. Eighty percent are women. Iowa has the highest percentage of centenarians ("Chances," 1999).

Immigration

Beginning in 2019, the net increase in the U.S. population from immigration is expected to be higher than the increase from natural births. Thus, the nation's ethnic and racial makeup will continue to shift. During the 1980s, about 570,000 legal immigrants and 200,000 illegal immigrants entered the United States each year.

In the 1990s, one in five new Americans joined the nation through naturalization (gaining U.S. citizenship). "Asians are more likely than immigrants from other regions to become U.S. citizens, as are better educated people and those who have lived here longer" (Mogelonsky, 1997, p. 45). In 1995, the

United States gained four million new citizens from birth and 1.1 million through naturalization.

Population Age and Composition

As a nation, the United States is growing older. Currently, the nation's population is the oldest it has ever been. The median age is 36.5 in the year 2000, up from approximately 32.3 years in 1990. After a slow decline from 27 million in 1988 to 24 million in 1995 and 1996, the college-age population (ages 18 to 24) began a steady rise, which will continue through 2005.

Gender ratios will also change. Between 1994 and 2000, there were more males than females in their twenties. Among those over age 75, women outnumber men by nearly two to one.

Minorities

Minority groups are the fastest growing segment of the U.S. population. One in three Americans is a member of a minority group. On average, minority populations are younger than other Americans and therefore have higher birthrates, and immigration is also increasing their numbers.

By U.S. Census Bureau definition, minority groups include American Indians, Alaskan natives, Asians, Pacific Islanders, blacks, and Hispanics. It is important to note, however, that minority populations include many subgroups. For example, there are 505 federally recognized Indian tribes in the United States, including 197 Alaska native village groups. Language, religion, culture, and economic conditions differ significantly among these various tribes and subgroups. Furthermore, the term *minority* is sometimes a misnomer because a group defined by the Census Bureau as a minority may actually be a majority group in some parts of the country. For example, in Honolulu, the majority of residents are of Asian descent and in San Antonio, Texas, the residents are 52 percent Hispanic.

Blacks (or African Americans) are the largest minority group in the United States. African Americans constitute 13.3 percent of the U.S. population, and one-third live in one of five states: Georgia, Florida, Texas, California, or New York. The average African-American family has 3.5 members. According to a Census Bureau report, 57 percent of black children are living with one parent who has never married compared with 21 percent of white children and 32 percent of Hispanic children.

Hispanics constitute 12.5 percent of the U.S. population. Most Hispanics in the United States are of Mexican origin; the remainder are of Puerto Rican, Central and South American, Cuban, or Spanish heritage. Mexican Americans are the fastest-growing group among Hispanics. The majority of Hispanics live in Arizona, New Mexico, Florida, Texas, and California.

Asian Americans constitute 3 to 4 percent of the nation's population. They are overwhelmingly urban. The Census Bureau's category of Asian and Pacific Islanders covers 17 countries. Most of the Asians entering the United States come from Indochina: Vietnam, Laos, and Kampuchea (formerly Cambodia). There are also sizable groups with Japanese, Korean, Chinese, Taiwanese, and Filipino heritage.

Of the three largest minority groups, Asian Americans are the most highly educated. Thirty-four percent of Asian Americans have college degrees compared to 20 percent for the overall American population, 11 percent for African Americans, and 8.6 percent for Hispanics. Full-time college participation rates among young adults is rising for all groups, especially blacks (Crispell, 1997).

Households and Families

The number of households is increasing in the United States, but the number of persons per household is decreasing. Household change parallels population change. Household growth in the 1990s was fastest in Nevada, especially for 25- to 34-year-olds. Four other fast-growing states also saw gains in householders aged 25 to 35: Arizona, Georgia, Utah, and Delaware. Nearly three in five households have no children, and this trend toward smaller families is expected to continue. One reason for the decline in household size is lower fertility. Another reason is the increase in the number of elderly persons. Male-headed households are expected to be the fastest-growing type of household through the year 2000.

Single-parent households represent 25 percent of all family households. Nonfamily households, consisting of two or more unrelated persons living together, are also on the rise.

Marital Status

Young people are waiting longer to get married, and the marriage rate itself is decreasing. According to the Census Bureau, men and women are delaying marriage, with the median age of first marriages rising. Historically, 90 percent of Americans have married at some time in their lives, but that rate is declining. The divorce rate is also declining after having reached a peak in 1984. The highest divorce rate is for couples in their twenties, and divorced people are waiting longer to remarry.

THE NATURE OF CHANGE

Roosevelt Thomas Jr., in his book *Redefining Diversity*, provides an interesting perspective on change within American society. He says that, increasingly, we see America's strength in its diversity—a mixture of colors and creeds bringing their different backgrounds to a common endeavor. Yet, he says diversity is not confined to race and gender, rather, it applies to intangibles such as ideas, outlooks, and procedures.

Change means to cause to be different, to alter, or to transform. A change can be categorized into two general types, internal and external. **Internal change** originates within the family. Births, marriages, divorces, and deaths are all examples of internal changes. In contrast, **external change** is fostered by society or the outer environment. Tornadoes and recessions are examples of external changes. An individual or a family may experience internal and external changes at the same time.

The ability to cope with change is called **adaptability**. Adaptability is an example of a human resource that everyone has, but in different quantities. People's temperaments and usual ways of reacting (rapid versus slow) to new situations affect their response to change. The actual circumstances, such as whether an event is expected or unexpected, will also influence the response.

Because of these personality, behavioral, and situational factors, each person approaches change differently.

Most changes occur gradually over a period of time. This transition period can be helpful because it allows individuals to take stock of the situation and consider possible alternatives. Effective managers take advantage of transition time to think through a situation and make plans to deal with it. Changing one's job or residence involves transition time. This is discussed in the next section, which explores moving as an example of change.

Mobility

Nearly all individuals and families have to cope with the problems and decisions associated with moving. The technical term for changing residences is **mobility.** Statistics on mobility trends are surprising. According to a survey conducted by the U.S. Census Bureau, the typical householder moves every five or six years. The average distance moved is six miles, and renters move more than homeowners.

Mobility has several major effects on individual and family behavior. First, it affects finances. When people move, they spend money on household furnishings, moving services, and utility deposits. They may use the services of realtors and mortgage companies. Second, moving can be a stressor. Many household services must be changed and rescheduled when relocating—telephone, electric, water, and mail service, to name just a few. Children may have to change schools. Parents may change jobs. Third, moving affects individual or family morale. Moves may be disruptive or present opportunities. They may mark the end of valued relationships or signify a fresh beginning or both.

The general trend in the twentieth century was the movement from rural areas to suburbs and cities. The largest city in the United States is Los Angeles, with nearly 10 million people, followed by New York City, then Chicago. In the last census, 80 percent of Americans lived in cities that claimed 16 percent of the country's land (Edmondson, 1997).

Certain states have more mobile populations than others. Nevada has the fewest natives, followed by Florida. At the other end of the spectrum is Pennsylvania, where 80 percent of residents were born in the state.

Managing Change

Managing change is inherently messy.

> It is always complicated. It invariably involves a massive array of sharply conflicting demands. Despite the best-laid plans, things never happen in exactly the right order— and in fact, few things rarely turn out exactly right the first time around. . . . Change means new patterns of power, influence, and control . . . and that's why it's so hard. Change is far too important, pervasive, and complicated a phenomenon to be taken for granted. Every manager may be aware of it; that doesn't mean he or she knows how to handle it. (Nadler, 1998, pp. 3, 5, 11)

Each family and each organization is a complex social system. There are several components (adopted from Nadler, 1998), that need coordinating including:

◆ The work or the task.

◆ The people.

◆ The formal organization. The structure, the processes, the systems, and the identity (i.e., the Clark family or the Tech Systems Company).

◆ The informal organization. The collective values, attitudes, beliefs, communication and lines of influence, and accepted standards of behavior.

The challenge is to sustain momentum, to move forward. Sustaining any profound change process requires a fundamental shift in thinking. Participants need to understand the nature of growth processes (forces that aid efforts) and how to catalyze them. But, they also need to understand the forces and challenges that impede progress, and to develop workable strategies for dealing with these challenges (Senge, 1999, p. 10).

In an article in *Marriage and Family Review,* Kathryn Rettig observed:

> Management is a thoughtful adaptation to the opportunities and demands of life. It involves problem-solving and decision-making, as well as carrying out actions to implement decisions. The consciousness of the deliberations that occur prior to decisions about how to use resources and the controlled implementation of decisions in order to reach valued-goals will distinguish management from other adaptive responses. The need for conscious problem-solving and decision-making is created because of changes that are wanted by individuals and families (proactive management) or because internal and/or environmental changes occur that require different responses (reactive management). (1993, p. 191)

The management problems and decisions inherent in change must be addressed because households and families are living in an increasingly complex web of internal and external changes. For example, many functions that were once the domain of households and families, such as child rearing and meal preparation, are now purchased to some degree outside the home—from child care centers, restaurants, and grocery stores. How many people today bake bread from scratch? A hundred years ago, the average household would have devoted many hours a week to this activity.

Before the 1950s, the study of management emphasized internal household processes. Today, management encompasses the interaction of the inside and outside activities and the lives of individuals and families within the greater environment. For example, a working mother may purchase a precooked dinner at the store and add a salad or a dessert at home. Thus, she is combining home-prepared with store-prepared food—an increasingly common method of meal preparation. Although this combined effort might seem to imply less need for resource management skills, in actuality these skills are more necessary than ever because coordinating inside and outside activities takes time, effort, and planning. As more people, services, and environments become involved and time becomes tighter, more complex problem solving and decision implementation are necessary.

MEETING INDIVIDUAL, FAMILY, AND SOCIETAL NEEDS

Along with all the external changes that are occurring, the family itself has become a more diverse institution. Collectively, single-person households, single-parent families, and two-income families outnumber traditional one-income families with both parents sharing a residence. Even though the family is taking on diverse forms, it still remains an important stabilizing force in the rapidly changing, often chaotic outside world. The word *family* implies a safe harbor, a place to come home to, and people who care.

The remainder of this chapter explores the special management needs of certain populations. This information is based on aggregate data, so specific individuals and families may not fit the generalizations given.

Dual-Earner and Dual-Career Families

Perhaps no phenomenon has had a greater effect on the fabric of American society than the increasing number of women in the labor force. The influx of women into the workplace has altered the way families live, the products they buy, and the way they spend their time. In 1990, there were approximately 33 million **dual-income** or **dual-earner** households, where both spouses had income-producing jobs, up from 26 million in 1980 (Spain & Nock, 1984). Dual-income households on average have more money than single-income households. However, many dual-income families need both incomes to maintain a minimum standard of living. The idea that dual-earner families are affluent and use the extra money for luxuries and vacations is far from reality: many of these families are earning just enough to make ends meet. The term *dual income* needs to be distinguished from *dual career*. In **dual-career** families, not only do both spouses work outside the home, but both have made a long-term commitment to a planned series of jobs leading toward an ultimate career goal. Not everyone who is working thinks of himself or herself as a career person.

Dual-earner families usually report that they are happy and satisfied (Runyon & Stewart, 1987). Family resources, such as spousal or partner support and sensitivity, play a key role in the satisfaction levels of dual-earner families (Gilbert, 1993). Tahira Hira (1987) found that satisfied dual-earner families (versus dissatisfied dual-earner families) have more money in their savings accounts, save larger proportions of their annual income, and have smaller monthly debt payments. Such families are also less likely to have an auto loan or outstanding balances on their credit cards. Having two incomes also reduces the fear of unemployment since the family will have one income to fall back on in case of a recession or company downsizing.

Dual-earner families are also better educated, more mobile, better spenders, and more likely to own their own home than one-earner families (Rubin & Riney, 1994). The lifestyle is not perfect, however. Dual-earner families also report that they have less leisure time and less time for children and friends. Their pace of life is quicker. Jobs requiring extensive travel and numerous transfers increase stress for dual-income families, especially those with children. Spouses may enter into long-distance commuting relations, live halfway between two cities, or relocate for short periods of time to take advantage of a career opportunity (Gilbert, 1993). Dual-earner couples try to adjust their work or vacation schedules to maximize their time together.

Dual-earner couples may face various management problems, including difficulty setting priorities and saying "no," budgeting, and making joint financial decisions. Dividing household tasks equitably so that everyone is content may also be a problem. Open communication and dealing with changes before events become overwhelming will help dual-income families keep ahead of their workloads.

The overriding management problem that dual-income families face is how to handle both their jobs and family responsibilities. Lucia Gilbert advises young adults who want to marry and work to plan ahead, which "means thinking about expectations for yourself and a future spouse and communicating these early on in serious relationships" (1993, p. 75). The next three chapters on managing time, work and family, and stress and fatigue will provide additional insight into the management problems of dual-earner families.

Children and Child Care

Child care is a broad issue with numerous ramifications for families and for society in general. Providing financial support for children is a form of child care. So is physical and emotional care. As both parents increasingly are working outside the home, child care is becoming a more and more critical issue for many families. Families manage child care in several ways: one parent may stay home, or neighbors, relatives, and friends may provide care. Family day-care homes and child care centers in the community or at the parents' work sites are other options. If children are school age, parents may enroll them in before-school and after-school programs and summer camp. Parents often combine several of these methods. A Yale University study found that many parents prefer home-based care for infants and toddlers and child care centers for older children (Cheskis-Gold, 1988).

Young families with children often have more management problems than other types of families. For example, studies show repeatedly that families with young children have the most time management problems because young children require so many hours of physical and nurturant care. These problems may be exacerbated in young families where parents may be completing their own education or launching their careers at the same time that they are having children. Employers, realizing that working parents need support, offer a wide range of child care options including resource-and-referral services and on-site child care.

In the 1990s, women aged 30 and older accounted for 33 percent of the total births. Older mothers tend to be highly educated, to be members of high-income families, and to have professional occupations (Langer, 1985). Their careers are well underway before they have their first child. Furthermore, in such families many financial arrangements and assignments of household tasks have been settled before children come along. When the children arrive, the division of labor will have to be renegotiated, but at least initial patterns have been established.

One controversial aspect of child care and human capital development is the small amount of time American children spend in school compared to children in other countries (see Figure 8.3). The issue is controversial because some parents and educators believe our schools should continue to be closed in the summer, a tradition that originally was intended to allow children time off to help on the family farm. Less than 2 percent of American families live on farms now, however, and educators and parents think it is time for a change. The relatively low number of days spent in school may have implications for societal well-being if U.S. children are receiving less formal education than children in other industrialized nations. Some U.S. school districts are experimenting with longer school days and fewer vacation days or split schedules. From the perspective of time management and family relations, the fact

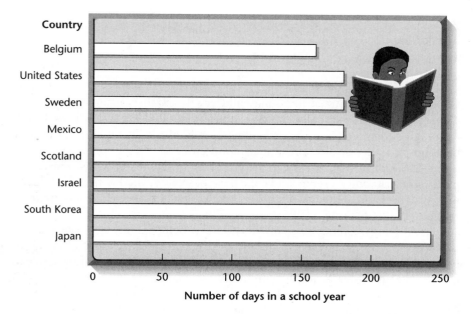

FIGURE 8.3
Number of Days in School
Source: Adapted from National Association of Elementary School Principals, 1615 Duke Street, Alexandria, VA 22314.

that children's school days and vacations often do not coincide with parents' work schedules makes it difficult for families to spend time together or to offer secure home-based child care. Any changes that are made in the timing and length of childrens' school days should focus first on what is best for the children and their education given today's global society and future workforce demands.

Parents are interested not only in the quantity of time they spend with their children, but also in the quality of time they have with them. Enjoying each stage of development, being present for school plays and activities, and encouraging children toward independent and fulfilling lives are common parental goals. Former First Lady Barbara Bush spoke at the Wellesley College commencement in 1990 and told the graduates:

> For several years, you've had impressed upon you the importance to your career of dedication and hard work. This is true, but as important as your obligations as a doctor, lawyer or business leader will be, you are a human being first and those human connections—with spouses, with children, with friends—are the most important investments you will ever make. At the end of your life, you will never regret not having passed one more test, not winning one more verdict or not closing one more deal. You will regret time not spent with a husband, a friend, a child or a parent. . . . Fathers and mothers, if you have children . . . they must come first. You must read to your children, you must hug your children, you must love your children. Your success as a family . . . our success as a society . . . depends not on what happens at the White House, but on what happens inside your house.

Although parenting and family life are rewarding, no matter how hard parents try they often experience problems with children, particularly during the teen years. Drugs, alcohol, child neglect, and abuse are examples of adolescent and family problems.

The roots of abusive parental behavior across all periods of childhood can be traced to five broad areas (Azar & Siegal, 1990):

1. Maladapative interpretive processes, including unrealistic expectations of children, poor problem solving, and negative interpretations of child behavior

2. Poor parenting strategies

3. Poor impulse control

4. Poor stress coping

5. Poor social skills

Child abuse is not limited to young children. Researchers estimate that 22 to 47 percent of abuse cases involve abused adolescents (Pagelow, 1989). Although parental stress is associated with child abuse, it is important to note that most parents do not abuse their children even when experiencing stress (Azar & Siegal, 1990). Stress can lead to other problems, however. For example, infant irritability, crying, and colic have been associated with parental feelings of depression, helplessness, anger, and exhaustion, as well as with marital tension (Wilkie & Ames, 1986).

Developing better management skills can help parents deal with stress. Well-developed management skills bring a sense of mastery and a feeling of being in control. A parent who has developed these skills will find it easier to form strategies, solve problems, and adjust to change.

An interesting trend related to child care is the growing number of 18- to 24-year-olds who are moving back home. Active parenting starts at birth, but it is becoming less clear when active parenting ends. More young adults are living with their parents now than at any time since the Great Depression of the 1930s (Riche, 1990).

Through an analysis of the Census Bureau's Survey of Income and Program Participation, demographers found that most people aged 20 or 21 remain in their parents' home, while most people aged 22 to 24 have left. Women leave home earlier than men (Riche, 1990). Demographers also found that many young adults move in and out of their parents' homes and that men are more likely to return after age 25. The main reasons children return home are economic difficulties, marital failure, prolonged education, and job market insecurity. According to Riche (1990), the return of adult children to their parents' homes is called **boomeranging**; it is regarded as a rational response to changes in the society and economy.

Elderly, Elder Care, and Aging

One in four U.S. households is involved in the daily care of an elderly parent. As many as 40 percent of Americans who care for their parents also have dependent children. Middle-aged Americans, who care for both their children and their elderly parents are called the "sandwich generation." Although the need for child care has been widely publicized, the need for elder care is less well known. The number of available caregivers is dwindling because many adult women are in the workforce and the number of children in families has decreased. The majority of caregivers are daughters, wives, or other females (see Figure 8.4).

The caregiver role can bring with it a mixture of joy, guilt, service demands, and emotional and financial burdens. The difficulty of the role depends on many factors: the health of the elderly dependent person, the personalities of the elderly person and caregiver, their mutual resources, and the social support they receive from relatives and community groups. Caregiving can take place gradually over several years and require only a few phone calls or visits, or it can be a 20-year daily commitment to the physical and emotional care of another. From a management viewpoint, the need for caregiving may develop

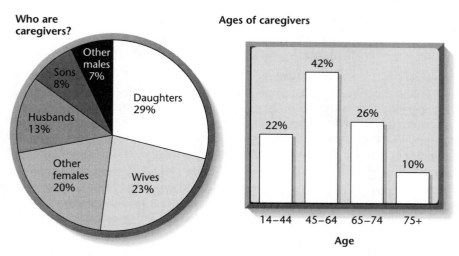

Who are caregivers?

Ages of caregivers

FIGURE 8.4
Majority of Caregivers to the Elderly Are Middle-Aged Women

Source: National Center for Health Services Research, (1989).

slowly, allowing a family to adjust and plan for it, or it can arise from a sudden crisis that completely depletes the family's emotional and financial reserves. A midnight phone call from 1,000 miles away about a stroke or an accident is a crisis that requires an immediate response.

From a management perspective, caregiving for dependent elderly can precipitate a number of resource allocation problems. Time, energy, and money may all be strained in caregiving situations. In addition, caregivers have to maintain a sense of humor and be sensitive to the elderly person's desire for independence and dignity. Compounding these needs is the difficulty elderly parents have in letting a child take charge. The adult child may also feel awkward managing her or his parents' affairs and avoid this task until the health or safety of the parent requires it.

Understanding the aging process and the needs of the elderly can help caregivers perform their role more effectively. The aging process has three aspects: physical or biological, social, and psychological. To date, most gerontological research (**gerontology** is the scientific study of the aging process) has focused on the physical aspects, but the others are important as well. Aging involves both growth and decline (Cavanaugh, 1990). Most elderly people are self-reliant and require little or no caregiving. Many maintain active, independent lives well into their nineties. Health, wealth, and attitude have a lot to do with the degree of independence they can maintain. The idea that elderly people are often depressed is a myth; in fact, evidence suggests that depression decreases in old age (Cavanaugh, 1990). Many more myths about aging will be exposed as scientists learn more about the aging process. Even what constitutes old age is being questioned as researchers learn more about the elderly. Commonly, old age is defined as beginning at age 65, but this is an arbitrary boundary because chronological age is a poor indicator of a person's social, economic, physical, or mental condition.

One of the most important life changes people make is adjusting to retirement. Regardless of how much workers plan and anticipate this change in work role, it can still be difficult because jobs give people a routine, companionship, and a sense of accomplishment. Retired people can feel aimless and useless. Without roles, people feel a sense of loss and a lack of direction, and the loss of work routine can be disconcerting. Declining health exacerbates the problem. To counteract this feeling of loss and provide extra income, many "retirees" take on part-time or seasonal work. If they are self-employed, they may never retire.

In many companies, human resource departments assist older employees in the transition period to retirement and help middle-aged workers find home health care for their aged parents. According to an article in *American Demographics:*

> Home health care is an important concern of middle-aged workers. Most providers help elderly relatives preserve their independence. Helpers are usually women, but men are likely to shop and pay the bills. Out-of-pocket spending accounts for one-third of this $21 billion industry, and caregivers also face a time crunch. As the population ages, employers will offer eldercare benefits to attract and keep good workers. (Braus, 1994, p. 38)

In addition, some companies offer retirement planning programs; others allow employees to work part-time to ease into retirement. Many retirees choose to do volunteer work. Others travel or go back to school to finish degrees or to take continuing education courses.

As with all age groups, older adults have varying lifestyles and, therefore, differing management needs. Too little time may be as much a problem as too much time. Other resources that may be affected in the later years include the emotional, health, human energy, and financial resources of both caregivers and elder dependents. Money is a particular problem for many older persons because income may not keep pace with inflation and increases in health care costs. The elderly most likely to be poor are those who rely solely on Social Security for their incomes. About 26 percent of the elderly population fall into this category, and the majority are women (United Way Strategic Institute, 1989). Increasingly, aging is considered within the context of total well-being, which requires a careful balance between emotional and physical health. This balance becomes more precarious as we age. Besides reexamining changing perceptions of aging, people need to enhance their mental and physical vitality by focusing on active strategies that can extend life and improve the quality of life. These management strategies (adapted from *Healthy Living,* 1999) may include:

◆ Thinking over what is essential and what is controllable

◆ Identifying strategies to help prevent health problems or poor quality of life

◆ Applying a proactive approach to diet, attitude, and activity levels

◆ Using practical techniques to incorporate improved lifestyle changes in everyday life

In addition to valuing independence, older adults value comfort, security, convenience, and a sense of purpose. They want to eliminate problems, receive personal service, and feel good about themselves. Airline and car advertisers appealing to the elder market may emphasize comfort over speed and appearance. As more of our population falls into the elderly category, businesses and service providers will have to adjust their approaches to better meet the needs of older adults.

The Homeless

Although from the media coverage one would assume homelessness is a new societal problem, it is not. There have been homeless people in the United States since colonial times. What is new is that they are more numerous than ever before and more visible (Baum & Burnes, 1993). There are more homeless now in the United States than at any time since the Great Depression of the 1930s (Lamar, 1988). Researchers predict that by the year 2003, the U.S. homeless population will reach 18 million (United Way Strategic Institute, 1989). The majority of the homeless are single males, although the number of homeless women and children is growing (United Way Strategic Institute, 1989). Families constitute an estimated 23 to 30 percent of the homeless population (Martin, 1991; Burt & Cohen, 1989). The number of homeless varies because homelessness can range from a temporary situation of a few days to a chronic situation of several years. Chronic homelessness is linked to poverty. However, it is important to distinguish between the homeless and the poor. According to Baum and Burnes (1993):

> Homelessness is more than being poor and without a home; homelessness is a condition of disengagement from ordinary society—from family, friends, neighborhood, church, community. Perhaps most importantly, it is a loss of self. A homeless man we know told us, "The first time, I felt like this is not me. I felt less than a man." Homelessness means being disconnected from all of the support systems that usually provide help in times of crisis; it means being without structure; it means being alone. (p. 23)

The rise in the number of homeless people is not limited to the United States—it is a worldwide problem. In 1999, thousands of people were displaced from their homes in Kosovo. Thus, homelessness can affect individuals or families or, on a wider scale, nations.

One study of the educational plight of homeless children in England found that changing schools constantly threatened educational stability, hindered educational progress, caused emotional insecurity, and promoted educational disadvantage (Lines, 1992). The study recommended that liaisons be formed between schools and homeless families so that the transition to each new setting is easier.

The growing rate of poverty, the declining supply of low-income housing, and a rise in drug addiction and alcoholism have all contributed to the rise in homelessness (Rubin, Wright, & DeVine, 1992). An estimated 65 to 85 percent of all homeless adults in the United States suffer from one or more of the

Families displaced from their homes in Kosovo.

disabling conditions of alcoholism, drug addiction, and mental illness, complicated by serious medical problems (Baum & Burnes, 1993). Other factors affecting the rise in the number of homeless in the United States include cutbacks in public housing, mental health, and social programs.

Families become homeless for numerous reasons, including fire, eviction because of failure to pay rent, eviction because of unfit housing, cuts in assistance programs, scarcity of low-income housing, unemployment, and internal strife in countries. Homelessness can be devastating for children who are suffering a loss of education and security. Naturally, the length of time spent in a homeless condition will affect the severity of these effects. Children in homeless families are less likely to have successful peer interactions, a factor that may also lead to poorer attitudes toward school (Winborne & Murray, 1992).

The response to the growing number of homeless has been sporadic. Recommended measures that could aid the homeless include day care for children, setting goals and providing support with job training, low- or no-cost mental health and medical clinics, public policy changes, transitional housing for those leaving shelters, better coordination of social services, and innovative programs to provide low-income housing. The 1992 report of the Federal Task Force on Homelessness and Severe Mental Illness suggested the following services: needs assessment, diagnosis and treatment planning, counseling and supportive therapy, hospitalization and medication management, 24-hour crisis response services, habilitation and social skills training, and improved hospital discharge procedures. As has been pointed out, the homeless problem cannot be separated from other problems, including poverty, unemployment, and mental illness. Each of these problems needs to be tackled if the number of homeless is to be reduced. A study reported in the *American Journal of Psychiatry* found that high levels of mental distress are common to all homeless persons and suggests that the focus of treatment should be on empowerment, consumerism, entitlement, community-level interventions, and closer alliances with other advocates for the homeless (Cohen & Thompson, 1992). According to another study, the major cause of family homelessness is the relative inability of heads of homeless families to function independently (Ellickson, 1990).

Some efforts are being made to help homeless families. For example, in the United States, the Stewart B. McKinney Homeless Assistance Act guarantees homeless children the right of access to an education (Eddowes & Hranitz, 1989). Besides legislation, communities, hospitals, and substance abuse treatment centers are working together to find successful ways to help the homeless. Since not all homeless persons have the same problems, an effort is being made to tailor programs and alternatives to the individual and the family.

Individuals with Disabilities

More than 43 million Americans have some type of disability (Emanoil, 1999). Slightly less than half of these have a severe impairment. A **disability** is a long-term or chronic condition medically defined as a physiological, anatomical, mental, or emotional impairment resulting from disease or illness, inherited or congenital defect, trauma, or other insult (including environmental) to mind or body (Wright, 1980). Often, the word *disability* is used as a synonym for *handicap,* but the terms are different. A **handicap** is a disadvantage, interference, or barrier to performance, opportunity, or fulfillment in any desired role in life (e.g., social, educational, vocational, familial), imposed upon the individual by limitation in function or by other problems associated with disability and/or personal characteristics in the context of the individual's environment or role (Wright, 1980). Thus, a handicap can occur as a result of disability, but a disability does not always necessitate a handicap. For example, a deaf person has a hearing disability, but she or he is not handicapped when it comes to sewing because deafness does not affect one's ability to sew. It is important to understand that disabled individuals may have certain limitations, but they can function wholly and well in many ways.

Individuals with disabilities prefer to be recognized as a person first and only secondly as a person with a partially disabling condition. Community prejudice and resistance may reduce opportunities for disabled persons. People with disabilities have been fighting for years to overcome prejudice so that they can have equal access to jobs, schools, and services.

One important aspect of home management is the ability to perform routine tasks. Persons with disabilities may face problems associated with the home, including the loss of mobility, decreased strength, decreased reach, coordination impairment, one-handed use, lack of hand muscles, and visual impairment (Pickett, Arnold, & Ketterer, 1990). The hindrance or negative effect in the performance of household tasks or activities is referred to as a **functional limitation.** Wright (1980) offers five examples of functional limitations that may affect task performance:

Access to buildings is a concern of the disabled.

1. Activity restrictions due to the danger of unexpected unconsciousness

2. Inability to follow rapid or frequent changes in instruction due to slow learning

3. Restrictions in mobility due to neuromuscular impairment

4. Difficulty in interpersonal relationships associated with peculiar behavior

5. Necessity of avoiding respiratory infection or dusty conditions due to hypersensitivity reactions

As this list suggests, there is a wide range of disabilities.

A disability in a family raises several critical questions. Is the disability temporary, such as a broken arm, or long term? Are family resources adequate to handle the disability? For example, is there enough insurance to cover medical and rehabilitation costs? After an assessment has been made of the severity of the disability and the level of support and resources, a management plan needs to be formulated. In the case of permanent handicapping conditions, critical changes in the family support system and the home environment may need to be made. Ramps, lower sinks, braille markings on appliances, easier access to bathrooms and kitchens, and levers instead of doorknobs are examples of possible changes. Specific alterations depend on the needs and desires of the disabled individual. The nature and timing of the handicapping condition are also important. Was the disabling condition a shock, or did the individual and family have time to make gradual accommodations to the condition? Are adequate social, health, and public services available in the community?

As more baby boomers cross the middle-age threshold and become more at risk for heart disease and other impairments, the ranks of the disabled will grow rapidly (Waldrop, 1990). In addition, medical advances have kept many more people with disabilities alive longer than in the past. Fortunately, the public today is much more aware of disabilities, including those that are not physically apparent, such as learning problems, and is prepared to adjust to and accommodate the needs of disabled individuals. Every person, disabled or not, needs a safe, functioning environment in which to live and work.

Single-Parent and Blended Families

As has been noted throughout this text, the composition of the typical American family and household is changing. Single-parent families have special management needs. Raising children is a difficult task in itself, but raising children alone can be even more challenging. The single parent finds no relief and has no one to share ideas with or turn to for help with discipline. Reduced income is another problem most single parents must face, in part because many fathers fail to make child support payments (Kissman & Allen, 1993). Only about one-third of single mothers receive child support (Goodrich, Rampage, & Ellman, 1989). Family income in general drops sharply at the end of marriage because of the splitting up of resources, maintenance of two households, legal fees, and so forth.

Another change in the structure of the U.S. family is the increase in blended families. **Blended families,** which are also called stepfamilies or reconstituted or combined families, are new families that include children from previous relationships. They commonly result when some of the more than a million Americans who divorce each year remarry (Lauer & Lauer, 1991). *Newsweek* magazine recognized the phenomenon of blended families when it devoted a special issue to the family of the twenty-first century. An article in the issue on stepfamilies began as follows:

> The original plot goes like this: first comes love. Then comes marriage. Then comes Mary with a baby carriage. But now there's a sequel: John and Mary break up. John moves in with Sally and her two boys. Mary takes the baby Paul. A year later Mary meets Jack, who is divorced with three children. They get married. Paul, barely 2 years old, now has a mother, a father, a stepmother, a stepfather and five stepbrothers and stepsisters—as well as four sets of grandparents (biological and step) and countless aunts and uncles. And guess what? Mary's pregnant again. This may sound like an unusually complicated family tree. It's not. Some demographers predict that as many as a third of all children born in the 1980s may live with a stepparent before they are 18. (Kantrowitz & Wingert, 1990, p. 24)

In blended families, stepparents are more likely than biological parents to perceive strains on the marriage from the parenting experience. Studies show that marital satisfaction is significantly lower when both spouses bring children to the marriage (Lauer & Lauer, 1991). Generally, there is more stress, less cohesion, and less adaptability in blended families (Lauer & Lauer, 1991). According to Patricia Papernow (1993):

> The new stepfamily is also complicated by in-laws with long relationships with and concomitant loyalties to the previous spouse, which make it difficult to welcome a new adult in their children's and grandchildren's lives. Furthermore, children in stepfamilies experience biological parents and stepparents very differently. For children the stepparent may be not another nurturing adult but an intruder who threatens to disrupt their close single-parent-child relationship, thereby influencing yet another loss. Stepparents also place children in a loyalty bind: If I care about mom's new husband, am I betraying my father? Children in first-time families almost always want their original parents to stay together. (p. 49–50)

Single-parent and blended families also exhibit special strengths. Blended families succeed if they have a clear understanding of each family member's feelings and needs and if they engage in open communication. Before remarriage, it is suggested that the adults forming a combined family realize that their commitment to one another will be the base upon which their new family will be built (Kaufman, 1993). In single-parent households, the child may find that having one person make all parenting decisions leads to consistency and stability. If the original marriage involved spousal, substance, or child abuse, being a single parent could be a relief. Since circumstances vary widely, each family must be looked at individually to determine its resource management needs. There are many types of single parents, ranging from unwed teenagers to middle-aged men whose wives have left them. Single parenthood can arise from never having married, from being abandoned, widowed, or divorced, or from a single person opting for adoption.

Additionally, both single-parent and blended families must contend with various legal, social, personal, economic, and psychological issues. These family types have to contend with all sorts of small and large indignities because they live in a society built around two-parent first-marriage families. For example, a graduating senior may be allotted only two high school graduation tickets but be from a blended family with two biological parents and two step-parents and eight grandparents. Who receives the tickets in this case? In a mother-headed household, whom does the son invite to a father-son picnic? Schools and community organizations are becoming more sensitive to these issues and are putting fewer children and families in awkward positions. Laws and legislation are making it easier for new family forms to function and are providing better protection for family members.

Poverty and Low-Income Families

Poverty is the state of being poor and the inability to provide for basic needs on a consistent basis. The United States has the highest average income in the world, but also the highest percentage of what the United Nations Development Program calls human poverty, taking into account many factors, including illiteracy, among industrialized countries (Vo, 1998).

For families, poverty is defined as a family income less than half the national median. In the United States, women with children are the fastest-growing segment of the poor (United Way Strategic Institute, 1989). It is recognized that it costs less, and is more effective, to get children on the right track than to change adults (Huey, 1989). Early nutrition, health, and educational programs are positive first steps.

Poverty, like homelessness, is not necessarily a permanent state. There are gradations in income, and income may be temporarily low as a result of sudden unemployment. Low-income families may also experience seasonal variations in income. Migrant workers may have food and shelter during harvest seasons and none during other times. The poverty class (i.e., those with very low or nonexistent incomes) may include low-paid service workers, the elderly poor, illegal immigrants, and abandoned families. In addition, size of family and size of debt affect poverty status.

In the United States, a strong economy in the latter half of the 1990s meant that more of the poor were working and consuming at a higher rate. The lifestyles of many of the poor in the United States would be considered middle-class or even high-income in other countries. For example:

> Almost three-quarters of families living below the federal poverty line own at least one car, up from 64% in the mid-1980s. The percentage of poor households with washing machines has risen to 72% from 58% in 1984; with dryers, to 50% from 36%. Two out of three poor families have microwave ovens, up from one out of eight in 1984. Ninety-seven percent of poor households have color televisions, and three of four have VCRs. In 1970 only one in 50 poor people had a credit card; now, one in four does. (Cox & Alm, 1999, p. A21)

The federal government helps low-income families through a variety of programs. One way is through transfer payments such as food stamps, Aid to Families with Dependent Children, and Supplementary Security Income, all of which help the aged, blind, and/or disabled. **Transfer payments** are monies or services given for which the recipient does not directly pay. To receive these benefits, household income or assets must fall below a specified level. The welfare-to-work laws in the United States have changed many of the traditional ways of supporting the poor. More people are encouraged to work and be less dependent on the government.

The terms *poverty* and *low income* are defined not only by the government, but also by the families themselves based on previous income levels and lifestyles. The strains that result from the lack of money or assets can have negative effects on family life regardless of whether the source of the economic stressor is unemployment (Perrucci & Targ, 1988; Voydanoff & Donnelly, 1988), or recession (Elder & Caspi, 1988; Liker & Elder, 1983). According to several studies, women in particular have a difficult time with the negative effects on the quality of family life related to economic hardship (Duncan et al., 1988; Wilhem & Ridley, 1988; Rettig, Danes, & Bauer, 1993).

Planning for long-term goals can seem like a luxury. Returning to Maslow's hierarchy of needs in Chapter 1, the emphasis in helping low-income families should be placed on providing for the most basic needs first, in particular such physiological needs as food, water, and shelter. Low-income families often spend over half of their income on housing. Therefore, securing safe, affordable housing is a particular concern for low-income families. Because of the lack of adequate housing and other daily living problems, over time many very low-income families become pessimistic about the future and feel that they have little control over what their lives will bring (Wilkie, 1986). This feeling, termed **fatalism,** means that all events are thought to be shaped by fate. A belief in fatalism can lead to low expectations and a sense of hopelessness. Recognizing the possible existence and influence of this phenomenon is helpful in designing appropriate and effective aid for low-income families.

Electronic Resources

The United Nations Human Development Report, with data on life expectancy, poverty and consumption levels, and environmental conditions worldwide, can be found at **www.oup-usa.org**. The U.S. Census Bureau Web site is **www.census.gov/population/www**. National mortality statistics are available at **www.cdc.gov/nchswww/nchshome**. The Web site of the Centers for Disease Control and Prevention (**www.cdc.gov**) has worldwide health data and disease warnings. Web sites about the elderly, aging, elder care, and the disabled include:

◆ American Association of Retired Persons: **www.aarp.org/**

◆ Caregiver Alliance: **www.caregiver.org**

◆ National Aging Information Center: **www.aol.dhhs.gov/naic**

◆ Senior Law Page: **www.seniorlaw.com.80**

◆ The Sandwich Generation: **members:aol/com/sandwich-gen/index**

◆ National Alliance of the Disabled: **www.naotd.org**

◆ Worldwide Virtual Community of the Disabled: **www.linkable.org**

www.cdc.gov/

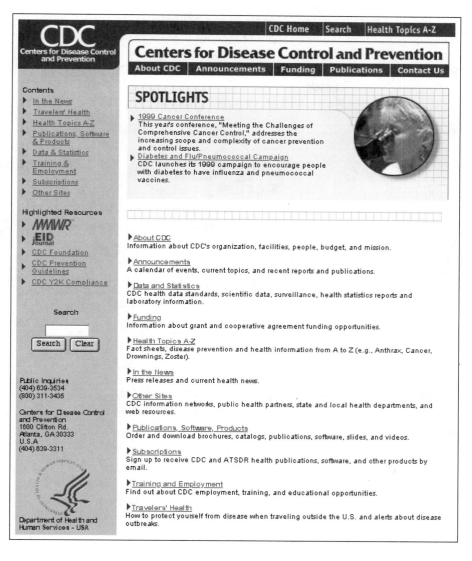

Summary

This chapter has examined special problems regarding the management of human resources. Population growth, changes in family structure, mobility, the baby boom tidal wave, and the "aging of America" were discussed. All of these changes are having an effect on family life. By understanding the nature of change, families may be able to react to it more effectively. In addition to exploring these themes, the chapter examined the management needs of specific population groups.

The U.S. population is becoming older and more diverse. If the population stays on the predicted course, there will be a larger percentage of minorities, single-parent families, blended/stepparent families, low-income families, individuals with disabilities, elderly persons, and homeless individuals and families in the future. In summary, the U.S. and the world populations are growing, and consequently, there are more human resource problems to address.

Striving for a certain quality of life is not just a theoretical construct, but a very real day-to-day concern for people. Effectively managing human resources and increasing human capital are a fundamental part of the overall study of resource management. The next chapter explores the particular problems associated with managing time.

Key Terms

adaptability
blended families
boomeranging
change
demographics
demography
disability
dual career
dual income or dual earner
external change
fatalism

fertility rate
functional limitation
gerontology
handicap
immigration
internal change
mobility
mortality
poverty
transfer payments

Review Questions

1. How has the world population changed since 1900? Where do most people live today? In the United States, what are the largest cities?

2. Worldwide, are fertility rates rising or falling? What sorts of factors influence fertility rates?

3. According to the chapter, managing change is inherently messy. Why is that?

4. What do you think are the benefits and deficits of the 180-day school year for children? Where do you stand on this issue?

5. Choose one of the groups discussed in the section "Meeting Individual, Family, and Societal Needs" and discuss their resource management needs (explain what they have or do not have and what they need).

References

Azar, S. & Siegal, B. (1990). Behavioral treatment of child abuse. *Behavior Modification, 14*(3), 230–249.

Baum, A. & Burnes, D. (1993, Spring). Facing the facts about homelessness. *Public Welfare,* 20–27, 46, 48.

Braus, P. (1994). When mom needs help. *American Demographics,* 38–46.

Burt, M. & Cohen, B. (1989). *America's homeless: Numbers, characteristics and programs that serve time.* Washington, DC: Urban Institute.

Cavanaugh, J. (1990). *Adult development and aging.* Belmont, CA: Wadsworth.

Chances. (1999, June 16). *The Wall Street Journal,* A1.

Cheskis-Gold, R. (1988, February). Child care: What parents want. *American Demographics,* 45–46.

Cohen, C. & Thompson, K. (1992). Homeless mentally ill or mentally ill homeless? *American Journal of Psychiatry, 149*(6), 816–823.

Cox, W. & Alm, R. (1999, April 6). The good times will last. *The Wall Street Journal,* A21.

Crispell, D. (1997, November). Depending on college. *American Demographics,* 39.

Duncan, S., Volk, R., & Lewis, R. (1988). The influence of financial stressors upon farm husbands and wives' well-being and family life satisfaction. In R. Marotz-Baden, C. B.

Hennon, & T. Brubaker (Eds.), *Families in rural America: Stress, adaptation and revitalization*. St. Paul, MN: National Council on Family Relations.

Eddowes, E. & Hranitz, J. (1989, October). Educating children of the homeless. *The Education Digest*, 15–17.

Edmondson, B. (1997). Where America lives. *American Demographics*, 16–17.

Elder, G. H., Jr. & Caspi, A. (1988). Economic stress in lives: Developmental perspectives. *Journal of Social Issues, 44*, 25–45.

Ellickson, R. (1990, Spring). The homeless muscle. *The Public Interest*, 45–60.

Emanoil, P. (1999, Spring). Employment policy for people with disabilities. *Human Ecology Forum*, 14.

Federal Task Force on homelessness and severe mental illness. (1992). *Outcasts on Main Street*. Washington, DC: HHS and the Interagency Council on the Homeless, 43–44.

Gilbert, L. (1993). *Two-career/one family*. Newbury Park, CA: Sage Publications.

Goodrich, T., Rampage, C., & Ellman, B. (1989). The single mother. *Family Therapy Networker, 13*, 55–56.

Hager, M. (1998, November 2). How demographic fatigue will define the population. *Newsweek*, 12.

Healthy Living. (1999, May/June). Tallahassee Memorial Health Care, 21.

Hira, T. (1987). Satisfaction with money management: Practices among dual-earner households. *Journal of Home Economics, 79*(2), 19–22.

Huey, J. (1989, April 10). The war on poverty. *Fortune*, 125–136.

Kantrowitz, B. & Wingert, P. (1990, Winter/Spring). Step by step: Who will be? *Newsweek* (Special Issue), 24–34.

Kaufman, T. S. (1993). *The combined family*. New York: Plenum Press.

Kissman, K. & Allen, J. (1993). *Single-parent families*. Newbury Park, CA: Sage Publications.

Lamar, J. (1988, October 24). The homeless: Brick by brick. *Time*, 34–38.

Langer, J. (1985, July). The new mature mothers. *American Demographics*, 29–31, 50.

Lauer, R. & Lauer, J. (1991). *The quest for intimacy*. Dubuque, Iowa: Wm. C. Brown, 570–571.

Liker, J. K. & Elder, G. H., Jr. (1993). Economic hardship in the 1930s. *American Sociological Review, 48*, 343–359.

Lines, S. (1992). Educational disadvantage in the primary school: Children living in temporary accommodation. *Support for Learning, 7*(1), 8–13.

Longman, P. (1999, March). How global aging will challenge economic well-being. *U.S. News & World Report*, 30–31.

Martin, J. (1991). The trauma of homelessness. *International Journal of Mental Health, 20*(2), 17–27.

Mogelonsky, M. (1997, March). Naturalized Americans. *American Demographics*, 45–49.

Nadler, D. (1998). *Champions of change*. San Francisco: Jossey-Bass.

Pagelow, M. (1989). The incidence and prevalence of criminal abuse of other family members. In L. Ohlin & M. Tonry (Eds.), *Family violence*. Chicago: University of Chicago Press, 263–314.

Papernow, P. L. (1993). *Becoming a stepfamily*. San Francisco: Jossey-Bass.

Perrucci, C. C. & Targ, D. B. (1988). Effects of a plant closing on marriage and family life. In P. Voydanoff & L. C. Majka (Eds.), *Families and economic distress: Coping strategies and social policy*. Newbury Park, CA: Sage Publications, 55–71.

Pickett, M., Arnold, M., & Ketterer, L. (1990). *Household equipment in residential design* (9th ed.). Prospect Heights, IL: Waveland Press, 401–402.

Rettig, K. (1993). Problem-solving and decision-making as central processes of family life: An ecological framework for family relations and family resource management. *Marriage and Family Review, 18*(3/4), 187–222.

Rettig, K., Danes, S., & Bauer, J. (1993). Gender differences in perceived family life quality among economically stressed farm families. *Resource Theory: Exploration and Applications*. Academic Press, 125.

Riche, M. (1990, May). Boomerang age. *American Demographics*, 25–30, 52–53.

Rubin, B., Wright, J., & Devine, J. (1992). Unhousing the urban poor: The Reagan legacy. Special Issue: The Reagan legacy and the American welfare state. *Journal of Sociology and Social Welfare, 19*(1), 111–147.

Rubin, R. & Riney, B. (1994). *Working wives and dual-earner families*. Westport, CT: Praeger.

Runyon, K. & Stewart, D. (1987). *Consumer behavior* (3rd ed.). Columbus, OH: Merrill, 224–227.

Senge, P. (1999). The dance of change. NY: Doubleday.

Spain, D. & Nock, S. (1984, August). Two-career couples, a portrait. *American Demographics*, 25–27, 45.

Toffler, A. (1970). *Future shock*. New York: Random House.

United Way Strategic Institute. (1989). *What lies ahead: Countdown to the 21st century* (Research Report). Alexandria, VA.

Usdansky, M. (1992, May 30). Diverse fits nation better than normal. *USA Today, 10*(181), International Edition, 2A.

U.S. Bureau of the Census. (1989). *Money, income and poverty: Status of families and persons in the United States: 1988* (Series P. 60, No. 165). Washington, DC: U.S. Government Printing Office.

U.S. Department of Commerce, Bureau of the Census. (1989 and 1990). *Statistical Abstract of the United States.* (Washington, DC: U.S. Government Printing Office).

Vo, M. (1998, November 6). A look at the world by the numbers. *The Christian Science Monitor,* 8–9.

Voydanoff, P. & Donnelly, B. W. (1988). Economic distress, family coping and quality of family life. In P. Voydanoff &

L. C. Majka (Eds.), *Families and economic distress; Coping strategies and social policy.* Newbury Park, CA: Sage Publications, 97–115.

Waldrop, J. (1990, April). From handicap to advantage. *American Demographics,* 33–35, 54.

Wilhelm, M. & Ridley, C. (1988). Unemployment induced adaptations, relationships among economic responses and individual and marital well-being. *Lifestyles: Family and Economic Issues, 9,* 5–20.

Wilkie, J. (1986). *Consumer behavior.* New York: John Wiley & Sons, 617–675.

Wilkie, C. & Ames, E. (1986). The relationship of infant cries to parental stress in the transition to parenthood. *Journal of Marriage and the Family, 48,* 545–550.

Winborne, D. & Murray, G. (1992). Address unknown: An exploration of the education and social attitudes of homeless adolescents, *High School Journal, 75*(3), 144–149.

Wright, G. (1980). *Total rehabilitation.* Boston: Little, Brown.

chapter **9**

Managing Time

MAIN TOPICS

TIME AS A RESOURCE
DISCRETIONARY VERSUS NONDISCRETIONARY TIME
PERSONAL COMPUTERS AND TIME
THE ABC METHOD OF TIME CONTROL
TIME PERCEPTIONS
PERCEPTIONS OF TIME ACROSS CULTURES
BIOLOGICAL TIME PATTERNS

QUANTITATIVE AND QUALITATIVE TIME MEASURES
DEMANDS, SEQUENCING, AND STANDARDS

Did you know that...?

... The average amount of time spent at lunch is 36 minutes.

... The average U.S. office worker sends or receives 201 messages each day.

All my possessions for a moment of time.
—*last words of Queen Elizabeth I*

DO YOU HATE waiting in lines?
Do you multitask every chance you get?
Do you check your e-mail and voicemail often?
Is your computer just too darn slow?
Do you want everything now?

Welcome to the time-stressed twenty-first century. People are feeling more determined and are working and playing harder than ever before. The computer, 24-hour television, extended stock market hours, and 24-hour toll-free lines have aided in creating this hurry up, around-the-clock environment. For example, an advertisement for CBS MarketWatch.com says it has the "tool to fuel your obsession" by "bringing you the hottest financial stories, market data in real time, and expert analysis you need to stay ahead of the market." The message is if you wait you will be behind the game. What implications does this sped-up time have for individuals and families and how are they dealing with it? This is the subject of Chapter 9.

An analysis of time begins with awareness.

Waking to the shrill clattering of an alarm clock, checking clocks and watches throughout the day, going to bed at 11 o'clock—these are all examples of how our lives are synchronized around time. The hours of the day, weekends, holidays, and seasons provide a rhythm and a framework for people's lives.

One of the recurring themes of this book is how individuals and families make choices. The management of time, a resource that everyone has in equal amount (24 hours a day), affects life choices. According to Luciano L'Abate and Tamar Harel:

> To understand how we allocate time and energies from one setting to another we need to invoke the concept of priorities. These priorities stem from definite choices we make about what is important in our lives. How important is a person, an object, or an activity to us? (1993, p. 252)

Time is a measured or measurable period. A central management concept is **time displacement,** which is concern over how time spent in one activity takes away from time spent in another activity (Mutz, Roberts, & Van Vuuren, 1993). For example, choosing to watch television rather than studying will affect the goal of academic achievement. Thus time, as a resource, is related to the fulfillment of wants, needs, and goals.

Awareness of time is an important part of the human consciousness. **Time management** is the conscious control of time to fulfill needs and achieve goals. The way time is allocated is based on an individual's values, what is important to that person. If a family values a shared dinner hour with a multicourse meal, then family members will set aside time for meal preparation and eating together. If the family values school, work, and community activities more, then activities will become their time focus, and they will eat meals in shifts. In today's time-pressured societies with so many scheduling and demand conflicts, sit-down family-style dinners are becoming increasingly rare, at least in families with older children. According to Leonard Berry, a retailing expert:

> The Norman Rockwell image of a family seated around a dinner table eating a roast beef lovingly prepared at home no longer accurately reflects America's eating habits. More likely, people are grabbing a quick restaurant meal, buying takeout food, and using the microwave oven. Restaurants now capture more than 40 cents of every dollar spent on food in the United States, up from less than 20 cents in the 1960s. Americans spend about 15 percent of their food dollar on ready-to-eat food prepared for off-premise consumption, according to FIND/SVP of New York City. And Americans are spending in the neighborhood of $1 billion a year on foods for the microwave. (1990, p. 32)

Time is a resource that can be measured in units (i.e., minutes, hours, days), but comprehending it can be difficult because individuals' perceptions and use of time affect the way they think about it. Time has been the subject

*Time-pressured families have
hurried mealtimes.*

of philosophical debate (e.g., "If no one measures time, does it still exist?" and
"Has time a beginning or an end?") and also the subject of psychological,
mathematical, and economic inquiry. In the fifth century A.D., Saint
Augustine said, "What then, is time? If no one asks me, I know what it is. If I
wish to explain it to him who asks me, I do not know." The best way to
measure time remains a subject of debate, with choices ranging from the use
of simple time diaries and complex psychographic inventories to consumer
focus groups and actual drawings of time (Kaufman & Lane, 1993). Time is
thus the most familiar of concepts, yet at the same time the most elusive.

TIME AS A RESOURCE

In economics, time is considered a resource because it is a scarce commodity
(Graham, 1981). It is saved, spent, and allocated to get something wanted. Time
has not always been thought of in this way. Some cultures, even today, challenge
the notion of thinking of time in terms of the discrete beats of mechanical linear
"clock time." Senge, in his book *The Dance of Change,* states that:

> It is important to remember that the mechanical clock was only invented five hun-
> dred years ago, in the fourteenth century. Before that, human beings did not think
> of time in constant, fixed increments that keep adding in a steady linear progres-
> sion. Today, you can almost hear the machine's wheels grinding relentlessly: sixty
> minutes to each hour, then another sixty minutes make another hour, then another
> sixty minutes makes another hour, then another, then another. . . . Nature's time is
> different. (1999, p. 57)

A resourceful person uses time effectively or imaginatively, especially in
difficult situations. Notice that unlike money, time is a nonrenewable resource
and thus might be considered the more valuable resource. In fact, money is

sometimes traded off for time, as when a busy person hires someone to clean the house or take care of the yard. As another example of the tradeoffs between time and money, a 1998 survey by the Union Bank of Switzerland used the price of a Big Mac (because it is served worldwide) as its standard of time worked. An American would work 11 minutes to earn enough money for a Big Mac; a worker in Zurich, 14 minutes; Vienna, 17 minutes; Berlin, 18 minutes; London, 20 minutes; Moscow, 2 hours; and Nairobi, 3 hours. The global average was 37 minutes.

Attitudes affect how one feels about time. For example, an article in *American Demographics* reported that:

> Feeling rushed may have more to do with one's attitudes than with one's activities. People who get more than 15 minutes of exercise a day are only half as likely as others to feel rushed, 22 percent versus 44 percent. . . . People are more likely to feel rushed if they also say they are dissatisfied with themselves, unable to do things as well as others, feel useless, or don't have much to be proud of. (Godbey & Graefe, 1993, pp. 26–27)

DISCRETIONARY VERSUS NONDISCRETIONARY TIME

Time can be categorized as discretionary or nondiscretionary. **Discretionary time** is the free time an individual can use any way she or he wants. **Nondiscretionary time** is the time that an individual cannot control totally by himself or herself. For example, class times are nondiscretionary because they are set by the school or college. Opening and closing times of banks, restaurants, post offices, and stores are also nondiscretionary. In the course of the day, nearly all people have some discretionary time when they can take breaks, use the bathroom, eat meals, and come and go between activities. Evenings and weekends generally offer the most discretionary time.

Usually, children have more discretionary time (e.g., free time, play time, sports and recreation time) than adults, but this situation may be changing. David Elkind, in his book *The Hurried Child,* makes the point that children today are overcommitted and are growing up too fast and too soon. He argues that they have too little free, unstructured, discretionary time. This lack of free time leads to stress. According to Elkind:

> Today's child has become the unwilling, unintended victim of overwhelming stress—the stress borne of rapid, bewildering social change and constantly rising expectations. The contemporary parent dwells in a pressure-cooker of competing demands, transitions, role changes, personal and professional uncertainties, over which he or she exerts slight direction. (1988, p. 3)

Discretionary time allows the individual to make choices about whom to be with and what to do. These choices are not made in a vacuum, however—an individual's time use and needs must be weighed against what others want and need. Learning time management skills can help individuals maximize their time and use it optimally. The following suggestions can help in managing both discretionary and nondiscretionary time:

- ◆ Make a daily "things to do list" or keep a calendar.
- ◆ Say "no" to requests for time that keep one from finishing projects already under way.

compromise standards

◆ Make use of the telephone and the computer whenever possible.

◆ Delegate.

◆ Keep a flexible schedule that allows for unexpected events.

◆ Ask, "Is this the best possible use of my time at this moment?"

◆ Lessen interruptions, such as unnecessary meetings, visitors, and telephone calls.

For example, regarding lessening interruptions, a family may have a rule that outsiders are discouraged from calling after 9 o'clock at night. In offices, because they are public settings, interruptions are more difficult to manage. According to one study, the average U.S. office worker sends or receives 201 messages each day. The majority of the messages are by telephone (50), e-mail (35), and voice mail (22). Other messages are received by postal mail, interoffice mail, pagers, cell phones, express mail, post-it notes, telephone message slips, and couriers or messengers (Clark, 1999). The problem with so many messages is that workers spend nearly all their time responding and receiving and have very little time left to think, write reports, and so on.

Nearly half of office workers surveyed said they had difficulty keeping up with their work and were feeling overwhelmed. The director of the study's research team said, "We found that it was very much an interrupt-driven style of work that was emerging. . . . For too many people, information is proving to be more of a burden than a resource" (Clark, 1999, R4).

Personal Computers and Time

In the United States, personal computer (PC) ownership is up, but usage of PCs is off according to a recent survey of 5,500 consumers. Arbitron NewMedia says that home penetration of PCs surged to 54 percent in 1999 from 29 percent in 1995, but the percentage of adult consumers who said they were using their PCs fell, over the same period, to 53 percent from 90 percent ("PC Usage in Homes Found to Have Dropped Sharply," 1999). The drop may be explained by the fact that many people now have computers at work and when they come home they do not want to use them. Another factor is that PCs are still hard to use, "the patience factor is wearing thin" according to the study's research director.

In the past, the introduction of printing and telephones required adjustments, and the computer is no different in this regard. Today, people in a variety of occupations feel overwhelmed, but so did the monks 500 years ago when the Gutenberg printing press brought a 20-fold increase in the number of texts they had to study. As people attempt to fit their lifestyles within the context of the information and technological explosion, experts and entrepreneurs are looking for solutions—applying the very tools that caused the data glut in a mission to help alleviate it. For example, e-mail filtering or organizing devices for computers (just as answering machines were for telephones) are possible solutions.

The ABC Method of Time Control

The pressures of modern society have led to the publication of many books suggesting ways individuals and families can improve their use of time. One of the best-known books is Alan Lakein's *How to Get Control of Your Time and Your Life,* which explains how to set short-term and long-term goals, establish

FIGURE 9.1

Chris's Thursday Schedule

This example uses Lakein's ABC priority method in which A activities are top priority, B activities are less important, and C activities are to be done if there is time.

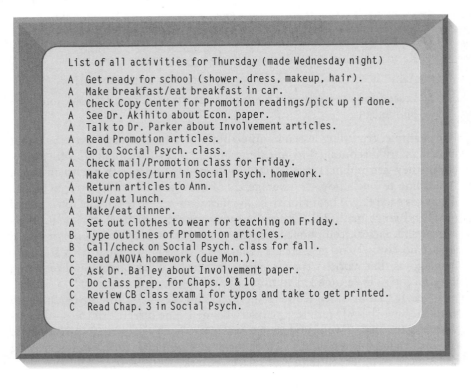

List of all activities for Thursday (made Wednesday night)

A Get ready for school (shower, dress, makeup, hair).
A Make breakfast/eat breakfast in car.
A Check Copy Center for Promotion readings/pick up if done.
A See Dr. Akihito about Econ. paper.
A Talk to Dr. Parker about Involvement articles.
A Read Promotion articles.
A Go to Social Psych. class.
A Check mail/Promotion class for Friday.
A Make copies/turn in Social Psych. homework.
A Return articles to Ann.
A Buy/eat lunch.
A Make/eat dinner.
A Set out clothes to wear for teaching on Friday.
B Type outlines of Promotion articles.
B Call/check on Social Psych. class for fall.
C Read ANOVA homework (due Mon.).
C Ask Dr. Bailey about Involvement paper.
C Do class prep. for Chaps. 9 & 10
C Review CB class exam 1 for typos and take to get printed.
C Read Chap. 3 in Social Psych.

priorities, organize a daily schedule, and achieve better self-understanding. Lakein encourages the use of the ABC priority method in which the most important activities are designated "A," medium-value activities are "B," and low-value activities are "C." An individual using this method writes down all his or her activities for a given day, rates each activity as A, B, or C, and then tries to accomplish the A's first, the B's next, and turns to the C's if there is time. Figure 9.1 shows how Chris, a 28-year-old doctoral student and teaching assistant, used the ABC method during one busy Thursday.

Another important concept in Lakein's book is that daily time use should be directly related to goals. Chris describes her life goals and lifestyle goals in Figure 9.2. Are there connections between Chris's Thursday "to do" list and her goals?

Time Perceptions

Perception refers to the process whereby sensory stimulation is translated into organized experience. Understanding how time is perceived is necessary because, as noted earlier, time is more than simply clock time; an individual's perception and use of time are also important. Because perception is not observable, researchers have to rely on people's self-reports of their perceptions. **Time perception** is the awareness of the passage of time. Since 1850, social and behavioral scientists have been trying to determine why people's sense of the length of a period of time can differ from the precise measurement. They have found that many factors come into play in time perception. For example, drug and alcohol consumption alter time perception. Changes in body temperature and lack of exposure to natural daylight have been shown to affect a person's sense of time. Besides these physiological influences, temperament, culture, environment, and absorption in the task at hand may also affect perception.

FIGURE 9.2
**Chris's General Life Goals and
Lifestyle Goals**

General Life Goals
My general life goals are (1) to complete my doctorate work and earn a
Ph.D., (2) to marry the man of my choice, (3) to obtain a professional
position at a large state university, (4) to have at least 2 to 5 articles
accepted for publication each year, (5) to be published at least twice
in a premier journal, (6) to establish myself as one of the leading
academicians in my field, (7) to earn the respect of both my colleagues
and my sisters, (9) to earn enough money to take care of my parents and
my husband's parents, (10) to truly make a difference in the life of at
least one of my students, (11) to establish myself as a consultant,
(12) to establish myself as a consumer rights advocate, (13) to get
tenure, and (14) to improve my health.

Lifestyle Goals
My lifestyle goals are (1) to live in a new house in an upper-class
neighborhood in the suburbs, (2) to live near, but not in, a major city
with cultural events, great shopping, and other universities, (3) to
drive a Saab or an Alfa Romeo, (4) to be able to buy clothes without
worrying about the cost, and (5) to be able to fly/drive to getaway
weekends to fun places or visit old friends and family.

Estimating Duration

Without watches, clocks, newspapers, radio, or the television to serve as a
guide, people would have to use other means of estimating how much time has
passed. Several factors influence a person's estimation of time. Being active
seems to make time go faster than being passive. For example, the driver of a
car may think a trip goes faster than a passenger because the driver has something to do besides look passively out the window. An individual who is motivated is able to concentrate longer on a task and enjoy it more. Time seems
to move faster when one is not bored.

In addition, research studies reveal marked individual differences in the
ability to estimate time. Age appears to be one factor. Elderly people tend to
find time shorter than younger people. According to Jean Piaget's theory of
concrete cognitive operations, children's time estimates become more accurate
after the age of 7 or 8. This is why younger children irritate their parents on a
family vacation by repeatedly asking when they are going to arrive at the destination. Children do not mean to be irritating; they simply do not understand
time as an adult does.

Practical Uses of Time Measurement

Although perceptions and estimations of time vary from person to person, time
itself is one of the most accurately measured physical quantities. Indeed, the
study of time can be a very practical subject. In the twentieth century, time and
motion studies were conducted in offices and factories throughout the United
States. The studies evaluated industrial performance and analyzed the time
spent in producing a product such as a car. As discussed in Chapter 2, the early
study of factory efficiency was closely associated with the work of Frederick
Taylor (1911), who is widely considered to be the father of time and motion
studies. Taylor's studies later led to the discipline of management as it is taught

in business schools today. He introduced the idea of measuring time precisely in order to examine specific activities with the intent of finding ways to reduce the amount of time they required. Thus these studies aimed at improving efficiency through saving time and human energy. Each job on a factory production line would be divided into different operations, and each operation would then be analyzed in terms of time and energy used. As a result of the findings, assembly line work in factories became more standardized and efficient.

Many of the principles and methods derived from industrial performance studies, such as those conducted by Taylor, were applied to household efficiency studies. Chapter 2 examined some of these studies in the discussion of work simplification. The time and product use of individuals and families continue to be studied by manufacturers and marketers of appliances, food, and household products. They are interested in identifying trends in who does what in the home and learning how many minutes a day are spent in preparing food, eating, cleaning up, and washing clothes so that they can tailor their advertising and their products to fit current household practices and, hence, increase sales by better meeting consumer needs (see Figure 9.3 for an example). They are also interested in eating behaviors away from home. Restaurant chains, grocery stores, and office furniture manufacturers may want to know

FIGURE 9.3
An Appliance Advertisement Tailored to the Practices of Modern Households
Source: Reprinted by permission of Whirlpool Corporation.

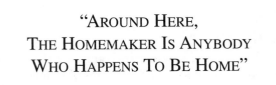

how workers spend their lunch hours and what they eat (see Figure 9.4). For example, a fast food chain might use several methods of inquiry, including in-restaurant consumer surveys, **focus groups** (selected groups of people who are questioned by a discussion leader or moderator about what they think about different topics, in this case products and services), observations, and self-reports. Companies also rely heavily on point-of-sale information obtained when bar codes from products are entered into a cash register. The data in Figure 9.4 and findings from other studies reveal that lunchtime is shrinking and more people are eating at their desks.

Time measurement also has practical applications in evaluating skills such as word processing (number of words per minute), sales (number of sales per month), library use (number of books checked out per week), and so on. Mall and store hours are determined by the number of customers per hour. During the holiday season, stores remain open longer to meet increased customer traffic and boost sales.

In addition, the amount of Social Security retired people receive is based on the number of years they were employed and how much they earned. Divorce settlements take into account the number of years of marriage. On a daily basis, people try to determine if they will be on time for work, school, or

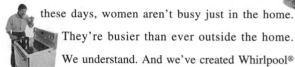

Faster Food

Average amount of TIME SPENT AT LUNCH: **36 minutes**

Percentage of American office workers who SKIMP ON LUNCH to keep up with an increasing workload or to get ahead: **40**

Percentage who take 15 MINUTES OR LESS for lunch every day: **56**

Percentage who EAT LUNCH AT THEIR DESKS or on the go: **42**

Percentage who SKIP LUNCH 1 or 2 times a week: **63**

Percentage who take an HOUR BREAK just to eat lunch: **less than 8**

Percentage who engage in activities BESIDES EATING during their lunch hour: **55**

What's on Their Plate Instead

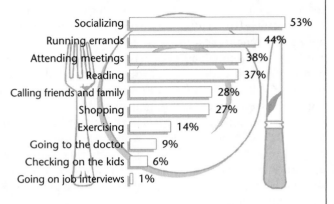

Socializing	53%
Running errands	44%
Attending meetings	38%
Reading	37%
Calling friends and family	28%
Shopping	27%
Exercising	14%
Going to the doctor	9%
Checking on the kids	6%
Going on job interviews	1%

Lunch Money

Percentage who eat lunch at a restaurant every day: **25**

Percentage who brown bag it at least once a week: **50**

Number of expense account lunches in the U.S. annually: **23.2 million**

Drop in expense account lunches in the U.S. since 1989: **8.3 percent**

Percentage who woo clients at mid-priced restaurants: **77**

Percentage who conduct business at upscale restaurants: **11**

Percentage who clinch deals over fast food: **5**

You Are What You Eat

Percentage of women who eat a vegetarian lunch: **4.2**

Percentage of men who eat a vegetarian lunch: **0.8**

Household income of workers who prefer vegetarian lunches: **$50,000+**

Percentage of working Americans who buy lunch from a vending machine or food cart at least once a week: **9.2**

Sales of gastrointestinal products: **$1.2 billion**

FIGURE 9.4

Does Skipping Lunch Make Us Less Productive?

Sources: National Restaurant Association, Kentucky Fried Chicken/Market Facts, Steelcase Workplace Index, Smithkline Beecham

appointments, if they will have enough time to eat lunch or prepare dinner, if they will be able to read the newspaper or watch the television shows they want to, and so on. In other words, people are engaged in time management from the moment they wake up until they go to sleep. Even sleeping is a timed event ending when one awakens at the sound of a radio or an alarm clock.

Perceptions of Time across Cultures

As mentioned earlier in the chapter, individuals perceive time differently due to many factors. For example, a widely held concept in anthropology is that time perceptions are strongly influenced by culture. The person most associated with studying how culture influences the way people think about time is E. T. Hall, the author of *The Silent Language*. The three anthropological models of time—linear-separable, circular-traditional, and procedural-traditional—were introduced by Hall (1959) and further delineated by Robert Graham (1981) and Alma Owen (1991). These models define time in the context of various activities, life stages, or time of year. By doing this, the models illustrate what time means to different cultural groups and also the ways in which they process and structure time.

Linear-Separable Model of Time

Most Western European cultures and other cultures that have been strongly influenced by Western Europe view time as linear. Linear-separable time processing is related to economic time. An investment in time today is expected to have a payoff in the future. Long-term planning is accepted as normal in the linear-separate model. When most U.S. residents are asked to think about the future, for example, they think in terms of 5 to 25 years (Hawkins, Best, & Coney, 1986). The model also treats the past, present, and future as distinct entities that are broken down into units. Thus, in linear-separable time orientations, stories, steps, and procedures are usually told in chronological order. Speed of preparation is valued, so time-saving products such as cake mixes and canned soups are accepted.

Time is measured by clocks and calendars. Appointments are kept on time. Furthermore, it is assumed that the future will bring better things. The linear-separable model represents an optimistic point of view because improvements are expected over time.

Procedural-Traditional Model of Time

The procedural-traditional perception is very different from the linear-separable model. Individuals with a procedural perception consider the actual steps, event, or procedure to be more important than the time spent in the activity. Being prompt is not as critical as doing things correctly or when conditions are right. Several tribes of American Indians and Alaskan Eskimos ascribe to a procedural perception of time. Procedural time processing is characterized by staying with a task until it is completed no matter how much time it takes. Scientists looking for cures and people who quilt or do other arts and crafts may subscribe to procedural-traditional models of time. They are focused on taking the right steps and finding a solution or making an end product regardless of how long it takes. In the United States, Martha Stewart, an icon of home decorating and gourmet cooking, is known for taking elaborate steps to produce something of unusually high and unique quality—prepared cake mixes are not her forte; cooking from scratch the old-fashioned way is. Beauty and taste are more important than time.

Circular-Traditional Model of Time

A circular or cyclical perception emphasizes the repetitive nature of time; this model assumes that today will be much like yesterday and tomorrow will be more of the same. Time follows a rhythmic pattern with regular beginnings and ends, but without discrete units of past, present, and future. In the circular perception, things may move forward or may remain the same. The circular perception is often associated with poverty because life for the poor, regardless of country, may change little from day to day. People living in primitive or agricultural subsistence cultures may also subscribe to the circular perception since they may be born, live, raise their families, and die on the same land as their grandparents. Time is not saved or spent; it just is, and life is lived day by day.

Some Effects of Cultural Differences

None of these models of time perceptions is good or bad; they simply illustrate cultural differences that affect managerial and consumption behavior. It is also important to note that many countries use a combination of the models or include cultural groups that ascribe more to one model than another. In Western Cultures, all three models exist, although the linear-separable model is dominant. Guy Claxton, an English psychologist specializing in the structure of the human mind and the author of *Hare Brain Tortoise Mind,* says that Western hurry-up methods have their drawbacks because slow ways of knowing exist and are useful:

The individuals and societies of the West have rather lost touch with the value of contemplation. Only active thinking is regarded as productive. Sitting gazing absently at your office wall or out of the classroom window is not of value. Yet many of those whom our society admires as icons of creativity and wisdom have spent much of their time doing nothing. Einstein, it is said, would frequently be found in his office at Princeton staring into space. The Dalai Lama spends hours each day in meditation. Even that paragon of penetrating insight, Sherlock Holmes, is described by his creator as entering a meditative state "with dreamy vacant expression in his eyes." (1997, p. 4)

Latin America provides an example of how perceptions of time can affect consumption behavior. Latin Americans generally view time as less concrete and less subject to scheduling than do North Americans. Consequently, appointments and meetings rarely start at the scheduled time. Since eating fast in an impersonal setting is not valued in Latin America, fast-food outlets popular in the United States and Great Britain, such as Wimpy, Kentucky Fried Chicken, and McDonald's, had difficulty penetrating Latin-American markets (Penteado, 1981), although this is gradually changing. Convenience foods such as boxed cereals sell well in North America because quick breakfasts that save time are highly valued. They are less successful in unhurried cultures.

In the circular perception, the concept of the future is vague. Southeast Asians, for instance, tend to think of the future in terms of hundreds or thousands of years (Hawkins, Best, & Coney, 1986). This perception leads to a different sense of urgency. In Asian countries, businesses are planned for the long run over several decades rather than for the short term. On the other hand, the Japanese have been very receptive to many American-European time-saving convenience goods.

Research studies have tried to establish the validity and monitor the cultural changes in the three types of time perceptions. A study of 48 East and Southeast Asian students (men and women from Thailand, Japan, and Malaysia) attending a large midwestern university found that they most frequently used procedural processing, followed by circular processing, and rarely used linear processing (Lindquist, Tacoma, & Lane, 1993). In contrast, U.S. students appeared to use linear processing most, followed by procedural processing, and then circular processing (Lindquist, Tacoma, & Lane, 1993). The U.S. students were more likely to view time as a valuable and limited commodity—something to be scheduled—whereas the Asian students were more concerned with the task itself rather than time.

Naturally, people with different time perspectives may find it difficult to understand each other. Often, people from the United States who become restless when waiting are viewed as rude by people from non-Western cultures. Conversely, people who are always in a hurry may think cultures that are slower and less orderly are behind the times. To be effective in international business and education, one must be sensitive to and adjust to the dominant time orientation.

Biological Time Patterns

Cultural perceptions of time use provide insight into how different groups of people perceive them. Another important aspect of time is how individuals perceive time. Each person has an internal clock that tells her or him when to wake, go to sleep, and eat. **Circadian rhythms** are the daily rhythmic activity cycles, based on 24-hour intervals, that humans experience. The word *circadian* comes from the Latin words *circa* meaning about and *dies* meaning

Also in families Some always need to get things done ... Some are who is a dreamer.

day. Before birth, babies are exposed to these daily rhythms from their mother's eating and sleeping patterns.

Jet lag and the disorientation caused by changing work shifts are examples of how humans react when their rhythms are disturbed. In the case of jet lag, people experience psychological dislocation and disruption of bodily rhythms caused by high-speed travel across several time zones in an airplane. Their sleeping and eating patterns are thrown off. Changing work shifts have been found to be a stressor for individuals and families.

QUANTITATIVE AND QUALITATIVE TIME MEASURES

Perceptions have to do with people's estimations of time, but time can also be measured in units. **Quantitative time measures** refer to the number, kind, and duration (e.g., minutes, hours, day) of activities that occur at specific points in time (Goldsmith, 1990). A quantitative time researcher would be interested in how many minutes a day an individual spends in food preparation, shopping, eating, driving, grooming, playing, child care, elder care, and working. Table 9.1 shows daytime activity results from several studies. Most quantitative time-use data are gathered in four ways:

1. In the *self-report* or *diary method,* individuals record their own time-use data on a form provided by the researcher (Walker & Woods, 1976).

TABLE 9.1
Where Does Time Go?

Based on **daytime activities** reported by representative adults and teenagers in recent U.S. studies. Percentages will differ by age, gender, social class, and personal preference—minimum and maximum ranges are indicated. Each percentage point is equivalent to about one hour per week.

Productive Activities		**Total: 24–60%**
Working at work, or studying	20–45%	
Talking, eating, daydreaming while at work	4–15%	
Maintenance Activities		**Total: 20–40%**
Housework (cooking, cleaning, shopping)	8–22%	
Eating	3–5%	
Grooming (washing up, dressing)	3–6%	
Driving, transportation	6–9%	
Leisure Activities		**Total: 20–43%**
Media (TV and reading)	9–13%	
Hobbies, sports, movies, restaurants	4–13%	
Talking, socializing	4–12%	
Idling, resting	3–5%	

Source: Csikszentmihalyi, M. (1998). *Finding Flow,* NY: Basic Books, p. 9.

2. In the *recall method,* individuals are asked to think back (recall) and explain in detail a previous day's activities to an interviewer in person, or over the telephone, or by self-report on a form provided by the researcher.

3. In the *observation method,* a trained researcher observes and records the precise way, duration, and sequencing of an individual's activities (Nelson, 1963; Diana, 1983). This method has been used extensively in anthropology and child development.

4. The *self-observational control-signalling method* is rarely used for collecting data on household time use, but is used extensively in business management studies. In this method, subjects are asked to record their time use at a given signal, such as when a bell sounds, a telephone rings, or a light flashes. In most previous studies, the data were recorded at work with the permission of the company's management (Carroll & Taylor, 1968). The method incorporates a self-report, but the reports in the control-signalling method are required at random times and are less expected and less time-consuming for the subject than are the lengthy ongoing diary self-reports. Because the signals occur sporadically and the subject responds immediately, some researchers conclude that the control-signalling method produces more accurate data than the other methods.

Using a combination of methods with built-in cross-checks is generally considered to be the best way to obtain accurate data (Denzin, 1970; Goldsmith, 1977; Hamilton, 1989). Examples of extensive quantitative household time-use studies are the 1967–1968 Walker-Telling study of 1,296 families in Syracuse, New York, and the 11-state spinoff studies (Walker & Woods, 1976; Walker, 1983). These studies used 24-hour recalls as told to interviewers and diaries. Among other things, the New York study established that the presence of young children in the home dramatically increased the amount of household work. In 1994, in another time-use study, Allen Martin and Margaret Sanik reported that women spent more time in household production if there was a young child or a teenager in the household and that men contributed more time to household production as they aged.

In *The Second Shift,* sociologist Arlie Hochschild wrote that many employed women work at a job during the day and go home and work until bedtime at household chores and child care—in other words, women work two jobs. Through interviews and observations, she found that in some marriages where the husband earned more, he justified doing less housework because he contributed more monetarily; she also found marriages where the wife earned more, felt guilty, and therefore did more housework. Hochschild concluded that rarely is housework evenly divided between working parents and that there is a gap between their ideals and the reality of their busy lives. In her followup book, *The Time Bind,* Hochschild explored further the interchange between home and work lives. She says that "the more attached we are to the world of work, the more its deadlines, its cycles, its pauses and interruptions shape our lives, and the more family time is forced to accommodate to the pressures of work" (p. 45).

Qualitative time measurement investigates the meaning or significance of time use as well as how individuals feel about their time use, that is, the satisfaction it generates. It also measures who they are spending time with. Consider the following comment by the Duke of Windsor who abdicated the British throne to marry an American divorcée in 1937. "You know what my day was today?" asked the former king, "I got up late and then I went with the Duchess and watched her buy a hat" (Menkes, 1987).

The "who" part of how time is spent is important because daily life is not defined solely by what we do, but also by who we are with. Mihaly Csikszentmihalyi (1997) estimates that people spend roughly equal amounts of time in three social contexts:

1. Strangers, coworkers, fellow students. This is "public" space where one's actions are evaluated by others and where one competes for resources.
2. Family and friends. This is a place of kinship, special bonds, and home.
3. Solitude. Time spent alone.

In technological societies, more time is spent alone than was common in tribal societies, where being alone was often considered dangerous. Many people are uncomfortable being alone, but it is important to learn to tolerate solitude or else the quality of our lives is bound to suffer (Csikszentmihalyi, 1997). The popularity of chat rooms and e-mail may be partially explained by this need to connect with others even if physically alone.

Prior to the 1970s, nearly all time-use measurement was quantitative. Since then, several studies have used qualitative measures as well as a combination of quantitative and qualitative measures. The increased use of qualitative measures is a response to the growing recognition that simply knowing how many minutes are spent washing dishes or diapering a baby does not provide as meaningful time-use data as knowing how persons performing the task feel or how they interact with others involved in the task. Asking qualitative questions also lets the researcher know how the individual feels; thus, the burden of interpretation is no longer on the researcher where obvious bias or perceptual errors could occur.

As an example of a study investigating the qualitative aspects of time use, Hafstrom and Paynter (1991) studied data collected on farm wives in seven states and found that although farm wives (many of whom were employed off the farm) appeared to assume a large share of the workload—a combination of home, farm, and labor force—they remained satisfied with management in the home and on the farm. Hafstrom and Paynter also found that satisfaction with time use was affected by a variety of factors, including the wife's sense of control over her own life. So, even though the wives reported being overloaded with work and family demands, they still were relatively satisfied with their lifestyle and accepted its complexity.

Demands, Sequencing, and Standards

Three concepts introduced earlier in this book—demands, sequencing, and standards—are an integral part of the discussion of time from a managerial perspective. Since time is a limited resource, individuals have to make decisions about how to allocate their time. Demands, sequencing, and standards affect these decisions.

Demands

As lives become more complicated, increasing demands are placed on time. Demands are events or goals that necessitate or motivate action. For example, schools demand attendance, workplaces demand a certain number of hours of work, parents demand a safe neighborhood for their children, the children's coach demands that they spend time practicing, and citizens demand fair government. Many of these demands may not be met, but they are goals or ideals worth striving for.

One would assume that saving time is the main reason that people buy and use appliances, but research has shown that appliances do not always lessen time demands (see Table 9.2). In the United States, the average woman aged 18 to 50 spends 57 minutes a day cooking. The difference between women with microwave ovens and those without is just four minutes (Robinson & Milkie, 1997).

Demands on time within families and organizations may conflict. One child may want the parents to attend her school play while a sibling wants them to come to his soccer game. At work, employees find several tasks competing for their attention. Stretching limited resources, including time, to meet conflicting demands is a dilemma all people experience.

Families with young children or disabled family members may face even greater demands on their time. Teenagers and dependent elderly may put high emotional demands on the family, and meeting those demands takes time. Unfortunately, demands are often strongest when resources are weakest, as in the case of young married couples who are trying to set up a household, have children, and become established in their careers—all at the same time. Time demands are also high for families trying to balance more established careers and home responsibilities.

Besides demands external to the person, there are internal demands as well. All individuals have a **tempo**, meaning a time pattern or pace that feels comfortable to them. One person may be described as "high energy, always on the go, or hyper," whereas another is described as "slow, thoughtful, and de-

---

TABLE 9.2
Taking Time For Tasks

Time spent by women aged 18 to 50 on household tasks after adjusting for gender, age, work hours, marital status, and parental status, for those with and without appliances.

	Minutes per day
Cooking Meals	57.0
With microwave	55.0
Without microwave	59.0
Meal Cleanup	7.7
With dishwasher	6.7
Without dishwasher	8.0
Laundry	18.4
With washing machine	19.0
Without washing machine	13.6
With clothes dryer	18.0
Without clothes dryer	20.4
All Housework	17.4

Other things being equal, women with microwave ovens spend just 4 minutes less per day fixing food than those who don't. Those with washing machines spend even more time than average doing laundry.

Source: Americans' Use of Time Project, University of Maryland. Robinson, J. and Milkie, M. (1997, January). "Dances with Dust Bunnies: Housecleaning in America," *American Demographics,* p. 40.

liberate." Successful organizations thrive on having members with both types of temperaments.

Sometimes demand for time is uneven and difficult to manage. For example, bicycle stores may be empty during weekdays, but crowded on Saturdays with children and parents. Tennis courts and golf courses are usually overbooked on weekends. Thus, demand can range from none at all to excessive and can be irregular as well. When shopping, consumers try to gauge when demand will be low, lines short, and stores uncrowded. As these examples illustrate, the concept of demand can be applied to time as well as to other constructs and contexts, such as shopping demands and energy demands.

Sequencing

A sequence is a following of one thing after another in a series or an arrangement. Examples of sequences are sharpening a pencil before writing with it, unlocking a door before entering a house, or making an appointment before going to the dentist. Individuals' daily lives are filled with many such sequences. Sequencing refers to the order of activities in time, as in a series of events. Sequencing may be simple or complex. In a simple sequence, one person performs one task. A complicated sequencing plan involves many people and many tasks. Obviously, a large family with children at different ages will have more trouble completing tasks and holding to a set sequence than a person living alone.

Schedules, which are sets of time-bounded activities, are made up of two mental processes—sequencing and time-tagging. **Time-tagging** is a mental estimation of the sequences that should take place, the approximate amount of time required for each activity in the sequence, and the starting and ending times for each activity (Avery & Stafford, 1991). Repeatedly following the same sequences with the same starting and ending points leads to procedural routines where the person no longer has to think about the individual steps in the sequence. Remember learning how to drive a car or use a computer? At first, you were slow and had to think carefully about each step. In time, the sequence became faster and felt more natural. Schedules and sequences can be mental or they can be written, as in a schedule of college classes or a program of forthcoming events.

As has been mentioned earlier, many individuals and families feel overwhelmed by demands on their time—they are living in a time drought, a barren land with little relief. They feel short of time because of the phenomenon of multitasking, which is becoming more and more the norm. As described in Chapter 6, tasks can be divided into three main categories: interdependent, dovetailed, and overlapped. In *interdependent* activities, one task must be completed before the next task can begin. An example of an interdependent activity is mailing a letter. The letter has to be written and the envelope stamped and addressed before mailing. Doing two or more activities at once is called *dovetailing*. A person may, for example, fold laundry and watch television at the same time. In fact, people are so used to having the radio or the television playing in the background that they do not consider these as competing activities. Many dull, repetitive activities lend themselves to dovetailing. The one drawback to dovetailing is that if you do too many activities at one time, the end results may be less than desired. A meal can be burned, a deadline missed, or a message misinterpreted if a person is trying to do too much at once. *Overlapping* involves giving intermittent attention to two or more activities until they are completed. For example, a parent might put a baby to bed, then read while partly listening to hear if the baby is falling asleep. On any given day, people use all three types of sequencing. Along this same line of thought, Claxton warns that:

There is an old Polish saying, "Sleep faster; we need the pillows," which reminds us that there are some activities which just will not be rushed. They take the time that they take. If you are late for a meeting, you can hurry. If the roast potatoes are slow to brown, you can turn up the oven. But if you try to speed up the baking of meringues, they burn. If you are impatient with the mayonnaise and add the oil too quickly, it curdles. If you start tugging with frustration on a tangled fishing line, the knot just becomes tighter. (*Hare Brain Tortoise Mind,* 1997, p. 1)

Each individual may favor a certain type of sequencing based on his or her style, pace, or tempo. Most people go through a certain sequence of events when they first awaken in the morning. They perform routine activities such as putting on a bathrobe, going to the bathroom, taking a shower or washing their face, combing their hair, watching the morning news programs or reading the newspaper, dressing, and eating breakfast. As the day progresses, they move into more complicated sequencing involving dovetailing and overlapping activities. At bedtime, they revert back to a more habitual sequential mode, essentially reversing the morning routine with a snack, brushing teeth, going to the bathroom, undressing, reading or watching television, and going to sleep.

A **routine** is a habitual way of doing things that saves time and energy for other activities. Routines and habits provide stability to our lives. Young children thrive on routines at home and in preschool. Learning logical ways of sequencing activities is part of the socialization process. Some of us need more routine than others. The roots of this need probably stem from childhood socialization patterns, personality, and temperament.

Standards

A standard is an acknowledged measure of comparison or a criterion. The notion of standards incorporates the concept of value. It can be said that people have a certain set of standards, meaning that they conduct their lives in a particular way. Standards serve as guides or measures of human behavior. As discussed earlier, a more detailed definition of standards by DeMerchant (1993) describes them as quantitative and/or qualitative criteria, or measures of values and goals, that reconcile resources with demands and affect how certain tasks or activities are completed.

Standards are relevant to this chapter on managing time because in today's fast-moving world, individuals and families often do not have enough time or energy to meet the standards they would like to in keeping their homes clean, exercising regularly, eating appropriately, meeting family needs, and accomplishing work. Great demands on time are experienced in other countries besides the United States. An article about daily time use in rural households in India reported that women, including pregnant women, worked an average of 14 to 16 hours per day (Singal, Srinivasan, & Jindal, 1993). Their hours were split between a variety of jobs in the home and farm and livestock management. Clearly maintaining standards in all areas under these conditions is difficult.

Standards have both quantitative and qualitative aspects. Quantity refers to a measurable amount. Quality refers to a degree or grade of excellence, the essential character or nature of something. Quantitatively, a teacher may set a standard of grading 50 math papers an hour. Qualitatively, a person may want her or his food prepared to a certain standard of nutrition, taste, and attractiveness. Conflict arises in homes and organizations when people have different standards. For example, if a teacher expects to grade 50 math papers an hour, an intern assigned to the teacher who can grade only 5 papers an hour will fall below expectations. In a restaurant, if food is not prepared to the expected standard, a customer may send the food back to the kitchen.

In a home, some family members may be perfectly happy living in a mess that other family members cannot tolerate. One of the values of living on a college campus is the opportunity to experience how many different ways people can live and the different standards they have.

Standards of quality and quantity form the criteria for action. Demands lead to an alteration of standards. Students cramming for a test will not have time to cook dinner or to go to movies with friends. Preparing for the test demands all their time and attention, so household work and friends have to wait.

The more complex the lifestyle and the greater number of people involved, the more regular standards have to be if everyone involved is going to survive and thrive. The military is an example. Beds must be made a certain way, and rooms are inspected. Everyone wears uniforms. When 1,000 service people must be fed in one hour, food lines have to move efficiently. Because of the vast numbers of people and the complexity and seriousness of their tasks, there is little room for individual choices or variations in standards.

Electronic Resources

www.gallup.com/poll/releases/

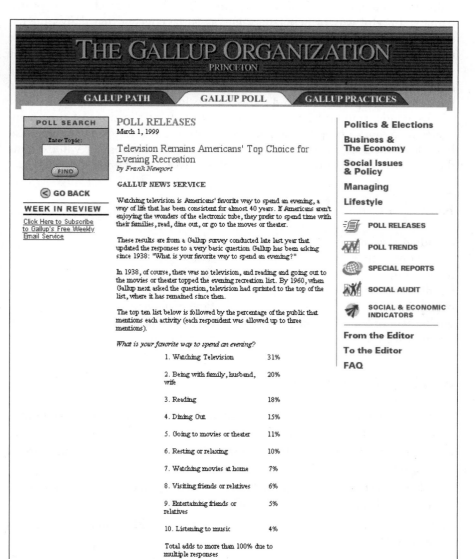

For a report on "The New Millennium American" by PaineWebber that includes information on stressless leisure and time-efficient leisure (activities that cram a lot into a limited amount of time, such as quick getaways) go to **www.painewebber.com**. This site also has information on multitasking and its implications for investments and consumption patterns. For the latest public poll information from the Gallup Organization, check their Web site at **www.gallup.com**. For an example of how one company is offering variable work hours, go to IBM's Web site at **www.ibm.com/diversity**.

Summary

This chapter focused on time and time management. Time is a limited, nonrenewable, scarce resource. Consequently, it is valuable. It has also been the subject of much philosophical debate. Time perceptions vary from individual to individual and within and between cultures. The ABC method of time prioritizing is a useful way of managing time, as is the concept that daily time use should be related to goals sought. Both quantitative time measures (i.e., those using units such as seconds, minutes, hours, and days) and qualitative time measures (feelings about time use) provide useful information for managing households and businesses. Time-use data have many practical applications to the home, the marketplace, and the work world.

Demands, standards, and sequencing provide applications of time management to work and other activities. Too little time and too much responsibility lead to stress, the subject of Chapter 11. The next chapter will examine the complexity arising from trying to balance work and family life.

Key Terms

circadian rhythms   routine
discretionary time   tempo
focus groups   time
nondiscretionary time   time displacement
perception   time management
qualitative time measurement   time perception
quantitative time measures   time-tagging

Review Questions

1. In your opinion, in what ways are today's societies subjected to more time pressure than those in the past?

2. What is your reaction to the quotation from Leonard Berry about hurried mealtimes (see p. 200)?

3. What is the balance in your life between discretionary and nondiscretionary time? Which do you have more of?

4. What is your opinion of the quotation from David Elkind about today's hurried child (see p. 202)?

5. According to Mihaly Csikszentmihalyi in *Finding Flow*, people spend roughly equal amounts of daytime in three social contexts (i.e., with strangers or coworkers/students, with family and friends, and alone). Is your time similarly spent? If you could change your time use in any way, what would you change? Explain your answers.

References

Avery, R. & Stafford, K. (1991). Toward a scheduling congruity theory of family resource management. *Lifestyles: Family and Economic Issues, 12*(4), 327.

Berry, L. (1990, February). Market to the perception. *American Demographics, 12,* 30–33.

Carroll, S. & Taylor, W. (1968). A study of the validity of a self-observational central-signalling method of work sampling. *Personnel Psychology, 21,* 359–364.

Clark, D. (1999, June 21). Managing the mountain. *The Wall Street Journal,* R4.

Claxton, G. (1977). *Hare brain tortoise mind.* New York: W. W. Norton.

Csikszentmihalyi, M. (1997). *Finding flow.* NY: Basic Books.

DeMerchant, E. (1993). Standards: An analysis of definitions, frameworks and implications. *Proceedings of the Eastern Regional Home Management—Family Economics Conference,* Blacksburg, VA.

Denzin, N. (1990). *Sociological methods: A source book.* Chicago: Aldine Press.

Diana, M. (1983). The relationship between observation of affiliative behavior patterns for parents and toddlers and parental reports of caregiving, play, and support-control behaviors. Unpublished Ph.D. thesis, Michigan State University, East Lansing.

Elkind, D. (1988). *The hurried child.* Reading, MA: Addison-Wesley.

Goldsmith, E. (1977). Time use of beginning families with employed and unemployed wives. Unpublished Ph.D. thesis, Michigan State University, East Lansing.

Goldsmith, E. (1990). The effect of women's employment on quantitative and qualitative time-use measurements: A review and synthesis. *Home Economics Forum, 4*(2), 18–20.

Godbey, G. & Graefe, A. (1993, April). Rapid growth in rushin' Americans. *American Demographics,* 26–27.

Graham, R. (1981). The role of perception in consumer research. *Journal of Consumer Research, 7,* 335–342.

Hafstrom, J. & Paynter, M. (1991). Time use satisfaction of wives: Home, farm, and labor force workload. *Lifestyles: Family and Economic Issues, 12*(2), 131–143.

Hall, E. T. (1959). *The silent language.* New York: Fawcett World Library.

Hamilton, J. (1989). Epistemology and meaning: A case for multi-methodologies for social research in home economics. *Home Economics Forum, 4,* 12–14.

Hawkins, D., Best, R., & Coney, K. (1986). *Consumer behavior* (3rd ed.). Plano, TX: Business Publications.

Hochschild, A. (1989). *The second shift.* New York: Viking.

Hochschild, A. (1997). *The time bind.* New York: Henry Holt.

Kaufman, C. & Lane, P. (1993). Role overload and the perception of time pressure, *Proceedings of the Atlantic Marketing Association,* Orlando, FL, 25–30.

L'Abate, L. & Harel, T. (1993). Deriving, developing, and expanding a theory of developmental competence from resource exchange theory. In U. Foa, J. Converse, K. Tornblom, & E. Foa (Eds.), *Resource theory: Explorations and applications.* San Diego: Academic Press, 233–269.

Lakein, A. (1973). *How to get control of your time and your life.* New York: New American Library.

Lewis, J. (1993). *How to build a winning project team.* New York: American Management Association.

Linquist, J., Tacoma, S., & Lane, P. (1993). What is time: An exploratory extension toward the far east. In M. Levy and D. Grewal (Eds.), *Developments in marketing,* Vol. 16, Proceedings of the Annual Conference of the Academy of Marketing Science, Miami Beach, FL, 186–189.

Martin, A. & Sanik, M. (1994). Determinants of married men's and women's time spent in household production in 1985. *Proceedings of the 1994 Conference of the Eastern Family Economics and Resource Management Association,* Pittsburgh, PA, 1–17.

Menkes, S. (1987). *The windsor style.* Topsfield, MA: Salem House.

Mutz, D., Roberts, D. & Van Vuuren, D. (1993, February). Reconsidering the displacement hypothesis. *Communication Research, 20*(1), 51–75.

Nelson, L. (1963). Daily activity patterns of peasant homemakers. Unpublished Ph.D. thesis, Michigan State University, East Lansing.

Owen, A. (1991). Time and time again: Implications of time perception theory. *Lifestyle: Family and Economic Issues, 12*(4), 345–359.

Penteado, J. (1981, May 25). U.S. fast foods move slowly. *Advertising Age*, S–8.

PC usage in homes found to have dropped sharply. *The Wall Street Journal*, B6.

Robinson, J. & Milkie, M. (1997). Dances with dust bunnies: Housecleaning in America, *American Demographics*, p. 40.

Senge, P. (1999). *The Dance of Change*, NY: Doubleday.

Singal, S., Srinivason, K. & Jindal, R. (1993). Women's work status and their time use pattern in rural households of Haryana. *Journal of Consumer Studies and Home Economics*, *17*, 99–104.

Taylor, F. (1911). *The principles of scientific management.* New York: Harper & Brothers.

Walker, K. (1983). An interstate urban/rural comparison of families' time use: Introduction. *Home Economics Research Journal, 12*(2), 119–121.

Walker, K. & Woods, M. (1976). *Time use: A measure of household production of family goods and services.* Washington, DC: American Home Economics Association.

chapter 10

Managing Work and Family

MAIN TOPICS

OVERVIEW OF WORK AND FAMILY
THE PROBLEM OF WORK AND FAMILY CONFLICTS
RESOLVING WORK AND FAMILY CONFLICTS
FAMILY-SUPPORTIVE WORKPLACE POLICIES

THE MEANING OF WORK AND LEISURE
THE WORK ETHIC
WORKAHOLISM
THE THREE P'S: PROCRASTINATION, PARKINSON'S LAW, AND
    PARETO'S PRINCIPLE
WORKFORCE TRENDS INCLUDING HOME-BASED BUSINESSES
VOLUNTEER WORK
LEISURE

Did you know that...?

...A typical American holds 8.6 different jobs between the ages of 18 and 32.

...Forty-two percent of teens see at least an 8 in 10 chance of working at home as adults.

To affect the quality of the day, that is the highest of arts.
—Henry David Thoreau

VERY FEW PEOPLE are immune from the problems of trying to balance work and family life, the subject of this chapter. For example,

> Just a few years ago, Krishan Kalra worked as fast and as furiously as any other Silicon Valley CEO. The founder of a biotech company called Bio-Genex Laboratories, the 55-year-old native of India pushed himself, his 150 employees and his family to the breaking point. Finally, with his marriage in crisis and the kids feeling neglected, Kalra dropped out for three months. . . . Today, back at work Kalra meditates during the day and, at night religiously ignores the temptations of the fax, laptop and phone to be with his family. "I've started to pay attention to all aspects of my life," he says, "Once you become a whole person, you tend to be more creative and productive." (Stone, 1999, p. 68)

Dowonia Goodwin, a school bus driver and a single mother with three children, should by all accounts also be a casualty of the work and family battleground, but she is coping quite well with the help of her nine brothers and sisters. She says without them, "I would totally fall apart" (Shellenbarger, 1999, May 12, B1). She also relies on a child care center for her youngest.

These are just two examples of the millions of families who are trying to manage the important life roles of work and family. With the increasing number of women joining the labor force worldwide and the increasing number of people working at home, management experts have turned their attention to the problems individuals and families face in trying to meet work and family responsibilities. The focus of this chapter is on the resource management problems and solutions associated with balancing work and family or life roles. Since statistics indicate that most college graduates will marry and work full-time, the problems of combining work and family are not just societal issues, but personal issues of significance for the readers of this chapter.

If one were to believe recent media outpourings, one might think that the "superwoman" and "superman" model of working and loving is a new phenomenon. It is not. People have been combining several roles for a long time. They have worked split shifts, served in the military, or in some other way worked a variety of hours or jobs or in more than one location, while at the same time trying to raise a family and have a personal life. Individuals may be friends, siblings, parents, children, workers, employers, caregivers, neighbors, students, teachers, volunteers, and many more roles, depending on choices and circumstances. Perhaps of all these roles, work and family stand out as the most important to an individual's self-image and are the most demanding of her or his time. Adults spend most of their time sleeping (one-third of our lives), at home alone or with families or friends, or at work. When Sigmund Freud was asked his recipe for happiness, his short answer was "work and love."

OVERVIEW OF WORK AND FAMILY

Although both men and women work, the rapid influx of women into the labor force since the 1970s has caused a shift in the public's perception of the interchange between work and family. According to a United Nations' report ("The World's Women 1970–1990"):

> Women everywhere contribute to economic production. As officially measured, 46 percent of the world's women aged 15 and over—828 million—are economically active. At least another 10–20 percent of the world's women are economically productive but not counted as part of the labour force because of inadequate measurement. . . . Although women spent less time in activities officially counted as economically productive and make much less money, they spend far more in home production. If a woman spends more time in the labour force, she still bears the main responsibility for home and family care, and sleep and leisure are sacrificed. . . . Men's participation in the labour force has fallen everywhere. Women's by contrast, has fallen significantly only in sub-Saharan Africa, where economic crises have been most widespread. Women's share in the total labour force is increasing in most regions.

More and more families are feeling pressured for time and stressed from coping with conflicting work and family demands. In response, employers wanting the most satisfied and productive workers possible are reexamining child and elder care policies and providing flextime and other schedule changes to accommodate family needs.

Several facts, figures, and research findings about the work and family interchange follow:

- Although baby boomers are known for paying their career dues through long hours and other sacrifices, postboomers are more diverse. Some Gen-Xers work almost around the clock, while a second, polar-opposite group resists, leaning more towards nesting, family, and community (Shellenbarger, 1998). Coming up behind GenX, the baby boomlet will further rewrite the work-life book, with technology as its tool. Children using the Internet rose 63 percent to 16 million in the past year, according to Cybor Dialogue.

- There is a gender gap between the earnings of men and women. Currently, in the United States, women on average earn about 76 cents to each dollar men earn, up from 74 cents in 1996. Internationally, the earnings gap between men and women is larger.

- A growing number of teenagers are getting a big dose of training in balancing work and family life in high school (Shellenbarger, 1999, Feb. 24).

- More than 80 percent of all U.S. high school students hold jobs before their high school graduation (Greenberger & Steinberg, 1986).

- Forty-two percent of teens see at least an 8 in 10 chance of working at home as adults (Shellenbarger, 1998).

- Families with two earners, one parent, or young children, are likely to experience work/family conflict and job tension (Kelly & Voydanoff, 1985; Voydanoff, 1988; Voydanoff & Kelly, 1984; Voydanoff, 1993).

- The more positive fathers' work experiences, the higher their self-esteem, which affects their parenting styles (Grimm-Thomas & Perry-Jenkins, 1994).

- Spousal support has a direct positive relationship with job commitment (Orthner & Pittman, 1986).

- Commuter marriages have become more common (Anderson, 1992).

- The problems of combining work and family are worldwide concerns that will become increasingly important as more nations become industrialized and more women leave the home to enter the labor force (Goldsmith, 1993).

- Future families will break the mold in their quest for better ways to blend work and child rearing (Shellenbarger, 1998).

The Problem of Work and Family Conflicts

At the center of the work and family debate is the concern that a person who is heavily involved in one domain (work or family) may not be psychologically or physically available for the other. Work and family conflict may arise when a person is torn between work and family demands, and frustration develops. It may also arise when spouses, coworkers, employers, and children differ over how work and family time should be divided.

As one way to manage work and family demands, more parents are choosing to have children later in life. Babyboom women have married late, delayed childbearing, and spaced their births farther apart. Although some parents choose not to work outside the home when their children are young, the general trend is toward increased employment participation for mothers of infants and young children. Employment rates for mothers with children under the age of 2 increased from 31 percent in 1970 to 54 percent in 1985, and employment for mothers of infants less than a year old rose 100 percent between 1970 and the mid-1980s, when it reached 49 percent (Rapoport, 1985; Schroeder, 1988). It has risen further since.

Voydanoff (1989) identified several job demands that are related to work/family conflict:

- ◆ Role ambiguity (doubt or uncertainty)
- ◆ Role conflict
- ◆ Intellectual or physical effort
- ◆ Rapid change
- ◆ Pressures for quality work
- ◆ Pressure to work hard and fast
- ◆ Heavy workload

This list implies that work is a stressor on the family. It can be, but work also benefits families. Most women in the labor force work primarily because they or their family needs the money and secondarily for their own personal self-actualization. Promotions, praise, awards, and raises are other benefits of work that can increase self-esteem. In addition, several studies indicate that performing the multiple roles of worker, spouse, and parent is positively related to women's physical and mental health (Voydanoff, 1989).

On the negative side, work pressures and constant travel strain family relations. An extreme example of work absorption was documented by therapists, David Ulrich and Harry Dunne. In *To Love and Work: A Systemic Interlocking of Family, Workplace, and Career,* they describe a session with a busy executive, who "glancing at his watch as he sat down for his first and only interview, announced that he could take one hour to decide whether or not to divorce his wife" (1986, p. 129). These authors also say that many workers treat the home as a "pit stop," or a refueling place for the main purpose in life, getting ahead at work. Spouses and children are virtually ignored in the "pit stop" approach to home and family life.

Resolving Work and Family Conflicts

Individuals or families may find the following approaches helpful in reducing work and family conflict:

1. Manage the conflict so that different ideas, opinions, and approaches are brought out for discussion.
2. Resolve conflict when it becomes too disruptive.

The first option is a preventive strategy, and the second can be used when conflict already exists and needs to be addressed immediately.

The second strategy comes into play when the conflict interferes with family members' ability to get their work done and threatens the security and the functioning of the family as a whole and of individual family members. It is not unusual for individuals and families to hope that work and family conflicts, in particular, time conflicts, will go away (e.g., things will be better next week when my report is finished), but they seldom do. If the pressure builds to the point of explosion, someone in the couple or family will have to deal with a crisis. To cope with the crisis, the persons involved have to examine the cause of the frustration. According to Lewis (1993, p. 145), conflict usually arises from one or more of the following:

◆ *Values*. What we deem important. These include our work ethic, our sense of family responsibility, and similar issues.

◆ *Facts*. Our perception of what the facts are.

◆ *Role perceptions*. How different people view a role. Differing role perceptions can lead to role conflict.

◆ *Methods*. Disagreements about the best or the right way to do something are common.

◆ *Objectives*. Differences over what the objectives should be and their relative importance.

From a family management perspective, the way work and family conflicts are resolved depends on the answers to the following questions:

1. How strong is each individual's concern with satisfying her or his own interests in the issue?

2. How strong is each individual's concern with satisfying the interests of his or her spouse or children (adapted from Lewis, 1993, p. 145)?

Obviously, compromise is one solution to a couple's or a family's work and family conflicts. In **compromise** each person makes concessions, giving in a little in order to gain a valued settlement or outcome (e.g., harmony, an intact, functioning family). Accommodation is another solution wherein the needs of each person are accommodated or adjusted to as best they can be. Since work and family time conflicts can be a lifelong battle and work and family demands change over time, the people involved should not rush the process. Once they agree on when to leave for work in the morning, for example, each person should regularly check to see if the agreement is still working or if a new schedule is needed.

Unemployment and the Family

The problems of combining work and family can become even more complex when unemployment is involved. What happens to the work and family interchange when a breadwinner suddenly is out of work? Going from eight hours of work per day to zero requires an adjustment of time, ego, and family as well as an adjustment to the loss of income. Most of the studies on unemployment were done in the Great Depression of the 1930s and focused on men. Since the recession of the 1980s and the downsizing of companies in the 1990s, studies have focused on the effects of unemployment on both men and women.

Larson, Wilson, and Beley (1994) found that stress stemming from job insecurity is related to marital and family dysfunction and a host of family problems. Unemployment is a crisis event affecting all aspects of a person's and a family's life including resource management and social support systems. In a study of 216 unemployed women in Louisiana, the researchers found that the women sought and successfully obtained assistance from relatives and friends

(Retherford, Hildreth, & Goldsmith, 1989). The women's parents were especially helpful in providing emotional support. Overall, the way people react to unemployment depends on the length of the unemployment period, the circumstances surrounding the unemployment, and the potential for future employment, as well as the strength of the family support systems and financial status of the unemployed person.

Due to changes in the U.S. economy, increasing numbers of blue-collar workers in the steel, automotive, rubber, textile, apparel, and electronic industries have been vulnerable to extended unemployment, permanent job loss, or reemployment at lower wage and benefits levels (Smith & Price, 1992). A study of women workers who lost their jobs in textile and apparel plants in Georgia provides insight into how the loss of work affects families. The researchers found that the stage in the family life cycle and the demands of combining productive work and family responsibilities contributed to women's experience of unemployment and their labor market participation (Smith & Price, 1992). For example, one woman in the study observed:

> It's kind of nice, really, being at home with children. I spent 20 years working and my mother-in-law raised the kids because I had to work. My husband likes it too. He likes me cooking for him, being at home when he comes home and not running around trying to clean and cook and take care of the children. (p. 67)

Another participant in the study reacted differently:

> After you've worked all this time and paid for things, you feel guilty, like you're not doing your part. It's hard to get used to not carrying your own weight. You worry about emergencies if you've only got one insurance carrier, lose a sense of security. I miss being independent. When we go on vacation I would put my own portion in the pot. It's really a change—I've learned to be dependent. I guess I've learned who was in charge. Just giving up the independence [from] bringing home a good salary was something. (p. 69)

The Interchange between Work and Family

As the previous quotations indicate, the interchange between work and family involves many issues. It is not only a gender issue or a husband versus wife issue. According to Voydanoff:

> In recent years researchers have recognized that it is necessary not only to understand relationships between work and family roles for either the husband or wife but also to examine the combined effects of husbands' and wives' work role characteristics on family life. Preliminary research has begun to address joint effects in terms of amounts and scheduling of work time, relative socioeconomic attainment of husbands and wives, work-related geographic mobility, and commuter marriage. (1989, p. 8)

Generally, far more is known about the effects of work on family than vice versa. Ulrich and Dunne (1986) observed that many of the ways that people react to work, employers, and coworkers are based on early childhood experiences, especially relationships with parents and siblings. The boss may serve as a parent figure, and how the employee responds to that boss may have a lot to do with how she or he perceives authority. Loyalty to parents and the family unit may spill over into loyalty to the firm. Relationships between coworkers may be a reliving of the childhood give and take between brothers and sisters.

Going beyond childhood experiences into the present day, it is acknowledged that marital satisfaction and family responsibilities affect work performance and a person's motivation to work. Thus, severe personal or family problems affect work performance. Someone going through a difficult divorce or having problems with children may talk about his or her problems at work and be distracted from the tasks at hand. Many employers offer Employee Assistance Programs (EAPs) to help workers and families with emotional, financial, and legal difficulties and problems with alcoholism and drug abuse. For example, more than 70 percent of the nation's largest companies (e.g., AT&T, Dupont, McDonnell Douglas, and General Motors) offer EAPs (Symonds et al., 1991).

Family-Supportive Workplace Policies

EAPs are one example of the increased commitment of work organizations to provide family-supportive policies and practices. Employers can also provide the following:

- ◆ Access to outside services. For example, help workers find (and in some cases pay for) child and elder care. BP-Amoco provides as much as $1,500 a year for child care for nonroutine business trips, including flying Grandma in to help out if costs are reasonable (Shellenbarger, 1999, May 12).

- ◆ On-site seminars from financial planning to stress prevention. Joo and Garman (1998) found that personal financial wellness affected work productivity in a study of 447 clerical workers.

- ◆ Private coaches to help employees sense where they need to draw the line on work hours and carve out personal time.

- ◆ Wellness programs. These might include on-site fitness centers, free on-site health check-ups, exercise classes.

- ◆ Flexible hours. Let employees make up their own schedules within a range of acceptable hours. Sue Shellenbarger, writer of the "Work & Family" column for *The Wall Street Journal,* says, "Regardless of the source of the flexibility, the need is clear. Everyone concerned needs to cut families a little slack up front, to avoid tearing the delicate fabric of family life" (1999, May 12, B1).

- ◆ Days to work at home.

- ◆ Achievement awards. These should go beyond plaques and into usable items such as movie passes, restaurant vouchers, and bonuses.

- ◆ Dry cleaning services, food shops, child care centers on-site.

- ◆ Drop-in centers. These mini-offices (satellite offices) in the suburbs allow employees to avoid the commute into the city every weekday.

- ◆ On-site educational services. Free or subsidized classes, for example, Master of Business Administration classes, so that employees with bachelor's degrees who are moving into management positions can get higher degrees.

How successful are these methods? Companies report that they lower absentee rates and improve employee retention, especially in highly mobile fields such as technology. Absentee rates shot up 25 percent from 1997 to 1998 and increasingly the reason people skip work is stress (Stone, 1999). Therefore, programs and services that relieve stress should diminish absenteeism.

Ideally, employees should have input into which options are offered. Consistency within companies and across companies would also be helpful to employees who transfer or change jobs.

Family and Medical Leave Act of 1993

In recognition of the difficulty of combining work and family, many nations and companies have developed specific policies regarding employee leave for personal, family, or health reasons. The policies vary greatly by country and by employer.

In the United States in 1993, President Bill Clinton signed the Family and Medical Leave Act, which allows workers at companies with more than 50 employees to take up to 12 workweeks of unpaid leave to care for newborns and newly adopted children or to care for ill family members, or themselves. Prospective parents who meet the qualifications set out in the act no longer have to be concerned about whether they will be allowed to be away from work before, during, and after the birth of their children (leave) or whether they will have a job to come back to (job security). Adoption and foster care are covered as well as the illness of a child, spouse, or parent. More details of the act are given in Table 10.1.

Many employers had policies in place long before the passage of the Family and Medical Leave Act. Two of them, Johnson and Johnson and AT&T, reported that their family-supportive policies boosted morale and worker productivity (Galen, 1993). In a January 1993 survey of 524 companies, 7 of 10 respondents said they already offered leave to employees for adoption, family illness, or childbirth, and that costs of such policies were insignificant ("Most Small Businesses Appear Prepared to Cope with New Family Leave Rules," 1993). The *Wall Street Journal* article that reported the survey quoted one employer's comments:

> As far as we're concerned, it's not a problem, says Bill Parsons, president of Palmer Johnson Inc. The Sturgeon Bay, Wis., boat builder already grants family leave to its 350 employees. "In an era where companies are competing for employees, the enlightened companies have already thought about how to handle and treat employees with respect," he adds.

THE MEANING OF WORK AND LEISURE

The next part of this chapter explores the meaning of work and its managerial implications. **Work** is effort expended to produce or accomplish something or activity that is rewarded, usually with pay. **Effort** is exertion or the use of energy to do something (Goldsmith, 1994). Because so many hours are spent in work, it makes a tremendous difference to one's overall sense of contentment and growth. Thomas Carlyle, a nineteenth-century British historian and essayist, wrote, "Blessed is he who has found his work; let him ask no other blessedness."

Around 1900, a six-day workweek was common. In 1938, President Franklin D. Roosevelt signed the Fair Labor Standards Act, which established a 44-hour workweek, which was reduced to 40 hours by 1941. In Japan and other countries around the world, a workweek of five and a half (five weekdays and Saturday morning) to six days is still common. A generation ago, the conventional wisdom among economists was that America was turning into an "affluent society," in which ever more efficient technology would produce an abundance of wealth requiring less and less labor. This did not happen for a variety of reasons, but the end result is that U.S. workers are working more at this point in American history than was predicted. The four-day workweek is still elusive. In fact, workload for many has increased over the last decade.

TABLE 10.1
Family and Medical Leave Act of 1993

The Family and Medical Leave Act applies to all public agencies, including state, local, and federal employers, local education agencies (schools) and private-sector employers employing 50 or more employees in 20 or more workweeks in the current or preceding calendar year within a 75-mile radius.

◆ Covered employers must grant an eligible employee up to a total of 12 workweeks of unpaid leave during any 12-month period for the birth or placement of a child for adoption or foster care, for the care of a seriously ill child, spouse, or parent, or in the case of his or her own serious illness.

◆ Employers have to continue health care coverage for the employee during the leave.

◆ Employers have to guarantee that employees will return to either the same job or a comparable position.

◆ Employers can refuse to reinstate certain highly paid "key" employees after their leave. Such employees are defined as the highest paid 10 percent of the workforce and whose leave would cause economic harm to the employer.

◆ Employers can exempt employees who have not worked for at least one year and who have not worked for at least 1,250 hours, or 25 hours a week, in the previous 12 months.

◆ A doctor's certification has to be obtained to verify a serious illness. Employers may require a second medical opinion.

◆ Employers can substitute an employee's accrued paid leave (such as sick or annual leave) for any part of the 12-week period of family leave.

◆ Under some circumstances, employees may take the leave intermittently, by taking leave in blocks of time or reducing their normal weekly or daily work schedule.

◆ Employers are permitted to require an employee taking intermittent leave for planned medical treatments to transfer temporarily to an equivalent alternative position.

Source: E. Goldsmith, *Family Leave: Changing Needs of the World's Workers,* United Nations, Occasional Paper Series, No. 7 (1993): 6.

The fact hit home for me when I returned to the U.S. in 1996 after a decade abroad. I began to notice that not one of the other seven people in my office left their desks at lunchtime, the way folks used to . . . the Bureau of Labor statistics reports that since 1985 paid vacation time has declined, and so has the average time that workers take off sick. Not surprisingly, more than one third of the people in the FWI survey said that they often or very often feel used up at the end of the workday. (Hunter, 1999, p. 38)

The Work Ethic

The work ethic in the United States has changed along with other changes in the overall culture (Quilling, 1990). The **work ethic** is the degree of dedication

Scott Adams, creator of Dilbert, pokes fun at workplace management.

or commitment to work. **Commitment** refers to the degree to which an individual identifies with and is involved in a particular activity or organization (Goldsmith, 1994). The work ethic is alive, well, and even flourishing in the United States (Quilling, 1990; Brokaw, 1999).

The work ethic is part of an individual's value orientation and, hence, is linked to managerial behavior. Individuals who adhere to a strong work ethic appear to be more polite, responsible, and conservative; they also tend to resist social change and to be rigid (Furnham, 1987; Tang & Tung, 1988). Predictability, discipline, and order are also associated with a strong work ethic (Feather, 1984).

More recently, however, the work ethic has been redefined based on the switch to the knowledge economy. The new workplace requires specific skills (often computer-related) and a great deal of employee discretion. Many organizations reward employees who have the ability to interpret and respond to change, including the unpredictable moods and actions of other people. Thus, discipline remains an important attribute, but striving to learn, to conquer new problems, and to find solutions are more likely to generate success than is dutiful drudge work. "The knowledge economy gives us not only the opportunity but the obligation to reunite work with independent thinking, self-expression, and even joy" (Postrel, 1998, A10). Even Scott Adams, the creator of the comic strip "Dilbert," which pokes fun at the workplace, says that "I'm not at all sad about the state of work right now. I think people are generally happier than they've been in a long time" (Stafford, 1998, 2E).

Since the work ethic is based on values, adherence or nonadherence to the work ethic is a form of self-expression and definition. People develop a work ethic or not depending on what they feel is important. Educators and parents influence the development of the work ethic in children by rewarding work performance. The overall culture, the economy, and work environments further contribute to the development and the sustenance of the work ethic.

Workaholism

Workaholism refers to the inability to stop thinking about work and doing work and the feeling that work is always the most pleasurable part of life. Most workers are not workaholics. True workaholics may have trouble sleeping, relaxing, going on vacation, or spending time alone or with their children and spouse. In terms of Freud's definition of happiness as a combination of work and love, the constant workaholic may be neglecting the "love" side of life in favor of the "work" side. At the beginning of the chapter, the founder of the biotech company, Krishan Kalra, showed classic signs of workaholism.

One myth about workaholics is that they are the most productive workers in a home or an organization. This is usually not true because workaholics are addicted to work, not necessarily to goal attainment. They lack organization and their energy is not channeled properly. Workaholics often suffer from fatigue and stress and may experience health problems from a lack of exercise and rest. They also lack a sense of balance, and this deficiency may spill over into a failure to understand why other employees or family members do not also work constantly. In short, workaholics may be difficult to live with at home or at the office.

The Three P's: Procrastination, Parkinson's Law, and Pareto's Principle

In contrast to a workaholic who constantly works or thinks about work, a **procrastinator** puts off work and postpones decisions. Procrastinators are also difficult to work with because they seldom finish tasks on time and consequently often disappoint their coworkers and employers. They are difficult to live with too because they often forget or fail to meet family obligations.

Everyone procrastinates now and then, but procrastination is excessive when it is pervasive across all arenas of life. When this happens, procrastination is more than a bad habit—it has become a lifestyle. Procrastination is a way to escape responsibility and resist the structure of growing up. It may be related to a fear developed in early childhood or to an unresolved conflict. Sometimes, a person procrastinates because he or she really does not want to do whatever is required. A child who dislikes playing the piano will delay practicing. A child who continually avoids practicing may be signaling he is no longer interested. In that case, perhaps the piano lessons should stop and another activity substituted. Someone who constantly procrastinates on work assignments may be in the wrong job and would be happier elsewhere.

Some individuals (e.g., students putting off studying for a test and pulling an all-night cramming session) say they like the feeling of rushing to meet deadlines and the excitement of the last-minute push; they insist that they perform best when living on the edge. This approach may work for them some of the time, but what if others are relying on them for information (e.g., a team report for a class), if there is a family crisis, or if they become ill the night before an assignment is due? Procrastination can be overcome if the procrastinators are willing to change by rearranging their approach to assignments and rewarding themselves for planning ahead and being on time.

Another concept related to the organization of work is called Parkinson's law. In 1957, the English historian C. Northcote Parkinson studied the Royal Navy and found that the more people hired, the more work they created, without necessarily increasing the organization's output. His observation led to the formulation of **Parkinson's law,** which states that a job expands to fill the time available to accomplish the task. This law illustrates the elasticity of time and work.

Parkinson's law is evident in people who have a lot of time on their hands. They may take all day to mail a letter or to go grocery shopping. They stretch a routine task that could be completed in half an hour into an all-day expedition.

The third P of working and its organization is the Pareto principle. Vilfredo Pareto, a nineteenth-century Italian economist and sociologist, discovered that in any series of elements to be controlled, a selected small fraction of the elements always accounts for a large fraction of effectiveness. The **Pareto principle,** also known as the 80–20 rule, states that 20 percent of the time expended usually produces 80 percent of the results, while 80 percent of the time expended produces only 20 percent of the results. According to this principle, the bulk of an individual's time is wasted in low-productivity activities. The solution to this phenomenon is to recognize that it exists and to focus more of one's attention on the activities and relationships that matter and to put less time and energy into things that do not.

Workforce Trends Including Home-Based Businesses

There is a joke: A guy reads a headline saying, "The president creates 8 million jobs," and he cracks wearily, "Yeah, and I got three of 'em." Many people have two jobs and 13 percent have three jobs (Hunter, 1999). So, one trend is simply more working in a variety of settings.

The average full-time job although officially 40 hours is in reality about 47 hours per week, according to Juliet B. Schor's book *The Overworked American,* and can go to the extreme of 60 hours or more. Workers also report long commutes, chirping cell phones, e-mails that never quit, and lost weekends. The "lost weekends" concept (time spent reading reports, grading papers, answering e-mail, etc.) illustrates the blurring of the distinction between work and leisure.

Another trend is that the workforce is aging as the baby boomers move forward through life. In the year 2000, workers age 55 through 64 will be the fastest growing segment of the workforce. The Age Discrimination Act of 1967 protects most workers age 40 and older from discrimination in the workplace.

A worldwide trend is a redefinition of work space, whether at home or in more traditional workplaces. The move is away from individual offices and cubicles into shared spaces, shared computers (many on wheeled tables), workstations, and so forth. It's all about mobility. "People are working in a variety of different settings. They're moving constantly, both within the office and outside the office" (Powers, 1998, p. 21). An early experimenter with reducing office space was Anderson Worldwide, which reduced the office-to-employee ratio from 1:1 to 1:5.3 in its San Francisco office, thus saving on the cost of rent, furnishings, and utilities. As more and more companies scatter their employees around the globe, they will be relying more on technology to bring people together rather than on a physical space.

Mobility is also evidenced by people moving from job to job, and therefore from location to location, more often today than in the past, according to Phyllis Moen of Cornell University. She says that "The lock-step template of American life is obsolete. . . . This has enormous consequences for policy, employers, communities, families, and individual lives" (Powers, 1998, p. 14). For young people, job hopping is very common. A typical American holds 8.6 different jobs between the ages of 18 and 32, with most changes before the age of 27, according to the Bureau of Labor Statistics. For example, Felix Batcup, 26,

Futuristic workplaces have fewer walls, partitions on wheels, and more open spaces.

associate art director at *Women's Sports and Fitness* magazine, had five jobs in five years and tripled his starting salary in those years ("What's News," 1998).

The point at which a worker on the rise becomes a worker who's consigned to history is coming earlier in people's careers, usually around age 44, according to the Bureau of Labor Statistics. To avoid plateauing, workers are encouraged to try new projects, mentor younger workers, take assignments abroad, and/or get fresh training in order to keep their careers lively, interesting, and challenging.

Another trend is **downshifting,** opting for a simpler life, usually less pay, less stress, more time, in a more personally satisfying occupation. Basically, in downshifting, a person decides that more is not always better. Their reduced income is offset by a more frugal lifestyle. Obviously, downshifting is not for everyone. Someone whose self-worth is measured by status and money would have a hard time turning his or her back on a large income. So, who should consider downshifting? Not those who truly love their careers and enjoy consuming to the hilt:

> But others, like Jacque Blix, just feel trapped in that world. For years, an unhappy Ms. Blix couldn't leave the AT&T marketing job that brought her a good salary and the status of succeeding in a nontraditional role for women. "I felt if I took less money I'd be taking a step backward and denying my potential as a human being," she says. Eventually, she and her husband, David Heitmiller, a corporate product manager, did downshift, saving 30% of their income over three years to finance their corporate exits. They tell their tale in their book, *Getting a Life.* "We saw that we could live with less income and still be happy," she says. (Lancaster, 1998, B1)

A final trend is a return to home-based work. The information age, with its emphasis on computers and electronically transferred information, has made it possible for more people to work from their homes. Naturally, working at home has implications for family relations and involves management considerations such as the arranging of child care and the allocation of time, money, and space (Heck, Saltford, Rowe, & Owen, 1992; Heck, Winter, & Stafford, 1992; Loker & Scannell, 1992; Owen, Carsky, & Dolan, 1992; Rowe, Stafford, & Owen, 1992; Stafford, Winter, Dundan, & Genalo, 1992; Winter, 1992). Time management methods, such as the dovetailing and overlapping of activities described earlier in this book, will come into play as home-based workers juggle their work and family responsibilities. Owen, Carsky, and Dolan (1992) provide this insight into home-based work:

> Even the choice of a home-based occupation over a market job may reflect a commitment or priority by the worker to meeting the needs of the family, especially when family demands are high, such as when young children are present. The degree to which home-based workers can control the various aspects of time may influence the satisfaction derived from the work and from the family/work interface. (p. 136)

The stereotype of a home-based business is a female-owned enterprise, such as a child care center. But that is inaccurate; a recent survey revealed that 59 percent of home-based workers are male. The typical person is about 44 years old, married, and employed in a white-collar profession such as marketing, sales, or technology, for example, software engineering. Kathryn Stafford, a professor at Ohio State University who worked on the study with Barbara Rowe of Purdue and George Haynes of Montana State, said, "We found that most home-based workers are men performing traditional work in fields like sales and construction" (DeLisser & Morse, 1999). They also found that home-based business owners were better educated and more affluent than the rest of the population. A further finding was that 88 percent of home-based owners sell most of their products or services within their state or an hour's drive from their homes. For example, in Ohio, home-based work contributes more to the state's personal income rolls than farming.

In the late 1990s, 30 million Americans were working at home at least some of the time; the highest share among those aged 18 to 29 (Allen & Moorman, 1997). Are home-based businesses the nirvana people hoped for? In some cases yes, but in others a number of problems are surfacing:

> Many home-office workers feel as though they're working in a vacuum. They feel isolated and struggle with a perception that they're not quite 'legit.' They lament the loss of support staff, employer-provided educational opportunities, health insurance, pension plans, and paid vacation time. They scramble to find suitable places to meet with clients. Those who run businesses also run the risks of running into zoning and IRS audits. (Allen & Moorman, 1998, p. 57)

So, home-based businesses, along with all the other trends, have their pluses and minuses. The next decade will reveal how these trends play out, which ones succeed, which ones do not, and in what ways they will be altered as people search for new options.

Volunteer Work

So far this chapter has focused on paid work. Another type of work that requires time, energy, and commitment is **volunteer work,** or work that does not generate pay. Half of all Americans volunteer in the nonprofit sector, (Mackin, 1998). People perform volunteer work for a number of reasons, but one of the most important is their sense of social consciousness. They want to contribute to their family's well-being (e.g., by volunteering for Boy Scouts or Girl Scouts or the PTA) or to contribute to others and to the community. Volunteer work also provides a sense of self-worth and self-esteem and heightened social and leadership skills. A survey conducted by the Gallup Organization revealed who volunteers and why (see Table 10.2). Some businesses and government agencies allow workers to take time off to perform volunteer work such as tutoring or helping with school events. Volunteerism used to conjure up an image of a kindly lady volunteering at the hospital or through her garden club. Today, volunteers come in all ages, races, and income levels.

High schools and universities are offering courses and credit for volunteer service. The courses teach students how to work as volunteers and managers of organizations that have goals other than making a profit. For example, Donald Tobias and Stephen Watson teach such a course at Cornell University. The goal of their course is to introduce students to the management practices and principles in public sector and nonprofit organizations.

> "At Cornell we aren't just turning out students who will be actively involved in careers," Tobias says, "We also are helping to produce people who will be citizens in their communities. Many of our students may become members of boards of directors for not-for-profit organizations, so they need to know how those organizations work and how to think strategically about management decisions and strategies based on the mission of the organization." (Mackin, 1998, p. 10)

Leisure

Leisure is defined as freedom from time-consuming activities, tasks, duties, or responsibilities. Leisure time is interspersed throughout people's lives and

TABLE 10.2
Who Volunteers and Why

◆ Time given to volunteer work averaged 4.2 hours a week.

◆ People 45 to 54 volunteered the most (5.2 hours a week), followed by those 35 to 44 (4.8 hours).

◆ People with household incomes of $60,000 to $75,000 volunteered most often, followed by those earning $30,000 to $40,000.

◆ People volunteered because they were asked by someone (43.3%), through their participation in an organization (40.3%), because a family member or friend would benefit (26.5%), or because they sought out a volunteer activity on their own (21.8%).

Source: From a 1994 survey for the Independent Sector conducted by the Gallup Organization.

is formally designated in vacation time. The amount of time typically designated for vacations varies considerably by country. The United States has no vacation laws, and the usual vacation is two or three weeks after several years of employment with the same company. In Germany, Italy, Austria, France, and other industrialized countries that have laws governing minimum vacation time for employees, the usual allocation is five to six weeks of vacation a year. Why do U.S. workers trail Europeans in vacation time? Labor experts say Europe's powerful unions, in negotiating hard for more vacation time, have enjoyed political support as time off has become intertwined with economics. Though it's a matter of intense debate, some European governments argue that the combination of more holiday time and a shorter workweek translates into more jobs. U.S. workers, on the other hand, have focused more on pay increases, accepting less time off as part of the bargain (Shapiro, 1999).

Weekends are usually times of increased leisure. As Table 10.3 shows, men have more leisure time for themselves and spend less time than women do on weekend household chores. Interests and hobbies garner the most weekend leisure activity time for both men and women; playing with children comes second.

Although one would assume that leisure time has increased over the last two decades, Julia Schor, author of *The Overworked American,* says that the amount of time Americans spend at their jobs has risen steadily. She also notes that when surveyed, respondents report that they have only 16.5 hours of leisure a week after taking care of their job and household obligations. Surprisingly, studies of household labor beginning in the 1910s and continuing through the 1970s do not show a marked decrease in time spent in household labor, despite the improvements in household technology. Schor observes that household work has expanded to fill available time. Instead of the extra time being devoted to leisure, it apparently is being put back into work and higher standards of household labor. Perhaps this lack of leisure time is all part of the time squeeze; it reflects the increased value that is put on time and the fact that leisure time is not valued as much as work time. ·

In *The Harried Leisure Class,* Linder argues that high hourly earnings make time so precious that many people cannot afford the time it takes to enjoy life on a daily basis and are forced to eat meals on the run, cut short the foreplay of lovemaking, attend short religious services, and browse or

TABLE 10.3
Weekend Leisure and Chores:
Where Do the Hours Go?*

Working women begin the weekend with less energy than their husbands do. But catching up on sleep or spending extra time with the kids is often just a sweet dream. As shown in the following charts—which document how men and women spend their weekends—women spend most of their Saturdays and Sundays taking care of family responsibilities while their husbands have more time for themselves.

| | Time Spent (hours) | |
Weekend Leisure Activity	Women	Men
Interests/hobbies	3:19	4:09
Playing with kids	3:08	2:21
Visiting friends	2:38	3:12
Visiting relatives	2:30	1:45
Reading	1:58	2:03
Dining out	1:39	1:50
Entertainment	1:31	1:52
Exercising	1:00	1:58
Gardening	:52	:55

Men have, on the average, a full hour and a half more leisure time on weekends than women do. In fact, women scored higher only in those leisure activities that were family-related: visiting relatives and playing with the children.

Lesiure activities men spent most time on were pursuing hobbies or other personal interests, reading, exercising and visiting friends.

| | Time Spent (hours) | |
Weekend Chores	Women	Men
Cleaning	2:57	1:35
Working at job	2:42	3:07
Errands	1:51	1:35
Laundry	1:48	:46
Grocery shopping	1:08	:51
House repairs	:37	1:51
Bills	:33	:35

(Continued)

glance at books rather than read them. For example, a college professor named Neil says he reads movie and book reviews but rarely has time to see a movie or read a book cover to cover. By reading reviews, Neil can still converse with his colleagues. He is not distressed by his busy lifestyle and says that at this stage in his life he really values work over leisure. He spends most of his time in work-related pursuits, most of which he finds stimulating and pleasurable.

In view of such approaches to work and leisure, what part does leisure play in human life? People must answer this question for themselves. One person's idea of leisure is gardening; another prefers to play tennis. Leisure was once associated mostly with social or recreational activities (e.g., snowmobiling, boating, swimming), but it now includes relaxation and meditation as well as more lively pursuits. In its broadest context, leisure is a state of mind

TABLE 10.3 (Continued)
**Weekend Leisure and Chores:
Where Do the Hours Go?***

Weekend Chores	Time Spent (hours)	
	Couples with Kids	Couples without Kids
Cleaning	3:05	1:51
Working at job	3:23	2:37
Errands	1:57	1:35
Laundry	1:40	1:06
House repairs	1:28	1:03
Grocery shopping	1:04	:57
Bills	:42	:30

Women spend an average of 1 hour and 16 minutes more on household chores each weekend than men do. And what are men doing? They are primarily catching up on job-related work and making repairs around the house. Women's chores include housecleaning, laundry, grocery shopping, and running errands.

Couples with kids spend more time on weekend chores—a total of 3 hours and 40 minutes more—than do couples without kids, who average 9 hours and 39 minutes. Cleaning consumes an extra hour and 14 minutes for parents, laundry an additional 34 minutes, grocery shopping an additional 7 minutes and running errands an additional 22 minutes. And, since it's women who do the lion's share of household chores and jobs, they are, no doubt, the ones most likely to handle this extra load.

*The survey cited was conducted for the Hilton Corporation by R. H. Bruskin Associates, a New Brunswick, New Jersey, research firm. It is based on a projectable (to the total population) sample of approximately 1,000 men and women over the age of 18.

Source: Alice Fleming, "Quality Mommy Time," *Redbook* (June 1990). Survey data reprinted with the permission of Hilton Hotel Corporation. ©1990 Hilton Hotels.

rather than a use of time or an activity. It follows, then, that the location of leisure is also being rethought. Must one go away to engage in leisure activities? Not everyone has the time or the resources to go elsewhere to enjoy recreation and leisure. Consequently, there is a growing worldwide recognition of the need to provide leisure facilities, such as parks and fitness trails, in housing developments, especially in crowded urban areas (Woods & Strugnell, 1993).

Electronic Resources

Congress is considering ways of expanding the coverage of the Family and Medical Leave Act. One idea is to increase the coverage to include employees of small businesses. For more information on this, go to **www.nationalpartnership.org**.

The AFL-CIO has put together a Web site (**www.aflcio.org/women/equalpay.htm**) that breaks down the pay gap between men and women by occupation and by state. According to this site, female lawyers, for example, earned a median $959 a week in 1998, 24 percent less than men in the same profession.

www.aflcio.org/women/
equalpay/htm

The Women's Bureau of the U.S. Labor Department is the only agency that has a congressional mandate to promote the welfare of working women. Created in the 1920s, it is responsible for informing working women of their rights. Their site at **www.dol.gov/dol/wb/** provides government reports about equal pay issues and the state of child care resources, statistics on women's occupations, and the bureau's strategic plan. Another site identifying child care resources is **www.parentsplace.com/readroom/ACS/ daycare.html**.

For midcareer and late career advice visit the AARP Web site at **aarp.org/working_options/home/html**. This site also provides links to America's Job Bank, which is useful to adults seeking employment.

A resource for home-based work is the American Association of Home-Based Businesses at **www.aahbb.org**, a national nonprofit group that provides support and development information on starting and operating a home business, taxes, and insurance.

Cyberspace is having a profound influence on how volunteer programs are managed and how volunteers are recruited. For example, Hewlett Packard Company employees mentor high school students in math and science through HP Mentors, an e-mail exchange program. Examples of volunteer organizations who are online include:

◆ Big Brothers Big Sisters of America: **www.bbbsa.org/**
◆ Corporation for National Services: **www.cns.gov/**
◆ Points of Light Foundation: **www.pointsoflight.org/**
◆ YMCA of the USA: **www.ymca.net/**
◆ YWCA of the USA: **www.ywca.org/**

Summary

This chapter focused on the problems of managing work and family life roles and provided solutions to work and family conflicts. Employers and countries are reexamining child care, elder care, and family medical leave policies to accommodate the needs of employees with families. The Family and Medical Leave Act of 1993 is an example of such a policy.

The three P's—procrastination, Parkinson's law, and Pareto's principle—are important to understanding the organization of time and work. So are the work ethic and workaholism. Today's workforce includes more women and members of minority groups as well as more home-based workers. Not all work is paid; volunteer work is an important part of many people's lives. Just as work is changing, so is leisure. Indeed, the amount of leisure time may be decreasing. Too little time and too much responsibility can lead to stress, the subject of the next chapter.

Key Terms

commitment	leisure	volunteer work
compromise	Pareto principle	work
downshifting	Parkinson's law	workaholism
effort	procrastinator	work ethic

Review Questions

1. Do you agree or disagree with Freud that the recipe for happiness is "work and love"? Should anything else be added? If so, what? Explain your answer.

2. How can individuals and families resolve work and family conflict?

3. What is the difference between Pareto's principle and Parkinson's law?

4. The traditional image of volunteers and the reality of today's volunteers are different. What is the difference? Why do high schools and colleges give credit for and have courses on community service?

5. What is your definition of leisure? Do you agree with Julia Schor's observation that people have less leisure today than they did a few years ago?

References

Allen, K. & Moorman, G. (1997, October). Leaving home: The emigration of home office workers. *American Demographics, 57.*

Anderson, E. (1992). Decision-making style: Impact on satisfaction of the commuter couples' lifestyle. *Journal of Family and Economic Issues, 13*(1), 5–22.

Brokaw, T. (1999, May–June). The way we worked. *Modern Maturity,* 42–43, 49.

DeLisser, E. & Morse, D. (1999, May 18). Enterprise. *The Wall Street Journal,* B24.

Feather, N. (1984). Protestant ethic, conservatism, and values. *Journal of Personality and Social Psychology, 45*(5), 1132–1141.

Furnham, F. (1987). Work-related beliefs and human values. *Personality and Individual Differences, 8*(5), 627–637.

Galen, M. (1993, June 28). Work and family. *Business Week,* 80–88.

Goldsmith, E. (1993). Family leave: The changing needs of the world's workers. Occasional Paper Series, No. 7, International Year of the Family, United Nations: Vienna.

Goldsmith, E. (1994). Work efficiency and motivation. *Encyclopedia of Human Behavior, 4.* San Diego: Academic Press, 547–553.

Greenberger, E. & Steinberg, L. (1986). *When teenagers work.* New York: Basic Books.

Grimm-Thomas, K. & Perry-Jenkins, M. (1994). All in a day's work: Job experiences, self-esteem, and fathering in working-class families. *Family Relations, 43,* 174–181.

Heck, R., Saltford, N., Rowe, B., & Owen, A. (1992). The utilization of child care by households engaged in home-based employment. *Journal of Family and Economic Issues, 13*(2), 213–237.

Heck, R., Winter, M. & Stafford, K. (1992). Managing work and family in home-based employment. *Journal of Family and Economic Issues, 13*(2), 187–212.

Hunter, M. (1999, May–June). Work, work, work, work! *Modern Maturity,* 36–41.

Joo, S. & Garman, T. (1998). The potential effects of workplace financial education based on the relationship between personal financial wellness and worker job productivity. *Personal Finances and Worker Productivity, 2*(1), 163–174.

Kelly, R. & Voydanoff, P. (1985). Work/family role strain among employed parents. *Family Relations, 34,* 367–374.

Lancaster, H. (1998, January 20). 'Downshifters' find more balance in life by shrinking careers. *The Wall Street Journal,* B1.

Larson, J., Wilson, S., & Beley, R. (1994). The impact of job insecurity on marital and family relationships. *Family Relations, 43,* 138–143.

Lewis, J. (1993). *How to build and manage a winning project team.* New York: American Management Association.

Linder, S. (1970). *The harried leisure class.* New York: Columbia University Press.

Loker, S. & Scannell, E. (1992). Characteristics and practices of home-based workers. *Journal of Family and Economic Issues, 13*(2), 173–186.

Mackin, J. (1998, Summer). Learning to be an effective volunteer. *Human Ecology Forum,* 10–14.

Most small businesses appear prepared to cope with new family-leave rules. (1993, February 8). *Wall Street Journal,* B1–B2.

Orthner, D. & Pittman, J. (1986). Family contributions to work commitment. *Journal of Marriage and the Family, 48,* 573–581.

Owen, A., Carsky, M., & Dolan, E. (1992). Home-based employment: Historical and current consideration. *Journal of Family and Economic Issues, 13*(2), 121–138.

Postrel, V. (1998, September 4). The work ethic, redefined. *The Wall Street Journal,* A10.

Powers, M. (1998, Spring). The new template of American life. *Human Ecology Forum,* 13–32.

Quilling, J. (1990, Fall). Dimensions of ethics: The work ethic. *Home Economics Forum,* 13–16, 20.

Rapoport, R. (1985). Normal crisis, family structure, and mental health. *Family Process, 2*(1), 68–80.

Retherford, P., Hildreth, G., & Goldsmith, E. (1989). Social support and resource management of unemployed women. In E. Goldsmith (Ed.), *Work and family: Theory, research, and applications.* Newbury Park, CA: Sage Publications.

Rowe, B., Stafford, K. & Owen, A. (1992). Who's working at home: The types of families engaged in home-based work. *Journal of Family and Economic Issues, 13*(2), 159–172,

Schor, J. (1991). *The overworked American.* New York: Basic Books.

Schroeder, P. (1988). Parental leave: The need for a federal policy. In E. Zigler and M. Frank (Eds.), *The parental leave crisis: Toward a national policy*. New Haven, CT: Yale University Press.

Shellenbarger, S. (1998, December 30). Future work policies may focus on teens trimming workloads. *The Wall Street Journal*, B1.

_____. (1999, February 24). Students get lessons in how to manage a well balanced life. *The Wall Street Journal*, B1.

_____. (1999, May 12). New research helps families to assess flaws in work plans. *The Wall Street Journal*, B1.

Shapiro, E. (1999, January 11). The life of leisure. *The Wall Street Journal*, R37.

Smith, S. & Price, S. (1992). Women and plant closings: Unemployment, re-employment, and job training enrollment following dislocation. *Journal of Family and Economic Issues, 13*(1), 45–72.

Stafford, D. (1998, October 28). New "Dilbert" book chronicles "Joy of Work," *Tallahassee Democrat*, 2E.

Stafford, K., Winter, M., Duncan, K., & Genalo, M. (1992). Studying at-home income generation: Issues and methods. *Journal of Family and Economic Issues, 13*(2), 139–158.

Stone, B. (1999, June 7). Get a life! *Newsweek*, 68–69.

Symonds, W., Ellis, J., Siler, J., Zellner, W., & Garland, S. (1991, March 25). Is business bungling its battle with booze? *Business Week*, 76–78.

Tang, T. & Tung, Y. (1988). *Some demographic correlates of the Protestant work ethic*. Tulsa, OK: Southwestern Psychological Association. (ERIC Document Reproduction No. ED 300 702).

The world's women 1970–1990: Trends and statistics. (1991). A publication of the United Nations, Social Statistics and Indicators, Series K, No. 8, New York.

Ulrich, D. & Dunne, H. (1986). *To love and work: A systemic interlocking of family, workplace, and career*. New York: Brunner/Mazel.

Voydanoff, P. (1988, August). Work role characteristics, family structure demands, and work/family conflict. *Journal of Marriage and the Family, 50*.

_____. (1989). Work and family: A review and expanded conceptualization. In E. Goldsmith (Ed.), *Work and family: Theory, research, and applications*. Newbury Park, CA: Sage Publications.

_____. (1993). *Men, family, and work*. Newbury Park, CA: Sage Publications.

Voydanoff, P. & Kelly, R. (1984). Determinants of work-related family problems among employed parents. *Journal of Marriage and the Family, 46*, 881–892.

What's New. (1998, September). *The Wall Street Journal Classroom Edition*, 3.

Winter, M. (1992). At-home income generation: Introduction. *Journal of Family and Economic Issues, 13*(2), 117–120.

Woods, S. & Strugnell, C. (1993). Leisure provision and usage in recently redeveloped areas of Belfast. *Journal of Consumer Studies and Home Economics, 17*, 343–353.

chapter **11**

Managing Stress and Fatigue

MAIN TOPICS

STRESS: DEFINITION, THEORY, AND RESEARCH
CRISES AND ADAPTATION TO STRESS
DECISION MAKING AND STRESS
THE BODY'S RESPONSE TO STRESS
DIET, EXERCISE, AND STRESS

STRESS MANAGEMENT
TECHNIQUES FOR REDUCING STRESS
BURNOUT
STRESS AND NON-EVENTS
PARENTS, CHILDREN, AND STRESS
COLLEGE STUDENTS AND STRESS

FATIGUE: DEFINITION AND SOURCES
THE BODY AND FATIGUE
SYSTEMS THEORY: SLEEP, ENERGY, AND FATIGUE

Did you know that...?

...Although a man's blood pressure rises more sharply in response to stress, women react to a wider range of stressors and say they feel stress more often.

...The average American now sleeps 7 hours a night; before electric lights were invented, that number was 10.

> Don't sweat the small stuff. . . . And it's all small stuff.
> —*Richard Carlson*

THE TWENTY-FIRST CENTURY will be characterized as the era of family transformation and stress (McCubbin et al., 1997). Diverse family forms, more work demands, care of the chronically ill and disabled, and other pressures on individuals and families will stretch human resiliency as far as it can go. People exhibit stress in lots of ways: replying angrily to an innocent question, experiencing a pounding headache at the end of a hard day at work, or drumming their fingers on the steering wheel in a traffic jam (Powell & Enright, 1990). Daily hassles that build up stress include annoying practical problems, disappointments, disagreements, and family and financial concerns (Garrison et al., 1994). Contributing to this everyday stress are the new technologies, and constant streams of information. For example, due to fax machines and e-mail, messages that once took weeks now arrive in seconds and require instant responses. The pressure to respond immediately is enormous.

Managing stress and fatigue is the subject of this chapter. Rapid information transfer is just one example of the many stresses encountered in today's world. Fatigue, a concept covered extensively in early management books and courses, has reemerged as a significant management/wellness problem. People are not getting enough rest and relaxation. They spend their weekends running around getting ready for the next workweek. There is just too much to accomplish in too little time. In addition to examining the effects of stress on families and society, this chapter will offer suggestions on ways to manage stress and fatigue.

STRESS: DEFINITION, THEORY, AND RESEARCH

The word *stress* has many definitions, but for the purposes of this book, **stress** refers to the nonspecific response of the body to any demand made upon it (Seyle, 1974). Stress usually involves a state of tension. It is considered a process rather than an end state. A process implies that changes occur over time and across different situations. A person who is stressed experiences several stages or levels of stress. For example, getting ready to give a speech involves many stages: preparation, writing, rehearsal, and delivering the speech. Stress may occur at any or all of these stages.

Some stress is inevitable. Although there seems to be more stress today than ever before, stress is timeless. It exists in all societies no matter how primitive. In fact, the potential for stress exists whenever one person interacts with another or with the environment. An approaching hurricane or tornado is stressful, so is an approaching belligerent ex-boyfriend or ex-girlfriend.

As these examples suggest, stress may occur when a person feels threatened or scared. When the potential for harm is high or people feel they lack the resources to reduce the threat, stress increases. **Stressors** are situations or events that cause stress. Stressors can be categorized as relational or environmental. Most of the literature emphasizes relational stressors, but environmental stressors are equally important. Noise, pollution, poor lighting and ventilation, crowding, isolation, vibration, lack of adequate parking, static, litter, car fumes, and poorly insulated and designed homes, factories, and offices are examples of environmental stressors. School and work are particularly stressful because these environments are central to most people's lives and they view their self-worth in terms of their success or failure in these areas (McLellan, Bragg, & Cacciola, 1992).

At the same time, stress is culturally and personally defined. What is stressful in India may not be considered stressful in the United States and vice versa. Individuals vary in their reactions to stress, too. What is acutely stressful for one person may not affect another person at all. In other words, stress is ultimately in the eye of the beholder (House, 1983). Stress also varies in degree from everyday, normal stress to more prolonged serious stress that can lead to troublesome symptoms (Powell & Enright, 1990).

Stress can be explained within the context of systems theory because stress comes from a variety of sources (inputs) and has a variety of outcomes (outputs). Since it is a process, stress is generally considered a throughput, but stress can also be an input as it enters the system or an output because one person's actions may cause stress in another person. For example, worrying is a process that is stress producing. The cause of the worrying may be an outside stressor being input to the system. What the worrier finally decides to do may transfer the stress to another person. For example, a retiring chairperson of a committee may gleefully pass on a thick file of past committee business and procedures to the incoming chairperson and in so doing pass the stress on to another person.

There is evidence of a gender difference in reaction to stress. Men's blood pressure rises more sharply in response to stress than do women's. But, women react to a wider range of stressors and say they feel stress more often, perhaps because they take a holistic view of everyday life (Kalb & Rogers, 1999).

Crises and Adaptation to Stress

Crises, which are sudden events that require changes in normal patterns of behavior, often cause stress. Getting a flat tire while driving to work is a crisis. The driver must deviate from his normal pattern and fix the tire. How the driver reacts to the crisis will depend on many factors—the time, his expertise at changing tires, whether he has a spare tire or not, how far he is from a service station, and so forth.

Several researchers have developed models and scales that illustrate how individuals and families adapt to crises. These models and scales show the systematic interaction of crises, resources, pileup, and adaptation. **Stress overload** or **pileup** refers to the cumulative effect of many stresses building up at one time. For example, using the rating scale in Table 11.1, individuals can determine how much stress they have experienced in the past year. The originators of the scale, Holmes and Rahe, claim that substantial stress pileup can increase the incidence of illness. Note that the highest stressor event is the death of a spouse (100 points) and the lowest stressor event on the scale is a minor violation of the law (11 points). Scores of 100 to 200 are normal, but scores over 300 are considered high and indicative of trouble ahead.

As the Holmes and Rahe scale illustrates, stress levels can rise as a result of one major life change or from a series of small changes. Fixing a flat tire on the way to work may not be a big problem by itself, but as the day continues and the driver loses his keys, fights with his boss, and forgets an important meeting, stress pileup can occur. The individual may feel he cannot handle any more stress. Likewise, families experience stress pileup: too many conflicting appointments and too many demands on time, energy, emotions, and money will cause stress to build up to the point where the family cannot cope.

David Dollahite (1991) developed the ABCD-XYZ Resource Management Model of Crisis/Stress (see Figure 11.1). His model emphasizes how individual and family decision making, adaptive coping, and management behavior can be activated to lessen the impact of crisis/stress situations. This model has seven key parts:

- ◆ A   The stressor event or situation, the stimulus that forces some response
- ◆ B   The coping resources
- ◆ C   The definition of the situation
- ◆ D   The demands of the situation
- ◆ X   The crisis or stress
- ◆ Y   The cognitive coping and management
- ◆ Z   The adaptive behavior, which entails growth and change and leads to a better fit between the environment and the person or family

The oval surrounding ABCD-XYZ places individuals and families within their historical, economic, technological, cultural, legal, political, religious,

TABLE 11.1
Social Readjustment Rating
Scale: The Stress of Adjusting
to Change

Events	Scale of Impact	Events	Scale of Impact
Death of spouse	100	Son or daughter leaving home	29
Divorce	73	Trouble with in-laws	29
Marital separation	65	Outstanding personal achievement	28
Jail term	63		
Death of close family member	63	Spouse begins or stops work	26
Personal injury or illness	53	Begin or end school	26
Marriage	50	Change in living conditions	25
Fired at work	47	Revision of personal habits	24
Marital reconciliation	45	Trouble with boss	23
Retirement	45	Change in work hours or conditions	20
Change in health of family member	44	Change in residence	20
Pregnancy	40	Change in schools	20
Sex difficulties	39	Change in recreation	20
Gain of new family member	39	Change in church activities	19
Business readjustment	39	Change in social activities	19
Change in financial state	38	Mortgage or loan less than $10,000	17
Death of close friend	37	Change in sleeping habits	16
Change to different line of work	36	Change in number of family get-togethers	15
Change in number of arguments with spouse	35	Change in eating habits	15
Mortgage over $10,000	31	Vacation	12
Foreclosure of mortgage or loan	30	Christmas	12
Change in responsibilities at work	29	Minor violations of the law	11

Life change is stressful. To determine how much stress you have experienced from life changes in the last year, add up the points for each of the events listed that you have experienced in the last year. Then refer to the following chart to determine how serious your condition is. For example, if you get married, get pregnant, buy a house, take a vacation, and celebrate Christmas, your total would be 50 + 40 + 31 + 13 + 12 = 146.

Life Change Score	Chance of Illness in Next Year
0–150	37%
150–300	51%
300+	80%

Scores of 100 to 200 are common; 300-plus is high.

Source: Reprinted with permission from *Journal of Psychosomatic Research* 11, T. H. Holmes and R. H. Rahe, "The social readjustment rating scale," (1967) Elsevier Science Ltd. Pergamon Imprint, Oxford, England.

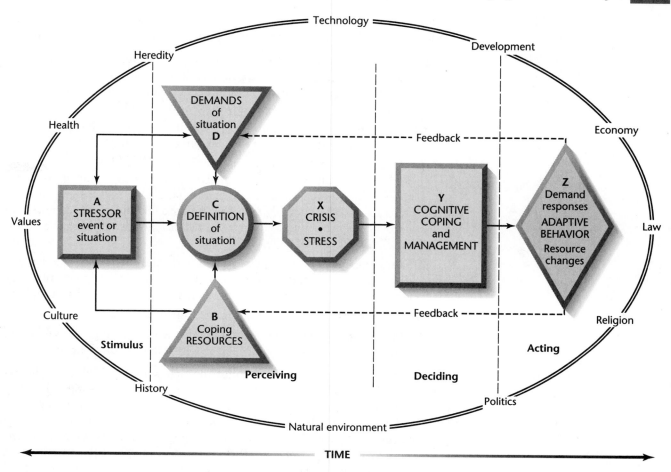

FIGURE 11.1

ABCD-XYZ Resource Management Model of Crisis/Stress

Source: David C. Dollahite (1991). Family resource management and family stress theories: Toward a conceptual integration. *Lifestyles: Family and Economic Issues, 12*(4), 265. Reprinted with permission.

and natural environmental contexts. Health (mental and physical), values, heredity, and development (stage of life cycle) form other important contexts.

The ABCD-XYZ Resource Management Model of Crisis/Stress illustrates that stress and stressors cannot be studied in isolation; they are part of an interactive system involving individuals and families in a larger environmental context.

Outsourcing

One of the ways to adapt to stress is to try to reduce it. To lessen stress, Americans increasingly are outsourcing traditional homemaking and child care functions, a trend driven by three factors: more women working, an older population, and a growing affluent class. **Outsourcing** is defined as paying someone else to do one's work.

> Outsourcing is a logical extension of David Ricardo's 1817 theory of **comparative advantage.** Individuals, no less companies, do best when they focus on activities in which they can add the most value, and outsource other activities to specialists. And since housework has traditionally not been counted as an economic activity, the impact on the economy of extending outsourcing into the huge household-services sector will be massive (Sheth & Sisodia, 1999).

The potential results of outsourcing include increasing employment and higher tax revenues, putting more individual effort into higher work productivity, and investing remaining time into hobbies or other preferred activities. Following are some examples of activities and tasks that are being outsourced:

- Meal preparation/cooking: increased use of restaurants, home delivery, take-out, personal chefs, and prepared foods from supermarkets. In the year 2001, supermarket home meal replacement food sales are expected to reach $176 billion a year (Sheth & Sisodia, 1999).

- Cleaning: between 1986 and 1996 the number of households using an external cleaning service rose by 33 percent (Sheth & Sisodia, 1999).

- Child care, elder care (including home-based assisted living), and pet care. For example, "Family caregivers, who must balance work responsibilities, stretch their budgets and handle the added stress of looking after an elderly family member or friend, are an emerging market in need of respite services, targeted consumer goods and financial planning" (Braus, 1998, p. 1).

- Shopping: personal shoppers, buying over the Internet, using services that will pick up and deliver—such as shoe repair, firewood, film, dry cleaning, videos, and mail packages (in short, less in-person shopping).

- Yard work, pool cleaning, and home improvements.

- Organizing. Personal service companies who rearrange closets, clean garages, or wait for the cable TV repairperson are on the rise.

Contrary to popular belief, it is not the rich who are driving up the demand for these services (they already have them), it is the time-starved middle class who are taking outsourcing to new heights. The hesitation to outsource has eased as more people have extra income and place a higher value on their personal time. Do they want to spend it cleaning house or mowing the lawn? Or, would they prefer to pay for these services and spend their time doing something else? How much they outsource has a great deal to do with their comfort level with the idea, a subject to be explored next.

Comfort Zones and Internal and External Stress

Stress is present in all human relationships and activities and only becomes harmful when there is an imbalance that causes natural coping mechanisms to become strained (Capel & Gurnsey, 1987). Stress reduction is a means of restoring balance in lives. As mentioned in Chapter 2, in systems terminology the return to balance is called homeostasis. When a system becomes unbalanced, the homeostasis mechanism is triggered and an attempt is made to reach a comfort zone. A **comfort zone** is a combination of habit and everyday expectations mixed with an appropriate amount of adventure and novelty. It represents that space in which the level of stress feels right for the individual—the quantity of work is enough to make life interesting, but is not so burdensome as to produce discomfort or other undesirable effects.

Families and organizations have comfort zones just as individuals do. For example, a sudden drop in the stock market may shake the comfort zones of Wall Street brokerage firms as well as those of families who have invested in the stock market. The passage of stress from Wall Street to the family and individual level is an example of the **domino effect**. Another example of the domino effect is the impact that a company president's personal problems may have on the entire organization. The anxiety at the top may rumble downward through the organization leading to a long list of workplace problems: diminished worker satisfaction, decreased productivity, subgroup conflict, misuse of authority, role confusion, scapegoating, and substance abuse (Ulrich & Dunne, 1986). In situations such as this, where stress is brought on from outside the individual, people are said to be experiencing **external stress**.

External stress may come from any of three kinds of experience:

1. *Acute major stress.* Stress resulting from a recent event such as a car accident, job loss, or death of a loved one.

2. *Ongoing, role-related stress.* Stress caused by chronic difficulties in one's work or family roles.

3. *Lifetime trauma stress.* Stress resulting from having undergone severe trauma, such as early-childhood loss of one or both parents or exposure to calamitous strains such as wartime or natural disasters (*Two New Landmark Studies,* 1991).

In contrast, **internal stress** originates in one's own mind and body. An ambitious person may bring on internal stress by setting too high a standard for achievement (e.g., expecting to win every award, title, or promotion). Or, a person may be stressed about her or his body image or lack of friends. Adolescents are particularly sensitive about their physical appearance (McLellan, Bragg, & Cacciola, 1992).

Everyone tries to balance internal and external stresses. Some stress is necessary to drive behavior—to get individuals out of bed in the morning and get them going. In this sense, stress serves as a motivator. Too much stress can be debilitating, however, and leads to immobilization.

Hans Seyle: Founder of Stress Research

Despite the long-standing fascination with stress, it was not until this century that a scientific explanation for stress and its effects on the body was developed. Hans Seyle, formerly a professor at the University of Montreal, has been called the father or founder of stress research. He pointed out that everyone lives with some degree of stress all the time and that complete freedom from stress is death. Perhaps his greatest contribution was in showing that there are two types of stress: harmful stress—called **distress**—and beneficial stress—called **eustress** (from the Greek *eu,* meaning good, as in euphoria). A person who gets on an airplane and feels sick with fear and anxiety is distressed. A fellow passenger feeling a sense of adventure and excitement is experiencing eustress. Both people are in the same situation, but they react differently. As this example illustrates, to understand the stress reaction, one must consider the person involved and not just the situation or crisis. The example also shows that not all stress is upsetting or damaging. As Seyle (1976) wrote, normal activities such as a game of tennis or a passionate kiss can produce stress without causing conspicuous damage.

Seyle studied the body's adaptive response to stress and reported that the stress syndrome is fundamental to virtually all higher forms of animals. He developed a comprehensive theory of the body's adaptive processes, based on a three-stage general adaptation syndrome. He was also the first scientist to identify the main organs and hormones involved in the stress response. His concept of stress led to new avenues of research in degenerative diseases, including coronary thrombosis, brain hemorrhage, hardening of the arteries, high blood pressure, kidney failure, arthritis, peptic ulcers, and cancer.

His experiments led him to theorize that to eliminate stress and individual's adaptive reactions would be to eliminate all change, including growth, development, and maturation. Without stress human lives would be at complete rest—rather boring to say the least.

Seyle was often asked what can be done to reduce distress. He advised individuals to watch for signs that they are becoming too keyed up. On a personal note, he said that he tried to forget immediately everything that was unimportant because trying to remember too many things is a major source of psychological stress.

Decision Making and Stress

Seyle's conscious decision to forget unnecessary information was one method he used to reduce stress. Delegating work or decisions to others is another way to reduce stress. For example, using the services of travel agents to arrange trips can lessen stress for a frequent traveler. In efficient households, chores can be delegated to spouses and children. A third way to reduce stress is to postpone decisions when there is no hurry. Most good decisions are not made in a hurry. Taking the time to think out all the alternatives and identify the best use of resources leads to sounder decisions. In addition, individuals, employees, and families can use many other methods to reduce stress. As an example, Toffler (1970) observed:

> I have seen a woman sociologist, just returned from a crowded, highly stimulating professional conference, sit down in a restaurant and absolutely refuse to make any decisions whatever about her meal. "What would you like?" her husband asked. "You decide for me," she replied. When pressed to choose between specific alternatives, she still explicitly refused, insisting angrily that she lacked the "energy" to make the decision. (p. 324)

In an employment situation, a way to reduce stress is to surround oneself with competent workers. Consider how carefully a newly elected president of the United States selects the members of the cabinet. A navy admiral expressed his thoughts on the importance of employee selection:

> If you have the capability to do this, surround yourself with competent, capable people. I found that if I have people that are working for me of this caliber, that makes my job much easier. . . . you try to get the best performer you can get—the best qualified, the best experienced. It gives you confidence in what they are doing and that it's going to be correct. (Quick, Nelson, & Quick, 1990, p. 55)

How to react to stress is a decision involving conscious problem solving. Because stress permeates all aspects of individual and family life, everyone needs to master these problem-solving skills: sound decision making leads to improved lifestyles and senses of well-being. As Chapter 8 pointed out, potential stressors for individuals and families include poverty, lack of adequate housing, and disabling conditions. Each of these stressors provides ample opportunity for decision making.

Psychological Hardiness

Decision-making style is based on the personal characteristics and strengths of the decision maker. For example, when Debra, a 35-year-old bride, learned the morning of her wedding day that the dry cleaners had ruined her "going away dress," she quickly drove to the nearest clothes store, grabbed a half dozen dresses in her size, tried them on, and bought one. Was it what she had planned? No. Was she stressed? Yes. Was she calm? Yes, according to store clerks who waited on her. They reported she bought a dress in under 10 minutes and left happy.

Debra exhibited a personality characteristic called psychological hardiness. In looking back, she said, "I was so happy to be getting married, nothing was going to bring me down." **Psychological hardiness** describes people who have a sense of control over their lives; are committed to self, work, relationships, and other values; and do not fear change. Such people may suffer fewer health consequences from crises or traumas.

Debra's experience with the ruined dress was a **nonnormative stressor event**. These events are unanticipated experiences that place a person or a family in a state of instability and require creative effort to remedy. **Normative stressor events** are anticipated, predictable developmental changes that occur at certain life intervals. For most college students, registering for classes is a normative stressor event. Flunking out of school is a nonnormative stressor event.

Some people are extremely resilient when faced with either type of stressor event. According to psychologist Suzanne Kobasa, people who are likely to be resistant to stress have a disposition composed of the three C's: commitment, control, and challenge (Kobasa, 1982). They have a sense of purpose, are committed to their work and their families, rely on others, and know that others count on them. Psychologically hardy people realize that stress and challenge are normal parts of life and that they have the resources to deal with them. Individuals who perceive less stress and express more hardiness report significantly greater work/life satisfaction (Nowack, 1991).

Theory of Adaptive Range

Someone once jokingly said that the only person who really welcomes change is a wet baby. But the theory of adaptive range suggests that some level of change is vital to everyone's health and well-being, although too much unwanted change can be damaging. As mentioned earlier, everyone's life includes a comfort zone in which certain things and relationships do not change.

Consider the example of James, a 40-year-old male who has gone through a series of relationships and has been divorced twice. He likes to travel, eat different foods, visit with friends, and see the latest movies. If something new is happening, he is there. He wears "in" clothing and has the latest exercise equipment. He has a high intellect and is easily bored. On the surface, he looks like the epitome of change and adventure, but in a later interview James reveals that he has had the same job and house for 15 years and has a 10-year-old Irish setter he loves.

The moral of this story is that most people opt for stability and consistency in certain areas of their lives and opt for change or novelty in others. James opts for stability in his work and home, but wants change in his appearance, entertainment, and relationships. As a footnote to this story, James says he is tired of dating and is looking for a stable, lasting relationship. Is this believable? Is he ready for change? Before exploring further ways to manage and accommodate change and stress, an examination of how the body responds to stress is necessary, because stress has as its base a physiological response.

The Body's Response to Stress

What happens to a person's body when he or she experiences stress? First, an alarm reaction takes place. The alarm response begins when the brain perceives a threat to the sense of equilibrium. Something is not right. A loud siren, a sudden clap of thunder, or any other such disturbance serves as an alarm signal.

After the brain is alerted, a chain of events ensues as both hormones and nerves bring about a state of readiness. In 1932, Walter Cannon of Harvard Medical School coined the phrase **"fight or flight syndrome"** to refer to this alerted condition of the body as it quickly prepares for physical battle or energetic flight to escape the situation. A threatened or alerted person will experience some or all of the following physical actions:

- Pupils of the eyes widen
- Muscles tense
- Heart races or pounds
- Hearing sharpens
- Breathing quickens
- Hair may stand on end
- Hands feel clammy
- Mouth becomes dry

These actions, when synchronized, provide support for emergency physical response, if needed. In the meantime, the brain is trying to process how to react next.

The second stress stage is called resistance. In this stage, the body adapts to the demand. If a woman driving a car hears a siren, she will become alert to a threat and try to find the source of the noise. If the siren is coming from an ambulance behind her, she will pull over to let it pass. After the ambulance goes by, her body will relax and return to normal.

Stress can be an energizer. For instance, people go to adventure movies and car races that give them a quick, but safe, brush with stress. Each person needs stimulation to survive. Staying in a safe, comfortable job for 20 years is one way to keep stress and stimulation low. Changing jobs or applying for a promotion increases stress and provides stimulation.

The third stage of the stress reaction is the exhaustion stage. Once the danger and the excitement have passed, the body may feel tired and possibly susceptible to various illnesses (see Table 11.1 at the beginning of the chapter). A family as well as an individual can reach the stage of exhaustion, leaving family members susceptible to various disorders and feelings of discontent or restlessness. For example, a family may feel let down, exhausted, or bored after a busy holiday season. It has been estimated that over half of all illnesses are related to stress (Schwartz, 1982).

For an example of a test used by researchers to measure stress levels, see Figure 11.2.

Diet, Exercise, and Stress

Stress research and theory have generally focused on the negative aspects of stress (or distress). Because people are eager to reduce these negative aspects, they invest in the many stress-reducing products and regimens offered in the marketplace. But, consumers should remember the cautionary phrase *caveat emptor,* meaning "may the buyer beware."

Before investing any money in a miracle vitamin or food, consumers should know that the best nutritional preparation for stress is a balanced and varied diet as part of a lifestyle that includes regular exercise (Hamilton, Rolfes, & Whitney, 1990). No known singular food, vitamin supplement, or herbal remedy will eliminate stress. During stress all three

Exercise is a healthy way to manage stress.

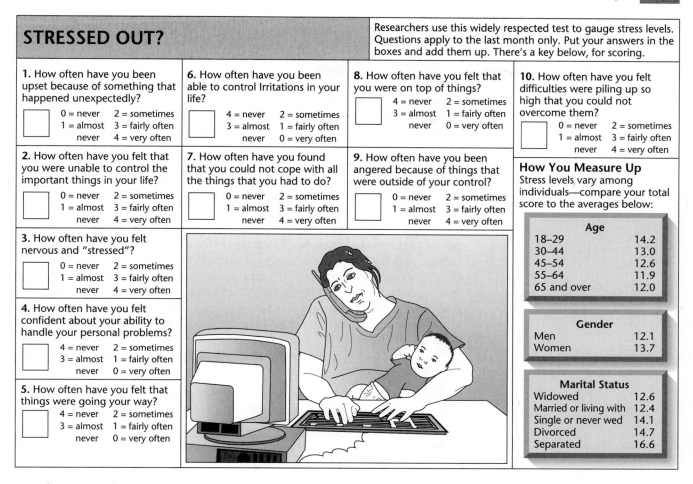

STRESSED OUT?

Researchers use this widely respected test to gauge stress levels. Questions apply to the last month only. Put your answers in the boxes and add them up. There's a key below, for scoring.

1. How often have you been upset because of something that happened unexpectedly?

0 = never   2 = sometimes
1 = almost   3 = fairly often
never   4 = very often

2. How often have you felt that you were unable to control the important things in your life?

0 = never   2 = sometimes
1 = almost   3 = fairly often
never   4 = very often

3. How often have you felt nervous and "stressed"?

0 = never   2 = sometimes
1 = almost   3 = fairly often
never   4 = very often

4. How often have you felt confident about your ability to handle your personal problems?

4 = never   2 = sometimes
3 = almost   1 = fairly often
never   0 = very often

5. How often have you felt that things were going your way?

4 = never   2 = sometimes
3 = almost   1 = fairly often
never   0 = very often

6. How often have you been able to control Irritations in your life?

4 = never   2 = sometimes
3 = almost   1 = fairly often
never   0 = very often

7. How often have you found that you could not cope with all the things that you had to do?

0 = never   2 = sometimes
1 = almost   3 = fairly often
never   4 = very often

8. How often have you felt that you were on top of things?

4 = never   2 = sometimes
3 = almost   1 = fairly often
never   0 = very often

9. How often have you been angered because of things that were outside of your control?

0 = never   2 = sometimes
1 = almost   3 = fairly often
never   4 = very often

10. How often have you felt difficulties were piling up so high that you could not overcome them?

0 = never   2 = sometimes
1 = almost   3 = fairly often
never   4 = very often

How You Measure Up
Stress levels vary among individuals—compare your total score to the averages below:

Age	
18–29	14.2
30–44	13.0
45–54	12.6
55–64	11.9
65 and over	12.0

Gender	
Men	12.1
Women	13.7

Marital Status	
Widowed	12.6
Married or living with	12.4
Single or never wed	14.1
Divorced	14.7
Separated	16.6

energy fuels—carbohydrates, fat, and protein—are depleted (Hamilton, Rolfes, & Whitney, 1990).

Individuals who eat well to obtain the nutrients needed and engage in regular exercise will be better prepared to withstand the impact of unavoidable stress than individuals with poor diets and low fitness levels. In general, exercise is recommended as a necessary part of a health-promotive lifestyle (Tanner, 1991). Moderate exercise has been shown to reduce stress because it raises the level of beta endorphins, chemicals in the brain associated with pain relief, which has a positive effect on mood and behavior (Hale, 1991). According to the American Heart Association, only 1 in 10 Americans follows a consistent exercise program. They suggest a daily goal of 30 minutes a day.

FIGURE 11.2
Stress Levels Test
Source: Kalb, C. & Rogers, A. (1999, June 14), "Stress," © 1999 *Newsweek*. Reprinted by permission.

STRESS MANAGEMENT

Beyond managing diet and exercise, what else can a person do to reduce the effects of stress? Other stress-reducing methods include:

- ◆ Getting more rest and relaxation
- ◆ Outsourcing (as discussed earlier)

◆ Meditation

◆ Massage

◆ Social support

Evidence suggests that stress relief and social support can prolong life. For example, in one study melanoma patients who received six weeks of structured group support suffered only half as many recurrences as their peers (Kalb & Rogers, 1999). In another study, patients with early breast or prostate cancer who attended stress management groups lived significantly longer than equally ill patients who weren't in groups (Elias, 1998).

Often a combined approach is best. Each individual must determine the stress management techniques that work best for them. Additional techniques will be given in the next section.

People with severe stress problems may seek individual treatment from a psychiatrist, psychologist, or physician, or they may join a support group or counseling workshop. These groups and workshops, which are usually offered at mental health clinics, hospitals, universities or through workplace Employee Assistance Programs (EAPs), may last from half a day to several days. Table 11.2 gives an example of an eight-session program for stress management.

Who attends these stress management programs? Men and women are almost equally likely to feel stress, but women are almost twice as likely to seek help (Waldrop, 1993). According to Cotton (1990), three categories of individuals tend to seek assistance with stress management:

1. People who are not experiencing any particular difficulty with stress, but are generally health conscious. They are interested in the preventive aspects of stress.

2. People who are distressed, anxious, or depressed. A distressed person is facing many ongoing stresses or hassles.

3. People with medical problems related to stress. These people are often Type A's and may be referred by their physician.

Researchers have established linkages among stress, illness, and certain types of personalities. One schema separates people into two groups of personalities: **Type A persons** are characterized by excessively striving behavior, high job involvement, impatience, competitiveness, desire for control and power, aggressiveness, and hostility, whereas **Type B persons** are more relaxed, easygoing, reflective, and cooperative.

The two most outstanding characteristics of Type A's are a sense of time urgency and hostility (Patel, 1991). Time urgency refers to the feeling that there is not enough time to do everything. It leads to impatience, tension, restlessness, preoccupation (e.g., inattentiveness to others), and rapid eating and talking. Hostility means evaluating people, events, or situations negatively and being suspicious, distrustful, aggressive, and competitive. Type A behavior is associated with cynicism, interpersonal negativity, and depersonalization (Nowack, 1991). In one study, Type A's were found to have low coping skills, and their depression and anxiety increased as their work stress increased (Greenglass & Burke, 1991). Type A's try to achieve goals without proper planning—they rush into their work without planning the steps necessary to achieve goals (Powell & Enright, 1990).

Type B's are characterized by an absence of the habits and traits associated with Type A's. They lack a sense of time urgency and its accompanying impatience. Type B's wait in line better than Type A's; they can relax without guilt,

TABLE 11.2
Stress Management: An Eight-Session Psychoeducational Program

Session	Content
1 What Is Stress?	◆ Defining stress ◆ Stress and illness ◆ How stress affects the individual
2 What Is Stressful?	◆ Types of stressors ◆ Life events versus hassles ◆ Identifying individual stressors
3 Dealing with Stress	◆ Where to start ◆ Planning and priorities ◆ Setting goals
4 Changing How You Feel	◆ How to relax ◆ When to relax ◆ Why to relax
5 Changing How You Think	◆ Identifying cognitive distortions ◆ Changing cognitions ◆ Effective problem solving
6 Changing How You Behave	◆ Identifying problem behaviors ◆ Self-monitoring ◆ Lifestyle behaviors ◆ Assertive behavior
7 Time Management	◆ Getting organized ◆ Setting time priorities ◆ Doing more with less time
8 Putting It All Together	◆ Where to go from here ◆ Making personal plans ◆ Rehearsing skills

Source: Reprinted with permission from *Stress Management: An Integrated Approach to Therapy* by D. H. Cotton. Published by Brunner/Mazel © 1990, p. 16.

are more cooperative with others, and take a break when fatigued. They are more likely to recognize signs of stress within themselves and to take time for fun. Type B's have goals and ambitions, but they have a confident style that allows them to wait for things to happen.

Several studies have linked Type A behavior to an increased rate of heart attacks and other diseases, but counterstudies indicate that the factors are more complex. Thus, there is no agreement on the health risks associated with Types A and B behavior. Similarly, the origins of Types A and B behavior are uncertain. It has been suggested that the Type A behavior pattern is established in childhood through the encouragement of high standards of achievement subconsciously imposed by adults, particularly parents (Matthews & Siegel, 1982). Despite these areas of uncertainty, researchers agree that stressors are experienced differently by different types of people and that coping responses vary by dominant personality type.

Techniques for Reducing Stress

Coping strategies to reduce everyday stress that is not chronic or disease related can be divided into two types: problem-focused coping and emotion-focused coping (Lazarus, 1991). Problem-focused coping attempts to alter the actual relationships and change behaviors or environments. Emotion-focused coping concentrates on regulating the emotional distress caused by harm or threat. Someone could do this by avoiding thoughts of the stressor, replacing negative thoughts with positive, by denial, or distancing. Positive thinking is used more by Type A's than Type B's as a coping strategy (Havlovic & Keenan, 1991). Emotion-focused coping requires a change in thinking or interpreting and a change in acting. Moderate stress can be relieved by first determining the cause of stress, then removing the stressor or moving out of the stressful environment, and, lastly, employing techniques that change the response to stress.

Specific techniques to help manage stress include the following:

◆ Plan and organize time to allow free time, time for enjoyment, relaxation, fun, hobbies, and exercise.

◆ Complete tasks that have been started.

◆ Develop a sense of humor.

◆ Indulge yourself.

◆ Find quiet environments and people who make one feel good about oneself. Build family and friendship bonds.

◆ Keep things in perspective. Stay flexible.

◆ Develop a positive attitude. Realize that one person cannot change everything. Much stress comes not from stressors but from perceptions of situations.

A study by pollsters Roper Starch Worldwide revealed that:

◆ Twenty-three percent of men and 15 percent of women take a day off from work when stressed.

◆ Nineteen percent of men and 36 perent of women buy clothing.

◆ Fifteen percent of men and 26 percent of women eat a special dessert (Crispell, 1997).

These techniques and study results may be useful, but how does a busy person find the time to relax? Consider the opening paragraph of an article on stress that appeared in *Parents* magazine:

> "We all know what we need to do about stress," says Alice, a legal secretary and the single mother of two young children. "We need to be good to ourselves, exercise regularly, eat well, get plenty of rest, and allow enough time for pleasure." Then she laughs and adds, "In other words, what we all really need is two weeks at a spa, complete with daily massage. Then when we return, we need a full-time maid, cook, and chauffeur." (Levine, 1990, p. 68)

As this quotation makes clear, reducing stress is more easily said than done. It is one thing to describe successful techniques for reducing stress; it is another thing to fit them into an already busy life.

Job Stress

According to the National Institute for Occupational Safety and Health (NIOSH), **job stress** is defined as the harmful physical and emotional responses that occur when the requirements of the job do not match the capabilities, resources, or needs of the worker. Job stress can lead to poor health and even injury. NIOSH differentiates challenge from stress. Challenge energizes people and motivates them to learn new skills. When a challenge is met, the reactions are satisfying and relaxing. Thus, challenge is a natural and healthy part of productive work. Job stress, however, results when job demands are not met, usually because of excessive workloads, there are no end results, only a sense of exhaustion and failure.

According to the NIOSH, job stress is on the rise. They cite the following study results as examples supporting this observation:

◆ One-fourth of employees view their jobs as the number one stressor in their lives (Northwestern National Life).

◆ Three-fourths of employees believe workers have more on-the-job stress than a generation ago (Princeton Survey Research Associates).

◆ Problems at work are more strongly associated with health complaints than are other life stressors—more so than even financial problems or family problems (St. Paul Fire and Marine Insurance Co.).

Karen Nussbaum, executive director of the Women's Bureau in the U.S. Department of Labor, says:

> I think of stress and working parents in two issues—time and work. When you are a parent who works outside the home—which is the case for more than 50 percent of all mothers of preschoolers—you have less time and more worry. And the combination results in high stress. (Levine, 1990, p. 68)

As Chapter 10 observed, stress is an inevitable result of work and family time conflicts. A study conducted by the Roper Organization found that 60 percent of the employed mothers surveyed reported a lot of stress from conflicting demands of work and family.

One of the conflicting demands that is causing stress for a lot of individuals and families is travel associated with work. More than 8 in 10 business travelers say that work travel is stressful (Fisher, 1998). Travel is hardest:

◆ On workers with young families. In one study, 6 in 10 married travelers said they experienced stress when missing family milestones, such as a birthday, a wedding anniversary, or a child's sporting event (Fisher, 1998).

◆ At night—workers especially miss their children at bedtime.

◆ On spouses who are left behind—the burden of household work and child care falls on them.

◆ When workers return to find piles of work waiting for them.

◆ On workers when things go wrong, such as cancelled flights, lost luggage, or reservations.

On the other hand, the most enthused travelers are those between the ages of 18 and 34. They enjoy seeing new places. Almost 70 percent say that overnight business travel makes them feel important and 68 percent say that trips provide a needed break from home and regular life (Fisher, 1998). So, travel can produce distress or eustress. A lot of the reaction has to do with the traveler's lifestyle, age, career stage, and other criteria—such as location of the travel destination and the meaning of the travel to their job success.

Typically, work and work-related activities, transportation time to and from work, and preparation activities take up over 40 hours a week. Boredom, overload, role ambiguity, underutilization of talent or skills, poor job design, lack of advancement, shift work, low pay, transfers, miscommunications, difficult bosses, too many meetings, high job turnover, poor labor-management relations, lack of control, and incompetence all contribute to job stress. Negative consequences or effects of stress may include anxiety, accident-proneness, lower productivity, and a host of other physical, mental, and behavioral problems.

Although work produces stress, remember that according to Hans Seyle, not all stress is bad. Work provides a purpose for living and provides challenges. According to Seyle (1974), work is a biological necessity. He wrote:

> [The] principal aim should not be to avoid work but to find the kind of occupation which, for you is play. The best way to avoid harmful stress is to select an environment which is in line with your innate preferences—to find an activity which you like and respect. (1974, p. 85)

Further, he said, one of the worst stressors is continuous leisure from enforced retirement or solitary confinement. Benjamin Franklin earlier expressed this same sentiment when he said, "There is nothing wrong with retirement as long as one doesn't allow it to interfere with one's work."

Another way of looking at work and stress is that the workplace may actually serve as a haven from the stress, disappointment, and problems encountered in home and family life. It may be a relief to go to an office where everyone is polite, well groomed, and courteous, if, for example, there are constant fights at home or a family member is an abusive alcoholic. A more popular image of the home is as a place where the wounds inflicted in "that jungle out there" can be soothed (Ulrich & Dunne, 1986). As these examples indicate, asking people where they work and what they do is not enough. Professionals interested in helping families should ascertain if work is a haven, a stressor, or a mixture of both for each individual in a given family.

Burnout

The word *burnout* is associated with being worn-out from doing too much work. Originally, burnout was used in the aerospace industry to describe the termination of rocket or jet-engine operation because of insufficient fuel. In resource management, **burnout** refers to emotional or physical exhaustion brought about by unrelieved stress. This all-inclusive definition shows that burnout can come from many sources. Burnout may be a result of fatigue or frustration with a cause, a way of life, or a relationship that has failed to produce the expected reward (Freudenberger, 1980).

In the 1970s, burnout was first associated with teachers, social workers, and others who worked in jobs involving considerable responsibility for the welfare of others. These jobs tended to have high turnover rates because workers were said to burn out after so many years on the job. In the 1980s, burnout was used to refer to just about anybody who was tired at the end of the day. During that decade, Charles Maslach (1982) published the Maslach Burnout Inventory, which defined burnout as the subjective experience of emotional exhaustion, depersonalization, and reduced personal accomplishment resulting from the continuous caring for needy clients in human service professions. Using the Maslach scale, two researchers discovered that day care workers who experienced emotional exhaustion and depersonalization tended toward learned helplessness and low self-esteem (McMullen & Krantz, 1988). In short, they found that many day care workers suffer from burnout.

In the 1990s, burnout continued to be used to refer to both everyday and long-term exhaustion. Regardless of how the word is used, the phenomenon should not be ignored. If burnout is acute, a person may have a breakdown in health, may not be able to continue performing at the expected pace, and may become discouraged and drop out of a profession, when what he or she really needs is a break, a chance for retraining, and perhaps a better job environment-person fit. Burnout can happen in friendships and marital relationships, too. Distance, vacations, a new setting, or a renewed commitment may all help reduce relationship burnout.

Burnout is generally regarded as a negative. But, like stress, burnout has its positive side. Burnout can be a signal for change, a deliberate dynamic in the psyche (mind) to reestablish balance and to stimulate growth (Garden, 1991). Viewed in this way, burnout can be a functional, positive developmental experience, rather than a dysfunctional, negative one. In 1997, Christina Maslach, a professor of psychology at the University of California, Berkeley, and coauthor of the book *The Truth About Burnout* concluded that:

> Most people think burnout is caused by work overload. . . . But while having too much to do can cause stress, it doesn't necessarily cause burnout. People will work long, hard hours willingly and happily if they love what they are doing, or if they can see it is making a difference. . . . Respect helps, too. (Smith, 1997, 11D)

Stress and Non-Events

Most of the stressors covered so far have been caused by events or reactions to events. An interesting line of research has focused on the stress caused by non-events—specific occurrences in people's lives that they look forward to and make plans around but that fail to materialize. Examples of non-events are cancelled weddings (these may be more stressful than divorces), postponed vacations, or not being invited to a follow-up job interview or an important social gathering. According to John Eckenrode of Cornell University:

> We know that unanticipated negative events are more stressful than anticipated ones. With an anticipated event, you can do some preparatory coping. You know it's going to happen and you can mobilize your resources. Things that just hit you out of the blue, on the other hand, are more stressful because you don't know they're coming. And when you've invested a lot of emotional buildup in whatever it is you're looking forward to, the effects can be huge. (Powers, 1995, p. 6)

Eckenrode says that many times people's plans are thwarted by others or something in the environment that is beyond an individual's control. He speculates that stress from non-events is just part of life, that disappointment is as normal an occurrence as the good things that happen.

Parents, Children, and Stress

The parent-child relationship can lead to stress for all concerned. Children are as vulnerable to stress and burnout as are adults. Hurried schedules and meals affect children as well as parents. Many experts think childhood stress in on the rise (Kalb & Rogers, 1999).

For parents, the stresses of child rearing may begin as soon as the newborn infant arrives home from the hospital. One study of parents of infants three to five months old identified a number of stressors. Thirty-five percent of the mothers and 20 percent of the fathers reported that a major stress was their infant's fussy behavior in relation to feeding or soothing techniques (Ventura, 1987).

Parental stress stemming from children is not limited to the children's preschool years. In one study of parents with children ranging in age up to young adulthood, 39 percent of the women respondents cited children as their primary source of stress (Mehren, 1988). Another study found that the Americans most likely to be stressed-out are women between the ages of 30 and 44 because they tend to be working mothers with young children (Waldrop, 1993). And at midlife, a major source of stress for the women surveyed was the return of adult children to the home for economic reasons. Another study found that single parents and their adolescents are under potentially significant amounts of stress due to family structure and developmental factors, such as the adolescents' movement toward independence (Houser et al., 1993).

Stress Warning Signs in Children

Stressed children give off many warning signs: poor appetite, excessive crying, headaches and stomachaches, withdrawal, clinging behavior, hyperactivity, moodiness, and sleep problems. Children can experience stress from homesickness, parental divorce, and family, friend, community, and school problems.

For example, Barbara Howard, a pediatrician at Johns Hopkins, says a quarter of her patients are there for stress-related problems. She says, "They'll come in with abdominal pain, urinary frequency, headaches . . . a whole variety of complaints which could be mistaken for medical problems and often are" (Kalb & Rogers, 1999, p. 63). In addition:

> Parents are frequently wrong about the sources of stress in their children's lives, according to surveys by Georgia Witkin of Mount Sinai Medical School; they think children worry most about friendships and popularity, but they're actually fretting about the grown-ups. "The biggest concern," she says, "was that the parents are going to be sick, or angry, or they're going to divorce." And "often and somewhat surprisingly," says Giedd (Jay Giedd of the National Institutes of Health), "children have very global worries"—wars, environmental issues and crime, the same things adults worry about. (Kalb & Rogers, 1999, p. 63)

Also, researchers report that "children who were neglected by their parents or raised in orphanages, tend to have higher levels of stress hormones and may be 'hot reactors' later in life. As adults, they may feel empty or bored when on edge" (Kalb & Rogers, 1999, p. 60). On the other hand, children raised in secure, loving homes learn to modulate stress reactions, according to Megan Gunnar of the University of Minnesota.

Children can experience stress and overload from competitive, win-lose, rule-bound situations just as adults can. Consequently, the nature and outcomes of highly structured, competitive team sports can be childhood stressors. It is generally agreed that this type of sports activity is too stressful for very young children. To help children through these and other stressful situations, parents should be sensitive to any change overload, responsibility overload, or emotional overload their children may be experiencing.

In *The Hurried Child*, David Elkind, professor of child development at Tufts University, says that today's children are pressured to grow up too fast. He gives this example of responsibility overload:

Janet is ten years old but has many adult responsibilities. In addition to taking care of her clothes and room, she must prepare breakfast for herself and her younger sister and make sure that they get off to school on time. (Her mother leaves for work an hour before Janet needs to get to school.) When she gets home, she has to do some housecleaning, defrost some meat for dinner, and make sure her sister is all right. When her mother gets home, Janet listens patiently to her mother's description of the "creeps" at work who never leave her alone and who are always making cracks or passes. After Janet helps prepare dinner, her mother says, "Honey, will you do the dishes? I'm just too tired," and Janet barely has time to do some homework. (1988, p. 150)

Janet is stressed not only from the work she has to do, but from the amount of responsibility placed on her shoulders at such a young age. In many one-parent and dual-career families today, children are required to take substantial responsibility for housework and child care. How much is too much is a question worth thinking about.

Elkind points out that not only are homes more stressful today, but schools are also more stressful. Besides the usual competition for grades and in sports, children are exposed to more threats and violence in schools than ever before.

Like adults, children can learn to moderate stress by following the techniques described earlier in the chapter—eating a balanced diet, engaging in regular exercise, enjoying free time, and being with people with whom they are comfortable. Elkind says that children can suffer from chronic stress, usually brought on by significant life changes, that can be lessened by reassurance and attention from parents and teachers.

College Students and Stress

Stress is a lifelong fact. However, it is generally assumed that the teen years are especially stressful. Therefore, college students, most of whom are in their teens and early twenties, are living in or emerging from a stressful life period. Boredom and school burnout are often stressors during the high school years. By college age, many of the boredom and burnout problems have been replaced by renewed enthusiasm for education because of the new setting and the opportunity to specialize. College students are usually dedicated and in school by choice—they enjoy school for the most part and want to keep learning. They have career ambitions and life goals. But for all the pluses, the college years also have some negatives—stressors in the forms of relationships, grades, and emotional and physical problems. Uncertainty about what lies ahead is an ever present stressor.

According to one study, the top academic stressors for college students were tests and finals, and the top personal stressor was intimate relationships (Murphy & Archer, 1996). Another study found that the most psychological distress was experienced freshman year and that it declined over the next four years (Sher, Wood, & Gotham, 1996). In response to this, many colleges and universities have put more effort in recent years into freshman orientation programs and specialized seminars for freshmen.

For certain individuals, mild test anxiety has been found to motivate and facilitate performance. But test anxiety is more commonly associated with negative motivation and poor test performance (Hill & Wigfield, 1984). One study of undergraduate college students tried to determine whether test anxiety could be significantly reduced through regular relaxation exercises or physical exercises (Topp, 1989). The students were divided into three groups: a nonmeditative relaxation exercise group, an aerobics dance group, and a control group who did not meet during the seven-week study. Both the relaxation exercise group and the aerobics dance students (who increased in fitness also) reported a significant decline in test anxiety; the control group did not experience any change in test anxiety. The results from this study suggest that exercise reduces test anxiety, so a student suffering from it should consider incorporating exercise into his or her life. Another stressor for college students is meeting deadlines—deadlines for term papers, for projects, for club reports, for registering for classes, and so on. Time management techniques, including prioritizing, allocating time as best one can, checking progress, and keeping a calendar, should help with the problem of meeting deadlines.

Not all college students are in their late teens and early twenties. More and more college students are over age 25. They are returning to school after serving in the armed services, raising a family, or being engaged in some other work or family activities that caused them to postpone entering or finishing college. In addition to the college life stressors already mentioned, older students have the problems involved with combining family life with student life, doubts about their ability to compete with younger students, more complicated financial situations, and other concerns about mixing a more mature lifestyle with the demands of college life. These students face such stressful choices as the following: Should I go to see my in-laws on Sunday or finish my term paper? Should I make dinner or study? Their self-doubt concerns may range from what to wear to the first class to how to study for a test after not having taken one for 20 years.

All college students, regardless of age or life stage, undergo a change in their usual lifestyle. And as explained previously, change is stressful. Since going to college is a new experience and the people and environment are new, it is not surprising to find many students feeling and acting shy (Greenberg, 1983). Making new friends, talking with professors and advisers, using the services of counselors in the student counseling center and dormitories, and attending stress management workshops should help reduce stress.

FATIGUE: DEFINITION AND SOURCES

College students experience fatigue as well as stress. Irregular hours, studying for final exams, and weekend parties all contribute to fatigue. **Fatigue** is the feeling of having insufficient energy to carry on and a strong desire to stop, rest, or sleep (Engel, 1970). This feeling can come from mental or physical exertion, work, or play. Fatigue may be related to stress or have nothing to do with stress. For example, at night you may be tired from a long day of activity and feel fatigued, but you are not necessarily stressed or tense. Short-term fatigue can be easily remedied with some rest, but long-term, chronic fatigue is more serious.

Besides being a feeling, fatigue can include the physical symptoms of dizziness, headaches, nausea, and tremulousness (Atkinson, 1985). These physical symptoms are extreme; generally, a fatigued person simply feels tired. Fatigue is a normal part of daily life, but sometimes a person is more keenly aware of it than other times. Fatigue can sneak up on an individual or build up to a point where the individual is not functioning well. It can also be dangerous, as when someone falls asleep at the wheel. Because of this potential danger, individuals need to recognize personal fatigue sensations and do something about them.

Fatigue comes from many sources. As Chapter 10 pointed out, the demands and conflicts arising from trying to achieve too much in the work and family realms can result in fatigue. A survey of 666 male and female clerical and professional employees revealed that fatigue levels were similar at home and at work. One male professional penciled in the following comment at the end of the survey: "Going home is just exchanging one set of problems for another." The study also revealed that professional women experienced significantly more fatigue and role overload than professional men (Goldsmith, 1989).

These findings have implications for those interested in personal and family management. What is happening in offices and homes that produces so much fatigue? And, why are researchers finding that home and family life is just another stressor rather than a reliever of stress and fatigue?

The Body and Fatigue

Like stress, fatigue originates as a physiological response, and it comes from both internal and external sources. Regardless of where the fatigue originates, it is always felt as a subjective sensation by the person (Atkinson, 1985). Menopause, aging, certain medications, menstrual cycles, various diseases (both mental and physical), certain injuries, and pregnancy affect fatigue.

Fatigue begins at an unconscious, microscopic level and progresses through stages until the person thinks, "I'm tired." At the final stage, the person experiences fatigue as a sensation (Atkinson, 1985). Because the mind is included at this level, psychological factors such as boredom, depression, and being upset are combined with the physiological ones that cause fatigue.

Systems Theory: Sleep, Energy, and Fatigue

Systems theory is relevant to the discussion of fatigue because fatigue is a sign of energy imbalance: too much energy is being expended and not enough is being conserved. One way to look at energy is to envision an energy pool with an imbalance of energy boosters (inputs) and energy drainers (outputs) (see Figure 11.3). The energy pool is depleted when there are more energy drainers (bad habits, overwork, mental strain, illness, and occupational hazards) than energy boosters (nutrition, exercise, good sleep, pleasure, and mastery).

Sleep

Sleep, a critical energy booster, is vital to maintaining well-being and enthusiasm for life. It plays a major role in preparing the body and brain for an alert, productive, psychologically and physiologically healthy tomorrow (Maas, 1998).

Even though everyone needs sleep, sometimes the amount and timing are difficult to control. For example, falling asleep after a stimulating day may be difficult even though you are very tired. At other times, you may feel drowsy, even though you want to stay alert, such as in an afternoon class.

As noted in Chapter 10, humans spend about one-third of their lives sleeping. The average American sleeps 7 hours a night; before electric lights were invented that number was 10 (Did you Know, 1998). At least 50 percent of the adult population is chronically sleep-deprived (Maas, 1998). Sleep is necessary for two reasons:

FIGURE 11.3
The Drained Energy Pool
Source: Atkinson, H. (1985). *Women and Fatigue.*
New York: G. P. Putnam, p. 25.

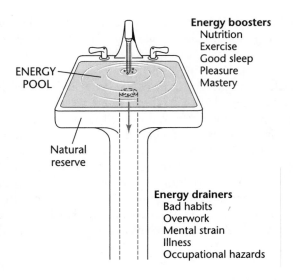

ENERGY POOL

Natural reserve

Energy boosters
Nutrition
Exercise
Good sleep
Pleasure
Mastery

Energy drainers
Bad habits
Overwork
Mental strain
Illness
Occupational hazards

◆ To restore energy levels

◆ To help the body to regulate and synchronize itself

Sleep provides rhythm to lives. Most people go to sleep and awake about the same time every day. While asleep, humans go through certain cycles of light and deep slumber. Figure 11.4 illustrates the rhythmic nature of typical sleep patterns.

There are two kinds of sleep: REM and NREM sleep. **REM** or **rapid eye movement sleep** occurs when the sleeper is in a light sleep; most dreams happen during REM. **NREM** or **non-rapid eye movement sleep** occurs when the sleeper is in an inactive, deep slumber. Through the night, the sleeper goes back and forth between REM and NREM sleep.

Insomnia is the inability to sleep. There are three kinds of insomnia: inability to fall asleep, inability to remain asleep, and early morning waking. When people are deprived of sleep for a long time or do not get the right balance of REM and NREM sleep, they can feel fatigued and irritable, and their abilities to make decisions and to concentrate are diminished. This is why fatigue and insomnia are an integral part of the study of resource management. Appropriate levels of sleep and rest are resources. For example, many athletes experience some form of precompetition stress that may result in insomnia during the night before their competition. This sleep withdrawal, even though temporary, has a negative influence on performance.

There are 365 sleep-disorder clinics accredited by the American Sleep Disorders Association. Clinic staff study sleep patterns and help people suffering from chronic insomnia. Among the discoveries of these clinics is that stress and anxiety can affect the length and quality of sleep.

Work schedules can also influence sleep patterns and insomnia. For example, studies have shown that shift workers get three hours less sleep than people who work a normal daytime schedule, and up to 90 percent of shift workers report sleep disturbances (Atkinson, 1985). Irregular and rotating shifts (for example, working nights one week, days the next) play havoc not only with the individual's health and sleep patterns, but also with family schedules. Sometimes a family may see shifts as an asset; for example, shifts may allow someone always to be home with the children. On the negative side, however, husbands and wives working on different shifts may rarely see each other. More intimate, face-to-face communication may be replaced with hurried phone calls and written messages.

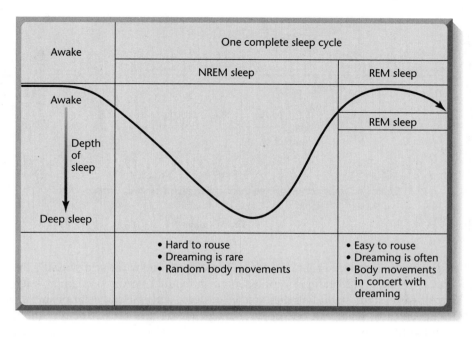

FIGURE 11.4

Two Kinds of Sleep: NREM and REM

Source: Atkinson, H. (1985). *Women and Fatigue.* New York: G. P. Putnam, p. 154. Illustration by Karen Ann Atkinson. Copyright © 1986 by Holly Atkinson.

According to James Maas (1998), the four golden rules of sleep are:

1. Get an adequate amount of sleep every night.
2. Establish a regular sleep schedule.
3. Get continuous sleep.
4. Make up for lost sleep.

Energy and Alertness

Getting adequate rest and sleep is an energy booster. An energetic person has the capacity to take on a job or an activity and complete it to the best of her or his ability. As the energy pool diagram in Figure 11.3 shows, there are many types of energy boosters. In addition, some individuals seem to be born with more energy than others. Research is incomplete as to why this difference exists.

Another little understood energy phenomenon is how people reenergize themselves during the day. Many people at one time ascribed to the drain theory, which asserted that individuals wake with a certain level of energy in the morning. As the day wears on, each activity takes away some of that energy until by nightfall the energy is depleted and the person sleeps. Then, according to the theory, sleep restores the person, and the pattern is repeated the next day. The problem with the drain theory is that not all people are highly energized on first waking up, and during the day such things as food, exercise, and excitement refuel people. Each person has typical energy rhythms or patterns during the day that can be altered by events. Figure 11.5 shows typical alertness patterns over 24 hours.

Fatigue Management

The purpose of this book is not just to describe life management problems (e.g., people do not get enough sleep or rest), but to also present possible solutions. Systems theory asserts that systems are connected: if one part of the system is affected, other parts are affected. The subjects of sleep, energy, and

FIGURE 11.5
Alertness across 24 hours
Humans experience ups and downs in alertness over the course of the day, even when nocturnal sleep is adequate. Alertness is quite strong in the morning (hence 10 o'clock classes are a good idea), quite weak midafternoon, and fairly strong from late afternoon until midevening.

Source: Adapted from James B. Maas (1998). *Power Sleep.* New York: Villard, p. 40. Reprinted by permission of Villard Books, a division of Random House, Inc.

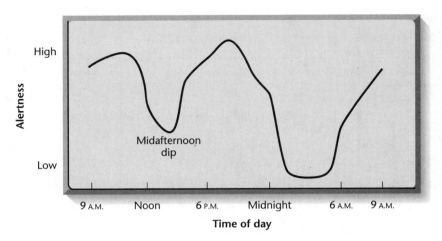

fatigue are so interlaced that it is difficult to discuss one without discussing the others. To cope with fatigue problems, an individual needs to examine each part of the system, including diet, exercise, sleep, activity, and relationships.

Specifically, what can one do to manage energy and fatigue better? First, an individual should be able to recognize his or her sleep and fatigue signs and assign time and energy accordingly. In other words, it is up to the individual to self-monitor. Successful people rarely go blindly into a new activity; they think first about how much of their time and energy will be required. Second, when fatigue is imminent, the individual should try to cope with it by napping or sleeping, relaxing, eating properly, changing activity, or whatever combination works best. Keeping a regular schedule and avoiding all stimulants such as coffee, tea, and soft drinks containing caffeine at least two hours prior to going to bed will help improve sleep (Powell & Enright, 1990).

Chronic Fatigue Syndrome

In recent years, an affliction known as **chronic fatigue syndrome** has become a public health concern. Because it was discovered only recently and research is still under way, chronic fatigue is a controversial topic. It is not clear what causes the disease or even if it is one disease or many. It may be a long-acting viral infection, a form of allergy, or something entirely different (*Two New Landmark Studies,* 1991). No one knows precisely how many people have chronic fatigue syndrome. Patients with extreme chronic fatigue cannot work and have little energy for anything.

People with chronic fatigue exhibit a variety of symptoms. The Centers for Disease Control (which defined the syndrome in 1988) has identified the main ones as chills or low-grade fever, sore throat, tender lymph nodes, muscle pain, muscle weakness, extreme fatigue, headaches, joint pain (without swelling), neurological problems (confusion, memory loss, visual disturbances), sleep disorders, and the sudden onset of symptoms (Cowley, 1990).

In addition to these symptoms, chronic fatigue differs from ordinary fatigue brought on by overexertion in several respects. In chronic fatigue:

◆ Rest is not restorative.
◆ Minimal physical activity can bring on significant exhausterbations (S. Straus, personal communication, August 24, 1989).

Chronic fatigue is long-lasting and affects children as well as adults. A good night's sleep or a leisurely vacation will not lessen true chronic fatigue.

Electronic Resources

For more information on sleep, go to **www.Sleepfoundation.org**. Publications and information on job stress are available from NIOSH's Web site at **www.cdc.gov/niosh/jobstress**. The American Psychological Association maintains lists of licensed psychologists who can help with stress-related problems. Their Web site is **helping.apa.org/refer**. The Bureau of Labor Statistics' Web site (**www.stats.bls.gov/**) reports on the number and percentage distribution of nonfatal occupational injuries and illnesses involving days away from work by nature of injury or illness. As part of this, the Bureau of Labor Statistics keeps track of stress-related injuries, illnesses, and days missed from work.

http://helping.apa.org/
work/stress6.html

| HOME | SITE MAP | SEARCH | FREE BROCHURE | FIND A PSYCHOLOGIST |

Psychology at Work
GET THE FACTS

The Road to Burnout

If in the beginning your job seems perfect, the solution to all your problems, you have high hopes and expectations, and would rather work than do anything else, be wary. You're a candidate for the most insidious and tragic kind of job stress—burnout, a state of physical, emotional, and mental exhaustion caused by unrealistically high aspirations and illusory and impossible goals.

Potential for burnout increases dramatically depending on who you are, where you work, and what your job is. If you're a hard worker who gives 110 percent, an idealistic, self-motivated achiever who thinks anything is possible if you just work hard enough, you're a possible candidate. The same is true if you're a rigid perfectionist with unrealistically high standards and expectations. In a job with little recognition and few rewards for work well done, particularly with frequent people contact or deadlines, you advance from a possible to a probable candidate.

The road to burnout is paved with good intentions. There's certainly nothing wrong with being an idealistic, hardworking perfectionist or self-motivating achiever, and there's nothing wrong with having high aspirations and expectations. Indeed, these are admirable traits in our culture. Unreality is the villain. Unrealistic job aspirations and expectations are doomed to frustration and failure. The burnout candidate's personality keeps him striving with single-minded intensity until he crashes.

Burnout proceeds by stages that blend and merge into one another so smoothly and imperceptibly that the victim seldom realizes what happened even after it's over.

These stages include:

1. The Honeymoon

During the honeymoon phase, your job is wonderful. You have boundless energy and enthusiasm and all things seem possible. You love the job and the job loves you. You believe it will satisfy all your needs and desires and solve all your problems. You're delighted with your job, your co-workers and the organization.

2. The Awakening

The honeymoon wanes and the awakening stage starts with the realization that your initial expectations were unrealistic. The job isn't working out the way you thought it would. It doesn't satisfy all your needs; your co-workers and the organization are less than perfect; and rewards and recognition are scarce.

As disillusionment and disappointment grow, you become confused. Something is wrong, but you can't quite put your finger on it. Typically, you work even harder to make your dreams come true. But working harder doesn't change anything and you become increasingly tired, bored, and frustrated. You question your competence and ability and start losing your self-confidence.

Summary

When individuals experience excessive stress and fatigue, they question their life choices and reevaluate their time use and commitments. They wonder if it is necessary to hurry all the time. And are they really achieving more by hurrying? In the rush, are families being shortchanged?

This chapter has largely been based on theories and research from psychology and the health fields. An important point is that moderate levels of stress and fatigue are a normal part of life. The ABCD-XYZ Resource Management Model of Crisis/Stress illustrated how individuals and families adapt to stress and crisis.

Hans Seyle was a major contributor to stress research. Among other things, he differentiated between two types of stress: distress (harmful) and eustress (beneficial).

Stress originates from two sources: internal and external. Stressor events can be normative (expected) or nonnormative (unanticipated). The body's response to stress and the fight or flight syndrome are important to understanding how stress works. An individual's personality and emotional state play significant roles in the evaluation and reaction to stress. Type A and Type B persons react differently to stress.

The meaning of burnout has changed over the years, but the phenomenon is serious and should not be ignored. Although stress exists throughout the life cycle, childhood stress and the stress college students experience are particularly troubling. David Elkind has observed that children today may be pushed to grow up too fast and assume adult responsibilities at an early age.

Energy boosters can have a restorative effect on persons suffering from fatigue. So can sleep. Sleep researchers have distinguished rapid eye movement sleep from non-rapid eye movement sleep. Ordinary fatigue can be reduced by sleep and rest.

Far more research is needed on the complex interplay among energy, fatigue, personality, and stress. Individuals can strive to maintain a balance of activity, rest, and energy, acquire the skills to understand themselves, and enjoy each other more. The next chapter covers another potential stressor and relaxer—the environment.

Key Terms

burnout
chronic fatigue
  syndrome
comfort zone
comparative
  advantage
crises
distress
domino effect
eustress
external stress
fatigue

fight or flight
  syndrome
internal stress
job stress
nonnormative
  stressor events
non-rapid eye
  movement
  (NREM) sleep
normative stressor
  events
outsourcing

psychological
  hardiness
rapid eye movement
  (REM) sleep
stress
stressors
stress overload or
  pileup
Type A person
Type B person

Review Questions

1. Explain what happens to the body during each of the three stages of the stress reaction.
2. Describe the theory of adaptive range.
3. Give two examples of nonnormative and normative stressor events.
4. Explain the concept of the comfort zone.
5. Describe the drain theory of human energy and explain why it is inadequate.

References

Atkinson, H. (1985). *Women and fatigue*. New York: G. P. Putnam.

Braus, P. (1998, September). When the helpers need a hand. *American Demographics,* 1–4.

Capel, I. & Gurnsey, J. (1987). *Managing stress*. London: Constable.

Cotton, D. (1990). *Stress management*. New York: Brunner/Mazel.

Cowley, G. (1990, November 12). Chronic fatigue syndrome. *Newsweek,* 62–70.

Crispell, D. (1997, November). Demo memo. *American Demographics,* 36.

Did you know. (1998, June 29). *Tallahassee Democrat,* 3D.

Dollahite, D. (1991). Family resource management and family stress theories: Toward a conceptual integration. *Lifestyles: Family and Economic Issues, 12*(4), 361–377.

Elias, M. (1998, March 26). Antistress groups seem to support cancer survival. *USA Today,* D1.

Elkind, D. (1988). *The hurried child*. Reading, MA: Addison-Wesley.

Engel, G. (1970). Nervousness and fatigue. In C. M. MacBryde and R. S. Blacklow (Eds.), *Signs and symptoms* (5th ed.). Philadelphia: J. B. Lippincott, 637.

Fisher, C. (1998, June). Business on the road. *American Demographics,* 44–47, 54.

Freudenberger, H. (1980). *Burnout*. Garden City, NY: Anchor Press.

Garden, A. (1991). The purpose of burnout: A Jungian interpretation. In P. Perrewe (Ed.), *Job stress*. Corte Madera, CA: Select Press, 73–93.

Garrison, M., Malia, J., Norem, R., & Hira, T. (1994). Developing a daily hassles inventory. *Proceedings of the 1994 Conference of the Eastern Family Economics and Management Association,* Pittsburgh, PA: Resource, 18–43.

Goldsmith, E. (1989). Role overload: Professional men vs. professional women. *Proceedings of the Southeastern Regional Association of Family Economics—Home Management Annual Meeting.*

Greenberg, J. (1983). *Comprehensive stress management*. Dubuque, Iowa: Wm. C. Brown, 265.

Greenglass, E. & Burke, R. (1991). The relationship between stress and coping among Type As. In P. Perrewe (Ed.), *Job stress*. Corte Madera, CA: Select Press, 361–373.

Hale, E. (1991, June). Taming menstrual cramps. *FDA Consumer, 25*(5).

Havlovic, S. & Keenan, J. (1991). Coping with work stress. In P. Perrewe (Ed.), *Job stress*. Corte Madera, CA: Select Press.

Hamilton, E., Rolfes, S., & Whitney, E. (1990). *Understanding nutrition* (5th ed.). St. Paul: West Publishing Company.

Hill, K. & Wigfield, A. (1984). Test anxiety: A major educational problem and what can be done about it. *Elementary School Journal, 85,* 106–126.

House, J. (1983). *Work stress and social support*. Reading, MA: Addison-Wesley.

Houser, R., Daniels, J., D'Andrea, M., & Konstam, V. (1993). A systemic behaviorally based technique for resolving conflict between adolescents and their single parents. *Family Behavior Therapy, 15*(3), 17–31.

Kalb, C. & Rogers, A. (1999, June 14). Stress. *Newsweek,* 54–69.

Kobasa, S. (1982). The hardy personality; Toward a psychology of stress and health. In J. Suls and G. Sanders (Eds.), *Social psychology and illness*. Hillsdale, NJ: Erlbaum

Lazarus, R. (1991). Psychological stress in the workplace. In P. Perrewe (Ed.), *Job stress*. Corte Madera, CA; Select Press, 1–13.

Levine, K. (1990, May). Coping with stress. *Parents,* 68–70.

Maas, J. (1998). *Power sleep*. NY: Villard.

Maslach, C. (1982). *Burnout: The cost of caring*. Englewood Cliffs, NJ: Prentice-Hall.

Matthews, K. & Siegel, J. (1982). The type A behaviour pattern in children and adolescents: Assessment, development and associated coronary risk. In A. Baum and J. E. Singer (Eds.), *Handbook of psychology and health,* Vol. 2. Hillsdale, NJ: Erlbaum.

McCubbin, H., McCubbin, M., Thompson, A., Han, S., & Allen, C. (1997, Fall). Families under stress: What makes them resilient. *Journal of Family and Consumer Sciences,* 2–11.

McLellan, T., Bragg, A., & Cacciola, J. (1992). *Escape from anxiety & stress*. New York: Chelsea House.

McMullen, M. & Krantz, M. (1988). Burnout in day care workers: The effects of learned helplessness and self-esteem. *Child & Youth Care Quarterly, 17*(4), 275–280.

Mehren, E. (1988, June 14). New study downplays the effects of menopause. *Los Angeles Times.*

Murphy, M. & Archer, J. (1996, January/February). Stressors on the college campus, *Journal of College Student Development,* 20–27.

Neuharth, A. (1991, June 14). Most stressful job? *USA Today,* IIA.

Nowack, K. M. (1991). Psychological predictors of health status. *Work and Stress, 5*(2), 117–131.

Patel, C. (1991). *The complete guide to stress management*. London: Plenum Press, 36–52.

Powell, T. & Enright, S. (1990). *Anxiety and stress management,* London: Routledge, 4–17.

Powers, M. (1995, Fall). Dashed expectations. *Human Ecology Forum,* 5–7.

Quick, J., Nelson, D., & Quick, J. (1990). *Stress and challenge at the top.* New York: John Wiley & Sons, 30.

Schwartz, J. (1982). *Letting go of stress.* New York: Pinnacle Books.

Seyle, H. (1974). *Stress without distress.* New York: New American Library, 14.

_____. (1976). *The stress of life.* New York: McGraw-Hill, 62, 472.

Sheth, J. & Sisodia, R. (1999, June 28). Outsourcing comes home. *The Wall Street Journal,* A26.

Sher, K., Wood, P., & Gotham, H. (1996, January/February). The course of psychological distress in college: A prospective high-risk study. *Journal of College Student Development,* 42–50.

Smith, C. (1997, December 24). A mismatch in the workplace sparks employee burnout. *Tallahassee Democrat,* 11D.

Tanner, E. (1991). Assessment of a health promotive lifestyle. *Nursing Clinicians of North America, 26*(4), 845–854.

Toffler, A. (1970). *Future shock*. New York: Random House.

Topp, R. (1989). Effect of relaxation or exercise on undergraduate test anxiety. *Perceptual and Motor Skills, 69,* 335–341.

Two new landmark studies. (1991). Survey Research Center, University of Michigan, Ann Arbor, 7.

Ulrich, D. & Dunne, H. (1986). *To love and work*. New York: Brunner/Mazel, 4.

Ventura, J. (1987). The stresses of parenthood reexamined. *Family Relations, 36,* 26–29.

Waldrop, J. (1993, September). Josie and the pussy cats beat stress. *American Demographics, 15*(9), 17.

chapter 12

Managing Environmental Resources

MAIN TOPICS

THE ECOSYSTEM AND ENVIRONMENTALISM
PROBLEM RECOGNITION
INDIVIDUAL AND FAMILY DECISION MAKING

ENVIRONMENTAL PROBLEMS AND SOLUTIONS
WATER
ENERGY
NOISE
WASTE AND RECYCLING
AIR QUALITY

Did you know that...?

...ninety-seven percent of the world's water is saline and unusable.

...American households recycle over 1.4 billion pounds of plastic bottles per year.

Ah, what a dusty answer gets the soul when hot for
certainties in this our life.

—*George Meredith*

THE SUBJECT OF this chapter is the current state of the environment
with an emphasis on the near physical environment, particularly the home.
During the twentieth century, the industrial and service revolutions created
thousands of products that made people's lives more comfortable. However,
these products did not come without a price, and often that price was a reduction in environmental quality and increased waste.

The twenty-first century challenge is to have products that make people's lives healthier and easier, but to do this with the goal of **sustainable
development**—a form of growth wherein societal needs, present and future, are met. Sustainable development requires the input and cooperation of
all segments of society, particularly producers and consumers. Toward this
end, today more careful decisions at every level are being made about the
products brought into the home and their use and disposal.

In this chapter the 3-Rs solution—reducing, reusing and recycling—will
be highlighted. It is increasingly being accepted worldwide as a means of
combatting negative effects on the environment. There is also a growing
recognition of the total product life cycle—from the resources used to make

Indoor pollution is not a new phenomenon, as this nineteenth-century engraving reveals.

the product, through its actual use, until its final disposal. The study of the life cycle of household products involves not only the material resources involved in their manufacture, distribution, and disposal, including energy use, but also the human resources involved (Uitdenbogerd, Brouwer, & Groot-Marcus, 1998). Thus, environmental problems are intertwined with trends, practices, preferences, and variations in human behavior.

Sigmund Freud, the founder of psychoanalysis, best known for his theories about the psyche (the mind) and social interaction, also made observations about humans in environmental contexts. *In Civilization and Its Discontents* (1930), Freud wrote that as civilizations become increasingly complex and modern, humans must renounce their innate selves. In 1987, Stephen J. Gould, Harvard paleontologist, added that humans are by nature selfish and aggressive, yet any successful civilization demands that we suppress our biological inclinations and act altruistically for common good and harmony. In 1988, J. Lovelock, another theorist, wrote that to be selfish is human and natural. But, he asserts, if we choose to be selfish in the right way, then life can be rich yet still consistent with a world fit for our grandchildren.

Thinking about others and the future of the planet is this chapter's theme. As Chapter 1 pointed out, the management process takes place within an environmental context, as illustrated in Figure 12.1. Building on the chapters on resources and managing human resources, time, stress and fatigue, this chapter gives practical examples about how to manage the environment, particularly the near environment that directly affects individuals and families. The resource chapters share the philosophy that the way individuals and families allocate resources has an impact on the state of the environment and global well-being. Certainly, decisions and actions at the household level collectively affect not only the present state of the world, but also the world that is to come. Even one simple behavioral change, such as driving the car less often or recycling plastic bags, affects the environment.

The present state of the environment is a result of developments and changes in the past. According to the best current estimates, the human

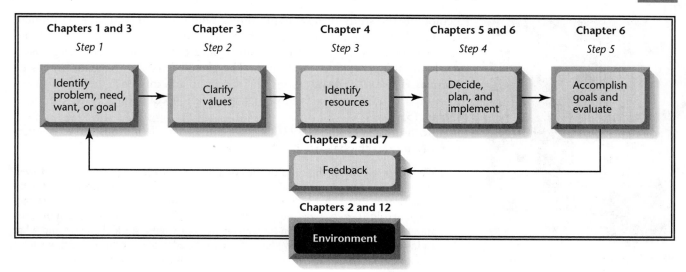

Chapters 1 and 3	Chapter 3	Chapter 4	Chapters 5 and 6	Chapter 6
Step 1	Step 2	Step 3	Step 4	Step 5
Identify problem, need, want, or goal	Clarify values	Identify resources	Decide, plan, and implement	Accomplish goals and evaluate

Chapters 2 and 7

Feedback

Chapters 2 and 12

Environment

FIGURE 12.1
**The Management
Process Model**

species, *Homo sapiens,* is 250,000 years old, and the earth is 4.5 billion years old (Gould, 1989). Phrasing it poetically, Gould says that in terms of the age of the earth, humanity arose just yesterday as a small twig on one branch of a flourishing tree. The realization of our minor place in earth's history gives us a sense of the magnitude of our responsibility to preserve what we have inherited. This responsibility is often referred to as **stewardship.** As stewards of the earth, we are committed to doing our part to sustain it for future generations. We are just beginning to understand both the limits and the potential of our planet and our role in its evolution. What separates us from previous generations is this greater awareness of the benefits and limits of our environment. The importance of the choices individuals and families make regarding the environment cannot be overstated. According to Al Gore, author of *Earth in the Balance:*

> This point is crucial: a choice to "do nothing" in response to the mounting evidence is actually a choice to continue and even accelerate the reckless environmental destruction that is creating the catastrophe at hand. (p. 37)

THE ECOSYSTEM AND ENVIRONMENTALISM

The systems approach used throughout this book emphasizes the interconnectedness and interactions between different systems. Systems are composed of living and nonliving things. Living systems (e.g., plants, animals, societies) are open systems that react to feedback. They can exist only in certain environments. Any change in the environment, such as a change in the temperature, air pressure, hydration, oxygen, or radiation outside a relatively narrow range, produces stress to which they cannot adjust. Under severe stress or deprivation, living systems cannot survive.

As discussed in Chapter 2, the family ecosystem is the subsystem of human ecology that emphasizes the interactions between families and environments.

Rachel Carson (1907–1964), an American biologist, was the author of Silent Spring, *a book published in 1962 that caused a worldwide awareness of the dangers of environmental pollution. Many credit her as the founder of the modern environmental movement.*

Ecology is the study of how living things relate to their natural environment (Naar, 1990). An **ecosystem** is the subsystem of human ecology that emphasizes the relationship between organisms and their environment. Organisms are living things—plants or animals. The place where an organism lives is its **habitat.** The external conditions that surround and influence the life of an organism, an individual, a family, or a population constitute its environment (Naar, 1990).

According to Gould (1998), beyond these basic definitions, there is a certain mystery to the balance of life. He says:

> We do not yet know the rules of the composition for ecosystems. We do not even know if rules exist in the usual sense. I am tempted, therefore, to close with the famous words that D'Arcy Thompson wrote to signify our ignorance of the microscopic world (*Growth and Form,* 1942 edition). We are not quite so uninformed about the rules of composition for ecosystems, but what a stark challenge and what an inspiration to go forth: "We have come to the edge of a world of which we have no experience, and where all our preconceptions must be recast." (p. 404)

Concern for the environment is called **environmentalism.** It can be found at all levels, from the individual—including activists such as Rachel Carson—to the family to community organizations to government and industry. Furthermore, the levels overlap. For example, individuals can work through institutions by banding together, boycotting products, writing letters, and voting for appropriate candidates. They can positively affect what industry produces by buying "green" (environmentally friendly) products. However, it should be pointed out that:

> Most consumers lack the scientific background to understand many environmental issues and few have relevant previous experience to guide them in assessing the relative environmental merits of market-place alternatives. Thus, the potential for consumer fraud and deception is great. (Cude, 1993, p. 207)

A major emphasis of environmentalism is how to retain existing environmental resources. These resources can be divided into two types: social and physical. **Social environmental resources** include an array of societies, economic and political groups, and community organizations. In each of these, people are united in a common cause, such as saving the manatees, or in a more general concern, such as reducing global warming. Global warming is caused when carbon dioxide and other gases collect in the air and trap heat radiated from the earth; over time, it can alter the earth's temperature, sea level, and storm systems (Pinchen, 1990). Carbon dioxide is released into the atmosphere by the burning of coal and oil and by the destruction of the forests.

Physical environmental resources include natural tangible (e.g., trees, soil, and ocean) and less tangible (e.g., air, sound, and light) surroundings. The latter part of this chapter will explore physical environmental management problems in the home and suggest eco-friendly practices.

Ecoconsciousness refers to the thoughts and actions given to protecting and sustaining the environment. **Conservation** is the act or process of preserving and protecting natural environments from loss or depletion. Individuals and families who are ecoconscious discuss environmental issues, recycle, conserve, reduce energy consumption and waste, buy "green" products, and support environmental causes and groups. The degree of ecoconsciousness varies, as shown on the continuum in Figure 12.2. Each person and each family fall somewhere on the continuum.

FIGURE 12.2
**Continuum of Environmental
Activism**

Problem Recognition

Differences between the ecological interests and practices of family members may be a source of conflict in families. One family member may go around the house turning on the lights while another follows carefully turning off the lights. Eventually, one of them is going to become irritated with the other's behavior.

Problem solving begins with a recognition that there is a problem to be solved. **Problem recognition** occurs when an individual or a family perceives a significant difference between their lifestyle and some desired or ideal lifestyle. The discrepancy must be large enough to push the individual to action. For example, Shannon and Dan enjoy fishing. One Saturday they go to a nearby lake and see a sign that says the fish in the lake are contaminated by high levels of mercury. Disappointed because they cannot fish, they recognize that water contamination is a problem affecting their choices and lifestyles. Shannon and Dan did not create the problem, but now they realize they are affected by it. What alternative courses of action do they have? They can quit fishing, go to another lake, or join others in an attempt to clean up the lake.

A problem can arise in one of two ways: need recognition and opportunity recognition. In **need recognition**, the person realizes how much he or she needs a certain product, service, or condition. In **opportunity recognition**,

Water contamination limits choices.

> **WARNING**
>
> ELEVATED LEVELS OF MERCURY
> HAVE BEEN DETECTED IN
> SOME FISH IN THESE LAKES.
>
> WE RECOMMEND *CATCH AND
> RELEASE OF ALL FISH*
>
> FOR MORE INFORMATION CALL
> THE ASSOCIATION OFFICE 668-3231

the individual realizes that she or he may have limited or no access to a product, service or condition. For example, suppose the price of gasoline soared to over $10 a gallon—this is definitely need recognition. Nearly everyone needs gasoline, but who could afford it? Now, suppose a gasoline shortage forces gasoline stations to close for a few days—this is an example of opportunity recognition. Drivers cannot purchase gasoline even if they want to, a situation that has occurred in the United States and other countries. Many environmental problems involve both need and opportunity recognition.

Communication plays a large part in environmental problem recognition. The sign warned Shannon and Dan not to eat the fish they caught. The federal government communicates environmental information through news releases, press conferences, warnings, and legislation. Television is a great communicator of environmental news, as are magazines, newspapers, and radio. Besides media sources, families communicate news about environmental conditions and behavior. Parents model littering or recycling behaviors for their children.

Once an environmental problem has been recognized, the individuals involved engage in an information search in order to resolve it. Information has been dubbed the ultimate **renewable resource** (meaning that it is essentially unlimited) because new technologies are constantly being devised to transmit, collect, store, process, package, and display it (Elkington, Burke, & Hailes, 1988). Through television, environmental disasters such as an oil spill are immediately transmitted to the public. This is one of the reasons that environmental awareness is greater now than ever before. Marshall McLuhan (1962), who coined the phrase the "medium is the message," said that the spread of electronic communications technology has established a global network. As individuals become more globally connected, they naturally become more globally aware. An example of the importance of global communications was the International Whaling Commission's decision, supported by the United States, to place a moratorium on commercial whale harvesting (Bohlen, 1990). Television reports on the plight of the whales undoubtedly played a part in the decision.

Saving Species

Each day 50 to 100 animal and plant species are being extinguished somewhere in the world (Elkins, Hillman, & Hutchison, 1992). These figures are estimates because no actual count of the total number of species exists. New insects are constantly being discovered, particularly in the tropics. In 1988, E. O. Wilson, a Harvard zoologist, estimated that there were 5 to 30 million species in the world. One of the chief causes of species extinction is the loss of habitat—and that loss is nearly always caused by human encroachment. As humans use more resources (land and water), less resources are available for other life-forms.

According to Gould (1987), in the long run many of the species saved will not be able to remain in their natural environments. Inevitably, zoos, which currently house about 540,000 mammals, birds, reptiles, and amphibians, will be the final home for many species (Conway, 1988). Fortunately, zoos are changing their function from institutions of capture and display to havens of preservation and propagation. Nevertheless, something is lost when an animal can no longer exist in its native habitat.

In Chapter 4, utility was defined as the use, value, or worth of a resource. In order for a substance, thing, or idea to be considered a resource (something useful for achieving an end purpose or goal), it must first be recognized as having current or potential utility. For example, at one time, uranium was considered a worthless, silvery white metal. Now it is used in research and nuclear fuel. One of the reasons animals, minerals, plants and habitats must be protected is that their potential use and their particular role in the total ecosystem may not be fully understood.

Many difficult decisions lie ahead as to which species will be saved and which will not. These decisions are part of a branch of study called environmental ethics. **Ethics** are systems of morals, principles, values, or good conduct. No discussion of environmentalism would be complete without considering the ethical issues involved. Each person has to decide what is the right course of action in personal situations as well as in the broader societal context. As Wilson (1988) said: "I suppose it will all come down to a decision of ethics—how we value the natural worlds in which we evolved and now, increasingly, how we regard our status as individuals" (p. 16).

Individual and Family Decision Making

Individuals and families are taking on a greater share of responsibility for their environment and are relying less on large institutions. Many people realize that government or business alone cannot be depended on to solve all the environmental ills that exist. The problems are too widespread to be remedied by one group. Furthermore, the boundaries of the problems are often difficult to discern. For example, consumption and disposal practices of individuals and families, as well as those of businesses and industry, contribute to the **waste stream** (all garbage produced). This blurring of the boundaries between the traditionally defined roles of the public sector and the private sector is a growing trend.

One of the most difficult aspects of environmentalism is determining what is a real, acute problem or shortage and what is not. The media often give out conflicting messages about the severity of a problem or the best solutions. Now more than ever before, critical thinking skills are needed to evaluate environmental information. Cross-checking the information by looking at several different reliable sources is one way of arriving at the truth of a situation.

Environmental decision making by individuals is complicated enough considering the range of values, resources, goals, and decision-making steps involved. Environmental decision making in families is necessarily all the more complicated. Not only may family members differ in their use of electricity, but some may want to recycle bottles, jars, and cans while others throw them away in the garbage, to cite just two examples of conflicting environmental behavior. Sometimes one family member takes on the role of environmentalist and sets the rules, turns down the thermostat, and turns off the television when not in use. With so much environmental education taking place in schools, it is not unusual to find a school-aged child rather than a parent taking on this role. Children may be better informed about environmental issues than their parents, and, with their youthful optimism, they are willing to try new ways of managing household waste or adjusting consumption patterns.

The Elbing model of viewing alternatives in a family decision situation, discussed in Chapter 5, includes the component "Z," which represents the effect of environmental factors on decisions. In this model, environmental forces include the natural and human environments existing when the decision is being made, that is, the physical, social, economic, and political conditions in place at that time. Deciding where to go to lunch may be a decision involving environmental factors. To save gasoline, a person may choose to walk to a nearby restaurant rather than drive. Distance is one type of physical environment constraint.

To summarize, within the same family there may be vast differences in types, styles, and levels of environmental awareness. Differences are even more evident between families and between communities. Some communities have active recycling programs that make it easier for people to recycle, and ease is a significant factor in the success of conservation programs.

ENVIRONMENTAL PROBLEMS AND SOLUTIONS

The balance of this chapter is divided into five parts: water, energy, noise, waste and recycling, and air quality. Each part describes the problems and presents solutions applicable to individuals, families, and households. To keep the chapter a manageable length, some important topics had to be omitted, including ocean pollution, ozone depletion, desertification, deforestation, climatic changes, and loss of soil. All of these are important avenues for future study and research. Many of them overlap. For example, desertification refers to the increase in dry, barren land that supports little or no vegetation. This happens for many reasons, including the loss of soil, overpopulation, overgrazing, deforestation and overcultivation. Common to all environmental problems is the widespread growth of pollution. **Pollution** is a general term referring to undesirable changes in physical, chemical, or biological characteristics of air, land, or water that can harm the health, activities, or survival of living organisms.

The information that follows is as accurate as possible, but it will be up to the reader to keep abreast of the very latest developments in the ever changing field of environmentalism.

Water

The two main problems associated with water are shortages and pollution. Since 1900 there has been a six-fold increase in worldwide water use. About one-fifth of the earth's population does not have safe drinking water. According to the Environmental Protection Agency (EPA), approximately 50,000 water contaminants have been identified, and more than 100 of these are regulated in the United States. All contaminants are potentially hazardous to human health. The five main types of contaminants in the U.S. water supply are chlorinated solvents, trialomethanes, lead, PCBs (or polychlorinated biphenyls, a class of compounds that have various industrial applications), and pathogenic bacteria and viruses (Foran, 1990).

Most water that comes from a public system must meet the standards set by the Federal Drinking Water Act and state and local regulations. Water is less likely to be officially tested if it comes from a well or a small system. In this case, a sample of the water can be tested at the local department of health, an independent state-certified laboratory, or a local college or university. The cooperative extension service can inform residents about testing services available.

Because of the fear of water contaminants, water-purifying businesses ranging from legitimate to quasi-legitimate are thriving. Each year, U.S. residents spend over a billion dollars on home purifying equipment and water filtration services. In addition, consumers spend billions on bottled water, some of which is unregulated and less pure than tap water. Before investing in any equipment or services, consumers should first have their water checked by legitimate testing services that are not selling a product. Consumers can also check with their local Better Business Bureau or consumer protection agency to see if there are any recorded complaints against the company from whom they are considering buying equipment or services.

Contamination of drinking water is not the only water-related issue. There are many others, including the following:

◆ *Drinking water:* Supply and conservation, treatment, and health considerations

◆ *Groundwater:* Availability and depletion, quality and contamination, consequences to public health, detection, and monitoring

◆ *Seawater:* Quality and quantity; preservation of sea life

◆ *Water for agricultural use:* Conservation and supply

◆ *Water for industrial use:* Supply and pollutants

◆ *Water for household use:* Supply and quality, conservation and water-efficient products

Because this book is concerned primarily with individual and family management practices, this discussion will focus on drinking water and household water use.

Water Consumption and Shortage

In the average household, toilets account for 35–45 percent of the water used, showers/baths for 20–30 percent, drinking/cooking for 5–10 percent, laundry for 8 percent, dishwashing for 5 percent, and garden/car for 2 percent (Pearson, 1989). Estimated per capita in-house water use ranges from 20 to 100 gallons per day (Seaker & Sharpe, 1988). As these statistics illustrate, the greatest water use is in the bathroom. Collectively, each day, U.S. residents flush more than five billion gallons of water down the toilet and shower away three billion gallons ("How to save water," 1990). In 1994, the Federal Energy Policy Act restricted all new household faucets and showerheads to 2.5 gallons per minute. The Act also restricted toilets, limiting flush capacity to 1.6 gallons compared to an earlier standard of 3.5.

Water used to be cheap, clean, and abundant, but in many metropolitan areas and in the dry Southwest and southern California, water has now become a limited resource. As a result, many areas are regulating water use through rules and legislation. Some cities have ordinances governing when cars can be washed or sprinklers used.

The amount of water available varies by region, season, and climatic factors. Droughts can be particularly serious in overpopulated areas. As the population grows, the need for water increases, and the present system of dams and aqueducts will have difficulty meeting the demand. Supply is only one side of the equation, however. On the other side, individuals and families will have to adjust their lifestyles to effectively manage the supply that is available to them.

Practical Ways to Reduce Household Water Use

Most homeowners cannot afford to replace their toilets, and this is certainly not practical for renters. Nevertheless, there are many low-cost or free ways to save water:

- Do not leave the water running while doing dishes, brushing teeth, or shaving.
- Run full loads in the washing machine and dishwasher. Also, new front-loading washers use 30–40 percent less than top-loaders.
- Install water-saving shower heads or take showers instead of baths (baths use more water than short showers).
- Fix leaky faucets and toilets.
- Landscape with native plants that do not require additional watering.
- Use only the water necessary for cooking and rinsing food.
- Water the lawn and garden early in the morning to avoid losing too much water to evaporation in the heat of the day. Watering cans use less water than hoses. Cover soil with compost or mulch to reduce evaporation.
- Use buckets of water to wash the car rather than running water continuously from a hose.

This list could go on, but these suggestions provide a starting point. The fact is that 97 percent of the world's water is saline and unusable, leaving a meager 3 percent to nourish and sustain life (Graves, 1990). Desalination research provides long-term hope for a larger water supply. Another solution is to grow crops that require less water. Currently, the world's human population continues to grow while the supply of fresh water remains constant. Learning how to conserve and apportion water will be one of the greatest management problems of the twenty-first century. Though the United States ranks sixth among water-rich nations in the world, it ranks third in water consumption and waste. Humans can live only a few days without water. As water becomes scarcer, its perceived value as a resource will increase. Learning to conserve now will begin a lifelong habit that will lead to saved money and a healthier environment.

Energy

Energy is the ability to do work, measured as potential or stored energy or as kinetic energy, the energy of motion (Naar, 1990). The main problems associated with energy are energy production, energy wastage, and pollution from the use of fossil fuels. **Fossil fuels** are the remains of dead vegetation, such as coal, oil, and natural gas, that can be burned to release energy (Naar, 1990). Fuel is used to provide physical comfort and mechanical power (Elkins, Hillman, & Hutchison, 1992). Because electricity is the main form of energy used in today's homes, the emphasis in this section is on electricity.

Historically, usable energy was most often produced by burning wood or a natural fuel such as coal or oil. Only in the late nineteenth and twentieth centuries was heat energy used to create another form of usable energy—electricity. In the United States, most electricity is generated by burning coal. Electricity is also produced by generators driven by steam, from other fossil fuels such as oil and natural gas, and from nuclear reactors. Hydroelectric power, which comes from generators turned by falling water, is another current source of energy. Dwindling fossil fuels and concern over potential accidental radioactive discharges from nuclear power plants have led to efforts to find alternative electric energy sources. Among the alternatives under consideration are solar batteries, geothermal power stations, nuclear fusion reactors, and magnetohydrodynamic generators. Whatever the source of power, electric energy is generated at a central point (e.g., a dam, an energy plant) and then transmitted to delivery points or substations, from which it is distributed to consumers. New forms of transmission are being investigated along with new ways to generate energy.

Energy Consumption and Home Energy Audits

The United States uses more energy per capita than most other countries, even countries with higher standards of living and colder winters than ours (Stein, Reynolds & McGuiness, 1986). An average-sized, conventional house uses 20,000 to 30,000 kWH (kilowatt hours) of energy each year (Pearson, 1989). Depending on the climate and the home's insulation, about 60 percent of energy goes to space heating and cooling, 20 percent to hot water, 10 percent to cooking/refrigerating, and 10 percent to lighting and appliances. The remainder goes to standing charges and maintenance. By improving insulation, weatherstripping, and making a few alterations in a home (e.g., adding storm windows, adding overhangs, shutting drapes and doors), a homeowner can save at least half the money spent on heating, air conditioning, and hot water.

In the average home, the greatest amount of air leakage is through cracks in walls, windows, and doors (*What to Know about a Home Energy Audit*, 1990). Sometimes the homeowner will not notice these hairline cracks, but trained specialists can detect them. Local utility companies or city or county utility offices may provide free or low-cost home energy audits. An energy audit is performed by a specialist who makes a one- or two-hour "walk through" inspection of the interior and the exterior of a home. Upon completion of the inspection or shortly afterward, homeowners receive an analysis of what they can do to improve the energy efficiency of their home. Auditors focus on determining where a house loses heat in winter and cool air in summer and identify appliances and heating/cooling systems that have better efficiency levels. College graduates who have studied resource management have been hired to work as home energy auditors for city and county government and utility companies and as energy educators and policy makers in state and national government.

Practical Ways to Reduce Household Energy Use

The home energy audit is a good way to find out about a specific home's energy use. This section provides several energy-saving ideas applicable to most homes.

Because air leaks are a major problem, insulation is an important way to reduce energy loss. Insulation comes in several forms: rigid panels or sheets of insulation, batts (fluffy fiberglass rolls of insulation), and blown insulation (mainly chopped fiberglass with air). A vapor-proof barrier of strong plastic can increase the efficiency of the insulation. The higher the **R-value** (R stands for resistance), the higher the insulation properties. Another solution is double- or triple-glazed windows to reduce heat loss or heat gain. Storm windows are usually triple-glazed. Weatherstripping around windows and doors will also seal leaks. Window awnings will reduce heat gain in summer, and drawn, insulated drapes will reduce heat loss in winter.

The **site** is the location or situation of a house. **Orientation** is the location or situation of the house relative to points on a compass. In selecting the site and the orientation of the house, the homeowner and builder should take the natural environment into account. Warmth and shelter can be enhanced if hills, trees, winds, water, and the sun are considered. The climate will influence the best site and orientation for a house. In states with hot climates, most houses should have few windows on the west side to avoid the afternoon sun. In states with predominantly cold climates, houses should have few windows on the north side to reduce the cold drafts.

Landscaping can also affect heat loss and gain. **Deciduous trees,** such as oaks and maples, that lose their leaves in the winter are good choices. Their leaves will shield the house in the summer, but let the sunshine through in the winter. Trees and bushes can also serve as wind barriers.

According to the Department of Energy, U.S. households spend more than $1,000 each year to run household appliances. The following suggestions can reduce this amount considerably:

- ◆ Install a computerized thermostat.
- ◆ Turn the thermostat down on water heaters. Each 10-degree reduction cuts water heating energy bills by 3–5 percent. To get dishes clean in a dishwasher, the water heater should not be set below 140°F (Fahrenheit) unless the dishwasher has its own water heating system.
- ◆ Keep the temperature setting in the refrigerator between 38°F and 42°F and the freezer between 0°F and 5°F. If the refrigerator and freezer are kept 10 degrees colder than this, energy consumption can increase as much as 25 percent. Clean refrigerator coils at least once a year. A filled refrigerator or freezer is more energy efficient than an empty or partially filled one.
- ◆ Use small appliances when possible because they require less energy than large ones. Microwave ovens and toaster ovens use less energy than conventional ovens. Coffeemakers, hairdryers, irons, and toasters do not consume very much energy overall; they draw a lot of power but are in use for short periods of time. Because refrigerators and freezers run constantly, they use far more energy than other kitchen appliances.
- ◆ Keep the refrigerator door open for a short time rather than opening and closing it frequently, which wastes more energy. Most of the cold air rushes out of the refrigerator as soon as it is opened.
- ◆ Replace old, inefficient appliances with new ones.
- ◆ Clean the dryer's lint screen after each use. Run full loads in the dishwasher and clothes washer rather than running small loads more often. Heating water accounts for 95 percent of the energy consumed for hot water in the clothes washer. Save money and energy by washing in cold water, unless the clothes require hot or warm water, and always use cold water rinse.

To help consumers select low-energy appliances, the Appliance Labeling program administered by the Federal Trade Commission requires major household appliances—those using the most energy—to have an Energy-Guide label (see Figure 12.3 for an example). Labeled appliances include water heaters, clothes washers, dishwashers, furnaces, refrigerator-freezers, freezers, heat pumps, and room air conditioners. Also, in cooperation with the EPA and the Department of Energy (DOE), most computer and television manufacturers have joined the Energy Star Program that promotes the design of equipment that uses less energy when turned on and off.

Reducing the amount of energy used by appliances is helpful, but it is a myth that turning off lights and the television is the best way to conserve energy in the home; in fact, these consume a small portion of the home's elec-

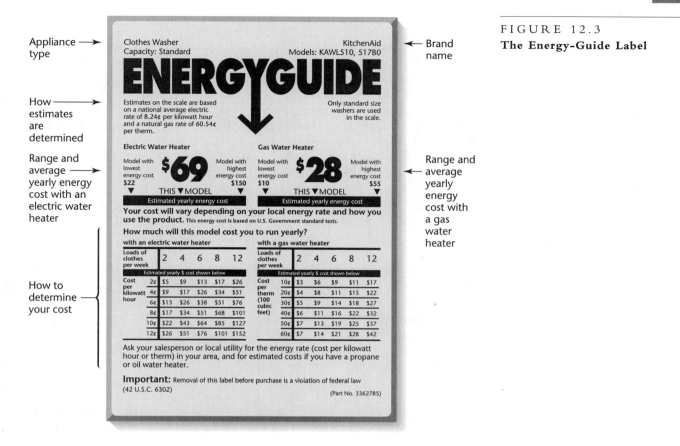

FIGURE 12.3
The Energy-Guide Label

tricity (Merline, 1988). Even small savings help, however, and consumers can reduce home energy consumption by:

◆ Installing dimmer switches.

◆ Lighting areas for specific needs.

◆ Installing fluorescent lights, which use 80 percent less energy than incandescent lights.

◆ Using light colors on ceilings, walls, floors, and furniture because they reflect more light and brighten a room.

◆ Replacing old lamps with new, more efficient ones. Dusting light bulbs and tubes increases light output and reduces the risk of potential pollutants.

◆ Turning off lights when not in use.

◆ Checking Energy-Guide or Energy Star labels before buying.

These suggestions can help, but it is important to remember that the greatest savings come from turning the thermostat down to 60°F in winter and turning it up to 80°F in the summer, or turning it off altogether and opening the windows in pleasant weather.

Energy company records reveal that energy use varies widely even in neighborhoods where houses are the same size and style. Efficient appliances and lighting and the management of human behavior (e.g., shutting windows when the air conditioning is on) can substantially affect the energy use in the home.

Noise

Far less information is available about noise pollution than about water and energy conservation. Noise pollution is less easy to delineate because people are not billed for the use of noise and each person is a producer as well as a consumer of noise. **Noise** is simply any unwanted sound. Sensitivity to noise varies from person to person. The intensity, or loudness, of sound is the amount of acoustic energy transmitted through the air; it is measured in **decibels (dB).** The lowest sound humans can hear is 1 dB. An average home on a quiet street has a dB level of 50 (Pearson, 1989). A noisy office, a preschool classroom, or an alarm clock can be as loud as 80 dB. At 120 dB the hearer experiences discomfort or pain; a jet taking off nearby or loud thunder can register this high (Pearson, 1989). Household appliances range from 60 to 90 dB with the food disposal being the noisiest at over 90 dB. Besides being harmful, too much noise can be annoying, making it difficult to concentrate or relax.

Homes, offices, and other environments should strive to offer a comfortable amount of noise. Research shows that people feel uneasy if they are deprived of environmental stimulation (i.e., too little sound, movement, or light) for too long. Too little sound may make a person feel uncomfortable or lonely. To counteract this effect, music is piped in to elevators, grocery stores, and dentists' offices. Many people go to sleep better at night with the hum of a fan or the drone of a radio in the background.

Too much noise is a more common problem than too little, however. Noise from loud neighbors, ringing telephones, barking dogs, and screaming children can become an intolerable burden. Often it is not the noise itself that is irritating or harmful, but the continuous nature of noise or the combination of noises (e.g., the noise of the vacuum cleaner, the blender, the television, and children slamming doors occurring at the same time). Poorly constructed buildings add to the noise level. Insulation and absorbing surfaces such as carpet, cork, or acoustical tiles can reduce noise. On common walls between apartments, brick, earth, and concrete reduce noise better than wood or aluminum siding. As a general rule, soft, porous surfaces absorb sound, and hard, smooth surfaces reflect sound.

Practical Ways to Reduce Noise

The following suggestions will help reduce noise in the home:

- Find housing away from noisy traffic, airports, schools, and factories.
- Plant barrier trees and hedges to reduce noise. High walls and earth mounds also cut noise.
- Place bedrooms in quieter parts of the house. Put the garage on the noisy side of the site.
- Buy "quiet" appliances—these have more insulation.
- Keep the volume on radios and televisions low.
- Draw heavy drapes and close blinds to shut out neighborhood noise.
- Weatherstrip windows and doors to prevent outside noise from entering the home. Inside the house, solid-core doors will reduce noise between rooms. On a busy street, use double- or triple-pane windows.

As the world becomes more crowded, noise pollution will become a greater management problem than it currently is. Finding a quiet, peaceful place may become more difficult. Decreasing noise is a way to de-stress life. Another way to reduce stress is to add sounds that are soothing and pleasant. The rustle of trees, the singing of birds, and the sound of ocean waves are soothing to many people. Bringing more of these natural sounds into one's life and removing some of the irritating, mechanical ones may increase a person's overall sense of well-being.

Waste and Recycling

A typical American creates 4.4 pounds of garbage a day. The problem is that the United States is running out of ways to dispose of garbage. Historically, landfills were cheap and readily available, but vacant land is no longer cheap and is becoming increasingly scarce around cities. Suburbs have sprung up where landfills used to be.

The skyrocketing cost of land, coupled with concern about environmental pollution and population growth, have led many people to suggest that new methods of waste disposal are needed. In particular, they recommend burying waste, burning it, recycling it, or not producing so much of it. Combining all four methods is called **integrated waste management.** In this system, waste products are sorted, recyclable items are reused, and the rest is burned cleanly in a furnace that also produces steam to generate electricity. Only the remaining ash goes to the landfill. According to the EPA, the breakdown of U.S. garbage is as follows:

- Paper and paperboard   38.6%
- Yard waste   12.8%
- Food waste   10.1%
- Plastics   9.9%
- Metals   7.7%
- Glass   5.5%
- Wood   5.3%
- Other (rubber, leather, textiles, etc.)   10.0%

In recent years, recycling has become more popular. The Environmental Protection Agency estimates that 30 percent of newspapers, 40–50 percent of cardboard, 10–15 percent of office paper, 50 percent of aluminum cans, 10 percent of glass bottles, and 2 percent of plastic products are recycled. Examples of recycling include the following:

- *Plastic:* Used for fiberfill for pillows, flowerpots, paintbrush bristles, fence posts, insulation, and docks. For example, according to the American Plastics Council, U.S. households recycle over 1.4 billion pounds of plastic bottles each year.
- *Paper:* Used for gameboards, puzzles, stationery, newspapers, toilet paper, paper towels, egg cartons, boxes, books, and tickets.
- *Glass:* Used for bottles, street paving, tiles, and bricks.
- *Aluminum:* Used for cans, lawn furniture, window frames, and car parts.

Although people in the United States have become more active in recycling, much still can be done to reduce waste.

Practical Ways to Reduce Waste

Households can adopt the 3-Rs solution to the waste problem:

1. *Reducing.* Avoid buying products with excessive packaging; use a coffee mug at work (avoid using styrofoam cups); buy in bulk (fewer packages); use lunch boxes instead of paper or plastic bags; and buy recycled paper products.

2. *Reusing.* Use both sides of sheets of paper; reuse old envelopes for messages and lists; reuse wrapping paper and ribbons; and reuse cardboard boxes and glass jars.

3. *Recycling.* Take recycling materials to recycling centers. Hand down clothes from child to child; alter and reuse existing clothes; and donate used clothing to charities or Goodwill Industries. Refinish, sell, or donate old furniture.

These three methods all involve management. Each requires time, energy, and commitment; decision plans must be made and carried out. Children can be taught the value of waste reduction in their families, schools, or in organizations such as Boy Scouts and Girl Scouts. Starting small and local makes the most sense for children. They can see the results of picking up litter in their playground and neighborhood. At home, children can separate waste into the appropriate recycling boxes and can help their parents take trash to community recycling bins. Children enjoy being part of a community effort, and parents can model good citizenship habits for the future. The fundamental message to children should be that each person can make a difference in the health of the environment.

Air Quality

Although humans can live a few days without water, they can only survive a few minutes without air. Therefore, clean air has to be given high priority in the list of environmental concerns. The pollutants that lead to deteriorating air quality come from many sources, not from a single source. Air quality is threatened by too much ozone, airborne particles, sulfur dioxide, lead, nitrogen oxides, and carbon monoxide. More than half of the nation's air pollution comes from mobile sources such as cars, trucks, motorcycles, airplanes, trains, buses, and boats. Stationary sources such as factories, drycleaners, homes, and oil refineries also pollute the air.

Air pollution contributes to many health problems and ecological problems, such as decreased quality of aquatic life and vegetation damage. Pollution is sometimes worse indoors than outside, particularly where buildings are tightly constructed or sealed to save energy or where they have poor ventilation systems. Sick building syndrome is caused by the presence of pollutants in the air compounded by inadequate ventilation systems. Harmful indoor pollutants may come from building materials, furnishings, space heaters, gas ranges, wood preservatives, aerosols, and cleaning agents. More than 90 percent of air-pollution deaths occur in developing countries. Eighty percent of these deaths are caused by indoor air pollution; many poor people lack access to clean fuel and burn dung and wood for cooking and heating (Vo, 1998).

In the United States, the top 10 indoor air pollutants according to the American Lung Association are:

1. Second-hand smoke.

2. Biological contaminants—including bacteria, viruses, animal dander, dust mites, cockroach parts, pollen, molds, and fungi. These are usually inhaled alone or by attaching themselves to dust that is then inhaled.

3. Particulates—including solid particles and liquid droplets such as dirt, dust, and smoke.

4. Household products—including cleansers, personal care products, and paint.

5. Carbon monoxide—an odorless and colorless gas, a product of combustion of fossil fuels and burning wood.

6. **Radon**—a naturally occurring gaseous by-product of the uranium in the earth—can enter a house through holes and cracks in the foundation, through cinder blocks or through loose-fitting pipes, floor drains, or pumps. Concentrations are likely to be largest in the basements of buildings. The Environmental Protection Agency estimates that between 10,000 and 40,000 lung cancer deaths a year in the United States are caused by radon ("Radon: The Problem No One Wants to Face," 1989). State environmental protection departments provide lists of approved contractors able to make radon-reducing modifications. A radon level of 4 picocuries per liter or more is considered dangerous.

7. Volatile organic compounds (VOCs)—the "new smell" from carpets, wood cabinets, plastics, etc. One of the most common VOCs is formaldehyde.

8. Pesticides.

9. Lead—found in paint and lead pipes. Before 1978 all homes used lead-based paint.

10. Asbestos—microscopic mineral fibers that are flexible, durable, and do not burn.

Practical Ways to Reduce Air Pollution

Air quality varies widely. The air quality index ranges from a low of 0 to a high of 500. Air quality from 0 to 49 is considered good; 300 and above is hazardous (Carpenter, 1989). Runners, construction workers, gardeners, children, and anyone else who is outdoors a lot need to be especially mindful of changes in air quality. Elderly people or younger persons with certain health conditions should be aware also. These suggestions can help improve air quality:

◆ Use roll-on or solid deodorants; liquid or "spritz" pump sprays for deodorants or hair sprays are recommended over the use of aerosols because chemicals from aerosols contribute to smog.

◆ Keep the car engine tuned. Use public transportation and bicycles when possible.

◆ Don't smoke. Encourage the designation of smoking and nonsmoking areas in businesses or eliminate indoor smoking completely.

◆ Air out houses and workplaces. Open windows at least once a week.

◆ Clean heater and air conditioner filters regularly. Use an air conditioner or dehumidifier to maintain an indoor relative humidity below 65 percent.

◆ When building or remodeling a house, use safe building materials and installation methods. For example, paint with brushes and rollers instead of sprayers. Be wary of asbestos, formaldehyde, and radon.

◆ Put green plants in homes and workplaces. Certain types of green plants are particularly effective in filtering out indoor air pollution. However, the Environmental Protection Agency suggests that rather than relying on plants, the focus on improving home air quality should be on removing the sources of unhealthy contaminants.

Electronic Resources

A global perspective on plants, gardens, botanical organizations, and land use issues is available through the Internet Directory for Botany Web site at **www.helsinki.fi/kmus/botmenu.html**. For a U.S. policy perspective on environmental issues go to the Environmental Protection Agency Web site at **www.epa.gov**. More information on air quality issues can be found on the American Lung Association Web site at **www.lungfla.org**. For information on Rachel Carson, author and key figure in the environmental movement, check encyclopedia Web sites and **www.rachelcarson.org/**.

Many environmental and scientific magazines and groups have Web sites. Examples are *Tomorrow* magazine at **www.tomorrow_web.com**, *Scientific American* at **www.sciam.com/**, *National Geographic* at **www. nationalgeographic.com** and EnviroLink at **envirolink.org/**.

In recognition that a single company cannot solve the world's environmental problems, Mitsubishi Electronic became a founding member of the Fortune 500 (**www.globalff.org**), a network of organizations interested in furthering industrial ecology and improving resource productivity. To find out more about what companies are doing to reduce waste and increase recycling, visit this Web site.

www.epa.gov/

Summary

Although this chapter has given practical suggestions for specific environmental problems relating to air, water, waste, noise, and energy, the overriding suggestion is to support legislation, research, and government policies that will improve all these areas of concern. This chapter has defined key environmental terms, discussed environmental issues, and suggested ways to conserve limited resources. People who incorporate several of these suggestions into their daily life management are practicing **positive ecology**. By shifting to less harmful energy sources, thinking more holistically, and being a "green" consumer, each individual can help create a healthier environment. Each person and each family should ask themselves, "What can I do to reduce waste and pollution?"

Although people rely to a degree on government, environmental organizations, and universities for solutions, ultimately they must look within for answers. As the actor Beau Bridges has said, "All the talk about how the environment is being ruined means nothing unless you're doing something about it in your own home."

Families need to consider the environmental messages and values they are passing down to their children. If the days of limitless clean air and water, low-cost energy, and abundant peaceful, quiet environments are gone, what will be put in their place? Will future generations view the twenty-first century as a turning point toward more positive ecology?

Key Terms

conservation
decibel
deciduous trees
ecoconsciousness
ecosystem
energy
environmentalism
ethics
fossil fuels
habitat
integrated waste
  management

need recognition
noise
opportunity
  recognition
orientation
physical
  environmental
  resources
pollution
positive ecology
problem recognition
radon

renewable resource
R-value
site
social environmental
  resources
stewardship
sustainable
  development
waste stream

Review Questions

1. Comment on the following statement by E. O. Wilson: "I suppose it will all come down to a decision of ethics—how we value the natural worlds in which we evolved and now, increasingly, how we regard our status as individuals." Do you agree or disagree? Include an explanation of the term *ethics* in your answer.

2. What are the two main problems associated with water in the home? What can be done to reduce water use?

3. What system uses the most energy in the home? Where does most heat loss occur? How can heat loss be reduced?

4. What is the 3-Rs solution to waste? How does the United States compare with other nations in waste production?

5. What is positive ecology? Give an example of how you practice positive ecology.

References

Bohlen, C. (1990). Report from the State Department, *EPA Journal, 16*(4), 15–16.

Carpenter, B. (1989, June 12). The newest health hazard: Breathing. *U.S. News and World Report.*

Conway, W. (1988). Can technology aid species preservation? In E. O. Wilson (Ed.), *Biodiversity.* Washington, D.C.: National Academy Press, 263–268.

Cude, B. (1993). Consumer perceptions of environmental marketing claims: An exploratory study. *Journal of Consumer Studies and Home Economics, 12,* 207–225.

Elkington, J., Burke, T., & Hailes, J. (1988). *Green pages: The business of saving the world.* London: Routledge, 156.

Elkins, P., Hillman, M., & Hutchison, R. (1992). *Green economics.* Doubleday: New York, 16.

Foran, J. (1990). Toxic substances in surface water. *Environmental Science Technology, 24*(5), 604–605.

Freud, S. (1961). *Civilization and its discontents.* (J. Strachey, Translator). New York: W. W. Norton (Original work published 1930).

Gore, A. (1992). *Earth in the Balance.* New York: Penguin Books USA, Inc.

Gould, S. J. (1987). *An urchin in the storm.* New York: W. W. Norton.

_____. (1998). *Leonardo's mountain of clams and the diet of worms: Essays on natural history.* New York: Harmony Books.

_____. (1989). *Wonderful life.* New York: W. W. Norton.

Graves, W. (1990, July). Water—the growing crisis. *National Geographic,* 1.

How to save water. (1990, July). *Consumer Reports,* 465–469.

Lovelock, J. (1988). The earth as a living organism. In E. O. Wilson (Ed.), *Biodiversity.* Washington, D.C.: National Academy Press, 486–489.

McLuhan, M. (1962). *The gutenberg galaxy.* Toronto: University of Toronto Press.

Merline, J. W. (1988, August). Energy smarts. *Consumers' Research,* 38.

Naar, J. (1990). *Design for a livable planet.* New York: Harper & Row.

Pearson, D. (1989). *The natural house.* New York: Simon & Schuster.

Pinchon, N. (1990, November 10). What causes global warming. Knight-Ridder Tribune News, 37.

Radon: The problem no one wants to face. (1989, October). *Consumer Reports,* 623–625.

Seaker, E. M. & Sharpe, W. E. (1988, August). *Water use in eight central Pennsylvania homes.* Washington, D.C.: American Water Resources Management, 283–292.

Stein, B., Reynolds, J. S., & MacGuiness, W. J. (1986). *Mechanical and electrical equipment for building* (7th ed.). New York: John Wiley & Sons.

Uitenbogerd, D., Brouwer, N., & Groot-Marcus, J. (1998). Domestic energy saving potentials for food and textiles: An empirical study. A report from Wageningen Agricultural University, Holland.

Vo, M. (1998, November 6). A look at the world by the numbers. *The Christian Science Monitor,* 8–9.

What to know about a home energy audit. (1990, January). *Consumer's Research,* 17.

Wilson, E. O. (1988). The current state of biological diversity. In E. O. Wilson (Ed.), *Biodiversity.* Washington, D.C.: National Academy Press.

chapter **13**

Managing Finances

MAIN TOPICS

WHAT IS FINANCIAL MANAGEMENT?
INDIVIDUALS AND FAMILIES AS PRODUCERS AND CONSUMERS
INCOME, NET WORTH, BUDGETS, SAVINGS, AND CREDIT
BANKING, INVESTMENTS, AND INSURANCE
EXPENSES RELATED TO CHILDREN
RETIREMENT PLANNING

FINANCIAL AND ECONOMIC CONCERNS
RECESSION, DEPRESSION, INFLATION, AND UNEMPLOYMENT
COLLEGE STUDENTS AND MONEY MANAGEMENT
THE GENDER GAP AND THE GLASS CEILING
POVERTY AND WEALTH
WHERE DOES MONEY GO?

Did you know that...?

. . . It costs about $300,000 to rear a child from birth to age 18.

. . . Three out of four college students expect to become millionaires.

Happiness seems to require a modicum of external prosperity.

—*Aristotle*

ONTROLLING FINANCIAL RESOURCES is one of the most important and practical aspects of management. Although this chapter begins
with theory, it moves quickly to the dollars and cents issues involved in
money management and ends with a discussion of current financial and
economic issues, including poverty and wealth, credit, the gender gap, and
the glass ceiling.

   This chapter is placed near the end of the book because it builds on
many of the principles covered in the previous chapters on values, attitudes,
goals, resources, and decision making. To reiterate, values are principles that
guide behavior, and goals are end results that require action. Thrift, for example, is a value affecting financial management, and saving for a car is an
example of a financial goal. Attitudes are concepts that express feelings in regard to some idea, person, object, event, situation, or relationship. They play
an important role in consumption because individuals have innumerable
consumer attitudes (e.g., preferring a particular brand, store, or product over
another). All people must make financial decisions, but their choices are limited by how much money they have. Money is a material resource, but how

a person chooses to spend it is a human resource. For example, while college students make up 5 percent of the U.S. population, they account for 35 percent of compact disk sales (Beiles, 1999).

Financial planning is an integral part of managing information systems and decision support systems. Individuals may choose to do their own financial planning or turn to experts for help. Financial advice can be obtained in a variety of ways: by consulting with experts in person, by reading newspapers or financial magazines, by watching television shows on finance, by accessing information on the Internet, or by talking with friends and family members. Case studies on calculating net worth and budgeting provide examples of how others manage. Space limitations prevent an exhaustive examination of personal and family finance, a topic to which entire books are devoted. Instead, this chapter provides an introduction to financial planning and related economic and lifestyle issues by focusing on families as producers and consumers and examining such concerns as what individuals and families do with their money and how they provide for retirement.

WHAT IS FINANCIAL MANAGEMENT?

Financial management is the science or practice of managing money or other assets. Financial management requires systematic and disciplined thought and action. Saving money rather than spending it, for instance, requires self-discipline and control, the ability to set goals, and a willingness to put future needs before current needs. The procedures followed at each stage of financial management must be methodological, sound, and planned for in advance to the extent possible. Essentially, financial plans are "a work in progress," subject to review and modification (O'Neill & Brennan, 1997).

In systems terminology, financial management is a transformation process involving the identification of financial goals, collection of information, analysis of resources, decisions about whether to spend, invest, or save, and evaluation of decisions. Management takes the perspective that money, like any other resource, can be controlled and used to achieve goals. As Figure 13.1 shows, the financial management process can be divided into three phases: planning, action, and postplanning.

FIGURE 13.1
Financial Management Model

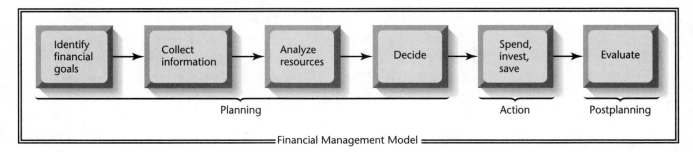

Financial Management Model

During the planning stage, individuals begin by defining their financial goals. They then identify potential financial opportunities and determine what information and funds are needed to take advantage of these opportunities. Once they have analyzed their resources and decided how to use them, they can proceed to the action stage, where they save, invest, or spend their money. In this phase, a **budget,** or a spending plan or guide, can be helpful by providing a visible means of controlling money. Finally, at the end of the process, as in any other management process, the decisions and their outcomes are evaluated. Throughout the process, money and other financial assets are treated as tools that can be used to enhance life and provide for growth and security.

Individuals and Families as Producers and Consumers

Individuals and families are both producers and consumers. Consumption choices include what food to eat, what clothes to wear, where to shop, and where to bank. Consumption decisions affect the present and future standard of living of an individual or family. An individual's or family's **level of living** is a measure of the goods and services affordable by and available to them. **Standard of living** is what an individual or a family aspires to. On the production side, families produce children and transform raw products into finished products through such activities as gardening, cooking, and sewing. In addition, families produce, process, manage, and provide a variety of other goods and services (e.g., child care, elder care, home maintenance, transportation, health care, and education for family members).

Households are both labor-intensive and highly productive. Nevertheless, household production is not included in the **gross domestic product (GDP),** which is the total market value of all goods and services produced by a nation during a specified period, usually a year. For example, tomatoes canned at home, though used the same way as factory-canned tomatoes, are not counted in the GDP. Similarly, an individual's work in completing his or her income tax forms is not counted in the GDP, but the services provided by an accounting firm doing someone's income taxes is included. Thus, although individuals and families are significant producing units, their home-based production is not counted in the U.S. GDP. Several reasons have been given for this omission, the most logical is that household production is difficult to measure accurately.

Income, Net Worth, Budgets, Savings, and Credit

Just as GDP is a measure of a nation's well-being, income is one of the measures of a family's well-being. **Income** is the amount of money or its equivalent received during a period of time. There are several different kinds of income:

◆ **Discretionary income:** Income regulated by one's own discretion or judgment.

◆ **Disposable income:** The amount of take-home pay left after all deductions are withheld for benefits, taxes, contributions, and so on. For example, college students have $100 billion in disposable income annually (Beiles, 1999).

- **Gross income:** All income received that is not legally exempt from taxes.

- **Psychic income:** One's perception or feelings about income; the satisfaction derived from income.

- **Real income:** Income measured in prices at a certain time, reflecting the buying power of current dollars.

Take special note of psychic income. When helping individuals and families formulate budgets or financial plans, it is important to know not only how much money they have to work with, but also how they feel about money in general. What one person regards as very little money, another may consider a fortune. An accurate assessment of people's income or lifestyle requires some knowledge of not only their actual income, but also how they perceive money and how much they feel they need to maintain an adequate level of living.

A personal tax levied on individuals or families on the basis of income received is called an **income tax.** In 1913, the Sixteenth Amendment to the U.S. Constitution was ratified making the personal income tax constitutional.

Figuring Net Worth

Net worth is determined by subtracting what is owed **(liabilities)** from what is owned **(assets).** An estimation of net worth is considered the best measure of one's material wealth. It is important to estimate net worth because it shows where a person stands financially. A net worth estimate should be made at least once a year.

Figure 13.2 provides a sample form that can be used for computing net worth. Notice the wide variety of assets: actual cash on hand and money in checking and savings accounts; investments such as certificates of deposit, stocks, bonds, and mutual funds; real estate, which includes one's house and any other real estate owned; pension benefits to which an individual is entitled; retirement accounts, such as employer-sponsored 401(k) and 403(b) plans and IRAs; the value of a business; personal property such as jewelry, furniture, and appliances; and any automobiles owned. Liabilities include the mortgage on one's home, the balance owed on installment loans, such as on a car or refrigerator, the balance owed on credit cards, unpaid bills, and any taxes owed.

The net worth statement of Pete Sawyer, a junior in college, appears in Table 13.1. Pete has some money in his checking and savings accounts that he earned from a summer job, a car, and various items of personal property, most notably a computer. Pete also has a number of liabilities, including his college loan, an outstanding balance on his credit card, library fines, and parking tickets he has not paid. When Pete's liabilities are subtracted from his assets, the result is –$2,609.97. Pete has a negative net worth—he owes more than his assets are worth. Actually, a negative net worth is not unusual for someone at Pete's life stage. College students and new college graduates often have college loans outstanding and might incur other financial obligations from moving and setting up a new lifestyle. As they begin to work full-time and their earnings increase, they are able to pay off their debts, and their negative net worth gradually declines, and then they begin to accumulate assets. Generally, college graduates earn substantial amounts of money, however, about one-third will have problems sometime during their life with credit card debt and, historically, as many as one-fifth of those with student loans will default on their loan repayment, causing financial and credit rating problems (Markovich & DeVaney, 1997). Specific advice on how college students can manage their money is given in an upcoming section.

Assets		
Cash on hand	$	
Checking accounts	$	
Savings accounts	$	
Money market funds	$	
Cash management accounts	$	
Certificates of deposits	$	
Stocks, bonds (market value)*	$	
Mutual funds	$	
Real estate (market value)	$	
Employer-sponsored retirement plans	$	
IRAs	$	
Vested company benefits	$	
Annuities (one-time investments paid upon retirement)	$	
Personal property** (market value)	$	
Automobiles (market value)	$	
Estate and trust values	$	
Cash value of whole life insurance	$	
Business venture values	$	
Debts owed to you	$	
Other	$	
Total assets	$	
Liabilities		
Loans (college, home, auto)	$	
Unpaid bills	$	
Personal debts (to friends, family)	$	
Other	$	
Total liabilities	$	
Net worth (total assets – total liabilities)	$	

*Market value means what the asset would be worth if it were sold immediately.
**This category includes nearly anything with a resale value, such as clothing, furniture, books, bicycles, computers, jewelry, televisions, and appliances.

FIGURE 13.2
Net Worth Statement
Net worth is calculated by subtracting liabilities (what is owed) from assets (what is owned).

Budgets and Saving

Whereas a net worth statement reveals current financial status, a budget helps individuals and families plan ahead and clarify their values and goals. As explained earlier, a budget is a spending plan. A budget should serve as a guide—one that the budgeter controls. It should be flexible and not put a straitjacket on spending. Many expenses, such as money spent on food, clothing, and entertainment, are flexible, whereas other expenses are fixed, such as rent and car payments. If budgets are too rigid, they will not allow for unexpected or variable expenses, such as medical or dental bills or the costs of home maintenance. For example, replacing a leaking roof or a faulty furnace for $3,000 is an expense that must be met but cannot be budgeted for in advance except in the most general way. Typically, budgets are based on average spending patterns. According to *American Demographics,* the average American household spends $90 a day, with housing expenditures being the biggest budget item, amounting to about one-third of expenditures. Homeowners average a little over $900 a month on housing and renters about $630 (Francese, 1997). If the low inflation rate continues, one would assume that American households in the early part of the twenty-first century will follow this pattern and spend about $100 a day.

TABLE 13.1
**Pete Sawyer's Net
Worth Statement**

Assets	
Cash on hand	$ 40.00
Checking account	465.02
Savings account	807.15
Personal property	
CD player and CD collection	225.00
Bicycle	125.00
Watch	135.00
Computer	1,000.00
Clothes and books	75.00
Automobile (9-year-old car)	3,500.00
Total assets	$6,372.17
Liabilities	
College loan	$8,655.00
Unpaid bills	
Balance on credit cards	122.00
Long-distance telephone bill	78.64
Library fines	32.50
Personal debts	
Loan from roommate	110.00
Other (parking tickets)	55.00
Total liabilities	$9,053.14
Net worth	$–2,609.97

One way to prepare for unexpected expenses is to budget a certain amount to be saved each month. Sometimes people forget to include savings in their budget because they think saving is not spending. Actually, saving is what makes future spending possible. How much should a person or family save? The answer depends on their present lifestyle, responsibilities, and goals and on the lifestyle they desire in the future. Generally, people in the United States save about 4–5 percent of their income, a rate that is lower than that of most other industrialized nations. To get ahead or to save for something, such as the down payment on a house, individuals may strive to save 10 percent or more. Another way to approach saving is to have the goal of building an **emergency fund** of three to six months income. An emergency fund could be used by a person to tide them over (i.e., pay the rent, buy food) during a time of unemployment or other crisis. In order to build savings "financial advisors recommend young professionals save regularly, even in small amounts, to enable them to accomplish short- and long-term goals such as the purchase of a home or retirement. The likelihood of having a successful investment program is increased with early and regular savings" (Markovich and DeVaney, 1998, p. 61).

Table 13.2 shows the budget of a young married couple, Tim Snyder and Mary Ann Kirby. As a young couple starting out, their sources of income and types of expenses are fairly limited. Their salaries are their biggest source of income, and their house and child care for their two-year-old daughter are their largest expenses. Notice that Mary Ann and Tim's budget does not leave any money for emergencies. They say they'll be able to start saving more in six months when Mary Ann finishes her training program at the bank and receives

TABLE 13.2
Monthly Budget for Tim Snyder and Mary Ann Kirby

Monthly savings (or losses) are determined by subtracting estimated monthly expenses from monthly income.

Income

Salaries

Mary Ann (management trainee at bank)	$2,102.74
Tim (part-time job while attending law school)	788.80
Dividends	22.00
Money gifts, scholarships (Tim's scholarship for law school)	600.00
Other (Mary Ann writes a weekly column on financial management for a newspaper)	60.00
Total income	$3,573.54

Expenses

Mortgage payment on house	$874.88
Food	380.00
Child care (for Kristin, their daughter)	860.00
Tuition/books	255.00
Gasoline/transportation	
Bus fare for Mary Ann	22.00
Parking at the university for Tim	15.00
Gasoline	40.00
Utilities (gas, electric, water, cable)	150.00
Telephone	25.00
Insurance (life, car, home—Mary Ann's employer pays for health insurance)	120.00
Clothing and personal care (haircuts, cosmetics)	80.00
Credit card payments	50.00
Entertainment	40.00
Loans	
College (Mary Ann)	190.00
College (Tim)	120.00
Automobile	239.85
Personal spending	65.00
Miscellaneous	35.00
Total expenses	$3,561.73
Total savings	$11.81

a substantial increase in salary and Tim finishes law school. In the meantime, they hope no emergencies arise.

In drawing up your own budget, checking account and credit card statements can help you obtain an accurate account of your money flow. Because expenses fluctuate from month to month, averaging several months' expenses will help you obtain a more accurate picture of typical monthly expenditures.

Evaluation of Finances and Managing Credit

Once an individual or a family figures out their net worth and their typical monthly expenditures, they can create a six-month or one-year spending plan.

By reviewing their net worth statement and monthly expenditures, people may be able to find places where they can spend less and save more.

One of the easiest ways to overspend is to misuse credit cards. **Credit** is time allowed for payment. A credit card authorizes the holder to buy something in advance of paying for it. Using credit instead of cash makes shopping more convenient and reduces the risk of loss or theft associated with carrying large amounts of cash. Although the savings rate is low in the United States, credit card use is on the rise due to broadened eligibility and ease of use. Managing credit is one of the biggest management problems individuals and families face. The following suggestions can help reduce the chances of credit mismanagement:

◆ Use only a few cards. It is hard to keep track of dozens of cards, and Visa or Mastercard can be used for most purchases. About 66 percent of households hold a Visa, Mastercard, or other credit cards, up from 43 percent in 1983 ("Cyclical Jobs," 1999).

◆ Pay off credit cards in full each month to avoid interest charges.

◆ Seek cards with the lowest annual percentage rates (APRs) and no additional fees.

◆ Check credit card statements carefully against receipts. Do not allow the unauthorized use of a credit card number.

◆ Keep a list of credit card purchases as they occur, similar to the check stubs in a checkbook.

◆ Keep a list of credit card numbers in a safe place, in case they are lost or stolen, along with a list of toll-free numbers of credit card companies to notify in case cards are lost.

Establishing Credit and Credit Bureaus

Under the **Fair Credit Reporting Act** of 1971, individuals who are denied credit, insurance, or employment because of their credit report have the right to obtain a free copy of their report within 30 days of denial. In the United States, credit reports are kept by credit bureaus that serve as clearinghouses of information on borrowers' credit histories. Potential lenders, such as department stores, may buy a report on a credit card applicant from the credit bureau.

A good credit rating can be established in a number of ways, including opening checking and savings accounts, paying bills promptly, and opening a charge account with an oil company or department store and promptly remitting the monthly balance due. Potential lenders who are considering whether to extend credit or not also look at several factors, including residential and job stability, education, income, and home ownership. Regardless of the criteria used, the **Equal Credit Opportunity Act** prevents a lender from discriminating against a person because of race, sex, age, color, marital status, or other related factors.

Deciding when to use credit and when to pay cash is part of the overall management problem of controlling money. The first step toward solving this problem is to define an attainable goal. Examples of specific financial goals include saving for a down payment on a house, college expenses, remodeling, a vacation, or additional investments and retirement. Once a financial goal is established and a plan drawn up, progress toward the goal should be reviewed to evaluate how well the financial planning is working.

Banking, Investments, and Insurance

Saving and investing can take many forms. For example, cash can be put in interest-bearing checking accounts, savings accounts, money market accounts, and low-risk, longer-term savings instruments. Regardless of the type of account, the goal is to maximize the earnings from the investment of cash and to avoid fees, payments, and extra charges. **Liquidity,** the speed and ease of retrieving cash or turning another type of investment into cash, is another important consideration.

Checking accounts from banks and share accounts from credit unions allow the holder to transfer funds from the account to pay for goods and services. Banks commonly charge a fee for this convenience in per-check charges or monthly service fees, but they may also pay interest on the money in the account. A savings account, also called a passbook account, typically pays higher interest than a checking account. A money market account pays an even higher rate of interest, and some offer check writing privileges. These accounts are commonly called NOW accounts and cash management accounts. Other low-risk possibilities for cash include government savings bonds and certificates of deposit (CDs). These typically pay higher interest than checking, savings, and money market accounts.

Investment is the commitment of capital to the achievement of long-term goals or objectives. Most people invest to build wealth and to secure a comfortable future. Investing is a process that involves planning, money, information, time, and an understanding of risk. Several chapters would be needed to discuss the pros and cons of the different kinds of investments available. For the purposes of this chapter, the focus will be on the subject of investing and the most common types of investments. These are:

- *Stocks:* Representing ownership in a company (e.g., Microsoft, IBM, Coca-Cola).

- *Bonds:* Investments in which a person lends money to an organization such as the government or a corporation.

- *Mutual funds:* Groups of stocks, bonds, or other securities managed by an investment company. Their chief benefits are diversification and professional management.

- *Real estate.*

- *Other:* A general category including such investments as Individual Retirement Accounts (IRAs), employer-sponsored retirement plans, precious metals (i.e., gold, silver), gems, and collectibles.

Before starting to invest, a person should have ample cash for daily and monthly expenses, an emergency fund set aside, paid off credit cards, and insurance. The purpose of insurance is to protect financial assets. A sound financial plan includes protection from major risks (e.g., auto accidents, natural disasters, health problems) that can threaten financial security. **Insurance** is a financial arrangement in which people pay premiums (payments) to an insurance company that reimburses them in the event of loss or injury. Usually, the most costly and the most important form of insurance is health insurance. Most employers offer health insurance as part of their benefits package. Other types of insurance include property, liability, automobile, disability, life, and long-term care insurance. Usually, group policies (insurance company contracts sold through organizations such as professional associations or alumni groups) are less expensive than individual policies. Decisions about insurance depend on how much protection is needed, how much can be afforded, and how much is given by employers. Insurance coverage should be appropriate to an individual's or a family's life stage, needs, and goals.

A course in personal finance or family financial planning will cover many of the points mentioned in this section in depth. Financial well-being is critical to a person's overall sense of well-being and success. Learning to manage money is a lifelong process begun in childhood. People between the ages of 45 and 54 have the highest median income of any age group, but they also have the highest expenses, because they may have children in college while they are also saving for their own retirement. Over the life span, individuals and couples have to reevaluate, update, and renegotiate their goals and spending and investing plans many times. For example, experts suggest that financial plans, in general, and, specifically, insurance policies and retirement accounts should be examined each year to determine if they still meet individuals' and families' needs.

Expenses Related to Children

Without a doubt, the costs of rearing and educating children add to the financial strain on families. Child-raising expenses can be divided into six main categories (Lino, 1990):

- ◆ Housing
- ◆ Food
- ◆ Transportation
- ◆ Clothing
- ◆ Health care
- ◆ Education, child care, and other miscellaneous expenses

The first year of life is particularly expensive; it is estimated that the highest cost then is usually child care, followed by furniture and food. Overall, in raising a child to age 18, however, housing is the most costly item, followed by education and child care (Lino, 1990).

Depending on the affluence of the household, the average estimated cost of raising a child from birth through age 18 range is $300,000. The specific costs vary by many factors, including the number of children in the family, the region of the country, and the affluence of the family. The more children in a family, the lower the costs per child. According to a government study, child-rearing expenses are highest in the urban West, followed by the urban Northeast, the urban South, and the urban Midwest (Lino, 1990). Housing costs contribute greatly to differences between regions, as do costs of child care and education. For example, parents in Boston on average pay nearly three times as much for day care as parents in Ogden, Utah ("Dollars for Day Care," 1991).

Children as Consumers

The study of children and money involves more than estimating how much it costs to raise them. Children are not passive consumers. From the first time they spit out strained peas, they are letting their parents know their preferences. Parents respond by buying what their children like, and later the children themselves collectively spend billions of dollars a year on cosmetics, toys, snacks, candy, gifts, athletic events and equipment, musical recordings and instruments, and other goods and services. They also influence their parents' expenditures on nearly all family-related purchases, including housing, cars, computers, vacations, breakfast cereals, and restaurant meals.

As part of the socialization process, children learn much of their spending behavior from their parents. For example, a study of elementary schoolchildren found that mothers who were restrictive and warm in relationships with their children were also more likely to use communication messages that promoted monitoring and control of children's consumption activities. Further, mothers who generally respected and asked for their children's opinions tended to utilize messages that fostered the development of consumption decision-making abilities in children (Carlson, Grossbart, & Stuenkel, 1992).

Schools and Economic Concepts

Along with families, schools, peers, and the media are important economic socialization agents for children (Rettig & Mortenson, 1986). As children age, teacher and peer opinions gain in importance. Increasingly, children are receiving consumer education in schools. Central to educational efforts in this area are the following curriculum concepts:

- ◆ That children from an early age realize that they make financial decisions and that they are an important part of the household's and the world's economy.
- ◆ That children be exposed to economic terms and concepts as soon as they are ready.
- ◆ That children should know the value of different coins (i.e., penny, nickel, dime, and quarter). This is taught in kindergarten and first grade.
- ◆ That children should be able to differentiate between generic and name brand products.
- ◆ That children should know how to make cost and quality comparisons.

In one innovative social studies curriculum used in the fifth grade, each classroom forms a minisociety in which economic decisions are made. Students are divided into production and consumption teams; some sell items that others buy, while others are bankers or stockbrokers. They use fake money that is useful only in their classroom for their transactions. In some communities, stores provide the classes with real goods to exchange or use as rewards, and local businesses provide consultants who advise the children on their enterprises.

Another innovative curriculum used in some high school family and consumer sciences classes, features simulated wedding ceremonies and the analysis of costs involved in weddings and in the first years of marriage. Students investigate the costs associated with renting apartments, insurance, childbirth, child care, cars, and other possible expenses.

Allowances and Money Management

Most children are ready to receive an allowance or handle a small amount of money as soon as they understand the concept of time. Readiness to handle money varies greatly from child to child, but usually comes around the ages of 7 or 8. Understanding time is important, because it enables children to wait for Saturday (a traditional day for handing out allowances). If they can wait for Saturday, then they will understand about waiting for money and parceling it out after they receive it. One method of training children for the responsibilities of adulthood is to encourage them to save part of their allowance, but again children's ability to do this varies with age and maturity. The younger the child, the more likely he or she will spend money quickly rather than save it for bigger items. The average 9-year-old will probably not be interested in saving for college—it is too far away. A teenager, though, may be able to manage a clothing budget.

Children need to learn that money is a tool—something they can use to get what they want. Along the way to disciplined money management, children will make mistakes, such as buying toys that fall apart or fail to live up to their expectations. Making poor or disappointing expenditures is part of the learning process. Both the mistakes and the successes of money management experiences in childhood will prepare children for the bigger expenses ahead.

Retirement Planning

At the other end of the spectrum from childhood costs are the costs of retirement. Americans have been retiring progressively earlier for about a century. However, that trend has flattened out; some say it's poised to reverse, leaving many Americans working later in life. With the massive baby-boom generation soon approaching retirement age, the question of how long they'll stay at their jobs is looming ever larger. On the job, they supply badly needed workers to one of the tightest labor markets in history and delay a rush on Social Security claims. Retired, they have the opposite effect (McDermott, 1999).

An examination of households with older Americans reveals profound diversity in their sources of wealth and financial abilities (Longino & Crown, 1991). The wealthiest elderly are most likely to be younger, working, and married, whereas the poorest are most likely to be nonwhite and female, often widows (Longino & Crown, 1991).

According to Virginia Junk, Laurie Stenberg, and Carol Anderson (1993), "generally, the goal of financial planning for retirement is to provide enough income in retirement to prevent living standards from dropping significantly from pre-retirement levels" (p. 6). Financial planning for retirement can begin at any age, but many individuals wait until they are in their 40s to become serious about it. Although people tend to think of retirement planning as being for themselves and their spouse, it can also involve providing for the financial needs of dependent aging parents. Individuals who provide or anticipate providing financial assistance to their parent or parents while also providing financial support to one or more children are known as the **sandwich generation** (Junk, Stenberg, & Anderson, 1993).

As mentioned earlier, types of investments include employer-sponsored retirement plans and IRAs. Before investing elsewhere, individuals should consider putting available funds into tax-sheltered plans to the maximum allowed. In so doing, income taxes will be reduced and wealth grows tax-free. For example:

- ◆ Most employers offer 401(k) or 403(b) plans. If $200 a month is put into a tax-sheltered account at 9 percent interest, the return is $73,327 in 15 years.
- ◆ If an employer does not offer such a plan, alternatives are to open an Individual Retirement Account, or a SEP or Keogh if self-employed. If $2,000 a year at 9 percent is invested in these types of accounts, the end result is $102,320 in 20 years.

Money can be automatically deducted from every paycheck toward a retirement plan, or monthly payments can be arranged from a bank account. As the examples show, the growth of a retirement fund depends on the amount invested, how often, and for how long. It also depends on how the fund is invested. More and more, individuals are having to make decisions about how their particular retirement fund is invested.

To determine retirement needs, financial planners or financial planning programs can run financial information through a computer. The information needed includes a person's age, salary, employer-sponsored retirement plans or IRAs, SEPs, or Keoghs, other investments, number of years employed, the percentage of salary being saved, projected retirement age, and the future income the person would like to have. Based on the analysis derived from this information, a person may choose to save more, change investments, or work longer. There are many variables, including the ups and downs in the economy and one's health, that will affect final retirement income, and calculations are at best estimates. The farther away from actual retirement the less accurate the estimate. Nonetheless, retirement planning is a necessary part of overall financial planning. Part of retirement planning is estimating Social Security income, the subject to be discussed next.

Social Security

Since the **Social Security Act** was enacted in 1935, Social Security has been one of the main sources of expected income for those reaching their retirement. Other sources of income include employer-sponsored retirement plans, savings and investments, and money from Individual Retirement Accounts (IRAs), SEPs, and Keogh plans. As might be expected, the higher the income of the retirees, the lower her or his reliance on Social Security. Although Social Security was designed to be a supplement to the retired person's savings and pensions, for many it is the sole or main source of income.

People become eligible for a reduced level of Social Security retirement benefits at age 62. In certain cases, Social Security benefits can begin earlier for disabled employees and survivors. For most people, full benefits normally begin at age 65. Beginning in 2003, the age for retiring with full benefits will climb one month per year until it reaches age 67 in 2027 ("Supplementing Retirement Income until Social Security Begins," 1990). By this change, the government hopes to encourage people to work longer and retire later.

To find out how much has been accumulated in a Social Security account, an individual can call the Social Security Administration (1-800-772-1213) and request the Personal Earnings and Benefits Statement form (Form SSA-7004). This will show how much credit the person has earned.

FINANCIAL AND ECONOMIC CONCERNS

When can I afford to retire? What happens if I lose my job? Will I be able to afford a house? All these questions involve financial concerns. Confidence in the state of the economy is an individual, family, and national concern. In the twentieth century, the United States struggled through several economic crises, most notably, the Great Depression that peaked in 1933. In the early 1990s, economic hard times in the form of slow economic growth hit the United

States and other countries around the world. The United States has been in a growth phase since the mid-1990s, and as this book went to press, the economy was strong, with low unemployment.

Recession, Depression, Inflation, and Unemployment

Since individuals and families live in an economic system, they are not immune to the changes in the economy. In the 1990s, many large corporations, including AT&T, Kmart, Boeing, Proctor and Gamble, and IBM, laid off thousands of workers. According to a professor at Northwestern University's business school:

> The newspaper says the banking industry will lose 100,000 jobs this year. That's 100,000 middle-class people who thought they were going to be in control of their lives. Manhattan is filled with 40-year-olds out of work, deep in debt and overextended on their apartments. They never thought it would happen to them. (Alder, 1992, p. 22)

The key phrases here are "people who thought they were going to be in control of their lives" and "they never thought it would happen to them." That unemployment is often unexpected makes it even more difficult to adjust to and manage.

Several terms often used to describe the general state of the economy are:

- ◆ **Recession:** A moderate and temporary decline in the economy.
- ◆ **Depression:** A drastic and long-lasting decline in the economy characterized by high unemployment, falling prices, and decreasing business activity.
- ◆ **Inflation:** Rising prices.
- ◆ **Unemployment:** Being out of work. An unemployment rate over 10 percent is considered severe.

Several of these terms overlap. A depression usually involves over 10 percent unemployment. At the worst of the 1930s depression, the unemployment rate was over 25 percent. The overall jobless rate provides a national picture of unemployment, but unemployment can also vary regionally. For example, the nationwide unemployment rate may be 4 percent, but when a factory closes in a small town, the unemployment rate for that area may well go above 25 percent.

Generally, the U.S. economy and living standards improved in the late 1990s. Unemployment went as low as 2.5 percent in some high-growth areas, such as Orlando, Florida. By 1999, more than 25 percent of all workers owned stocks and bonds through a retirement savings plan such as a 401(k) or 403(b). A record number, 66 percent of households, owned the homes they lived in and many of the goods inside had become cheaper. For example, since 1994, the prices for household appliances fell 3.5 percent and for home electronics equipment, 4.1 percent (Farrell, Palmer, & Browder, 1998). Two areas that went up significantly in cost in the 1990s were college tuition and health care.

Regarding the twenty-first century, "In an economy driven by innovation, it's clear that restructuring, reengineering, and downsizing—pick your favorite buzzword—will be a permanent part of management's tool kit. . . . Far from being left behind, the working and middle classes are reacting to the high-tech boom by getting training so they can prosper in the years ahead" (Farrell, Palmer & Browder, 1998, p. 75).

College Students and Money Management

As mentioned in Chapter 4, college students today have more money and credit than their parents did. More than half of college students at four-year colleges have cars and computers and two-thirds have credit cards and telephone calling cards (Speer, 1998). Generally, college students have favorable attitudes toward credit cards. One study found that students who are female, live on campus, major in consumer affairs and/or work less than 20 hours have more favorable attitudes toward credit cards than other students (Xiao, Noring, & Anderson, 1995). In a nationwide college survey, three out of four college students reported that they expect to become millionaires (Sebastian, 1999). Being in college brings with it new levels of freedom and also new responsibilities, including managing money. Students should beware of falling into a habit of debt that can follow them for years. After graduation, a bad credit record can hurt when the student tries to buy a car or a house. It can even hurt employment opportunities. Some employers are checking the credit records of applicants to determine their level of dependability.

Many of the money management principles already covered in this chapter apply to college students, but to reiterate, here are some tips for setting up a budget and maintaining a good credit record:

- Make a list of predicted monthly expenses and income. Ask yourself, how much money do I typically need?

- Set aside some money for savings or emergencies.

- Keep track of everything you spend. It helps you stick to your budget. Save receipts.

- Pay all bills on time—from the telephone to your credit card bill. Immediately open bills on arrival. They usually arrive about 15 days before they are due. Use automatic payment systems, wherein money for the bill is automatically withdrawn from your bank account.

- If you get into financial trouble, address it immediately; call creditors, contact parents.

Students can economize by:

- Living on less (e.g., sharing an apartment, eating out less).

- Working more.

- Joining co-op programs or getting paid internships.

- Applying for financial aid, loans, and scholarships.

- Living at home after graduation and during the summers between semesters, thereby reducing living expenses.

- Joining ROTC as a career option and as a way to finance school expenses.

While in school, college students are busy people. According to the Bureau of Labor Statistics, most college students work. Given the high cost of a college education, many parents and students might question whether it is worth it. From a financial perspective, the answer is yes. According to U.S. Department of Commerce data, education does provide an economic return in that most degrees beyond high school will result in higher income for that individual. Certain fields yield higher monthly incomes than others, and at each degree level, men earn more on average than women do. (For Web sites providing information on salaries and job trends, see the Electronic Resources section at the end of this chapter.)

Launching a career is a difficult task, especially for college students who are researching job opportunities, interviewing, and finishing coursework at the same time.

The Gender Gap and the Glass Ceiling

In the 1970s, when the concept of the **gender gap** (the difference in earnings between men and women employed full-time outside the home) first attracted attention, women earned approximately 60 percent of what men earned. By 2000, the gender gap had narrowed, and women were earning 76 percent of what men earned. The gender gap is closing. Researchers predict that it will be completely closed by the year 2010.

As women move up the corporate or government ladder, they often hit an invisible barrier that stops them from moving further. They can see the positions at the top that they want, but they cannot reach them. This phenomenon is known as the **glass ceiling.**

Studies are being conducted to determine why gender barriers exist and where they tend to be found. Generally, it is assumed that women want to move ahead and that corporations and other employers, for a variety of reasons, have imposed barriers impeding their advance. However, the glass ceiling may be caused by more than the barriers imposed by employers. One study found that the barriers might be at least partially imposed by the women themselves in that they have lower salary expectations even before they enter the job market. Researchers found that parents, especially fathers, have a strong positive impact on their daughters' career expectations (Hoffman, Goldsmith, & Hoffacker, 1992). Other studies indicate that schools may not provide as many opportunities for success for girls as they do for boys. Thus, supportive families and schools are important to the goal setting and potential career success of women students.

Because the gender gap is closing and the glass ceiling appears to be shattering (i.e., more women are moving up and commanding higher salaries), women's employment issues are rapidly changing. More studies will clarify the values, attitudes, and behaviors involved with these issues.

Poverty and Wealth

As Chapter 8 explained, *poverty* is the state of being poor and lacking adequate means to provide for basic material needs and comforts. **Wealth** is the state of being rich and having a high net worth.

> Of the 225 richest people on earth, 60 are thought to be Americans, far more than in any other nation. One estimate puts Bill Gates's personal wealth at $51 billion, more than the accumulated net worth of the lowest 40 percent of the U.S. population combined—that's right, one man is now worth more than 100 million Americans. (Gergen, 1999, p. 116)

As an update, when this book went to press Bill Gates's wealth was estimated at over $90 billion. America has had almost two decades of unprecedented growth in the technology sector. "Its largest three computer and software companies are worth more than all U.S. companies in the steel, auto, areospace, chemical, and plastics industries combined" (Gergen, 1999, p. 116).

Although overall there has been strong growth, poverty is still widespread especially in rural counties where the economic engine has broken down, in areas on the Texas-Mexico border, Appalachia, and the Deep South. Poverty is a serious problem because poverty in childhood can have lifelong repercussions:

> Poverty is the roadblock to educational progress of many disadvantaged youth. . . . Poor teenagers are four times more likely than nonpoor teens to have below-average basic academic skills. More than half of the 15- to 18-year-olds from fam-

ilies with incomes below poverty had reading and math skills that placed them in the bottom 20 percent of all teens. (Leidenfrost, 1993, p. 5)

Poverty can be either a temporary or a chronic state of living. If people are unemployed for a few months, they will experience a temporary decline in income, but if they have saved for a rainy day, their lifestyle will not be severely affected immediately. Likewise, college students may live at or below the poverty level, but this is a temporary state that will be remedied when they get their first full-time job. The mindset of a person who is experiencing temporary poverty is different from that of a person or family immersed in permanent poverty.

Because the study of management focuses on control and planning, educators and family facilitators need to be sensitized to the fact that not everyone has equal access to resources or the equal ability to use them. According to Rettig, Rossman, and Hogan (1992):

> People who are poor must devote their financial resources to meet basic needs. They have minimal freedom to allocate money, time, or human energy for other than immediate uses and have little to give toward planning for future needs. Families and individuals with lower levels of living have less freedom to decide, little control over resource access, fewer opportunities for human resource development, and their use of material resources is significantly diminished. Families can be "poor," not only in material resources, but also in human resources of imagination, initiative, self-discipline, and the ability to seek alternatives. (p. 35)

Most people in the United States fall into the middle class and derive their income largely from earnings, that is, wages or salaries from occupations. Wealthier people generally derive a considerable proportion of their income from investments; the higher the income, the higher the portion from investments tends to be. From a management standpoint, the goals of a middle-class family may be to educate their children and have a secure lifestyle rather than to accumulate vast wealth. The very wealthy, who have an abundance of money, property, and investments, spend a great deal of time trying to retain their fortunes so that they can pass on their money to their descendants. With the exception of highly successful athletes, business tycoons, entrepreneurs, and actors, most of the very wealthy have acquired their fortunes over a long period of time or through inheritances.

Where Does Money Go?

On average, one-third of the typical U.S. family's income goes to paying federal, state, and local taxes. **Taxes** are compulsory levies that are an important source of government revenue. Taxes help cover government expenses and, in the case of income tax, help redistribute income and wealth. In 1789, Benjamin Franklin wrote that "in this world nothing is certain but death and taxes."

After taxes, typically the remainder of a family's money goes first to housing, then transportation, then food, and on down the list to health/personal care, recreation, clothing, insurance, and other needs. The distribution of money varies greatly by the amount of income (for example, the lower the income, the higher proportion spent on food), savings, and other investments.

Financial Advice

Controlling personal or family finances need not be done in isolation. An avalanche of material is available to help investors track the status of their funds. Some information may come regularly through the mail, such as bank statements, stockbroker reports, mutual fund statements, IRA updates, and credit card statements. Additional free information on financial management is available from banks, the Internet, and the federal government. Financial advice for a price is also readily available through magazines, newspapers, and in-person services. According to a study by the Roper Organization, when U.S. residents want financial advice, they are most likely to turn to friends and relatives, then to their bank officer, lawyer and accountant, financial planner, real estate broker, and stockbroker.

Before investing in the services of a financial planner or other finance professional, a potential customer should check their credentials and see if any complaints against them are on file with the Better Business Bureau or the state Office of Consumer Affairs.

Electronic Resources

www.cnnfn.com/
This popular Web site offers general information on financial news.

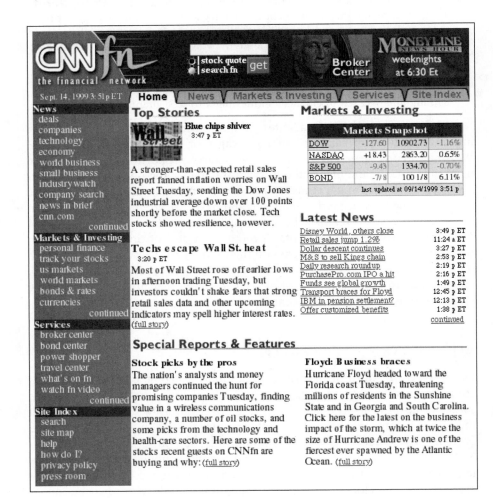

There are innumerable Web sites with a financial focus. A comprehensive site offering up-to-date stock quotes and financial news is available from Yahoo Finance at **financhance.yahoo.com**. Another comprehensive site is the The FinanCenter's at **financenter.com/**, a source for questions and answers and calculations regarding budgets, credit, savings, and purchasing automobiles, houses, and investments. To estimate savings needed for retirement, a calculator on the Web offers estimates at Financial Engines' Web site at **www.financialengines.com.**

Nearly all major banks, credit card companies, investment firms, and insurance companies have their own Web sites. They usually can be reached at www.companyname.com. Many offer financial planning work sheets and advice based on the information the site user provides. Computer software to assist with financial calculations and tax preparation can also be purchased over the Internet or at stores.

Current national economic and job trend statistics are available from **www.stats.bls.gov.** Salary and relocation information can be found at ESPAN's site at **www.espan.com.**

The following addresses offer a sampling of types of homepages related to searching for jobs on the Internet. As is the case for all Web sites and homepages in this book, the author does not take responsibility for the information contained therein, or any address changes. For current job openings, check:

- ◆ America's Job Bank: **www.ajb.dni.us** (mostly full-time listings)
- ◆ CareerPath: **www.careerpath.com** (newspaper employment advertisements)
- ◆ CareerSite: **www.careersite.com** (comprehensive services for job seekers and employers)
- ◆ JobTrak: **www.jobtrak.com** (listings for recent college graduates and alumni)

Summary

Financial management is a transformation process involving three phases: planning, action, and postplanning. Handling money is one of the most common managerial skills, but also one of the most difficult. The goal of financial management is to maximize net worth and satisfaction. Values and goals influence the way finances are managed. Savings and investments are important aspects of financial management. Saving for children's college education is an example of a long-range goal of many families. Not everyone has the luxury of planning for the future, however; low-income families must devote their financial resources to meeting basic daily needs. The typical family in the United States spends about one-third of its income on taxes, followed by housing and household expenses and transportation.

The individual and the family operate within the greater economy of the nation. Consequently, individuals need to understand how inflation, depression, and recessions affect them.

The last chapter of this book focuses on projected changes in demographics, the economy, the environment, and technology.

Key Terms

assets	emergency fund	gender gap
budget	Equal Credit	glass ceiling
credit	Opportunity Act	gross domestic
depression	Fair Credit	product (GDP)
discretionary income	Reporting Act	gross income
disposable income	financial management	income

income tax
inflation
insurance
investment
level of living
liabilities

liquidity
net worth
psychic income
real income
recession
sandwich generation

Social Security Act
standard of living
taxes
unemployment
wealth

Review Questions

1. What do families produce? What do families consume?
2. Do you think Benjamin Franklin's observation about the inevitability of death and taxes is still applicable today? Explain your answer.
3. What percentage of income do Americans generally save? How does the American savings rate compare to the savings rates of other nations?
4. How can college students manage their money better?
5. Why do you think more people turn first to friends and relatives for financial advice, then to professional financial advisors such as bankers, lawyers, and accountants?

References

Adler, J. (1992, January 13). "Down in the Dumps." *Newsweek*, 24.

Beiles, N. (1999, May 10). Common places' web strategy targets students. *Wall Street Journal*, B14A.

Carlson, L., Grossbart, S., & Stuenkel, J. (1992). The role of parental socialization types on differential family communication patterns regarding consumption. *Journal of Consumer Psychology, 1*(2), 31–52.

Current population survey. (1991, March). Bureau of the Census. Washington, DC: U.S. Department of Commerce.

Cyclical jobs. (1999, March 25). *The Wall Street Journal*, A1.

Dollars for day care. (1991, January). *American Demographics*, 10.

Farrell, C., Palmer, A., & Browder, S. (1998, August 31). A rising tide. *Business Week*, 75.

Francese, P. (1997, August). Big spenders. *American Demographics*, 51–57.

Gergen, D. (1999, March 29). No time for complacency. *U.S. News & World Report*, 116.

Hoffman, J., Goldsmith, E., & Hoffacker, C. (1992) The influence of parents on female business students' salary and work hour expectations. *Journal of Employment Counseling, 29*(1), 79–83.

Junk, V., Stenberg, L., & Anderson, C. (1993, Spring). Retirement planning for the sandwich generation. *Journal of Home Economics*, 4–11.

Leidenfrost, N. (1993, Fall). Poverty in the United States: Characteristics and theories. *Journal of Home Economics*, 3–10.

Longino, C. & Crown, W. (1991, August). Older Americans: Rich or poor? *American Demographics*, 48–52.

Lino, M. (1990). Expenditures on a child by husband-wife families. *Family Economics Review, 3*(3), 2–18.

Markovich, C. & DeVaney, S. (1997). College seniors' personal finance knowledge and practice. *Journal of Family and Consumer Sciences*, 61–65.

McDermott, D. (1999, July 12). Are baby boomers likely to retire early? *The Wall Street Journal*, A2.

O'Neill, B. & Brennan, P. (1997, Summer). Financial planning education throughout the life cycle. *Journal of Family and Consumer Sciences*, 32–36.

Rettig, K. & Mortenson, M. (1986). Household production of financial management competence. In R. Deacon and W. E. Huffman, (Eds.), *Human resources research, 1887–1987*. Ames, IA: College of Home Economics, Iowa State University.

Rettig, K., Rossman, M., & Hogan, J. (1992). Educating for family resource management. In Arcus et al., (Eds.), *Handbook of family life education*, Vol. 2. Beverly Hills, CA: Sage Publications.

Sebastian, P. (1999, March 25). Briefs. *The Wall Street Journal*, A1.

Speer, T. (1998, March). College come-ons. *American Demographics*.

Supplementing retirement income until social security begins. (1990). *Family Economics Review, 3*(3), 28.

Xiao, J., Noring, F., & Anderson, J. (1995). College students' attitudes towards credit cards. *Journal of Consumer Studies and Home Economics, 19*, 155–174.

Looking Ahead

part **4**

CHAPTER 14
FUTURE CHALLENGES

Future Challenges

MAIN TOPICS

TECHNOLOGY

COMPUTERS, HOME AUTOMATION, AND OTHER HOME
  INNOVATIONS

INFORMATION AND INNOVATION OVERLOAD

FAMILY AND GLOBAL CHANGE

QUALITY OF LIFE AND WELL-BEING

MULTICULTURALISM

ENVIRONMENT

TECHNOLOGY, SOCIETY, AND THE ENVIRONMENT

Did you know that...?

. . . Ninety percent of U.S. households have VCRs, and 91 percent
have microwave ovens.

. . . The average new house has over 2300 square feet.

My future is one I must make myself.

—*Louis L'Amour*

AFTER CONSIDERING THE advances of the last century, the temptation to speculate about the future is inevitable, though predictions about the future always bring with them a certain amount of risk. H. G. Wells, in his 1899 novel *When the Sleeper Wakes,* predicted color television and supersonic aircraft, but he made the less than successful prediction that hypnotism would replace conventional anesthetics in medicine. Likewise, Jules Verne, in *Twenty Thousand Leagues Under the Sea,* published in 1870, was visionary regarding the development of submarines, but missed on his prediction that automated baby-feeding machines would take care of the rising world population. According to Paul Raeburn (1999), some things are fairly easy to predict for the twenty-first century, such as:

- Smaller, faster, and cheaper computers
- Increased understanding of the human genetic code
- More space travel, including exploration of Mars or Jupiter's moon, Europa (see Figure 14.1)

◆ Medical advances, such as the reconnecting of severed spinal cords, and new ways to treat and prevent disease

But, what do these predictions mean for everyday life? Without a doubt, food preparation, transportation, and housing will change, and new institutions will emerge. The family will endure as it always has, but its form may be altered. Individuals and families will engage in more management activities than ever before, because the increasingly complex and diverse world in which they live will offer them so many choices.

This chapter builds on concepts introduced earlier in the book, namely values, decision making, goals, and resources. These four concepts work together to form the basis of a holistic construct called managerial judgment. **Managerial judgment,** defined as the ability to accept and work with change for the betterment of self and humankind, is this chapter's theme. So the ultimate goal of the manager today is the creation of a better tomorrow, but this is not an easy task. As Brian Twiss, the author of *Managing Technological Innovation,* says:

> If we are no longer sure of what the future will hold, it becomes increasingly difficult to manage any activity oriented towards the future. For we are now concerned with two dimensions of uncertainty—that of the innovation itself, and of the environment into which it will be launched at some future date. We can, however, detect a number of trends likely to play an important role in shaping the future. Some are already with us. Others are only just emerging. (1980, p. viii)

As explained throughout this book, management takes a proactive approach, meaning that through reasoning and decision making effective changes can be implemented. It has been suggested that the greatest future challenge for the field of resource management will be the continued integration of management with other theories to address socially relevant issues (Key & Firebaugh, 1989).

FIGURE 14.1
Mars (from NASA Web site)

A New Frontier Beckons

EXPLORING MARS AND BEYOND

As world history illustrates, humans are compelled to discover new frontiers. Our exploration of the space frontier has already begun. Robotic missions and new technology are the first steps toward expanding human presence in the solar system. Human missions to the Moon, Mars and beyond may become a reality in the 21st Century, and NASA is leading the way.

This chapter begins with a discussion of technological trends and then turns to the challenge of managing information and innovation overload. It concludes with an examination of possible changes in family life and the global community, with an emphasis on demographic shifts and environmentalism.

TECHNOLOGY

Robert Tucker, author of *Managing the Future,* says that in the future managing will mean identifying technological, social, cultural, economic, demographic, lifestyle, regulatory, and global trends and fluctuations to determine patterns of change. After identifying the patterns, the next step is to ride the forces of change in the direction in which they are headed. Effective managers, whether in the home or the office, are aware of changes and exploit them rather than waiting to react to them.

Technology is the application of the scientific method and materials to achieve objectives or another definition is knowledge systematically applied to useful purposes. Drucker says that:

> Technology is not nature, but man. It is not about tools; it is about how man thinks . . . but precisely because technology is an extension of man, basic technological change always both expresses our world view, and, in turn, changes it. (1989, p. 261)

In their book, *Innovation Explosion,* Quinn, Baruch, and Zien (1997) provide several terms and definitions useful in a discussion of technology:

- **Invention or discovery** involves the initial observation of a new phenomenon (discovery) or provides the initial verification that a problem can be solved (invention).

- **Innovation** consists of the social and managerial processes through which solutions are first translated into social use in a given culture. "Technological innovation involves a novel combination of art, science, or craft employed to create the goods or services used by society" (p. 3).

- **"Diffusion** spreads approved innovations more broadly within an enterprise or society" (p. 3).

- **System Understanding**, basically "know-how," involves understanding the interrelationship and rates of influences among key variables. "Some people may possess advanced skills but lack system understanding. They can perform selected tasks well but do not fully understand how their actions affect other elements of the organization or how to improve the total entity's effectiveness" (p. 2).

- **Intellect** means knowing or understanding, the capacity to create knowledge, the capability for rational or highly developed use of intelligence. "It includes (1) cognitive knowledge (or know what), (2) advanced skills, (3) system understanding, (4) motivated creativity, discovery or invention, and (5) intuition and synthesis" (perception and the ability to put information together), and the capacity to understand or predict relationships (p. 3).

In the twentieth century, no problem seemed too big to conquer—home, land, space, and communications were all the subjects of technological scrutiny and the beneficiaries of invention. Certainly, life was poorer and harder until the arrival of the technological innovations of the twentieth century. For example, consider the American home before 1940. More than one-fifth of the U.S. population still lived on farms, less than one-third of the farms had electric lights, and only one-tenth had a flush toilet. More than half of the households did not have a refrigerator, dryer, or dishwasher, and most lacked central heating. Air-conditioning did not become widespread until decades later. Fewer than half of the homes built in 1975 had central air.

The average new single-family home has grown from 1,645 square feet in 1975 to over 2,300 today. According to the National Association of Realtors, the most popular homes in the 1990s had three bedrooms and two bathrooms, central air-conditioning, a two-car garage, and one or more fireplaces (Mogelonsky, 1997). In addition, 56 percent had a dishwasher and 91 percent had microwave ovens. Unquestionably, everyday life for the majority of people has become physically easier in many ways.

The **technological environment** is the application of innovations, inventions, and knowledge based on scientific discoveries to the improvement of the quality of personal, family, and home life. New technology results in better goods and services and more cost-efficient means of producing and delivering these goods and services. An example of how the technological environment of the home has changed is the replacement of the wringer washer with the electric washing machine and the clothesline with the electric dryer—reducing laundry time from several days a week to several hours a week for the average-size family. Thus, time management and housing innovations are intertwined. When it comes to homes, emotions are also involved:

> Homes are not only the single biggest investment most Americans make, they are one of the most personal. This is probably why buying a home is considered one of life's most stressful experiences. People have a lot riding on making the right decisions. Those decisions have a lot to do with where people are in their lives. People's housing needs change as their lives do. (Mogelonsky, 1997, p. 31)

Computers, Home Automation, and Other Home Innovations

Given that people's housing needs change and that products change, what can be predicted about homes in the future? The main prediction is that home automation will continue to grow. The home automation industry predicts an average growth of 29% per year through the year 2005 (**www.homeautomation.org/**, July 19, 1999).

Two specific changes already under way are the proliferation of home computers and the increased use of microprocessors in consumer products for the home. The following time line shows some of the computer developments which have affected individual, home, work, and family life:

- ◆ 1977   Apple II is introduced.
- ◆ 1981   IBM PC (personal computer) comes on the market.
- ◆ 1984   Apple Macintosh popularizes mouse and graphical user interface.
- ◆ 1994   The World Wide Web emerges.
- ◆ 1997   Widespread use of e-mail for communication; e-commerce (buying over the Web) grows—particularly business-to-business sales, but also business-to-consumer sales.
- ◆ 2000   Worries about the millennium bug and an antitechnology backlash.

The following predictions have been summarized by William Buckeley (1998):

- ◆ 2003   Hand-held PCs offer speech recognition.

- ◆ 2005   Everyone in the developed world has Internet access.

- ◆ 2007   All business-to-business sales and 25 percent of retail sales will be over the Internet; substantial increase in distance learning courses and college degrees offered online to the extent that one-third of American colleges will go out of business. Peter Drucker adds that "long-distance learning, for instance, may well make obsolete within twenty-five years that uniquely American institution, the free-standing undergraduate college" (1999, p. 101).

- ◆ 2008   Translating telephones permit conversation with people speaking other languages; more electronic textbooks and newspapers replace paper ones; continued decrease in use of cash; increased use of cards for financial transactions.

Regarding home products with microprocessors, in the year 2000 and beyond there will be more hand-held devices for functions such as lighting, heating and cooling, and home entertainment, beyond the hand-held devices for televisions, radios, and VCRs that are already commonplace. Because hand-held devices are easily mislaid and clutter up houses, the trend will be to consolidate devices and functions into multipurpose devices or central controllers. These are already available, but the push will be on to make them more efficient and affordable. With central controllers, the basic functions that will be controlled in the home include lighting and appliances, security, temperature, intercoms, automatic lawn irrigation, and multiroom audio/video systems. The most common argument for home automation is its ability to support cross-product features such as whole-house scheduling. For example, someone returning home late at night can program the lights and the heat to go on at a certain hour.

Temperature controls will be particularly sophisticated. Houses will be divided into temperature zones that can be individually programmed to deliver heating and cooling during the times of day when the zones are used. Homeowners will set the temperatures for the zones using a touch-screen computer or hand-held voice controls that are linked to a central computer and to sensors in each zone. Temperatures will be held within a smaller range than with the old-fashioned thermostats, which conventionally allowed temperatures to vary within a six-degree range.

The most effective home automation systems will support both central and distributed control and communication standards such as those found in the CyberHome or the Smart House® System. The CyberHome is the name given to a building project cosponsored by *ComputerLife* magazine and a California builder. The CyberHome has an Ethernet local area network behind the walls that connects the computers in each room and has state-of-the-art appliances and entertainment equipment. The Smart House System is a project initiated by the National Association of Home Builders through their wholly owned subsidiary, the NAHB Research Center. In a Smart House, energy and data communications are brought together in a single system to centrally manage the most important lifestyle aspects in a home, such as security, energy management, entertainment, communications, and lighting and convenience features. Thus, the Smart House System offers features such as programmable heating and cooling and water heating, lighting controls, topflight security systems, advanced video surveillance, multimedia communications, and a home theater.

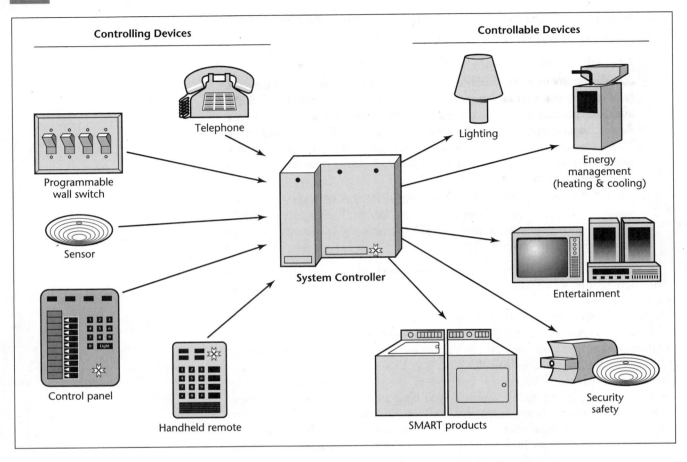

Controlling Devices

Telephone

Programmable
wall switch

Sensor

Control panel

Handheld remote

System Controller

Controllable Devices

Lighting

Energy
management
(heating & cooling)

Entertainment

SMART products

Security
safety

FIGURE 14.2
The SMART HOUSE® System
In the SMART HOUSE System,
energy and data communications are
brought together in a centrally
controlled system.

Reprinted by permission.

Televisions, telephones, cable television converters, and other consumer products will continue to get smarter. The distinction between consumer electronics and computers will continue to blur. One of the challenges the home electronics industry faces is keeping products simple enough to be easily used and repaired.

These developments in home automation are linked to management because individuals and families will have to decide which technologies to adopt and which to ignore. Consumers will also have to shop around for the best systems at the best prices and decide how to dispose of or recycle old systems. Once a system is in place, they may have to adapt their schedules and lifestyles to incorporate the technology.

This section has focused on home automation, but automated systems in libraries, stores, workplaces, and other community centers have made it easier to do everything, from shopping to conducting research at home. Computers, laser printers, copy machines, and fax machines have revolutionized the amount and kind of work that can be done at home and this trend will continue.

The trend toward shopping, working, and conducting other functions at home raises several questions. Researchers are trying to determine how working at home affects family relations, time management, and life satisfaction. Some are concerned that as people stay at home more, they will have less contact with people and feel isolated. But, as an earlier chapter pointed out, humans need social contact, so it is likely that they will seek out others for one reason or another. For example, when televisions, videocassette recorders, and movie rentals became available, movie producers and theater owners worried that people would not go to the movies as much. On the contrary, movie attendance is still strong, reflecting people's desire to get out of the house and their willingness to pay to see a movie with others. Likewise, major sporting events sell out even though they can be watched on television.

In the future, households, communities, and nations will be affected by the more efficient use of electricity. For example, better insulation materials will create a thermal shell so tightly closed that buildings can be heated and cooled with a smaller-capacity pump. Insulated ducts and improved insulation for windows will reduce air leakage by as much as 50 percent. The supply of electricity will also be more efficient due to advances in **superconductivity,** or the conducting of electricity with almost no power loss. Electricity will also be conserved by the use of compact fluorescent lights and E-lamps that will last far longer than present models.

All in all, tomorrow's homes will be more energy efficient, adaptable, affordable, and supportive of individual's and family's lifestyles. The race is on between companies to be the top suppliers of the new home systems and products.

Adopting Innovations and Applying Technology

As noted earlier, individuals and families will have to decide whether to ignore or adopt the new technologies. Persons considering a new technology or product will first become aware that it is available; then they will search for information, evaluate the information, and perhaps try out the product (e.g., test-driving a new car, trying out a computer in a store) to decide if they like it or not. Once consumers decide to adopt a new product, they move into the application phase, when they actually use the product. Even when consumers adopt a new technology, however, they do not necessarily use it to the fullest extent possible. For example, even though modern kitchens are more technologically advanced than ever before and meal preparation is easier, more meals are eaten out today than previously. However, this trend of eating out appears to be more closely associated with women's increased employment outside the home than with advances in home technology (Rapp & Collins, 1990).

Researchers of consumer behavior have found that the adoption of innovations follows a bell-shaped curve (see Figure 14.3). Some consumers are innovators and early adopters; they are eager to try new products. Others are laggards; they are very reluctant to try anything new. Most people fall in the middle of the curve as members of the early or late majority, depending on their willingness to adopt new technologies. They are interested in new products, but are wary of things that are brand new. They will wait for the product to be improved and for the price to drop. It is also possible for a person to be innovative in an area such as music and a laggard in another such as fashion.

Rodgers

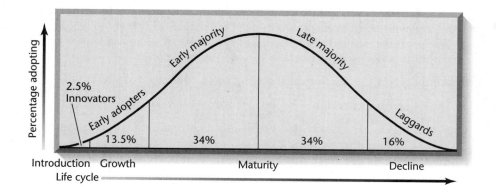

FIGURE 14.3

The Adoption of an Innovation
The bell-shaped curve indicates the rate at which new products, services, or ideas are typically adopted.

Source: Reprinted with permission of The Free Press, a division of Simon & Schuster, Inc., from *Diffusion of Innovations,* 4/e, by Everett M. Rogers. © 1995 by Everett M. Rogers. © 1962, 1971, 1983 by The Free Press.

Regarding the adoption of electronic technologies, some have taken 5 to 15 years to catch on with U.S. consumers. Among recent products, VCRs have achieved the highest acceptance level (about 90 percent of households). Other products with high levels of household penetration are cable TV (62 percent), personal computers (45 percent), and cell phones (30 percent) ("New Technologies Take Time," 1999).

Sources of New Technology

Extensive research and testing are necessary to develop new technologies. Government, industry, and universities contribute to the development of new technology. The general trend at all levels is to encourage mission-based team approaches to problem solving. The term **paradigm shift** refers to the process in which an individual or a team tackles a problem by jumping ahead to radically innovative solutions rather than taking a gradual step-by-step approach. As the pace of change accelerates, older conservative approaches to many situations may be inappropriate, and more drastic, rapid methods using paradigm shifts may be needed.

Clean Technologies

Accompanying these rapid advances in technology is a counterbalancing concern for the quality of the environment. As described in Chapter 12, a new concept in global industry is clean technologies, including processes and products that preserve the environment and do not pollute. International conferences have discussed the need for clean technologies, and several countries, most notably Japan, the United States, Australia and many in Western Europe, have given priority to their development.

Advertisements and company literature reflect consumers' concerns about the quality of their environment. A publication from Maytag observed that "as we move into the future, terms like 'a green marketplace,' 'the energywise consumer,' 'high efficiency appliances,' and 'energy standards' are becoming more and more a part of our everyday vocabulary" (*Consumer Connection,* 1994, p. 3).

Information and Innovation Overload

As consumers attempt to master the new technology, they must cope with a host of new data and information. But data and information are not necessarily the same as wisdom and knowledge as Kate Mullen of Harvard University explains:

> Data becomes information when it is crunched—systematically manipulated. Information, when conceptualized and "contextualized," leads to knowledge. Wisdom is the intelligence application of knowledge. Wisdom and knowledge are not the province of inanimate things—yet. (Mullen, 1994, p. 16)

Mullen diagrams the relationships among these concepts as follows:

Data → information → knowledge → wisdom

When consumers are bombarded with too much data and information, they may not be able to process all of it or use it to acquire wisdom and knowledge. In other words, as described in Chapter 7, they could experience information overload.

The information superhighway that is envisioned for the near future may contribute to information overload. Among other things, the information superhighway is expected to include as many as 500 television channels. But how many television channels can an individual successfully handle? Furthermore, will this variety lead to more creative programming? Or, will the slots be given over to endless rebroadcasts of a handful of hit movies and TV shows? Will more retailers use the television to demonstrate and sell their products increasing consumer confusion?

Rapid advances in technology are also leading to **innovation overload,** which is the "user's response to the ever increasing pace of information, knowledge, and innovations that are appearing on this earth" (Herbig, Milewicz, & Golden, 1993). An article in *Business Week* described the problems inherent in introducing too many innovations too rapidly:

> Otherwise highly competent men and women are driven to helpless frustration by the products around them. . . . New systems that were supposed to make work more efficient—computers, fax, electronic mail—often do the reverse. . . . Stress levels soar with VCRs, CDs, message machines, electronic thermostats, keypad burglar alarms, digital clocks, microwaves, programmable portable cellular phones for both the home and car, home computers. Their lives have become a nightmarish world of blinks and beeps. Too many companies wind up selling complex, overloaded gadgets that consumers can't figure out. (Nussbaum, 1991, p. 58)

According to Herbig, Milewicz, and Golden (1993), new products are being introduced at a numbing pace. During a single six-month period, Sony introduced more than a hundred new audio, tape, and video products in Britain alone, and Apple Corporation introduces one new product on average each week. Innovation overload refers not only to technological advances, but to any innovations—whether they involve social services (e.g., new child care providers), other services (e.g., new plumbers), or products (e.g., new books). Herbig, Milewicz, and Golden write that:

> One of the major reasons behind innovation overload and its negative effect upon adoption of many innovations is the risk factor. The degree of perceived risk is highly negatively related to the rate of diffusion. Risk is recognized as having a considerable influence on the purchase decision especially in the area of new products. (1993, p. 202)

Accordingly, one of the ways to reduce innovation overload is to reduce the amount of risk the individual perceives. As noted earlier in this text, information is one way to reduce a person's perception of risk. The more one knows about a product or service, the less risk is involved. Another way to reduce overload is to accept that it exists. Consumers need to decide how much overload they can successfully handle and adopt new products at a pace that feels comfortable. Innovations should provide clear-cut benefits to consumers. Before adopting an innovation, potential consumers should ask themselves, "Will this product or service make my life better?"

FAMILY AND GLOBAL CHANGE

One might wonder what will happen to individuals and families in the midst of all these changes. What does the future hold for families? The good news is that people are living longer and healthier lives. Life expectancy is over

70 years for men and women compared to just 35 years in 1776 (Rapp & Collins, 1990).

Chapter 8 on managing human resources, gave many family and global statistics. To review, the world population is 6 billion and the greatest concentrations of people are in Asia. Although there is a worldwide gain in population, certain countries are losing population. China is the most populous country, followed by India and the United States. Most of the world's population is concentrated in cities (straining natural resources such as clean air and water), and the trend is toward more urbanization. The largest city in the world in the year 2000 is predicted to be Mexico City. In the United States, families are smaller, there are more single-parent families, and, although there are more households, there are fewer people in them. At the same time, according to a Roper opinion poll, "the family is back and determined." Specifically, the Roper report said:

> Despite overwhelmingly pessimistic rhetoric pointing to the erosion of family values, the evidence suggests the future vitality of the American family. Partly this is due to simple demographics. The fact that the baby boom generation is in its family-forming and child-raising years has moved family life into the national foreground. The nature of the modern family, however, is irrevocably different from the "traditional" family. First, most families will have both parents working. Second, the average family size will be smaller than in previous generations. Third, the number of non-traditional family structures—single parents, step families, unmarried couples with children, grandparents with children, and so on—will continue to rise. (*The Public Pulse*, 1994)

The report adds that families, especially those lacking two parents, will expect more child-rearing help from schools and their communities. Balancing work and family responsibilities will continue to be a major concern for working parents.

Perhaps the only concrete thing one can say about the future is that change is inevitable. From an individual's standpoint, a change may be welcomed, as in a pay raise, or threatening, as in a job loss. Change upsets the status quo, disturbing those who are wedded to the known and experienced. Just as unsettling as not knowing what changes are coming is not knowing when they will occur. Peter Drucker says, "That major changes are ahead for schools and education is certain—the knowledge society will demand them and the new learning theories and learning technologies will trigger them. How fast they will come we do not, of course, know" (1989, p. 252).

Quality of Life and Well-Being

Urbanization, crowding, the economic growth, and the accelerated pace of life are already transforming where and how we live. Accelerated pace is part of a larger concept called the **acceleration effect,** which means that each unit of saved time is more valuable than the last unit. Therefore, time is becoming increasingly valuable.

According to Henry Sokalski, coordinator of the United Nations International Year of the Family:

> Although increased migration and urbanization are major trends in today's world, the complex reciprocal relationship between population movement and economic and social development is little understood. Some transitions, whether imposed by societal conditions or not, may require a sweeping reorganization of the family unit and its social network. In many cases families manage to cope, assisted by their own powers of adaptation. Too often, however, especially when faced with

poverty and lack of support from society, families unravel under the pressure of trying to sustain their members. (1994, p. 3)

Technology allows families to make better use of their time. For example, telephoning requires less time than sending a letter. Access to technology (telephones, computers, databases, publications) is not distributed evenly, however, nor will it be in the near future. The large gap between the haves and the have-nots is related to the **quality of life,** defined as the level of satisfaction with one's relationships and surroundings. Another definition of quality of life is simply one's well-being. One of the goals of management is to provide the ways and means to improve the quality of life for individuals and families.

A commonly used measure of quality of life is a country's Gross Domestic Product (GDP), which was discussed earlier in the book. The United Nations ranks countries by GDP. Realizing that economic data provide only one measure of quality of life, the United Nations and other organizations are working on developing more comprehensive measures. One such measure is the Human Development Index (HDI), which measures overall progress in 174 countries on three basic dimensions of human development: longevity, knowledge, and a decent standard of living (see Table 14.1). According to the latest HDI ranking, Canada ranked the highest, followed by France, Norway, the United States, and Iceland.

Well-being refers to a "state of being where all members of a community have economic security, are respected, valued, and have personal worth; feel connected to those around them; are able to participate in the decision-making process affecting them" (Marshall, McMullen, Ballantyne, Daciuk, & Wigdor, 1995, p. 1). There are many dimensions to the concept of well-being. The four conventionally discussed dimensions are economic well-being, physical well-being, social well-being, and emotional well-being:

◆ Economic well-being has to do with the degree of economic adequacy or security individuals and families have.

◆ Physical well-being has to do with the body and its needs. Keeping healthy and safe, eating right, getting enough sleep, and managing stress are all subtopics within this category.

◆ "Social well-being is the social space of the family as a group, whereas psychological well-being is the emotional space of an individual in the family. It is concerned with the social needs of the family played out in daily interactions in interpersonal relationships within the family groups and with the larger community, including the workplace" (McGregor & Goldsmith, 1998, p. 4).

◆ Emotional well-being has to do with the emotions (feelings) of an individual.

Recently, three other dimensions of well-being have emerged as topics in the literature and in everyday life. These are:

◆ Environmental well-being. This has to do with the level of environmental quality.

◆ Political well-being. This has to do with a person's internal sense of power, autonomy, and freedom, not necessarily involvement in politics.

◆ Spiritual well-being. Broadly and individually defined, spiritual well-being may include hope, faith, peace, joy in living, enlightenment, connectedness, and purpose.

TABLE 14.1
**Human Development
Index (HDI)**

The HDI measures overall progress for 174 countries in three basic dimensions of human development: longevity, knowledge, and a decent standard of living. It is measured by life expectancy, educational attainment, and adjusted income.

Top 5 Ranking Countries			Bottom 5 Ranking Countries		
Country	HDI Value	HDI Rank	Country	HDI Value	HDI Rank
Canada	0.960	1	Sierra Leone	0.185	174
France	0.946	2	Niger	0.207	173
Norway	0.943	3	Burkina Faso	0.219	172
USA	0.943	4	Mali	0.236	171
Iceland	0.942	5	Burundi	0.241	170

Source: Selected statistics from the Human Development Report 1998, published by Oxford University Press, **www.oup-ysa.org**. For the complete statistical database or the Human Development Report 1998 Background Papers, contact UN Publications at **www.un.org/Pubs/catalog.htm**.

A fundamental question to be addressed is which dimensions are most important to a specific person's sense of well-being? For example, an individual may value economic well-being over social well-being. In addition, levels and amounts may vary as well. An overriding question is why some people are content with very little, whereas others need a lot of "doing" "having" and "relating" to feel fulfilled. From an international comparison standpoint, the question is what measure is most appropriate. Can a measure be developed that is more comprehensive than the GDP and HDI in terms of reflecting more aspects of well-being? Answering these questions and better understanding human development, needs, and wants are all challenges for the future. According to Toffler, quality of life is something a person can attain by learning to cope with change. Copability, he suggests, is the main way a person can manage "future shock" (1990, p. 47). Further, he says to achieve their preferred quality of life, people need to consciously take control of change and guide their own evolution.

Multiculturalism

Among the most far-reaching changes in the twentieth century were the advances in communications and transportation that have caused people to extend their fairly isolated, insular concept of life to a wider worldview. They are more aware of the changes because of the improved information network. This more expansive worldview has helped to foster **multiculturalism,** or the expression by ethnic groups of their cultural heritage. The concept first began to attract the attention of educators, politicians, the media, and the general public in the 1980s. Inherent in the concept of multiculturalism is respect for each ethnic group and the willingness to recognize that "human society is a rich, multi-colored cultural and social mosaic" (Sokalski, 1994, p. 4).

Some advocates of multiculturalism see it purely as an ideal of intergroup tolerance. Others want to go beyond the theoretical and apply multiculturalism in government programs, schools, universities, churches, the media, and other institutions. The basic idea is that each ethnic group's contribution to the greater society should be acknowledged and preserved. "Thinking multiculturally requires collaborative activities and techniques that expand traditional pedagogy" (Winchip, 1997, p. 29).

Because Canada has two official languages (French and English), it is one of the world's leaders in multicultural research and government policy. As more nations embrace a model of multiculturalism, programs involving sociocultural integration and cultural retention will become more important. The main goals of such programs are to bolster cultural identity and self-esteem while promoting intergroup respect. Rather than being divisive, multiculturalism and ethnic diversity can be a source of national strength and identity. Ethnicity is a part of a society's cultural environment. Recognition of the differences as well as the commonalities among groups of people is all part of the more complex view of the world that we have today.

ENVIRONMENT

The crowding of our planet and its misuse have led to many family and environmental problems. According to Sokalski:

> Millions of families around the world continue to suffer from lack of shelter, clean water, adequate food and medical care. Yet, people everywhere are striving to improve their lives, to raise their children and care for their families, to enjoy their leisure-time, even if there is just a glimmer of hope for such aspirations to materialize. (1994, p. 2)

Environmental problems and solutions stem from many sources, including people's philosophical approach to life. For example, many people have the idea that more is better. As a result of this outlook, store shelves in some countries are crowded with essentially duplicate products, confusing consumers and making it difficult to shop in the store. At the same time, in other parts of the world, people are starving. The overcrowding of store shelves is not just a North American or Western European phenomenon. In Japan, 3,500 to 4,000 new products are introduced to food stores each year, and only 1 in 10 is believed to succeed (Rapp & Collins, 1990).

The more-is-better approach is changing somewhat, however. The desire to accumulate material things is giving way to a rising concern for a redefined quality of life in which better does not necessarily mean more. The shift from wanting to own all to owning only what is needed is an example of a paradigm shift. According to Rettig, Rossman, and Hogan (1992), this shift is not easy to make because the "compulsion to consume is so pervasive in many countries that educating people to think in alternative ways will be a monumental task which history suggests is impossible" (p. 39).

Technology, Society, and the Environment

According to the Roper report discussed earlier, the environmental movement has matured. Roper's nationwide opinion polls reveal that the current wave of environmentalism is expressed in action rather than words. For example, people are recycling more. The report also observes:

> One effect of Americans' new sense of personal responsibility is the realization that business is no longer solely responsible for environmental degradation. Yet, if people

are willing to accept more responsibility and take action, they are also likely to expect business to respond in kind. Adopting pro-environmental manufacturing processes and product designs will continue to be important for American industry. Far from being outdated, the best reasons for "going green" will continue to make sense for the foreseeable future. (*The Public Pulse,* 1994, p. 4)

Technology has been blamed for many environmental and societal ills, but it also holds the key to their solution. According to Stephen Lubar, we cannot really discuss our lives today without discussing technology and its impact in so many realms because:

> We are surrounded by new machines, new devices, new technologies that let us— or make us—deal with more information than ever before. We are also surrounded by new economic and social and cultural systems which support and made possible these machines, and which in turn are supported by them. Together our information culture and our information machines shape the way we live, work, and play, and change the way we think about the world around us. No aspect of our lives remains untouched. But we shape the machines, too, deciding what we want to use and how we will use it. We change along with the machines, and they change along with us. (Lubar, 1993, pp. 3–4)

In terms of solutions to environmental problems, technology can be used to achieve long-term ecological balance. Many examples of technology's positive impact on the environment could be cited, but one of the better known examples is technology's ability to increase the world's food supply.

The Food Supply

In the eighteenth century, Thomas Malthus predicted that the world's population would outgrow the food supply. Malthus, however, did not anticipate the advances in agriculture that have enabled the world population to grow to its current level. Among the recent advances in agriculture is genome mapping, or mapping the genes of plants and animals. **Genome maps** are blueprints that researchers use to investigate the development of an individual animal or plant from fertilization to maturity. Genetics research may provide the key to disease-free animals with more meat and less fat. Another practical use of genome mapping is to determine if genes exist or can be made that would make plants more photosynthetically efficient. This would allow light-sensitive plants to be grown in the shadow of other plants. Terry Sharrer (1992) points out that corn plants could then be grown in a space 3 inches square instead of requiring 5 inches between the plants and 40 inches between the rows. The result would be an approximately 1,000 percent increase in the plant population per acre.

Tomorrow's farms may be far different from the ones we see today in other ways as well. Already, farmers are experimenting with controlling watering, planting, fertilizing, and harvesting from a computer control panel in the house. Sensors in the ground let the farmer know immediately if the crops need more water or fertilizer.

Perhaps even more remarkable are the experiments in **hydroponics,** that is, growing plants in water without soil. Some of these experiments can be observed at universities and cooperative extension units of agriculture programs and at EPCOT Center in Walt Disney World in Orlando, Florida. The Land exhibit at EPCOT is the world's only major display of food and fiber crops from all climate zones under one roof. The exhibit is more than just an interesting display—it annually produces tons of fresh vegetables and fish for EPCOT restaurants. The goal of the exhibit is to demonstrate that intelligent and constructive land use can fulfill the world's future food needs.

The Land's staff, which includes college student interns, is working with NASA scientists from the Kennedy Space Center on agricultural research for space. In a spacecraft, plants are needed for food and also to replenish oxygen and water and for recycling of wastes. Lettuce, wheat, and potatoes are some of the crops selected for space study. Scientific research of this type may someday ensure an expanded food supply by allowing foods to be grown in space stations and on other planets. In this century, people may live on a self-sustaining moon base. Consequently, when discussing the future management problems and possibilities for individuals and families, one should keep in mind that soon not only will there be life on earth, but also the possibility of human life in space.

Electronic Resources

For information about the environment, contact the Environmental Protection Agency at **www.epa.gov**. For information about the space program, contact NASA at **www.nasa.gov**. The U.S. Dept. of Energy at **www.eren.doe.gov** covers all aspects of energy-saving in the home and offers an interactive program for assessing your own home's energy needs, including recommended insulation levels.

www.nasa.gov/

Home operating systems, including telecommunications, lighting, heating, and security, are described at **www.homeautomation.org**, the Home Automation Association Web site. Software is available on home automation from such companies as IBM. IBM's software is called Home Director; to view go to **www.us.pc.ibm.com/ibm/home**. Microsoft's Home Advisor at **homeadvisor.msn.com** offers remodeling advice and news about the latest computerized systems.

Web sites that offer nutrition and health information include:

- ◆ Tufts University Nutrition Navigator: **navigator.tufts.edu**
- ◆ The American Dietetic Association: **www.eatright.org**
- ◆ The International Food Information Council Foundation: **http://ificinfo.health.org**
- ◆ Medline: **www.nlm.nih.gov/databases/freemedl.html**
- ◆ National Institutes of Health: **www.nih.gov**
- ◆ The U.S. Food and Drug Administration: **http://vm.cfsan.fda.gov**
- ◆ Mayo Health Oasis (of the Mayo Clinic): **www.mayohealth.org**
- ◆ Johns Hopkins Health Information: **www.intelihealth.com/IH/ihtIH**
- ◆ World Health Organization: **www.who.int**
- ◆ Food & Agriculture Organization: **www.fao.org**
- ◆ Government healthfinder: **www.healthfinder.gov**

Summary

This chapter has examined future trends in technology, homes, and the environment. Each change presents its own challenges and opportunities for managerial judgment. Change starts with the individual clarifying his or her goals, making decisions, and using resources to reach solutions. Thinking ahead, planning, and a sense of self-responsibility are the hallmarks of management. Information and innovation overload, the acceleration effect, and quality of life issues present challenges that management can help solve. One of the purposes of this book has been to introduce various human and environmental problems and show ways of dealing with them through adapting, coping, planning, and managing.

As in any discipline, resource management has a history, a present, and a future. This chapter on the future concludes this book, which started with an overview of management, including its theoretical bases and history, progressed through chapters on specific concepts, and then applied those concepts to managing human resources, time, stress and fatigue, work and family life, the environment, and finances. Given this coverage from history to present to future, it is fitting to end this chapter and the book with a look back and a look forward:

> The past century was extraordinarily rich in innovation and scientific progress. There has never been a century like it, and we might worry that there can never be another. It is unlikely that we will ever again see the likes of Edison or Einstein, to mentioned two whose 20th century accomplishments far surpassed those of their colleagues. But Edison, Einstein, and other great innovators of this century would surely have shared the view that technological and scientific progress will continue. In that spirit, we might hazard one simple prediction: In the next 100 years, the only thing to be certain of is surprise. (Raeburn, 1999, 106)

Key Terms

acceleration effects
diffusion
discovery
genome maps
hydroponics
innovation (overload)
intellect

invention
managerial judgment
multiculturalism
paradigm shift
quality of life
superconductivity
system understanding

technological
   environment
technology
well-being

Review Questions

1. How can individuals and families cope with information and innovation overloads?
2. Why did the Roper opinion poll report conclude that "the family is back and determined?"
3. The chapter's introduction pointed out that making predictions is a risky business. For example, what is your reaction to the Buckeley comment that one-third of American colleges may go out of business by 2007 because of distance learning courses and online degrees, or Peter Drucker's prediction that in 25 years the American institution of the free-standing undergraduate college may be obsolete? What does learning and living on campus provide versus taking courses on computer?
4. How does the concept of quality of life relate to the study of resource management?
5. How will genetics research affect food supplies?

References

Buckeley, W. (1998, November 16). The course of change. *The Wall Street Journal*, R4.

Consumer Connection. (1994, January/February). A publication of Maytag, 3.

Drucker, P. (1989). *The new realities*. New York: Harper & Row.

_____. (1999). Management challenges for the 21st century. NY: Harper Business.

Herbig, P., Milewicz, J., & Golden, J. (1993). Information overload in review. *Proceedings of the Atlantic Marketing Association*, 199–204. Orlando, FL.

Key, R. & Firebaugh, F. (1989). Family resource management: Preparing for the 21st century. *Journal of Home Economics*, *81*(1), 13–17.

Lubar, S. (1993). *InfoCulture*. Boston: Houghton Mifflin Company.

Marshall, V., McMullen, J., Ballentine, P., Daciuk, J., & Wigdor, B. (1995). *Contribution to independence over the adult life course*. Toronto, ON: Centre for Studies of Aging, University of Toronto.

McGregor, S. & Goldsmith, E. (1998). Expanding our understanding of quality of life, standard of living, and well-being, *Journal of Family and Consumer Sciences, 90*(2), 2–6, 22.

Mogelonsky, M. (1997, January). Reconfiguring the American Dream (House), *American Demographics*, 31–35.

Mullen, K. (1994, February). We did not know that. *Forbes ASAP*, 16.

"New Technologies Take Time."(1999, April 19). *Business Week*, 8.

Nussbaum, K. (1991, April 29). *Business Week*, 58.

Quinn, J. B., Baruch, J., & Zien, K. (1997). Innovation explosion, NY: Simon & Schuster.

Raeburn, P. (1999, Summer). The next 100 years. *Business Week*, 106.

Rapp, S. & Collins, T. (1990). *The great marketing turnaround*. Englewood Cliffs, NJ: Prentice-Hall.

Rettig, K., Danes, S., & Bauer, J. (1993). Gender differences in perceived family life quality among economically stressed farm families. In U. Foa, J. Converse, K. Tornblom, & E. Foa

(Eds.), *Resource theory: Explorations and applications.* San Diego, CA: Academic Press, 123–155.

Rettig, R., Rossman, M., & Hogan, J. (1992). *Handbook of family life,* Vol. II. Arcus, et al., (Eds.). Berkeley, CA: Sage Publications.

Sharrer, G. T. (1992, Spring). Wonders and worries: A perspective on the future of American agriculture. Unpublished paper. Washington, DC.: National Museum of American History, Smithsonian Institution, 3. The comment noted in the text is based on Sharrer's conversations with John Fulkerson of the Cooperative State Research Service, U.S. Department of Agriculture, 1986.

Sokalski, H. (1994, June 20). The IYF in a world of change: Its global impact. Keynote address, 85th Annual Meeting of the American Home Economics Association, San Diego, CA.

The public pulse. (1994). Vol. 8, no. 5. Report of the Roper Starch Worldwide, Inc., New York.

Toffler, A. (1990). Toffler's next shock. *World Monitor,* 34–44.

Tucker, R. (1992). *Managing the future.* New York: G. P. Putnam's Sons.

Twiss, B. (1980). *Managing Technological Innovation,* (2nd ed.). London: Longman.

Winchip, S. (1997, Fall). Understanding multicultural perspectives through coursework. *Journal of Family and Consumer Sciences,* 28–31.

GLOSSARY

Absolute values Extreme, definitive values that are inflexible.

Abstract symbols Ideas rather than objects.

Acceleration effect Quickening of life's pace so that each unit of time saved is more valuable than the last unit.

Accommodation Reaching an agreement by accepting the point of view of the dominant person.

Actively acquired information Information the individual actively looks for, such as fashion coverage in magazines or news bulletins on television.

Actuating Putting plans into effect, action, or motion.

Adaptability The ability to cope with change.

Adjusting Checking a plan or activity and making appropriate changes.

Advocate or expert channels Experts in a field or people with a cause who are more likely to contact receivers through letters, speeches, or less direct forms of communication.

Affective domain Value meanings derived from feelings.

Artifacts Type, placement, or rearrangement of objects around a person.

Assessment Involves the gathering of information about results.

Assets What a person owns.

Attitudes Concepts that may express values, serve as a means of evaluation, or demonstrate feeling in regard to some idea, person, object, event, situation, or relationship.

Autonomic An equal number of decisions are made by each spouse.

Behavior What people actually do.

Blended families New families that include children from previous relationships. Also called stepfamilies or reconstituted or combined families.

Boomeranging The return of adult children to their parents' homes (Riche, 1990).

Boundaries Limits or borders between systems.

Brainstorming Group members suggest many ideas no matter how seemingly ridiculous or strange. Afterward, the group examines each idea separately to see if it has merit.

Budget A spending plan or guide.

Burnout Emotional or physical exhaustion brought on by unrelieved stress.

Change To cause to be different, to alter, or to transform.

Channel The medium or route through which the message travels from sender to receiver.

Checking Determining if actions are in compliance with standards and sequencing.

Chronic fatigue syndrome An affliction or disease exhibiting a variety of symptoms, including extreme long-lasting exhaustion.

Circadian rhythms The daily rhythmic activity cycles, based on 24-hour intervals, that humans experience.

Clarification The process of making clear, making easier to understand, or elaborating.

Cocooning The desire to remain at home as a place of coziness, control, peace, insulation, and protection (Popcorn, 1991).

Cognitive domain Value meanings derived from thinking about events, situations, people, and things.

Comfort zone A combination of habit and everyday expectations mixed with an appropriate amount of adventure and novelty.

Commitment The degree to which an individual identifies with and is involved in a particular activity or organization.

Communication The process of transmitting a message from a sender to a receiver.

Comparative advantage A theory that individuals, families, or companies do best when they focus on activities in which they can add the most value, and outsource other activities.

Compromise Each person makes concessions, giving in a little in order to gain a valued settlement or outcome.

Conflict A state of disagreement or disharmony.

Conflict resolution Negotiations to remedy the conflict.

Consensual decision making Reaching a mutual agreement equally acceptable to all individuals involved.

Conservation The act or process of preserving and protecting natural environments from loss or depletion.

Constructive conflict Focuses on the issue or the problem rather than on the other person's deficits.

Consume To destroy, use, or expend.

Contingency plans Backup or secondary plans to be used in case the first plan does not work out.

Controlling Things people do to check their course of action.

Credit Time allowed for payment.

Crises Events that require changes in normal patterns of behavior.

Critical listening   When the listener evaluates or challenges what is heard.

Cultural relativism   A comparative approach based on an understanding and appreciation of other cultures.

Cultural values   Generally held conceptualizations of what is right or wrong in a culture or what is preferred.

Culture   The sum of all socially transmitted behavior patterns, beliefs, arts, expectations, institutions, and all other products of human work and thought characteristic of a group, community, or population.

Decibel (dB)   A measure of the loudness of sound.

Decidophobia   The fear of making decisions.

Deciduous trees   Trees that lose their leaves in winter.

Decision making   Choosing between two or more alternatives.

Decision-making style   The characteristic way that a person makes decisions.

Decision plan   A long, complicated decision process that includes a sequence of intentions.

Decision rules   Principles that guide decision making.

Decisions   Conclusions or judgments about some issue or matter.

Decoding   The process by which the receiver assigns meaning to the symbols sent by the sender (Kotler, 1983).

De facto decision making   Characterized by a lack of dissent rather than by active assent.

Demands   Events or goals that require action.

Demographics   Data used to describe populations or subgroups.

Demography   The study of the characteristics of human populations, that is, their size, growth, distribution, density, movement, and other vital statistics.

Depression   A drastic and long-lasting decline in the economy characterized by high unemployment, falling prices, and decreasing business activity.

Destination   The receiver or audience.

Destructive conflicts   Interpersonal conflicts involving direct verbal attacks on another individual.

Diffusion   Innovations spreading within an enterprise or society.

Directional plans   Progress along a linear path to a long-term goal fulfillment.

Disability   A long-term or chronic condition medically defined as a physiological, anatomical, mental, or emotional impairment resulting from disease or illness, inherited or congenital defect, or traumas or other insults (including environmental) to mind or body (Wright, 1980).

Discovery   The initial observation of a new phenomenon.

Discretionary income   Income regulated by one's own discretion or judgment.

Discretionary time   The free time an individual can use any way she or he wants.

Disposable income   The amount of take-home pay left after all deductions are withheld for benefits, taxes, contributions, and so on.

Distress   Harmful stress.

Domino effect   The passage of stress from one source to another.

Dovetailing   Occurs when two or more activities take place at the same time.

Downshifting   Opting for a simpler life—usually less pay, less stress, and more time—in a more personally satisfying occupation.

Dual career   When both spouses have a long-term commitment to a planned series of jobs leading to desired career goals.

Dual-income or dual-earner households   Where both spouses have income-producing jobs.

Ecoconsciousness   Thoughts and actions given to protecting and sustaining the environment.

Ecology   The study of how living things relate to their natural environment.

Economic well-being   The degree to which individuals or families have economic adequacy.

Ecosystem   The subsystem of human ecology that emphasizes the relationship between organisms and their environment.

Effort   Exertion or the use of energy to do something.

Emergency fund   Savings equal to three to six months of income.

Empathetic listening   Listening for feelings.

Empathy   The ability to recognize and identify another's feelings by putting oneself in that person's place.

Encoding   The process of putting thought into symbolic form (Kotler, 1983).

Energy   The ability to do work, measured as potential or stored energy or as kinetic energy, the energy of motion (Naar, 1990).

Entropy   A tendency toward disorder or randomness.

Environment   The sum of the external conditions influencing the life of an organism or population (Naar, 1990).

Environmentalism   Concern for the environment.

Equal Credit Opportunity Act   Under this act, a lender cannot discriminate against a person because of race, sex, age, color, marital status, or related factors.

Equifinality   The phenomenon in which different circumstances and opportunities may lead to similar outcomes.

Ethics   A system of morals, principles, values, or good conduct.

Ethnocentrism   The tendency to interpret other cultures in terms of one's own dominant culture.

Eustress   Beneficial stress.

Evaluation   The process of judging or examining the cost, value, or worth of a plan or decision based on such criteria as standards, demands, or goals.

Expertise   The ability to perform tasks successfully and dependably.

External change   Fostered by society or the outer environment.

External motivation   The forces external to the individual that affect motivation.

External noise   Noise from the environment.

External search   Looking for new information from sources outside oneself.

External stress   Situations in which stress is brought on from outside the individual.

Extrinsic motivation   Outside rewards or motivation.

Extrinsic values   Values that derive their worth or meaning from someone or something else.

Extroverts   Overall types of character and response in which individuals are less interested in themselves and more interested in others.

Fair Credit Reporting Act   Under this act, individuals who are denied credit, insurance, or employment because of their credit report have the right to obtain a free copy of their report within 30 days of the denial.

Family   A group of two or more persons (one of whom is a householder) who are related by birth, marriage, or adoption and reside together (U.S. Bureau of the Census, 1989).

Family ecosystem   A subsystem of human ecology that emphasizes the interactions between families and environments.

Fatalism   The feeling that all events are shaped by fate.

Fatigue   The feeling of having insufficient energy to carry on and a strong desire to stop, rest, or sleep (Engel, 1970).

Feedback   Information that returns to the system.

Fertility rate   Yearly number of births per 1,000 women of childbearing age.

Fight or flight syndrome   Alerted condition of the body as it quickly prepares for physical battle or energetic flight to escape the situation.

Financial management   The science or practice of managing money or other assets.

Focus groups   Selected groups of people who are questioned by a discussion leader or moderator about their views on different topics.

Fossil fuels   The remains of dead vegetation, such as coal, oil, and natural gases, that can be burned to release energy (Naar, 1990).

Functional limitation   Hindrance or negative effect in the performance of household tasks or activities.

Gender gap   The difference in earnings between employed men and women.

Genome maps   Blueprints that researchers use to investigate the development of an individual animal or plant from fertilization to maturity.

Gerontology   The scientific study of the aging process.

Glass ceiling   As women move up the career ladder, they hit an invisible barrier that stops them from moving further.

Goals   End results that require action; the purpose toward which much behavior is directed.

Gresham's Law of Planning   Short-term concerns create priorities and deadlines that take managerial attention away from long-range concerns.

Gross domestic product (GDP)   The total market value of all goods and services produced by a nation during a specified period, usually a year.

Gross income   All income received that is not legally exempt from taxes.

Habitat   The place where an organism lives.

Habits   Repetitive, often unconscious patterns of behavior.

Habitual decision making   Choices that are made out of habit without any additional information search.

Handicap   A disadvantage, interference, or barrier to performance, opportunity, or fulfillment in any desired role in life, imposed upon the individual by a limitation in function or by other problems associated with disability and/or personal characteristics in the context of the individual's environment or role (Wright, 1980).

Homeostasis   The tendency to maintain balance.

Household   All persons who occupy a housing unit such as a house, apartment, or single room.

Human capital   The sum total of human resources; all the capabilities, traits and other resources that people use to achieve goals.

Human ecology   The study of how humans interact with their environment.

Human resources   The skills, talents, and abilities that people possess.

Hydroponics   Growing plants in water without soil.

Hypotheses   Predictions about future occurrences.

I-messages   Statements of fact about how an individual feels or thinks.

Immigration   The process in which people enter and settle in a country where they are not native.

Implementing   Putting decisions or plans into action.

Income   The amount of money or its equivalent received during a period of time.

Income tax   A personal tax levied on individuals or families on the basis of income received.

Independent activities   Activities that take place one at a time.

Indirect channels Message communication forms such as radio, television, magazines, newspapers, and signs.

Inflation Rising prices.

Information anxiety The gap between what individuals think they understand and what they actually do understand.

Information overload The uncomfortable state when individuals are exposed to too much information in too short a time.

Innovation overload The user's response to the ever increasing pace of information, knowledge, and innovations (Herbig, Milewicz, & Golden, 1993).

Inputs Whatever is brought into the system.

Insurance A financial arrangement in which people pay premiums to an insurance company that reimburses them in the event of loss or injury.

Intangible resources Resources that are incapable of being touched.

Integrated waste management A combination of methods to reduce environmental pollution.

Intellect Knowing or understanding; the capacity to create knowledge; the capability for rational or highly developed use of intelligence.

Interdependent activities When one activity must be completed before another can take place.

Interface The place or point where independent systems or diverse groups interact.

Interference Anything that distorts or interrupts messages.

Internal change Originates within the family and includes events that primarily affect family members.

Internal noise Noise occurring in the sender's and receiver's minds.

Internal search Looking within oneself for information for decisions.

Internal stress Originates in one's own mind and body.

Interpersonal conflicts Actions by one person that interfere with the actions of another.

Intrinsic motivation The underlying causes of and the internal need for competence and self-determination. The pleasure or value a person derives from the content of work or activity.

Intrinsic values Values classified as ends in themselves, having internal meanings.

Introverts Overall types of character or response in which individuals tend to think of themselves first and rely on inner-directed thoughts.

Intuition The sense or feeling of knowing what to do without going through the rational process.

Invention Provides the initial verification that a problem can be solved.

Investment Commitment of capital to the achievement of long-term goals or objectives.

Job stress The harmful physical and emotional responses that occur when the requirements of the job do not match the capabilities, resources, or needs of the worker.

Leisure Freedom from time-consuming activities, tasks, duties, or responsibilities.

Level of living The measure of the goods and services affordable by and available to individuals or families.

Liabilities What is owed.

Life management All decisions a person or family will make and the way their values, goals, and resource use affect their decision making. Includes all the goals, events, situations, and decisions that make up a lifestyle.

Lifestyle The characteristic way or pattern in which an individual conducts his or her life.

Liquidity The speed and ease of retrieving cash or turning another type of investment into cash.

Listening Hearing what is said and observing the actions communicated.

Low involvement Information that does not necessitate much thinking about or attention.

Macroenvironment The environment that surrounds and encompasses the microenvironment.

Management The process of using resources to achieve goals. It involves thinking, action, and results.

Management process Involves thinking, action, and results.

Management style A characteristic way of making decisions and acting.

Management tools Measuring devices, techniques, or instruments that are used to arrive at decisions and plans of action.

Managerial judgment The ability to accept and work with change for the betterment of self and humankind.

Material resources Include natural phenomena, such as fertile soil, petroleum, and rivers, and human-made items, such as buildings, money, and computers.

Message The total communication that is sent, listened to, and received.

Message construction Where information should be placed in a message to have maximum impact and how often information should be repeated in a message (Mowen, 1987).

Message content Strategies or information that may be used to communicate an idea or policy to receivers.

Microenvironment The environment that closely surrounds individuals and families.

Mobility Technical term for changing residences.

Morphogenic systems Adaptive to change and relatively open.

Morphostatic systems Resistant to change, stable, and relatively closed.

Mortality The technical term for death.

Motivation Movement toward goals or other desired outcomes.

Multiculturalism Respect for each ethnic group and the recognition that "human society is a rich, multicolored cultural and social mosaic" (Sokalski, 1994, p. 4).

Multifinality The phenomenon in which the same initial circumstances or conditions may lead to different conclusions or outcomes.

Need recognition Realization of how much an individual needs a certain product, service, or condition.

Needs Things that are required or necessary.

Negative feedback Information put into the system that indicates that the system is deviating from its normal course and that corrective measures may be necessary if the desired steady state is to be maintained.

Net worth Amount determined by subtracting liabilities from assets.

Noise Any interference in the communication process that prevents the message from being heard correctly; unwanted sound.

Nondiscretionary time The time that an individual cannot control totally by himself or herself.

Nonnormative stressor events Unanticipated experiences that place a person or a family in a state of instability and require creative effort to remedy.

Nonverbal symbols Anything other than words that is used to communicate.

Normative stressor events Anticipated, predictable developmental changes that occur at certain life intervals.

Norms Rules that specify, delineate, encourage, and prohibit certain behaviors in certain situations.

NREM or Non-Rapid Eye Movement Sleep Occurs when the sleeper is in an inactive, deep slumber.

Opportunity cost The highest-valued alternative that must be sacrificed to satisfy a want or attain something.

Opportunity recognition Realization by an individual that she or he may have limited or no access to a product, service, or condition.

Optimization Obtaining the best result.

Orientation The location or situation of a house relative to points on a compass.

Overlapping Activities Giving intermittent attention to two or more activities until they are completed.

Outputs End results or products, leftovers, and waste.

Outsourcing Paying someone else to do one's work.

Paradigm shift The process in which an individual or a team tackles a problem by jumping ahead to radically innovative solutions rather than taking a gradual step-by-step approach.

Pareto principle States that 20 percent of the time expended usually produces 80 percent of the results, whereas 80 percent of the time expended produces only 20 percent of the results.

Parkinson's law States that a job expands to fill the time available to accomplish the task.

Passively acquired information Information that one hears or sees but does not necessarily seek, such as billboard advertisements or airplane messages.

Perception The process whereby sensory stimulation is translated into organized experience.

Persistence A person's staying power; the personality trait of not giving up when faced with adversity.

Personality An extensive range of separate behavioral traits or overall types of character and response (Foxall, Goldsmith, & Brown, 1998).

Peter principle States that people are promoted beyond their level of competence.

Physical environmental resources Natural surroundings.

Plan A detailed schema, program, strategy, or method worked out beforehand for the accomplishment of a desired end result.

Planning A series of decisions leading to action or to need or goal fulfillment.

Pollution Undesirable changes in physical, chemical, or biological characteristics of air, land, or water that can harm the health, activities, or survival of living organisms.

Positive ecology Thinking and acting in such a way as to reduce waste and pollution.

Positive feedback Information put into the system that anticipates and promotes change.

Postpurchase dissonance After a purchasing decision, the buyer is likely to seek some reinforcement for the decision to reduce doubt or anxiety.

Poverty The state of being poor and unable to provide for basic needs on a consistent basis.

Prepurchase expectations Beliefs about the anticipated performance of a product or service.

Private resources Those owned and/or controlled by an individual, family, or group.

Proactive Taking responsibility for one's own life. Proactive people accept responsibility for their own actions; they do not blame others or circumstances for their behavior.

Probability The likelihood of a certain outcome.

Problem recognition When an individual or family perceives a significant difference between their lifestyle and some desired or ideal lifestyle.

Problem solving Making many decisions that lead to a resolution of a problem.

Problems Questions, dilemmas, or situations that need solving.

Process A system of operations that work together to produce an end result.

Procrastinator Someone who puts off work and postpones and delays decisions.

Proxemics Distance between speakers.

Psychic income   One's perception or feelings about income; the satisfaction derived from income.

Psychological hardiness   The characteristic way of people who have a sense of control over their lives; they are committed to self, work, relationships, and other values and do not fear change.

Public resources   Those owned and used by all the people in a locality or country.

Qualitative time measurement   Investigates the meaning or significance of time use, that is, the satisfaction it generates.

Quality of life   The level of satisfaction with one's relationships and surroundings.

Quantitative time measures   The number, kind, and duration (e.g., minutes, hours, days) of activities that occur at specific points in time.

Radon   A naturally occurring gaseous byproduct of the uranium in the earth.

Reactive people   Those overly affected by outside forces.

Real income   Income measured in prices at a certain time, reflecting the buying power of current dollars.

Receiving   Listening to the verbal messages and observing the nonverbal messages.

Recession   A moderate and temporary decline in the economy.

Reference groups   The people who influence an individual or provide guidance or advice are members of that person's reference group.

Reflective listening   Listening for feelings.

Relative values   Values that are interpreted based on context.

REM or Rapid Eye Movement Sleep   Occurs when the sleeper is in a light sleep; most dreams happen during REM.

Renewable resources   Resources that are essentially unlimited.

Resource stock   The sum of readily available resources an individual possesses.

Resourcefulness   The ability to recognize and use resources effectively.

Resources   Whatever is available to be used.

Responses   The individual reactions that follow a message.

Risk   The possibility of pain, harm, or loss from a decision; uncertainty.

Risk aversion   Avoidance of risk.

Routine   A habitual way of doing things that saves time and energy for other activities.

R-value   The level of resistance in insulation.

Sandwich generation   Individuals who provide or anticipate providing financial support for their parent or parents while also providing financial support for one or more children.

Satisficing   Picking the first good alternative that presents itself (Simon, 1959).

Scanning   An action in which individuals or families read the world searching for signals or clues that have strategic implications.

Scarcity   A shortage or insufficient amount or supply.

Scheduling   Specification of sets of time-bounded projected activities that are sufficient for the achievement of a desired goal set (Avery & Stafford, 1991).

Self-disclosure   The process in which one person tells another something she or he would not tell just anyone (Hybels & Weaver, 1989).

Sending   Saying what one means to say, with agreement between verbal and nonverbal messages.

Sequence   A following of one thing after another in a series or an arrangement.

Sequencing   When one thing follows another as in a series of events; ordering of activities.

Setting   The physical surroundings where messages are communicated.

Site   The location or situation of a house.

Social channels   Communication between people, such as between friends, neighbors, and family members.

Social environmental resources   People united in a common cause through an array of societies, economic and political groups, and community organizations.

Social Security Act   Under this act, retired persons and selected others receive money from the government.

Socialization   The process by which children learn the rules of society.

Source   The sender or communicator.

Spam   Unsolicited e-mail or junk mail on the Internet.

Standard of living   What an individual or family aspires to.

Standards   The quantitative and/or qualitative criteria that reconcile resources with demands (DeMerchant, 1993).

Stewardship   Responsibility to preserve the Earth.

Storyboarding   A planning technique used by advertisers and screenwriters to show the main scenes (in comic-strip style) of a commercial, television show, or movie.

Strategic plans   Use a directional approach and include both a practice search for new opportunities and a reactive solution to existing problems (Wheeler & Hunger, 1987).

Strategy   A plan of action, a way of conducting and following through on operations.

Stress   The nonspecific response of the body to any demand made upon it (Seyle, 1974).

Stress overload or pileup   The cumulative effect of many stresses building up at one time.

Stressors   Situations or events that cause stress.

Subsystem   A part of a larger system.

Superconductivity   The conducting of electricity with almost no power loss.

Sustainable development   A form of growth wherein societal needs, present and future, are met.

Symbols   Things that suggest something else through association.

Syncratic   Families in which the husband and wife share equally in making most of the decisions.

System   An integrated set of parts that function together for some end purpose or result.

System understanding   Know how. The understanding of the interrelationship and pacing rates of influences among key variables.

Tangible resources   Resources that are real, touchable, or capable of being appraised.

Taxes   Compulsory levies that are an important source of government revenue.

Technological environment   The application of innovations, inventions, and knowledge based on scientific discoveries to the improvement of the quality of life.

Technology   The application of the scientific method and materials to achieve objectives.

Tempo   A time patterning or pace that feels comfortable.

Theory   An organized system of ideas or beliefs that can be measured; a system of assumptions or principles.

Throughputs   The processing of inputs.

Time   A measured or measurable period.

Time displacement   Concern over how time spent in one activity takes away from time spent in another activity (Mutz, Roberts, & Van Vuuren, 1993).

Time management   The conscious control of time to fulfill needs and achieve goals.

Time perception   The awareness of the passage of time.

Time tagging   Mental estimation of the sequences that should take place, the approximate amount of time required for each activity in a sequence, and the starting and ending times for each activity (Avery & Stafford, 1991).

Transfer payments   Monies or services given for which the recipient does not directly pay.

Transformations   Transitions from one state to another.

Type A persons   Characterized by excessively striving behavior, high job involvement, impatience, competitiveness, desire for control and power, aggressiveness, and hostility.

Type B persons   Characterized by relaxed, easygoing, reflective, and cooperative behavior.

Uncertainty   The state or feeling of being in doubt.

Unemployment   Being out of work.

Utility   Value, work, applicability, productiveness, or, simply, usefulness of a resource.

Value orientation   An internally integrated value system.

Values   Principles that guide behavior.

Verbal symbols   Words people use.

Visible symbols   Symbols that can be seen.

Volunteer work   Work that does not generate pay, usually performed outside the home.

Wants   Things that are desired or wished for.

Waste stream   All garbage produced.

Wealth   The state of being rich and having an abundance of material possessions and resources.

Well-being   A "state of being where all members of a community have economic security; are respected, valued, and have personal worth; feel connected to those around them; are able to participate in the decision-making process affecting them" (Marshall, McMullen, Ballantyne, Daciuk, & Wigdor, 1995, p. 1).

Work   Effort expended to produce or accomplish something or activity that is rewarded, usually with pay.

Workaholism   The inability to stop thinking about work and doing work and the feeling that work is always the most pleasurable part of life.

Work ethic   The degree of dedication or commitment to work.

Work simplification   Improved, more efficient work methods in the home.

You-messages   Statements that often ascribe blame or judge others.

INDEX

ABC method of time control,
    203–204
Absolute values, 54
Acceleration effect, 328
Accommodation, 111
Actively acquired information,
    162
Actuating, 135–136
Adams, S., 159
Adaptability, 178
Adjusting, 136
Adoption of innovation, 325
Advertising, 142
Advocate or expert channel, 153
Affective domain, 53
Air quality
    indoor pollution, 290
    problems with, 290–291
    quality index, 291
    radon in, 291
    solutions, 291–292
Ajzen, I., 63, 64
Alder, J., 310
Alessandra, A., 138
Allen, J., 190
Allen, K., 236
Allowances, 307–308
Alm, R., 191
Alwin, D., 61
Ames, E., 184
Anderson, C., 308
Anderson, E., 225
Anderson, J., 311
Ansell, E., 17
Archer, J., 263
Arndt, W., 31
Arnold, M., 189
Artifacts, 151
Assessment, 137
Atkinson, H., 264–267
Attitudes, 53–54, 63–64
Autonomic, 111
Avery, R., 131, 215
Axinn, N., 40, 87
Azar, S., 183

Baby boom and boomlet,
    174–176
Balazs, A., 173
Ballentine, J., 329
Barker, J., 297
Bauer, J., 88, 192

Baum, A., 186, 187
Beck, A., 157
Beck, D., 15, 18
Beck, M., 18
Becker, G., 42
Begley, S., 150
Behavior, 53
Beiles, N., 299
Berger, P., 28
Berry, L., 200
Best, R., 209, 210
Bienvenue, M., 156
Bingham, J., 128
Birthrates, 174
Blieszner, R., 88
Blinder, A., 158
Blood, R., 111
Boomeranging, 184
Boundaries, 32
Bragg, A., 32, 246, 251
Brainstorming, 160
Braus, P., 186, 250
Brennon, P., 298
Bristow, D., 6, 88, 89
Broder, S., 310
Brown, S., 43, 44, 126
Brokaw, T., 232
Brouwer, N., 276
Bryant, K., 30
Bryant, W., 86
Bubolz, M., 18, 39, 41, 137
Buckeley, W., 323
Budgets, 299, 301
Burke, R., 256
Burke, T., 280
Burnes, D., 186, 187
Burnout, 260
Burt, M., 187
Burton, J., 12

Cacciola, J., 246, 251
Calvacca, L., 152
Cannon, W., 232
Capel, I., 250
Carlson, L., 307
Carpenter, B., 291
Carroll, S., 212
Carsky, M., 235
Caspi, A., 192
Castells, M., 31
Cavanaugh, J., 185
Central-satellite model, 104, 105

Chain model, 104, 105
Challenge, 68
Change
    definition of, 178
    managing, 179–180
    nature of, 178–179
Channels, 147, 152
Chartrand, J., 67, 71
Checking, 136
Cheskis-Gold, R., 182
Children and child care
    abuse, 183–184
    days in school, 182–183
    managing stress of, 184,
        262–263
    money and, 306–308
    returning home, 184
    time, 183
Choices, 3
Chronic Fatigue Syndrome,
    268–269
Circadian rhythms, 210
Clarification, 7
Clark, D., 203
Clayton, G., 209–210, 215–216
Cocooning, 163
Cognitive domain, 53
Cohen, B., 187
Cohen, C., 188
College students
    money, work, and, 311
    resources of, 80–81
    stress and, 263–264
    values and goals of, 70–72
Collins, T., 325, 331
Coltrane, S., 110
Comfort zone, 250–251
Commitment, 232
Communication
    as part of management,
        145–146
    cross-cultural, 158
    definition of, 146
    distance zones, 159
    families and, 154–156
    gender and, 156–157
    home, individual, and,
        163–164
    small groups and, 160
    technology and, 161–162
Comparative advantage, 249
Compromise, 227

Computers
    human capacity and, 163
    information and, 161–163
    time and, 203
Coney, K., 209, 210
Conflict resolution, 154
Conflict, 154
Consensual decision making, 111
Conservation, 278
Constructive conflicts, 156
Consume, 93
Consumption
    appliances, 93
    children's influence on, 113,
        306
    food, 82
    roles in families, 113
    U.S. and China compared,
        93
Contingency plans, 131
Controlling, 31, 136
Converse, J., 87
Conway, W., 280
Copes, M., 63
Cotton, D., 256
Covey, S., 3, 133–134
Cowan, R., 25, 26
Cowley, G., 268
Cox, W., 191
Crandall, E., 28
Cravatta, M., 72
Creamer, D., 71
Credit, 304
Crises, 247
Crispell, D., 178, 258
Critical listening, 149
Crown, W., 308
Csikzentmihalyi, M., 51, 65, 68,
    163, 213
Cude, B., 278
Cultural values, 59, 60
Culture, 91–92

Dalton, S., 117
Danes, S., 88, 192
Davey, A., 30
De facto decision making,
    111
Deacon, R., 28
Decibels, 88
Decidophobia, 108
Deciduous trees, 286

Decision(s) and decision making
  acronym DECIDE, 102
  as part of management,
    100–102
  avoidance of, 108
  consumer, 112–114
  criteria of, 99–100
  definitions of, 7, 100
  evaluation of, 102–103
  family, 109–112
  models, 105–106
  stress and, 252
  style, 101
Decision plan, 102
Decision rules, 104
Decision tree, 105
Decoding
Delaney, W., 108
Delisser, E., 235
Della Britta, A., 113
Demands, 34, 213–215
DeMerchant, E., 7, 130, 216
Demographics and demography,
  174
Denzin, N., 212
Depression, 310
Destination, 148
Destruction conflicts, 156
DeVaney, S., 300, 302
DeVine, J., 187
Diana, M., 212
Diffusion, 321
Dillard, J., 67
Directional plans, 133
Disability and disabilities,
  188–189
Discretionary time, 202
Distress, 251
Dolan, E., 235
Dollahite, D., 134, 247–249
Domino effect, 250
Donatelle, R., 107
Donnelly, G., 192
Dovetailing, 131
Downshifting, 235
Drucker, P., 5, 7, 10, 12, 15, 90,
  147, 323, 328
Dryfoos, J., 117
Dual-career and dual-earner
  families, 181–182
Duncan, S., 192
Dundan, K., 235
Dunne, H., 226, 228, 251, 260

Ebata, A., 60
Ecoconsciousness, 278
Ecology, 39
Economics and economic the-
  ory, 14, 26–27, 41–46
Ecosystem, 277–278
Eddowes, E., 188
Edison, T., 25, 72
Edmondson, M., 179

Elbing model, 111, 112
Elias, M., 256
Elder, G., 192
Elderly and elder care, 184–186
Electricity, 25–27, 284, *see also*
  energy
Elkind, D., 202
Elkington, J., 280
Elkins, P., 284
Ellickson, R., 188
Ellman, B., 190
Elstrom, P., 12
Emanoil, P., 188
Emergency fund, 302
Empathy, 149
Employee Assistance Programs
  (EAPs), 256
Encoding, 148
Energy
  appliance labels, 287
  consumption of, 285
  definition of, 284
  ways to reduce use of,
    285–287
Engel, G., 60
Enright, S., 67, 245, 246, 256,
  268
Entropy, 36
Environment
  definition of, 39
  problems and solutions,
    282–292
  3-Rs solution, 290
Environmentalism, 278
Equal Credit Opportunity Act,
  304
Equifinality, 36
Ethics, 281
Eustress, 251
Evaluation and evaluating, 137
Expertise, 129
External change, 178
External noise, 153
External stress, 116, 251
Extrinsic motivation, 73
Extrinsic values, 55
Extroverts, 128

Fair Credit Reporting Act, 304
Family and families
  changes in, 17–18
  definition of, 17
Family and Medical Leave Act,
  92, 230–231
Family ecosystem, 40
Fan, J., 105
Fatalism, 192
Fatique
  definition of, 264
  management of, 245,
    264–268
Farrell, C., 310
Fay, C., 114

Feather, N., 232
Feedback and feedback loop
  communication and, 153
  definition of, 7
  positive and negative, 35
Fertility rate, 174–175
Fight or flight syndrome, 254
Financial management
  advisors, 313–314
  college students and, 298, 311
  concerns, 309
  definition of, 298
  planning, 298
Firebaugh, F., 28, 320
Fishbein, M., 63, 64
Fisher, H., 18
Flanagan, C., 71
Foa and Foa resource model,
  87, 88
Focus groups, 207
Food purchasing, 82
Food supply, 332
Foran, J., 282
Forgue, R., 86
Foxall, G., 43, 44, 126, 128
Francese, P., 301
Frederick, C., 24
Freud, S., 224, 276
Freudenberger, H., 260
Functional limitation, 189
Furnham, A., 232
Future
  environment, 276
  predictions, 323

Galen, M., 230
Gallup polls, 237
Garden, A., 261
Garman, T., 86, 229
Garrison, M., 245
Genealogy, 44–45
Genalo, M., 235
Gender gap, 312
Genome maps, 332
Gergen, D., 312
Gerontology, 185
Giacquinta, J., 117
Gilbert, L., 181
Gilbreth, L., 24
Glass ceiling, 312
Global ecosystems, 40–41
Goals
  achievement, 69,70
  attitudes and, 54
  attributes of, 65
  college students', 70–72
  definition of, 6
  lifestyles and, 70
  obstacles to, 69–70
  roles and, 66
  setting, 67, 68, 146
  time and, 66
  types of, 66

Godbey, P., 202
Godwin, D., 112
Goebel, K., 30
Golden, J., 327
Goldsmith, E., 26, 30, 71, 85,
  154, 211, 212, 225, 227,
  232, 329
Goldsmith, R., 43, 44, 126, 128
Gotham, H., 263
Gould, S., 276, 277, 280
Graefe, A., 202
Graham, R., 201, 208
Graves, W., 284
Gray, N., 107
Greenberg, J., 264
Greenberger, E., 225
Greenglass, E., 256
Gresham's Law of Planning, 127
Grimm-Thomas, K., 225
Groot-Marcus, J., 276
Gross domestic product (GDP),
  299, 329
Gross, I., 28
Grossbart, S., 307
Gurnsey, J., 250

Habitat, 278
Habits, 65
Habitual decision making, 162
Hafstrom, J., 30, 213
Hailes, J., 280
Halberstam, D., 72
Hale, E., 158, 159, 208
Hall, O., 40, 87
Hamilton, E., 254, 255
Hammersla, J., 71
Handicap, 188
Hanna, S., 41–43
Happiness, 95
Harel, T., 156, 200
Havlovic, S., 258
Hawkins, D., 209, 210
Heck, R., 30, 235
Heitmeyer, J., 154
Hennon, C., 14
Hennon, D., 30
Herbig, P., 327
Hildreth, G., 227
Hill, K., 263
Hillman, M., 284
Hira, T., 181
Hochschild, A., 212
Hoffacker, C., 71
Hoffman, J., 71
Hogan, J., 313, 331
Holmes, T., 247–248
Home-based work, 233–236,
  324
Homeless, 186–188
Homeostasis, 36
House, J., 246
Household(s), householder
  chores, 110

definitions of, 17
expenditures, 301
families and, 15, 16, 178
history of, 25–27
housework time, 214
production/consumption of, 39
Houser, R., 262
Hranitz, J., 188
Hueber, G., 37
Huey, J., 191
Human capital
    definition of, 81
    resources and, 172
Human Development Index (HDI), 329–330
Human ecology, 39
Human resources
    categories of, 172
    definition of, 81
    population shifts and, 171–174
Hunter, M., 231
Hutchison, R., 284
Hybels, S., 160
Hypotheses, 31
Hydroponics, 332

I-messages, 151
Immigration, 174–176
Implementing
    blocks to, 135
    definition of, 7, 299
Income
    definition of, 299
    kinds of, 299–300
Income tax, 300
Independent activities, 131–132
Indirect channels, 153
Inflation, 310
Information anxiety, 162
Information overload, 162, 326
Innovations, 321–327
Inputs, 34
Insurance, 305–306
Intangible resources, 81
Integrated waste management, 289
Intellect, 321
Interface, 32
Internal change, 178
Internal noise, 153
Internal search, 116
Internal stress, 251
Interpersonal conflicts, 156
Intrinsic motivation, 73
Intrinsic values, 55
Introverts, 128
Intuition, 109
Investments, 305
Israelson, C., 30
Ivancevich, J., 133
Invention, 321

Jackson, J., 41
Jensen, H., 44
Jindal, R., 216
Job stress, 258–260
Johnston, S., 71
Jones, J., 51
Joo, S., 229
Junk, V., 308

Kalb, C., 247, 256, 261, 262
Kanter, R., 155
Kantrowitz, B., 190
Kanuk, L., 113
Kaplan, L., 14
Katz, E., 117
Kaufman, C., 190, 201
Kaufman, M., 71
Kay, I., 81
Keefe, D., 85
Keenan, J., 258
Keeney, R., 101
Kelly, R., 225
Ketterer, L., 189
Key, R., 320
Kissman, K., 190
Knoll, M., 28
Knowledge management, 4
Kobasa, S., 253
Krantz, M., 260
Kratzer, C., 85
Kronholz, J., 127

L'Abate, L., 156, 200
Lakein, A., 203–204
Lancaster, H., 235
Lane, M., 71
Lane, P., 201, 210
Langer, J., 182
Larson, J., 227
Latham, G., 67, 68
Lauer, J., 190
Lauer, R., 190
Lazarus, R., 258
Leidenfrost, N., 313
Leisure, 236–239
Level of living, 299
Levin, D., 63
Levine, K., 258
Levinson, J., 137
Lewis, K., 31
Lewis, J., 227
Liberman, R., 155
Life expectancy, 15
Life management, 14, 117
Lifestyle, 13
Liker, J., 192
Lindbergh, C., 51, 52
Linder, S., 237
Lindquist, J., 210
Lines, S., 187
Lino, M., 306
Liquidity, 305
Listening, 148–150

Lists, 131
Locke, E., 65, 67, 68
Loker, S., 235
Longino, C., 308
Longman, P., 174
Loudon, D., 113
Lovelock, J., 276
Low involvement, 162
Lubar, S., 332

Maas, J., 265, 267, 268
Mack, J., 236
Macroenvironment, 40
Management
    applied social science, 30
    definition of, 4
    eras of, 28
    financial, 298–313
    history of, 23–30
    interdisciplinary foundation of, 12–13
    legislation and research, 28–30
    process, 5–6
    second half of life, 14
    study of, 4–5
    style, 11
    tools, 8
Managerial judgment, 320
Markovich, C., 300, 302
Marriage, 178
Marshall, R., 18, 92
Marshall, V., 329
Martin, A., 212
Martin, J., 187
Martin, L., 51
Maslach, C., 260, 261
Maslow, A., 11, 129
Material resources, 81
Matteson, M., 131
Matthews, K., 257
McClellan, D., 70, 129, 251
McCubbin, H., 37, 245
McCullough, J., 30
McDermott, D., 308
McGoldrick, M., 38
McGregor, S., 85, 329
McGuiness, W., 285
McIntosh, W., 51
McLellan, T., 246
McMahan, L., 71
McMinn, D., 75
McMullen, J., 329
McMullen, M., 260
Mehrabian, A., 151
Mehren, E., 262
Menkes, S., 212
Merline, J., 287
Messages
    content, 152
    definition of, 150
Meyer, M., 17, 110
Microenvironment, 40
Milewicz, J., 327

Milkie, M., 214
Miller, J., 71
Minorities, 177–178
Mitchell, A., 57
Mitchell, T., 103
Mobility, 179
Moen, P., 234
Mogelonksy, M., 112, 176, 322
Mohanty, M., 112
Morphogenic systems, 33
Morphostatic systems, 33
Morse, D., 235
Mortality, 174, 175
Mortenson, M., 307
Motivation
    definition of, 72
    goals and, 72–73
    problem analysis and, 115
    rewards and, 73
Mowen, J., 6
Multiculturalism, 330–331
Multifinality, 36
Munz, D., 68
Murphy, M., 263
Murray, G., 188
Mutz, D., 200

N Ach Factor, 70
Naar, J., 39, 278, 284
Nadler, D., 179
Need recognition, 279
Need(s)
    definition of, 6
    fulfillment, 126–127
    hierarchy of, 11
    types of, 6
Negative feedback, 35
Nelson, D., 252
Nelson, L., 212
Net worth, 300–301
Newport, F., 37
Nock, S., 181
Noise
    decibels and, 288
    definition of, 153, 288
    ways to reduce, 288–289
Nondiscretionary time, 202
Nonnormative stressor event, 253
Nonverbal symbols, 150
Norcross, J., 69
Noring, F., 311
Normative stressor event, 253
Norms, 91
Nowack, K., 253, 256
NREM (non-rapid eye movement sleep), 266
Nunn, G., 6
Nye, E., 12
Nylen, D., 115

O'Neill, B., 208
Opportunity costs, 84

Opportunity recognition, 279
Optimization, 41
O'Reilly, J., 60
Orientation, 285
Orthner, D., 225
Outsourcing, 249–250
Outputs, 34
Overlapping activities, 131
Owen, A., 30, 208, 235

Pagelow, M., 184
Palkovitz, R., 63
Palmer, A., 310
Paolucci, B., 40, 87
Papernow, P., 190
Paradigm shift, 326
Pareto principle, 233
Parish, T., 61
Parkinson's law, 233
Parloa, M., 24
Passively acquired information, 162
Patel, C., 256
Payne, E., 67, 71
Paynter, M., 30, 213
Pearson, D., 283, 285, 288
Penteado, J., 210
Perception, 204
Perrucci, C., 192
Perry-Jenkins, M., 225
Persistance, 129
Personality
    definition of, 128
    planning and, 128–129
Peter principle, 108
Peters, T., 82
Phillips, S., 71
Physical environmental resources, 278
Pickett, M., 189
Pinchen, N., 278
Pittman, J., 225
Plan(s) and planning
    attributes of, 132
    definition of, 7, 125
    designing of, 124
    influences on, 128–130
    process of, 125–126
    stress and, 127
Pollution, 282
Popcorn, F., 163
Population
    age and composition, 177
    census, U.S., 173
    shifts, 173, 328
    terms and trends, 174–177
    world, 4, 171–172
Positive ecology, 293
Positive feedback, 35
Postpurchase dissonance, 103
Postrel, V., 232
Poverty and low income
    definition of, 191

families and, 190
problems of, 190–191, 312–313
Powell, T., 67, 245
Powers, M., 234, 261
Prepurchase expectations, 103
Price, S., 129, 228
Private resources, 85
Proactive, 133
Probability, 116
Problem solving, 9, 114
Problem(s)
    analysis of, 114
    definition of, 6, 114
    recognition, 114, 279
Prochaska, J., 69
Procrastination, 232–233
Proxemics, 151
Psychological hardiness, 252–253
Public resources, 85
Purnell Act, 28
Puspitawati, H., 30

Qualitative time measurement, 212
Quality of life, 328–329
Quantitative time measurement, 210–211
Quick, J., 252
Quilling, J., 231, 232

R-value, 285
Radon, 265
Raeburn, P., 319
Rahe, R., 247–248
Raina, M., 71
Rampage, C., 190
Rapoport, R., 226
Rapp, S., 325, 331
Ray, P., 61
Reactive, 133
Receiving, 148
Recession, 310
Recycling, 289–290
Reference groups, 106–107
Reflective listening, 149
Relative values, 54
REM (rapid eye movement sleep), 266
Renewable resources, 280
Resource Model of Motivation, 88, 89
Resource stock, 82
Resourcefulness, 81
Resource(s)
    allocation of, 85
    attributes and models, 85–89
    decision making and, 90
    definition of, 7, 80
    economics and, 82–83
    families and households, 92–93

financial, 297
    recognition of, 85
    regulation of, 85
    strategy, 94
    time as a, 201–202
    types of, 8–82
Responses, 148
Retherford, P., 227
Retirement planning, 308–309
Rettig, K., 18, 137, 180, 192, 307, 313, 331
Reynolds, J., 285
Riche, M., 184
Ridley, C., 192
Rigdon, J., 60
Riney, B., 181
Risk
    aversion, 43
    definition of, 43
    types of, 117
    uncertainty and, 116
Roberts, D., 200
Robbins, S., 67, 71, 73, 146
Robinson, J., 214
Rogers, A., 247
Rokeach, M., 55, 56
Rolfes, S., 254, 255
Rossman, M., 313, 331
Routine, 216
Rowe, B., 235, 256, 261, 262
Rubin, B., 187
Rubin, R., 181
Runyon, K., 181

Saar, L., 67, 68
Saltford, N., 235
Saluter, A., 17
Sandwich generation, 184, 308
Sanik, M., 30, 212
Satisficing, 42
Saving money, 302
Saving species, 280–281
Scanning, 135
Scanzoni, J., 112
Scarcity, 83
Scheduling, 131–132
Schiffman, L., 113
Schlossberg, A., 113, 114
Schnittgrund, K., 30
Schor, J., 83, 234, 237
Schram, V., 30
Schroeder, P., 226
Schumacher, E., 90
Seaker, E., 283
Seale, W., 12
Sebastian, P., 311
Seligman, M., 68, 69, 73
Seligmann, J., 72
Sending, 148
Senge, P., 4, 137, 180, 201
Sequencing, 34, 131–132, 215
Setting, 154
Seyle, H., 246, 251, 252, 260

Shapiro, E., 237
Sharpe, D., 34, 134
Sharpe, W., 283
Shaw, K., 67, 68
Shellenbarger, S., 38, 161, 223, 225, 229
Sher, K., 263
Sheth, J., 249–250
Sieburg, E., 34, 36, 155
Siegal, B., 183
Siegel, J., 257
Silver, W., 103
Simon, H., 42, 127, 133
Singal, S., 216
Singles, single-parent families, 15–16, 190–191
Sisodia, R., 249–250
Site, 285
Sleep, 265–267
Smith, A., 85, 129
Smith-Hughes Act, 28
Smith-Lever Act, 28
Smith, S., 228
Social channels, 153
Social environmental resources, 278
Social Security Act, 309
Socialization, 61, 307
Sokalski, H., 330, 331
Sontag, S., 39, 41
Source, 148
Spam, 164
Springer, K., 17
Srinivasan, K., 216
Stafford, D., 232
Stafford, K., 30, 131, 215, 235
Standard of living, 299
Standards, 7, 60, 216–217
Stein, B., 285
Steinberg, L., 225
Stenberg, L., 308
Stewardship, 277
Stewart, D., 181
Stone, B., 223, 229
Stoneman, B., 72
Storyboarding, 137
Strasser, S., 26
Strategic plans, 133
Strategy, 94
Stress
    body's response to, 252–254
    decision making and, 252
    definition of, 246
    jobs and, 258–260
    management of, 245–270
    parents and children, 261–262
    techniques to reduce, 258
    time and planning, 127
Stress overload and pileup, 247–248
Stressors, 246

Strugnell, C., 239
Stuenkel, J., 307
Subsystems, 33
Superconductivity, 325
Supply and demand, 84
Sustainable development, 275
Sweetman, M., 68
Symbols, 150–151
Syncratic, 111
System(s) and systems theory
    definition and description of, 32–36
    family, 37–38
    framework, 28
    household applications, 38–39
    personal, 37

Tacoma, S., 210
Tang, T., 232
Tangible resources, 81
Tannen, D., 156–157
Tanner, E., 255
Targ, D., 199
Taxes, 24, 25, 313
Taylor, F., 24, 205–206
Taylor, W., 212
Technology
    clean, 326
    definition of, 321
    environment and, 322, 331–332
    home automation, 323–324
    households and, 322
    innovations, 321
    White House and, 12
Tempo, 214
Theory
    definition of, 30–31
    functions of, 31
Theory of adaptive range, 253
Theory of planned behavior, 63–64

Thompson, K., 188
Throughputs, 34
Time
    as a resource, 200–202
    children and, 202
    cultures and, 208–209
    daily activities and, 211
    definition of, 200
    household tasks and, 214
    management of, 198–217
    measurement of, 210–212
    perceptions of, 204–205
    stress and planning, 127
    weekend, 234, 238–239
Time displacement, 200
Time-tagging, 215
Toffler, A., 173
Tokuno, K., 60
Topp, R., 264
Traditionalism, 61–63
Transfer payments, 192
Transformations, 34
Tung, Y., 232
Types A and B persons, 256–258

Uitenbogerd, D., 276
Ulrich, D., 226, 228, 251, 260
Uncertainty, 116
Unemployment, 227–228, 310
Usdansky, M., 18
Utility, 89–90

VALS and VALS 2 research, 57–59
Value orientation, 53
Values
    attitudes and, 52–53
    definition of, 7
    family and, 60
    formation of, 61
    lifestyles, consumption and, 54

societal and cultural, 59–60
    types of, 54
Van Vuuren, D., 200
Vats, A., 71
Ventura, J., 262
Verbal symbols, 150
Vickers, C., 28
Visible symbols, 150
Vo, M., 191
Volunteer work, 236–237
Voydanoff, P., 199

Waldrop, J., 189, 262
Walker, K., 30
Wallace, M., 114
Wants, 6
Warren, J., 30
Waste
    amount per household, 289
    ways to reduce, 283–284, 290
Waste stream, 281
Water
    households and, 282–284
    shortages and pollution, 282–283
    ways to reduce use of, 283–284
Waterman, R., 82
Wealth, 312–313
Weaver, R., 160
Well-being
    definition of, 329
    dimensions of, 329
    economic, 85, 306, 329
Wheeler, R., 68, 133
Whitehead, B., 92
Whitney, E., 254, 255
Whyte, W., 72
Wigdor, B., 329
Wigfield, A., 263
Wilhem, M., 199
Wilkie, C., 192

Wilkie, W., 175, 184
Williams, F., 145
Wilson, B., 12
Wilson, M., 30
Wilson, S., 227
Winborne, D., 188
Winchip, S., 331
Winer, R., 131
Winter, M., 30, 34, 129, 134, 235
Wolfe, D., 112
Woods, M., 30
Woods, P., 263
Woods, S., 239
Woolgar, C., 24
Work (workplaces)
    definition of, 230
    family and, 222–240
    home-based, 233–236
    job changing and, 234
    space redesign of, 234
    volunteer, 236–237
Workaholism, 232
Work and family. See also work, family
    conflicts between, 225–226
    facts, figures, research, 225
    interchange between, 228–229
    overview, 224–225
    workplace policies, 229–230
Work ethic, 231–232
Work simplification, 25
Wright, G., 188, 189
Wright, J., 187
Wurman, R., 162

Xiao, J., 105

You-messages, 151

Zick, C., 30

Photo Credits